Explaining War and Peace

This edited volume focuses on a common form of causal exp
of historical events, the use of "necessary condition counterfactuals",
which is neglected in the growing literature on the methodology of
qualitative analysis and case studies. The volume analyzes the causal
logics of necessary and sufficient conditions, demonstrates the variety
of different ways in which necessary condition counterfactuals are
used to explain the causes of individual events, and identifies errors
commonly made in applying this form of causal logic to individual
events. It includes discussions of causal chains, contingency, critical
junctures and "powder keg" explanations, and the role of necessary
conditions in each. The volume focuses in particular on the applications
of these concepts in a variety of competing explanations for two of the
defining events of the 20th century: the origins of World War I and the
end of the Cold War.

This book will be of great interest to students of qualitative analysis,
World War I, the Cold War, international history and IR theory in general.

Gary Goertz is Professor of Political Science at the University of Arizona.

Jack S. Levy is Board of Governors' Professor of Political Science at Rutgers University, and President of the International Studies Association
(2007–08).

Contemporary Security Studies

Stephen J. Cimbala, *Nuclear Weapons and Strategy: The Evolution of American Nuclear Policy*

Owen L. Sirrs, *Nasser and the Missile Age in the Middle East*

Yee-Kuang Heng, *War as Risk Management: Strategy and Conflict in an Age of Globalised Risks*

Jurgen Altmann, *Military Nanotechnology: Potential Applications and Preventive Arms Control*

Eric R. Terzuolo, *NATO and Weapons of Mass Destruction: Regional Alliance, Global Threats*

Pernille Rieker, *Europeanisation of National Security Identity: The EU and the Changing Security Identities of the Nordic States*

T. David Mason and James D. Meernik (eds.), *International Conflict Prevention and Peace-Building: Sustaining the Peace in Post Conflict Societies*

Brian Rappert, *Controlling the Weapons of War: Politics, Persuasion, and the Prohibition of Inhumanity*

Jan Hallenberg and Hâkan Karlsson (eds.), *Changing Transatlantic Security Relations: Do the U.S, the EU and Russia Form a New Strategic Triangle?*

Thomas M. Kane, *Theoretical Roots of US Foreign Policy: Machiavelli and American Unilateralism*

Christopher Kinsey, *Corporate Soldiers and International Security: The Rise of Private Military Companies*

Gordon Adams and Guy Ben-Ari, *Transforming European Militaries: Coalition Operations and the Technology Gap*

Robert G. Patman (ed.), *Globalization and Conflict: National Security in a 'New' Strategic Era*

James V. Arbuckle, *Military Forces in 21st Century Peace Operations: No Job for a Soldier?*

Nick Ritchie and Paul Rogers, *The Political Road to War with Iraq: Bush, 9/11 and the Drive to Overthrow Saddam*

Michael A. Innes (ed.), *Bosnian Security after Dayton: New Perspectives*

Andrew Priest, *Kennedy, Johnson and NATO: Britain, America and the Dynamics of Alliance, 1962-68*

Denise Garcia, *Small Arms and Security: New Emerging International Norms*

John Baylis and Jon Roper (eds.), *The United States and Europe: Beyond the Neo-Conservative Divide?*

Lionel Ponsard, *Russia, NATO and Cooperative Security: Bridging the Gap*

Tom Bierstecker, Peter Spiro, Chandra Lekha Sriram and Veronica Raffo (eds.), *International Law and International Relations: Bridging Theory and Practice*

James H. Lebovic, *Deterring International Terrorism and Rogue States: US National Security Policy after 9/11*

John Dumbrell and David Ryan (eds.), *Vietnam in Iraq: Tactics, Lessons, Legacies and Ghosts*

Jan Angstrom and Isabelle Duyvesteyn (eds.), *Understanding Victory and Defeat in Contemporary War*

Scot Macdonald, *Propaganda and Information Warfare in the Twenty-First Century: Altered Images and Deception Operations*

Derick W. Brinkerhoff (ed.), *Governance in Post-Conflict Societies: Rebuilding Fragile States*

Adrian Hyde-Price, *European Security in the Twenty-First Century: The Challenge of Multipolarity*

Reuben E. Brigety II, *Ethics, Technology and the American Way of War: Cruise Missiles and US Security Policy*

Joel H. Westra, *International Law and the Use of Armed Force: The UN Charter and the Major Powers*

Christian Enermark, *Disease and Security: Natural Plagues and Biological Weapons in East Asia*

Gary Goertz and Jack S. Levy (eds.), *Explaining War and Peace: Case Studies and Necessary Condition Counterfactuals*

Explaining War and Peace

Case Studies and Necessary Condition Counterfactuals

Edited by

Gary Goertz and Jack S. Levy

Routledge
Taylor & Francis Group

LONDON AND NEW YORK

First published 2007 by Routledge
2 Park Square, Milton Park, Abingdon OX14 4RN

Simultaneously published in the USA and Canada
by Routledge
270 Madison Ave., New York, NY 10016

*Routledge is an imprint of the Taylor & Francis Group, an informa
business*

© 2007 Gary Goertz and Jack S. Levy for selection and editorial matter;
individual chapters, the contributors. This book has been prepared
from camera-ready copy made with LaTeX and provided by the editors.

Printed and bound in Great Britain by Antony Rowe Ltd, Chippenham,
Wiltshire

British Library Cataloguing in Publication Data
A catalogue record for this book is available from the British Library

Library of Congress Cataloging in Publication Data
A catalog record for this book has been requested

ISBN10: 0-415-42232-9 (hbk)
ISBN10: 0-415-42233-7 (pbk)
ISBN10: 0-203-08910-3 (ebk)

ISBN13: 978-0-415-42232-1 (hbk)
ISBN13: 978-0-415-42233-8 (pbk)
ISBN13: 978-0-203-08910-1 (ebk)

For Alexander George,

Who made such a difference for so many.

Contents

Tables

Figures

Contributors

Stephen G. Brooks
Department of Government, Dartmouth College, Hanover, NH 03755, USA

Robert English
School of International Relations, University of Southern California, Los Angeles, CA 90089-0043, USA

Gary Goertz
Department of Political Science, University of Arizona, Tucson, AZ 85721, USA

Richard Ned Lebow
Department of Government, Dartmouth College, Hanover, NH 03755, USA

Jack S. Levy
Department of Political Science, Rutgers University, New Brunswick, NJ 08901-1411, USA

James Mahoney
Department of Political Science, Northwestern University, Scott Hall, Evanston, IL 60208, USA

Paul W. Schroeder
52E Mary Lane, Champaign, IL 61822, USA

William R. Thompson
Department of Political Science, Woodburn Hall 210, University of Indiana, Bloomington, Indiana, 47045-6001, USA

William C. Wohlforth
Department of Government, Dartmouth College, Hanover, NH 03755, USA

Acknowledgments

We would like to thank Andy Bennett for suggesting that many of the explanatory strategies we identified in the literature on World War I were also present in the literature on the end of the Cold War. We have benefited from feedback on Chapter 2 from numerous participants at the Institute for Qualitative Research Methods, where we presented this material. Parina Patel prepared the index for the volume, and we are grateful for her thorough and careful effort. We thank Andrew Humphrys at Routledge for his interest in the volume and his role in keeping the process moving in a timely fashion. For their assistance at various stages of the process we thank Marjorie Francois, Katie Gordon, and Alison Nick.

Chapters 1, 2, and 10 of this volume, along with the classroom exercises in the appendix, contain entirely new material. Chapters 3-9 represent revisions of previously published articles, in which the authors highlight and elaborate upon the role of necessary conditions in their analyses and in historical explanation more generally.

Chapter 3 was originally published as Jack S. Levy, "Preferences, constraints, and choices in July 1914." *International Security*, 15, 3 (Winter 1990-1): 151-86. We have reprinted substantial portions of that article with the permission of MIT Press. An earlier version of chapter 4 was originally published as Richard Ned Lebow, "Contingency, catalysts, and international system change." *Political Science Quarterly*, 115, 4 (Winter 2000-1): 591-616. We have reprinted substantial portions of that article with the permission of the Academy of Political Science. Chapter 5 originally appeared as William R. Thompson, "A streetcar named Sarajevo: catalysts, multiple rivalries, and 'systemic accidents.' " *International Studies Quarterly*, 47, 3 (September 2003): 453-74. We have reprinted substantial portions of that article with the permission of Blackwell Publishing. Chapter 6 was originally published as Paul W. Schroeder, "Embedded counterfactuals and World War I as an un-avoidable war." In Paul W. Schroeder, *Systems, stability, and statecraft: essays on the international history of modern Europe*, pp. 157-91, edited by David Wetzl, Robert Jervis, and Jack S. Levy. New York: Palgrave, 2004. We reproduce it with permission of Palgrave Macmillan. We

also thank MIT Press for their permission to reprint substantial portions of chapters 7–9, each of which appeared in *International Security*.
An earlier version of chapter 7 appeared as Stephen G. Brooks and
William C. Wohlforth, "Power, globalization, and the end of the cold
war: reevaluating a landmark case for ideas." *International Security*, 25,
3 (Winter 2000–1): 5–53. Chapter 8 originally appeared as Robert D.
English, "Power, ideas, and new evidence on the cold war's end: a reply
to Brooks and Wohlforth." *International Security*, 26, 4 (Spring 2002):
70–92. Chapter 9 was originally published as Stephen G. Brooks and
William C. Wohlforth, "From old thinking to new thinking in qualitative
research." *International Security*, 26, 4 (Spring 2002): 93–111.

Chapter 1

Introduction

Gary Goertz and Jack S. Levy

> The nose of Cleopatra; if it had been shorter all the face of the earth would have changed.
>
> *Blaise Pascal*
>
> There are ever so many ways that a world might be; and one of these many ways is the way that this world is.
>
> *David Lewis*

World War I and the end of the Cold War were two of the defining events of the 20th, with enormous implications for the subsequent evolution of politics, culture, and history in individual states and in the international system as a whole. Some scholars argue that had World War I not occurred the world might have been spared the Bolshevik revolution in Russia, the rise of Hitler, the outbreak of World War II, and the Cold War. Others argue that if the Cold War had continued it is quite unlikely that we would have witnessed the collapse of the Soviet Union and democratization in Eastern Europe, the collapse of Yugoslavia and the wars in the Balkans, the 1990-1 Persian Gulf, and the 2003 war in Iraq.

These are strong claims, and many scholars dispute them, but each involves a specific kind of causal logic, what we call a "necessary condition counterfactual."[1] The necessary condition counterfactual takes the deceptively simple form of "If X had not occurred or been

---

[1] One could almost call this simply the "counterfactual" approach, but alternative views of causation connected with statistical methods, e.g., King, Keohane, and Verba (1994), also have counterfactual components, though they play a much smaller role, see Holland (1986a, 1986b) and the responses to that article, notably Glymour (1986).

present, then Y would not have occurred."[2] It is a necessary condition because we can rephrase this as "X was a necessary condition for Y." It is a counterfactual because it expresses a "possible world" where X and Y did not actually happen (Lewis 1973).[3]

Counterfactuals about World War I made it into the wider press when Niall Ferguson published a controversial book (1999c) about Britain's role in the war. Boynton describes the argument in his *New Yorker* profile of Ferguson:

> Rather than joining the Allied war effect, he said, Britain should have maintained its neutrality and allowed the Germans to win a limited Continental war against the French and the Russians. In that event, he postulated, Germany, whose war aims in 1914 were relatively modest, would have respected the territorial integrity of Belgium, France, and Holland and settled for a German-led European federation. Had Britain "stood aside" he continued, it is likely that the century would have been spared the Bolshevik Revolution, the Second World War, and perhaps even the Holocaust. (Boynton 1999: 43)

As Paul Schroeder argues in his chapter, historians continually propose and use counterfactuals, if not always explicitly. Raymond Aron says the same thing: "*Tout historien, pour expliquer ce qui a été, se demande ce qui aurait pu être* [All historians in order to explain what actually happened ask themselves what might have happened]" (1986 [1938]: 202). They may not all take the form of a necessary condition counterfactual, but many do.

Scholars have applied necessary condition counterfactuals to the academic study of international politics as well as to historical events themselves. For example, Schweller and Wohlforth (2000) begin their essay on the end of the Cold War with a necessary condition counter-factual about the scholarship on the war:

> The end of the Cold War was a watershed for international relations theory. Before 1989, realism "ruled the theoretical waves," and scholars were preoccupied with a longstanding debate over the explanatory power of distribution of capabilities. The events of

---

[2] We should note that this volume examines *causal* necessary conditions and not definitional ones. For example, being male is necessary to become a king: this is true by the definition of a king.

[3] Any statement of necessary conditions implies a counterfactual, which we call a necessary condition counterfactual. For example, the statement X is a necessary condition for Y implies the necessary condition counterfactual that if X is not present then Y will not occur. Although all necessary conditions imply counterfactuals, not all counterfactuals imply necessary conditions. For example, if we say that if X is not present then Y will still occur implies that X is not a necessary condition for Y.

1989–91 pushed this debate aside and accelerated the turn toward culture, sociological, and domestic approaches to the study of world politics. If the Cold War were still raging, it is unlikely that an intellectual sea change of this scope and magnitude would have occurred. (Schweller and Wohlforth 2000: 60)

Our aim in this volume is to demonstrate the various ways in which necessary condition counterfactuals are used in the logic of causal explanation, and to do so by focusing on alternative explanations of the outbreak of World War I and the end of the Cold War, two of the critical events that frame the 20th century and that continue to be debated by historians and political scientists. We do not suggest that necessary condition counterfactuals are the only kind of causal explanation scholars use for individual events, just that they are very important ones. The reader will see in the next chapter and in each of the historical chapters the diverse ways in which scholars have invoked this kind of causal explanation in debates about World War I and the end of the Cold War. Necessary condition counterfactuals can be used to defend virtually any theoretical position, from the importance of individual variables to material structures or ideational factors.

With this volume we make an important contribution to the literature on the methodology of case studies. Counterfactual claims are a core, but underappreciated, part of the case study methodology and one that is rarely systematically discussed even in the expanding literature on qualitative methods in political science. An exception is Odell, who sees the close tie between case studies and counterfactuals:

A counterfactual argument is speculation, by definition. Nevertheless it is common, though often not explicit, throughout scholarship and political debate. When an author says "a hegemonic power structure in 1945 was necessary to reopen a liberal world economy," the statement must mean that if the power structure had not been hegemonic in 1945 – a counterfactual – a liberal world economy would not have been reopened.... A single case study that presents counterfactual thought experiments explicitly and carefully is likely to convince more readers than assertion or private intuition would. (Odell 2001: 164)

We have organized this volume for scholars and students alike. We include discussions of philosophical issues and more detailed examples of how political scientists and historians frequently make causal explanations. For example, we shall see how important it is to pay attention to the language of explanations, such as the use of terms such as window of opportunity, catalyst, powder keg, and the like. Each of these expressions and their variants suggest – implicitly or more directly – a necessary condition counterfactual. We shall see that causal explanations are just as often given via metaphor as in direct (and less colorful) language. By analyzing World War I and end of the Cold War counterfactuals we hope students learn to recognize these strategies and eventually use them in their own work.

We have chosen World War I and the end of the Cold War, not only because of their substantive importance in world history, but also because scholars writing on each subject frequently use necessary condition counterfactuals, and hence a common logical structure, in their historical explanations.[4] For example, in both cases the "window of opportunity" idea plays a central role. In both cases, we see strong arguments that individual persons (e.g., Gorbachev) or events (the assassination of Archduke Ferdinand) played a necessary role.

If one looks at the debate regarding the other most important events of the 20th century, such as the Russian and Chinese Revolutions and World War II, one can find scholars using the same sort of explanatory strategies. For example, in her classic *States and social revolutions* (1979) Theda Skocpol proposes that a state crisis was necessary for the occurrence of social revolution in China and Russia. In response to the common belief that after World War I and the unsatisfactory Versailles treaty another major war was inevitable, some make the necessary condition counterfactual argument that without Hitler World War II would not have occurred. Mueller (1991: 21; see also Mueller 1989: 64–8), for example, argues that:

> [H]istorical conditions in no important way required that contest, and that the major nations of Europe were not on a collision course that was likely to lead to war. That is, had Adolf Hitler gone into art rather than into politics; had he been gassed a bit more thoroughly by the British in the trenches in 1918; had he succumbed to the deadly influenza of 1919; had he, rather than the man marching next to him, been gunned down in the Beer Hall Putsch of 1923; had he been denied the leadership position in Germany; or had he been removed from office at almost any time before September 1939 (and possibly even before May 1940), history's greatest war would most probably never have taken place.

We suggest that the causal explanation of major events often use the necessary condition counterfactual strategies that are described in this volume.

We have designed the volume so that the chapters provide the basic background historical information about our two events. Hence the

---

[4]We started with World War I and we thank Andy Bennett for pointing out the many similarities in the literature on the end of the Cold War.

volume can be used in a classroom setting without additional readings. Levy gives a clear and detailed analysis of the basic positions of the key players in the period just preceding World War I along with the key events and decisions that led to the war. Schroeder provides the larger historical setting within which World War I occurred and describes the mentalities and general approaches to foreign policy of the major powers of the time. Brooks and Wohlforth give a good survey of the problems facing the USSR in the 1980s and 1990s, emphasizing the serious economic, military, technological problems confronting the Soviet Union. English in his chapter focuses more on the players, e.g., Gorbachev, the ideas and the policy options that key decision-makers used.

To make this volume more useful in a teaching setting we have constructed a webasite. This site provides a series of exercises using World War I and the end of the Cold War along with other important international events to help hone one's skills in seeing how other scholars have used the causal explanations that we cover here.[5] In almost all cases we give references to published works that are available electronically via library subscription (e.g., JSTOR). We will continue to add new exercises to our site as we find them: we also encourage readers to submit examples to us for incorporation.

Our focus in this anthology is on how scholars often use a certain family of causal explanations in their analyses of historical events, such as World War I and the end of the Cold War. The next chapter by Goertz and Levy serves as a survey of the various ways necessary condition counterfactuals appear in the literature on the causes of World War I and the end of the Cold War. We do not pretend to cover exhaustively these massive debates, but we have chosen prominent scholars whose work illustrates the various aspects of our central theme. While the idea of a necessary condition is simple, they show that there are extensive ramifications for research design, theory, and causal explanations.

Although necessary condition counterfactuals are the central focus of this volume, not all of the contributors agree that the concept is a useful one. In particular, Brooks and Wohlforth (this volume, chapter 9) argue that probabilistic approaches to explanation and causation are more useful. Thompson worries that an emphasis on necessary and sufficient condition causation will detract from the goal of evaluating the relative causal weights of different factors (see Goertz and Starr 2003 for a discussion of these two issues). So while Goertz and Levy show that the necessary condition explanatory strategy is widespread,

---

[5] An answer key for instructors is available on request from the authors.

this does not necessarily mean that it is without problems or that other alternative strategies do not exist.

Lebow in his provocative chapter illustrates most of the themes discussed by Goertz and Levy in their overview chapter. In particular, his claim about the central importance of the assassination of Archduke Ferdinand in the causes of World War I illustrates a very important issue in the analysis of events: what is the role of idiosyncratic events or individual people in causal explanations? The same issue arises in the debate about the end of the Cold War: how much importance should one attribute to Gorbachev and his ideas? English in his chapter makes a strong case for the importance of ideas and individuals in the end of the Cold War.

Not surprisingly, proponents of structural arguments dispute the significance of individuals. As Brooks and Wohlforth stress (this volume, chapter 9), one can downplay the importance of individuals by arguing that ideas, people, and particular events are *endogenously* produced by larger structural factors. They argue that the severity of material constraints almost inevitably pushed Soviet leaders to change policy. In the case of World War I, Thompson does not explicitly make the endogeneity argument, but both he and Schroeder suggest that given the multiple rivalries (Thompson) or the basic principles guiding foreign policy of states of this period (Schroeder) events like the assassination would occur. Similarly, while Lebow argues that had the assassination-induced war not occurred in 1914, adverse power shifts would have left Germany unable to fight a two-front war in Europe within three years, Levy argues that it was precisely such trends and the understanding of their consequences that would have led German leaders, in the absence of the assassination, to create another pretext for war while the opportunity was still available. So while all agree that the assassination is part of the explanation of the beginning of World War I or that Gorbachev carried out important reforms, some argue that the causal significance of these factors is reduced since they are themselves the *effects* of more basic processes.

The metaphor of the *powder keg* along with that of the *window of opportunity* are among the most widely used in the analysis of important international political events. Yet, these metaphors have almost never been explicitly and thoroughly analyzed in terms of what they imply for causal explanations. Goertz and Levy outline the key characteristics of the causal explanations that lie behind these metaphors. Powder keg ideas run through many of the chapters of this anthology. They are central to Lebow and Thompson's chapters, and they lie implicit in

English's contribution since it is material constraints (powder keg) and ideas/individuals (spark) that explain the collapse of the Soviet Union.

Levy's chapter starts the analysis of causal chains. The chain metaphor implies a series of necessary condition hypotheses. Levy explores some the causal chains of events or beliefs that led up to World War I. For example, he argues that the German belief in British eventual noninvolvment was absolutely essential for German support of the Austrians, which in turn was necessary for the Austrian ultimatum that led to the war. He explores many of the key "turning points" where certain beliefs, preferences or assumptions were necessary to continue on the path to war.

The metaphor of "causal chains" also implies, but more ambiguously, the presence of sufficient conditions. As Goertz and Levy discuss in the next chapter (see also Mahoney's chapter) the overall strength of a chain is really a sufficiency hypothesis. It is also possible, but perhaps less likely, that the hypotheses that compose each link are sufficient condition ones. However, it appears that hypotheses embedded in the individual links are typically necessary condition hypotheses and not sufficient condition ones.

One can move from *the* chain of events to a consideration of multiple causal paths. Lebow makes the idea of the intersection of multiple causal paths a central component of his explanation of World War I. Thompson as well focuses on the nonlinear interaction of multiple rivalries occurring around 1914.

Multiple causal path arguments illustrate a key concern about the *contingency* of important events. Lebow makes much of the contingency inherent in the intersection of complex and nonlinear series of events. In the "system accident" (Perrow 1984) approach of Thompson these occur as unpredictable events in complex systems. English stresses contingency inherent in the importance of individuals. Others (e.g., Evangelista 2000–1) have also argued that without Gorbachev's unique set of skills, beliefs, and values the events of the late 1980s would have been completely different. In various chapters, one gets outcomes that resulted from the complex interaction of many factors.

In contrast, many of the more structural approaches downplay the contingency of events. For example, Schroeder suggests that given the rules and norms of behavior of the major states World War I would have been very hard to avoid. In a very striking manner, Schroeder reverses the usual question of the causes of war and asks the counterfactual about the causes of continuing peace (or nonwar). He argues, in a masterful useful of counterfactual analysis, that it would have been almost impossible for leaders to do everything necessary to avoid World War I.

Similarly, Brooks and Wohlforth argue that there was no real alternative to what Gorbachev ended up doing. While not linking explicitly their analysis to counterfactuals, clearly they make claims that given the material problems there was no other plausible alternative.

Finally, James Mahoney evaluates and summarizes many of the themes that run throughout this volume. He provides outside expertise since he is not involved in the substantive debates concerning the causes of World War I or the end of the Cold War, but has worked extensively on the methodology of comparative historical studies (Mahoney 1999, 2000, 2004; Mahoney and Rueschemeyer 2003). While the debates and literatures regarding our two cases have run somewhat independent of each other, by putting them together we suggest that a comparative historical approach can shed light on both. Our fundamental thesis is that many of the same issues and responses appear in both cases. Hence, Mahoney transforms in part the analysis of two individual cases into the methodology of comparative historical studies.

With this volume we hope to furnish students and scholars alike with a set of theoretical and methodological tools that will allow them to better understand the causal claims which appear abundantly in the literature on the explanations of major political events, and to craft better and more explicit explanations of them.

Chapter 2

Causal explanation, necessary conditions, and case studies

Gary Goertz and Jack S. Levy

> "I know what you are thinking about," said Tweedledum; "but it isn't so, nohow." "Contrariwise," continued Tweedledee, "if it was so it might be; and if it were so, it would be; but as it isn't, it ain't. That's logic."
>
> *Lewis Carroll*

In this chapter we make no attempt to survey the various meanings of causation. We focus on necessary conditions as a particular kind of important cause. Necessary conditions are important causes because they directly imply a key counterfactual, such as, if X had not been present/occurred then the Cold War would not have ended. A probabilistic version is that if X had not occurred then the end of Cold War would have been very unlikely.

It turns out that this rather simple causal strategy has wide-spread ramifications for explaining individual events. We first take a look at simple necessary condition explanations and their intimate connection with counterfactuals. However, necessary conditions also play an essential role in multivariate explanations of events as well. For example, one frequently reads about historical *chains* of events. If we take this metaphor seriously then each "link" is a necessary condition factor: break one link and the chain is broken.

One cannot discuss necessary condition causal explanations without an analysis of sufficiency. Continuing with the chain metaphor we can ask about the sufficiency of each link. It is absolutely essential to realize that in almost all case studies the basic goal is to explain how the outcome came about. To use one of our main examples, we examine the causes of the end of the Cold War, by identifying the factors, events, or decisions that together were sufficient for this outcome to occur.

One can contrast the necessary condition counterfactual to a "contributing factor" view of causation. This kind of causal claim says the presence of X contributed to the occurrence of Y. We take this to mean that X was part of set of factors which were jointly sufficient for the outbreak of a particular event, or that made the probability of the event occurring very high. In statistical studies, where the aim is to explain or account for variation across outcomes in a larger number of cases, a contributory cause is often defined as a factor that increases the probability of a particular event (King, Keohane, and Verba 1994). For the purposes of this chapter we will define it as such: a contributing factor X is part of the set of conditions which are sufficient for Y but which is not necessary or sufficient by itself for Y.

We end this introduction with a couple of caveats about the scope and purpose of our analysis. We do not presume to do an analysis of what "cause" per se is. We do briefly discuss, however, how some philosophers and methodologists have defined cause in necessary condition counterfactual terms. We take as given that necessary conditions are an important *kind* of cause, but not the only kind. For example, our notion of a contributing factor is another kind of cause.

More generally, we use the logic of necessary and sufficient conditions as our basic explanatory framework. We shall argue, implicitly for the most part, that the necessary condition causal approach is a common causal explanation strategy in case studies. Not all explanations use necessary condition counterfactuals, but as we shall see in the cases of World War I and the end of the Cold War, they have been widely utilized.

The concept of cause in case studies

The topic of this anthology is *causal* explanations in case studies. It is worthwhile to briefly consider what counts as a cause, hence what one means by a causal explanation. It is all the more crucial to do so since views on causation within political science in general and qualitative methods in particular have been driven by philosophies of cause based on statistical considerations. These positions, typified by King, Keohane, and Verba (1994), have roots in Hempel's nomological, covering philosophy of science. Much less well-known to political scientists, but in fact more influential in contemporary philosophy, are positions that define cause in terms of necessary condition counterfactuals, a view associated with David Lewis (1986a) and others.

These two views of causation – the nomological covering law approach and the necessary condition counterfactual – represent the two primary and competing conceptions of causation in the literature, which are often confused. Wendt (1999: 79) provides one illustration of how scholars can combine the necessary condition counterfactual with the nomological in thinking about causation:

> In saying that 'X causes Y' we assume that: (1) X and Y exist independent of each other, (2) X precedes Y temporally, and (3) but for X, Y would not have occurred.... The logical empiricist model of causal explanation, usually called the deductive-nomological model or D-N model, is rooted in David Hume's seminal discussion of causality. Hume argued that when we see putative causes followed by effects, i.e., when we have met conditions (1) and (2), all we can be certain about is that they stand in relations of constant conjunction. The actual mechanism by which X causes Y is not observable (and thus uncertain), and appeal to it is therefore epistemically illegitimate. Even if there is necessity in nature, we cannot know it. How then to satisfy the third, counterfactual condition for causality, which implies necessity?

One immediately notes the necessary condition counterfactual condition, "but for X, Y would not have occurred." At the same time one can see the presence of nomological considerations in Wendt's discussion. Most scholars have associated the idea of covering laws or nomological relationships with Hume's idea of causation as inference from constant conjunction. Wendt fails to see the contradiction between the necessary condition counterfactual view and the nomological one which relies on constant conjunction (see Lebow 2000: 561 for another example).

This confounding of the necessary condition counterfactual with constant conjunction goes back to one of the most quoted passages in the history of Western philosophy:

> [W]e may define a cause to be *an object followed by another, and where all the objects, similar to the first, are followed by objects similar to the second. Or, in other words, where, if the first object had not been, the second never would have existed.* (David Hume *An inquiry concerning human understanding*)

The history of philosophy has shown that no one thinks that "in other words" expresses an equivalence between the two formulations. David Lewis is very clear on this point:

> Hume's 'other words' [see above] – that if the cause had not been, the effect never had existed – are no mere restatement of his first definition. They propose something altogether different: a counterfactual analysis of causation. (Lewis 1986a: 160).

Absolutely crucial in the context of this anthology is that the counterfactual school associated the necessary condition view of cause is very closely tied to the explanation of individual events, while the covering law, constant conjunction position has just as intimate a relationship with causal generalizations (e.g., statistical methods). Lewis is typical in linking the explanation of individual events to a view of causation as necessary condition counterfactuals:

> I shall confine my analyses to causation among *events* ... My analysis is meant to apply to causation in particular cases. It is not an analysis of causal generalizations. (Lewis 1986a: 161–2).

Not surprisingly Holland (1986b: the source of King, Keohane, and Verba's view of causation) rejects Lewis's view of causation as being fundamentally different from his:

> I must disagree with Glymour's [comments on Holland 1986a] paraphrasing of my (i.e., Rubin's) analysis, however, and with the counterfactual analysis of causation of Lewis described by Glymour. I believe that there is an unbridgeable gulf between Rubin's model and Lewis's analysis. Both wish to give meaning to the phrase '*A* causes *B*'. Lewis does this by interpreting "*A* causes *B*" as "*A* is *a* cause of *B*." Rubin's model interprets "*A* causes *B*" as "the *effect* of *A* is *B*." (Holland 1986b: 970)

In the analysis of individual events there is an inevitable pull toward Lewis's view of causation since we are, after all, trying to find the causes of an event.

Hence, it is quite common for philosophers to define causation in necessary and sufficient condition terms:

> It is a fundamental axiom in the study of nature that events do not just happen, but occur only under certain conditions. It is customary to distinguish between necessary and sufficient conditions for the occurrence of an event.... The word "cause" is sometimes used in the sense of necessary condition and sometimes in the sense of sufficient condition. (Copi and Cohen 1990: 377)

> We can [take] ... the statement *A* was the cause of *B* [to mean] that *A* was the set, from among all those conditions that occurred , each of which was necessary, and the totality of which was sufficient for the occurrence of *B*. (Taylor 1976: 298)

The first quote comes from one of the most popular philosophical textbooks on logic. The second quote links multiple necessary conditions and sufficiency.

It is not surprising that philosophers often think of cause in terms of logic, that is the formal, mathematical methodology in which all philosophers are trained. Similarly it is not surprising to see political scientists defining cause in statistical, probabilistic terms since that reflects their formal training.

In summary, there two basic schools of thought on causation that are relevant. One is the covering law, statistical/probabilistic causation school. The second is the necessary condition, counterfactual, approach. Very crudely, (1) the first school thinks of causation in terms of constant conjunction, while the second does so in terms of necessary conditions; (2) the first school thinks in terms of covering laws or generalizations, while the second thinks in terms of individual cases.[1]

To understand the implications of this difference in the context of explaining individual events it is useful to see how King et al. see the situation:

> [W]e have argued that social science always needs to partition the world into systematic and nonsystematic components, ... To see the importance of this partitioning, think about what would happen if we could rerun the 1998 election campaign in the Fourth District of New York, with a Democratic incumbent and a Republican challenger. A slightly [!] different total would result, due to nonsystematic features of the election campaign – aspects of politics that do not persist from one campaign to the next, even if the campaigns begin on an identical footing. Some of these nonsystematic features might include a verbal gaffe, a surprisingly popular speech or position on an issue, ... We can therefore imagine a variable that would express the values of the Democratic vote across hypothetical replications of this same election. (King, Keohane, and Verba 1994: 79; the systematic variable is incumbency effect)

Note that qualitative scholar focusing on explaining one election might well make the claim that *but for* the verbal gaffe the incumbent would have won. The statistical scholar is interested in general patterns ("mean effect") not the explanation of particular events.

It is not surprising then that many philosophers when thinking about the philosophy of history see causal explanations in terms of necessary condition counterfactuals. There is a long tradition starting at least with Max Weber (see Honoré and Hart (1985) for a very good history and analysis) that sees history as making necessary condition counterfactual claims. For example, Aron as well as Gallie clearly argue that causation in history is identified with necessary condition counterfactuals:

---

[1] There are a few who combined necessary condition hypothesizing with large-N statistical, methods, e.g., Bueno de Mesquita (1981), see Braumoeller and Goertz (2000) for some other examples.

> Si je dis que la décision de Bismarck a été cause de la guerre
> de 1866, que la victoire de Marathon a sauvé la culture grecque,
> j'entends que, sans la décision du chancelier, la guerre n'aurait pas
> éclaté ... que les Perses vainqueurs auraient empêché le "miracle"
> grec. Dans les deux cas, la causalité effective ne se définit que par
> une confrontation avec les possibles.[2] (Aron 1986 [1938]: 202)

> I wish to show that one kind of causal argument is peculiarly
> characteristic of historical explanation. Historians, I shall argue,
> sometimes explain events in a perfectly good sense of "explain," by
> referring us to one or a number of their temporally prior *necessary*
> conditions; they tell us how a particular event happened by point-
> ing out hitherto unnoticed, or at least undervalued, antecedent
> events, *but for which,* they claim on broadly inductive grounds,
> the event in question would not or could hardly have happened.
> (Gallie 1955: 161; he explicitly contrasts this kind of explanation
> with sufficiency and correlational explanations)

With examples like Weber, Aron and Gallie in hand, we suggest that
while there may be other ways of thinking about causation in case studies, the necessary condition counterfactual approach is an important
one.

In the philosophy of history those who take Hempel's covering
law view explanation almost always think of explanation in sufficient
condition terms. For example, White (1965) clearly sees narratives as a
chain of hypotheses, each supported by a covering law, each of which
has a sufficient condition nature:

> A statement of the form "A is a contributory cause of C" is true if
> and only if there is an explanatory deductive argument containing
> "A" as a premise and "C" as its conclusion. (White 1965: 60)

The deductive argument that White has in mind is the sufficiency one
associated with covering laws. These laws have the form of "If the
situation is A then because of covering law L then C will happen."
Because of equifinality, it is quite possible that there is covering law K
that can also produce C. It is not surprising then that White will argue
against necessary condition, counterfactual, or *sine qua non* approaches
to causation (White 1965: 151–63).

Let us emphasize in conclusion that we do not think that cause
should be defined in necessary condition terms or that there might not

---

[2]If I say that the decision of Bismarck was [a] cause of the war in 1866, that the victory
at Marathon saved Greek culture, I mean that without the decision of the chancellor
that war would not have broken out, that the victorious Persians would have prevented
the Greek "miracle." In these two cases, the effective cause can only be defined by
confronting possibilities. (Aron 1986 [1938]: 202; our translation)

be other types of cause. It may well be that there are events that have no necessary conditions.[3] Simply we would like to stress that making necessary condition counterfactuals is a core explanatory strategy in history and case studies. This is all the more important since the constant conjunction or covering law view of causation dominates the discussion in political science (again, in contrast to philosophy where there is a real debate between the probabilistic causation position, e.g., Salmon (1984), Humphreys (1989), and the counterfactual one defended by Lewis and many others).

Necessary conditions and counterfactuals

The extensive literature on counterfactuals has not treated the relationship between necessary conditions and counterfactuals (e.g., Elster 1978; Fearon 1991; Tetlock and Belkin 1996; though see Goertz 1994). We do not intend to discuss counterfactuals in general but only how they relate to a specific sort of causal explanation. Our general position is that the ease with which one can make counterfactuals and their validity depend to a large extent on the character of the theory or explanation used to make the counterfactual.

In the case of necessary conditions the link between a necessary condition explanation of a case and a counterfactual is built into the causal explanation itself. To say that X is necessary for Y means simultaneously the counterfactual that without X, Y would not have occurred. To assert a necessary condition is simultaneously to assert a counterfactual: they are bound together.

It is in large part because of the counterfactual implications of a necessary condition explanation that we consider necessary conditions to be important causes. If factor X is such that its absence would have prevented World War I then it certainly deserves to be considered a key cause of World War I.[4]

While necessary conditions are inseparably linked to counterfactuals, such is not the cause with other kinds of causes. If we take "contributing" factors or even sufficient conditions the ties to counterfactuals are much weaker. That X is sufficient for Y does not imply that if X had been absent then Y would not have occurred. As we discuss below, if an event is overdetermined, i.e., multiple sufficient causes are present, then we cannot make the natural counterfactual. Equifinality

---

[3] For example, linear regression models post no sufficient conditions.
[4] This assumes that it is not a "trivial" necessary condition, see Goertz 2004 for an extended analysis of the concept of a trivial necessary condition.

in its various forms such as INUS[5] causes (Mackie 1974) or Ragin's
fuzzy logic methodology (Ragin 2000) proposes that there are multiple
sets of sufficient conditions. This makes counterfactuals more difficult
because the absence of factors on one causal path does not exclude the
effects of other causal paths. In short, counterfactuals are hard with
equifinality, easy with necessary conditions.

One way to think of this is in terms of truth and entailment. The
truth of a necessary condition causal explanation directly entails the
truth of the corresponding counterfactual. The truth of a sufficient
condition proposition does not necessarily entail (though it may be
true in individual instances) the normal counterfactual. The truth of
a sufficient condition does entail the truth of some counterfactuals,
but these are not the counterfactuals that normally interest students
of case histories. The truth of "if X then Y" entails the truth of "if
not-Y then not-X". This counterfactual has not been the focus of much
attention at all in the analysis of individual cases.[6]

It is worth noting that the necessary condition counterfactual methodology is a *univariate* one. In many case studies the goal is to focus on
one important causal factor. The aim is not a "complete" explanation of
the event but rather a more modest one of exploring the consequences
of a key independent variable. The necessary condition counterfactual
methodology is thus a natural tool. Certainly if a good case can be made
for the necessity of X then X can be said to be an important cause of Y.

As we shall argue in more detail below, the necessary condition
counterfactual methodology really has two parts. First, one must
demonstrate that X is in fact necessary for Y. Second, one must show it
is a nontrivial necessary condition (see Braumoeller and Goertz (2000)
for this in a quantitative setting). While these are separate issues and
require different methodologies they are often discussed together in
case studies.

As one might expect it is not hard to find necessary condition
counterfactuals for World War I. As a matter of practice, scholars often
frame causal explanations using language that implies the necessary
condition connection. The counterfactual expression "Y would not have
occurred without X" probably appears more often than the phrase "X
is necessary for Y."

[5]A factor is an "INUS" cause if it is an insufficient but necessary part of a condition
which is itself unnecessary but sufficient for the result.

[6]One example of where the focus of attention has been on the sufficient – as opposed
to the necessary – condition version of the hypothesis is the democratic peace. The
proposition that joint democracy is sufficient for peace is more interesting to most
scholars than is the proposition that nondemocracy is necessary for war.

To get a taste for how this works in a concrete case here are some counterfactuals by prominent scholars for the origins of World War I[7]:

> Each decision, one can argue, led to the next, and in the absence of any one of them, the crisis [July 1914] might have been averted. (Williamson 1988: 806)

> If the Archduke had not been assassinated in 1914, giving rise to the unusual opportunity I have just described, it seems quite likely that Germany would have reached that fateful year of 1917 still at peace with its neighbors. (Lebow 1984: 168)

> The consequences of the cult of the offensive are illuminated by imagining the politics of 1914 had European leaders recognized the actual power of the defense.... Thus the logic that led Germany to provoke the 1914 crisis would have been undermined, and the chain reaction by which the war spread outward from the Balkans would have been very improbable. In all likelihood, the Austro–Serbian conflict would have been a minor and soon-forgotten disturbance on the periphery of European politics. (Van Evera 1984: 105)

These examples illustrate the tendency of many scholars to hedge (Lakoff 1973) their bets. Instead of strongly affirming the counterfactual, e.g., "was necessary for," one sees expressions like "might have been averted," or "probably would not have occurred." Often hedges take probabilistic form, e.g., very likely, but the use of hedges of this sort should not obscure the fundamental counterfactual, necessary condition character of the claim.[8]

Not surprisingly we can find many examples of necessary condition causes in the literature on the end of the Cold War. This approach can be found both in the arguments of the realists as well as those who stress the importance of ideas or individuals. For example:

> Oye argues that the pressures of international competition were a "significant permissive cause of political and economic liberaliza-tion within the Soviet Union" (Oye 1995: 58)

---

[7] One can also find important necessary condition-counterfactuals on other aspects of the war: "a nonrepressive, nonexclusionary Germany would have ended the war before 1918, with 1917 a likely termination year" (Goemans 2000: 315).

[8] Although some (Lieberson 2003) believe that necessary condition hypotheses are deterministic, we argue that necessary conditions can be either deterministic or prob-abilistic. For further discussion of the issues involved see Goertz and Starr (2003) and Goertz (2005). For a completely probabilistic view of necessary conditions see Cioffi-Revilla (1998).

> The growth of the specialist network, its institutionalization and involvement in setting the political agenda, in addition to personnel changes, created a political environment in which a withdrawal [from Afghanistan] could happen. (Mendelson 1993: 342)

These examples from the literature on the end of the Cold War illustrate the use of "possibility, permissive" language to express necessary conditions. The use of counterfactual language shows quite directly the necessary condition character of the explanation. In contrast, one can find the use of alternative modes of expressing necessary conditions. These include the language of "permissive conditions," or "make *X* possible." Implied in this language is the hypothesis that had the factor been *absent* then the outcome would have been *impossible*, or at least extremely unlikely. These words are just as often used by structuralists, e.g., realists in the end of the Cold War debate, as by social constructivists who emphasize ideas and norms.[9]

One indication of the usefulness of the necessary condition causal strategy is that one can find it in "structural" as well as "contingency" explanations. In the case of the end of the Cold War necessary condition, counterfactuals are used by those arguing for the importance of individuals (e.g., Gorbachev), ideas, and material decline. Some, such as Kahneman (1995), suggest that necessary condition counterfactuals are inherent in causal thinking. While not all causal explanations take the necessary condition counterfactual form, it does form a core explanatory tool in case study settings. We have also tried to illustrate the various ways in which scholars express necessary condition counterfactuals, particularly notable is the use of permissive cause or possibility language. We hope this volume will make readers and scholars alike more attentive to the language they use and its implication in terms of causal explanations.

---

[9]While some may use the language of "permissive cause" or "make possible" in a way that is equivalent to the concept of necessary conditions, which has a specific technical meaning, it is possible that scholars use this alternative language in a looser, non-technical sense. For example, by saying that a particular factor (Soviet material decline, for example) "made the end of the Cold War possible," some might allow for the possibility that there might be another factor that might also make the end of the Cold War possible, a possibility that would be precluded if the first factor were a necessary condition. Similarly, some might say that *X* was a "permissive cause" of an event and not preclude the possibility that *Y* was also a permissive cause of the event. The concepts of necessary and sufficient conditions lack this ambiguity, and it is their precision that makes their use preferable.

Sufficiency

A basic goal in historical accounts of events like World War I is to produce a causal explanation.[10] While we think sufficiency claims are rare in general (particularly compared to the commonness of necessary condition ones), the end of the Cold War debate provides a nice example where sufficiency concerns are core to the debate between the realist and ideational[11] positions. It is possible to give a sufficiency explanation that uses no necessary conditions. In a related fashion there is the possibility that events, notably World War I, might be overdetermined.

Whether it is accurate or not, those that argue for the importance of ideas often critique the realist position in terms of its claim of sufficiency.[12] While we do not intend to adjudicate the debate (readers can judge for themselves after reading the relevant chapters), we would like to expose in a skeletal fashion how sufficiency arguments appear in this debate.

One can find realists making claims about the importance of the material decline of the Soviet Union in sufficiency-like terms:

> In each area, policy went through three phases that closely tracked the severity of resource constraints. 1985–6 was the competitive phase, during which the Soviet leadership appears to have thought it had the resources to drive a hard bargain with the West. By 1988, however, Gorbachev's efforts to "accelerate" the Soviet economy by deploying the defense sector had failed, producing an escalating deficit, powerful inflationary pressures, and no measurable increase in competitiveness. The result was a second phase of radical new thinking in which Gorbachev and his colleagues were willing to make much larger concessions on the assumption that their interests would still shape the eventual settlement.... In 1990–1 [third phase], when the terms for ending the Cold War were finally settled, resource constraints were overpowering the Soviet policy process on all fronts ... Change in ideas similarly

---

[10]See Hexter (1971) for a critique of this and a counterproposal that what historians do is provide "credible stories"; see also Pennington and Hastie (1986) and Sylvan and Haddad (1998).

[11]Unfortunately, there is no commonly accepted label for theories that stress the importance of ideas, beliefs, values, or norms. Constructivists often emphasize these factors, but not all arguments employing these variables are constructivist. We use the term "idea" or "ideational" interchangeably to designate theories that stress the importance of these factors.

[12]Brooks has described neorealism in general in sufficiency terms: "Neorealists would likely argue that the preceding three factors [potential costs of war, focus on underlying capability for aggressiveness, focus on the possibility not probability of conflict] – which they assert can be traced to the anarchic state of the international system – necessarily induce rational states to adopt a worst-case/possibilistic focus." (Brooks 1997: 448–9).

tended to move in tandem with changes in policy that were necessitated by material pressure. (Schweller and Wohlforth 2000: 90–1)

In this passage Schweller and Wohlforth argue that changes in Soviet policy tracked, i.e., were caused by, changes in Soviet resource constraints. These changes were sufficient in the sense that one does not need recourse to other factors, notably ideational ones, to explain changes in policy.

In contrast, without exception, those who argue for the importance of ideas, norms, and the like grant that material constraints are part of the story but not the whole story; in other words, resource constraints might be a necessary cause of the end of the Cold War but they are not sufficient. For example,

Economic decline was clearly a necessary factor in the inception of Soviet reforms, and the authors (Brooks and Wohlforth this volume) have given us new insights into how such pressures also played an important facilitating role. But they are still far from establishing material forces as a sufficient condition. (English this volume, p. 259)

Typically then, the critique from an ideational position argues that material factors are important but "indeterminate," i.e., they narrow the range of options but do not select one (which would be sufficiency).[13] The realist explanation is too "deterministic," meaning that it specifies a particular outcome (one could consider that necessary conditions are also deterministic in the more usual sense of the word). Realists arguments are "underspecified" again saying that important causal variables are left out.[14] These, and the list is not complete, are various ways to phrase an argument against a sufficiency position. Similarly, Risse-Kappen states that realist theories are "notoriously insufficient if we want to understand the way actors define and interpret their interests" (Risse-Kappen 1994: 214).

---

[13] Kennedy raises the same sort of issue in the literature about World War I when he says that a structuralist approach "tells us why Wilhelmine Germany was expansionist at a certain time, but it has much less explanatory power when we move on to the equally important questions of what sort of expansionist policies were chosen, and why, and with what effects" (Kennedy 1982: 164).

[14] Waltz (1979) is more cautious than many other realists. He argues that international structures shape international outcomes by preventing certain outcomes from occurring, or at least making them extremely unlikely, rather than by forcing other outcomes to occur or by significantly influencing the foreign policy behavior of states. That is, Waltzian neorealism is a theory of constraints on international outcomes, not a theory of foreign policy.

Critics use the same strategy as Schweller and Wohlforth to argue against them. This strategy only really works if a sufficiency-like interpretation of realism is taken:

> But how a political leadership will respond to the strategy environment is indeterminate ... Virtually the same confluence of internal and external pressures that purportedly compelled the adoption of New Thinking had been present since the late stages of the Brezhnev regime without any significant changes in policy until 1985 (p. 277). Russia's growing assertiveness [ca. 1993] would seem to confound the expectations of realist theory.... how can they account for the Yeltsin government's increasingly nationalist course at a time when Russia is far weaker in both relative and absolute terms than in the late 1980s? (Herman 1996: 277, 312; see also Bennett 1999 chapter 2; Evangelista 1999 chap. 17)

Herman is saying that if we look at other periods of severe resource constraint we do not see policy shifts one would expect. For example, the early Yeltsin period was one of serious economic difficulty and Russian foreign policy got more belligerent.

A second common argument against sufficiency positions shows that alternative options existed and were quite possible outcomes. We discuss the importance of individuals below, but one can also argue that Gorbachev had other options than the one he chose:

> This suggests that Gorbachev could have attempted to appease both the MIP coalition and the yearning for economic and political reforms by espousing a combination of domestic reforms and hard-line, interventionist foreign policies. A number of possible linkages between domestic and foreign policy were open to him. If Soviet leaders during the drawn-out leadership succession in the 1980s had seen Soviet military interventions of the 1970s as successes rather than failures, Gorbachev might have competed for the mantle of "most interventionist" and sought the support of the very institutions that his reformist coalition downgraded. (Bennett 1999: 71)

Here, as with many of the arguments against sufficiency, one emphasizes that alternative possibilities and choices were available and that the potential sufficient condition cannot explain why a particular option or person was chosen.

Another way to express the difference between realists and their idea-based critics about the sufficiency of material factors is in terms of the distinction between adaptation and learning (Levy 1994). Realists concede the fact that Soviet leaders' beliefs changed in response to changing material circumstances, but argue that this was adaptation to structural change rather than genuine learning. Soviet leaders "learned," but learning had no causal effect, because the change of beliefs was endogenous to changing material structures. Critics like English (2000, and in this volume) and Bennett (1999) argue that belief change was not fully endogenous to structural change, but was based in part on autonomous ideas. While realists emphasize the sufficiency of structural adaptation, idea-based critics emphasize the necessity of causal learning. Many of the critics concede some role to structural change, however, and in the end argue that structural change and causal learning were each necessary conditions for the end of the Cold War.

Our point in this brief discussion is to illuminate the causal and empirical strategies that one uses in making and defending sufficiency-like claims. The end of the Cold War literature is one of the best and most prominent examples of this that we know of.

The end of the Cold War example is rare in that most sufficiency explanations are multivariate in character. Take, for example, the following explanation for World War I by Maier:

> The irreversible momentum toward general war in 1914 is usually seen as a result of three factors: the hopeless, long-term instability of the Habsburg empire, the rigid structure of opposing alliances, and the ineluctable pull of military preparations. (Maier 1988: 822)

As we have seen in the section on the concept of cause, a complete causal explanation can be taken to be all those conditions which are individually necessary and *jointly sufficient* for the outcome. We shall see below that the powder keg, or window of opportunity-catalyst model makes sufficiency claims.

However, the necessary condition part of this very general explanatory framework can be put into question if the event is overdetermined. Logically, it is possible for an event to be simultaneously overdetermined and yet have multiple necessary conditions.[15] Nevertheless, there is a feeling that if an event, such as World War I, is really overdetermined the emphasis on necessary conditions might be misplaced.

For example, Schroeder sees World War I as basically overdetermined:

> The difficulty arises in accepting the notion, implicit in all of Fischer's work and explicitly drawn by many historians as the chief lesson of it, that Germany's bid for world power was the *causa causans*, the central driving force behind the war.... the whole attempt to find a *causa causans* behind the multiplicity of contributing factors is misconceived.... one encounters a plethora of

---

[15] Think of two sets of variables, each of which is jointly sufficient for an outcome, and each of which has multiple (but different) necessary conditions.

"causes" far more than sufficient to account for the phenomenon one wishes to explain, clearly connected with it, and yet not "sufficient" in the sense that any set of them logically implies what occurred. The fact that so many plausible explanations for the outbreak of the war [World War I] have been advanced over the years indicates on the one hand that it was massively overdetermined, and on the other that no effort to analyze the causal factors involved can ever fully succeed. (Schroeder 1972: 320)

Maier is suggesting that these three factors were jointly sufficient for World War I. There appear to be causes "more than sufficient" to account for World War I. We can go back to Maier's three factors and ask if these are part of the "massive overdetermination" of World War I.

Recall that by definition necessary conditions are those factors for which there is no substitute within a given causal path. It is possible that say some factors of the causal explanation are massively overdetermined while others are very contingent. For example, the powder keg may be overdetermined because of the many factors pushing Europe into two camps and the many arenas, colonial, Balkans, and western Europe where conflicts occurred.

Nevertheless, there is a clear tension between overdetermination and the importance of necessary conditions. As the number of necessary conditions increase the contingency of events increases – *ceteris paribus* of course. If events are quite contingent, then they are not overdetermined.

Causal chains

One often reads of the "chain of events" leading up to some important outcome. The goal of this section is to begin an analysis of what that metaphor implies in terms of necessary or sufficient condition causal explanations. The chain metaphor also provides the occasion to introduce the topic of multivariate causal explanations. Potentially each link in the chain can be a cause of the outcome.

More generally, the chain metaphor permits us to tackle the question of narrative and causal explanation. History is traditionally – particularly in its classic form of political history – a narrative, i.e., a story, that ideally is also an explanation of why the event occurred.[16] Once again, we do not intend to survey the vast literature on history and

---

[16]Not all historical accounts of individual historical events take a narrative form. In his study of the origins of World War I, for example, James Joll (1992) begins with a narrative account of the July 1914 crisis, but then organizes his analysis (and subsequent chapters) around the following analytic themes: alliances and diplomacy, militarism and armaments, domestic politics, international economy, imperial rivalries,

narrative, but only to examine that part which is relevant to necessary condition causal explanations.

One frequently sees causal chains represented by $E1 \Rightarrow E2 \Rightarrow E3$. It is rarely made clear what causal interpretation to give to these arrows. Within the context of this chapter we can think of two interpretations, one is that the arrows represent a necessary condition, the second is that it represents a sufficient condition. To distinguish the two interpretations we shall use the subscripts N and S to differentiate the two, for example,

$$E1_N \Rightarrow E2_S \Rightarrow E3_{NS} \Rightarrow E3_N \Rightarrow E5$$

Key to our analysis of cause chains is the notion of the "strength" of the causal bond between links. We can rank links in terms of their strength from strongest to weakest, (1) necessary and sufficient, (2) sufficient condition and (3) necessary. Much of the debate about the relative importance of different factors relates to the kinds of relationships one finds between links in the chain.

Necessary condition causal chains

In a chain consisting of necessary conditions, if any link is absent then, counterfactually, the outcome would not have occurred. If an historical narrative describes a causal chain, then we would have a temporal series of necessary conditions for the event in question.

The classic chain metaphor does suggest one form of causal explanation in case studies. One potential multivariate causal explanation is a *temporal* series (chain) of necessary conditions, say, for World War I. For the purposes of this section the two key aspects are (1) the temporal nature of the series and (2) the components of the series are necessary conditions.

A traditional narrative focuses on key decisions in a process that over time leads to the event in question, e.g., World War I. While many narratives will include background and/or structural factors as part of the description we want to limit ourselves in this section to causal chains that invoke relatively specific decisions that link together to produce the outcome.

Levy (this volume) in summarizing his analysis of the decisions and factors that led to World War I gives this list:

---

and "the mood of 1914." Levy's chapter in this volume uses a different theoretical framework, one based on rational choice analysis, to structure an analytic narrative of the July crisis. For more on narrative and non-narrative historical explanations, see Levy (2001).

1. The German assumption of British neutrality during the early stages of a continental war was a necessary condition for German support for Austro–Hungarian military action against Serbia, for Germany's willingness to risk a continental war against Russia, and therefore for the outbreak of a World War I involving all of the great powers.

2. German support for Austria–Hungary was a necessary condition for a major Austro–Hungarian military action against Serbia, and consequently a necessary condition for a war of any kind in 1914.

3. Russian intervention in an Austro–Serbian war was a necessary condition for a continental war and consequently for a world war.

4. Russian Foreign Minister Sazonov's belief that a partial mobilization against Austria–Hungary would not lead to a general European war was a necessary condition for his willingness to push for mobilization.

5. Some form of Russian mobilization was a necessary condition for German mobilization.

Now not all of the factors listed here are "decisions" per se. For example, the German assumption of British neutrality is really a belief. Nevertheless, this list summarizes key aspects of individual links that Levy discusses in detail. The list is given in chronological order as one would expect of a causal chain. In addition, Levy says that each link was a necessary step on the path toward war.

One can see a chain of factors (maybe or maybe not necessary) in ideas arguments about the end of the Cold War. As we discuss in more detail below, many see Gorbachev as a necessary link in the causal chain. We can then work our way back by asking how Gorbachev got his ideas. For example, English makes this point:

> None [of the usual explanations], however, adequately addresses a critical, earlier, process that made such an endgame possible; the emergence, over the preceding two decades, of a Soviet intellectual elite holding sharply unorthodox beliefs about their country's development and proper place in the world community.... So while crisis and leadership transition were vital preconditions, so an earlier intellectual change – the rise of a global, "Westernizing" identity among a liberal policy-academic elite – was a sine qua non of the Cold War's sudden and peaceful end. (English 2000: 2, 3)

Checkel (1997) has argued strongly for the importance of various institutes like IMEMO and ISKAN as the source of Gorbachev's ideas. He argues that it was not just personal contacts or individual learning on the part of Gorbachev but rather the impact of organized, institutional-ized ideas:

> Despite these various changes and despite Arbatov's skills, IMEMO was a relatively uninfluential player in these security debates. Arba-tov was in fact a "policy entrepreneur" and a person like Yakovlev and Primatov had the necessary skills and connections to exploit open policy windows. Nevertheless, he failed to convert this en-trepreneurship into influence, even though he had the clear back-ing of his boss, Primakov. A key element in this failure was that Arbatov, in bringing his expertise in strategic affairs to IMEMO, was attempting to modify fundamentally the institute's basic mis-sion.... Moreover, his entrepreneurship was openly and actively resisted by various institute scholars. (Checkel 1993: 292–3)

Here Checkel uses an interesting strategy to make his case. He takes the example of Arbatov, someone without the (necessary) organizational support, and argues that this kind of personal contact did not result in policy change. Personal contacts *and* institutional support would influence Gorbachev but not just personal contacts alone.

We can continue to follow the causal chain back from Soviet pol-icy institutes. Evangelista (1999) has made a forceful case for the importance of transnational actors in influencing individuals and orga-nizations within the Soviet Union. So now the causal chain looks like Transnational groups ⇒ Soviet policy institutes ⇒ Gorbachev.

It is always important to remember that necessary condition causal chains are incomplete, while sufficient ones are not. The existence of a necessary condition makes the next link possible, but usually other factors must be included to explain why it in fact did happen.

Sufficient condition causal chains

We suspect when people use arrows to express causation that some sufficiency-like interpretation makes the most sense. This is because a sufficient condition actually produces the next link in the chain, whereas that is not the case for necessary condition links.

Consider the following causal chain of events (E) in the abstract:

$$E1_S \Rightarrow E2_S \Rightarrow E3$$

Since each link is sufficient we can say that the "intervening" link of $E2$ is not very important, the key cause is the first link of the chain $E1$. If Alice shoots Jane resulting in her death, the "immediate" cause of death is the bullet damaging Jane's heart ($E2$). However, since Alice's aiming the gun and pulling the trigger leads direct to $E3$ via $E2$ we find that the principal cause is Alice shooting the gun. So the first sufficient condition is important while the second is much less so.

Now consider a different causal chain where there are links that are not all sufficient:

$$E1_N \Rightarrow E2_N \Rightarrow E3_S \Rightarrow E4_S \Rightarrow E5$$

The strength of the bond between $E2$ and $E3$ is weaker because $E2$ is necessary but not sufficient for $E3$. Hence other factors have to be present for sufficiency to be achieved. The link between the two is weaker than the link between $E3$ and $E4$. Yet $E2_N$ is typically more important than the $E4_S$ sufficient condition. The key principle here is that each necessary condition in the link is equally important, while in chains of sufficient conditions it is the first sufficient condition that typically is the really important one. Hence, (1) the relative importance of sufficient conditions depends on where the sufficient condition lies in the causal chain, (2) necessary conditions are of roughly equal importance (see below for more on this), and (3) sufficient conditions at the beginning of causal chains are usually more important than necessary condition ones.

One commonly used example of these issues in the World War I case is the degree of linkage between mobilization plans. All have remarked upon the tight connection between Russian and German mobilizations. Trachtenberg poses a key question: "A mechanism of this sort [linked mobilization plans] clearly existed, but was it actually a *cause* of the war? It is important to think through what is implied by the claim that this mechanism of interlocking mobilization plans helped bring on the cataclysm" (Trachtenberg 1990-1: 121; see also Ferguson 1999a: 267). We suggest that the examples above of chains with differing levels of bonds between links provides a framework for looking at this question.

Trachtenberg then uses the tightness of sufficiency links in the causal chain to downplay the importance of mobilization plans as a cause of World War I:

> [I]f in 1914 everyone understood the system and knew, for example, that a Russian or German general mobilization would lead to war, and if, in addition, the political authorities were free agents – that is, if their hands were not being forced by military imperatives, or by pressure from the generals – then the existence of the system of interlocking mobilization plans could hardly be said in itself to have been a "cause" of war because, once it was set off, the time for negotiation was cut short. But if the working of the system was understood in advance, a decision for general mobilization was a decision for war; statesmen would be opting for war with their

> eyes open. To argue that the system was, in such a case, a "cause"
> of war makes about as much sense as saying that any military
> operation which marked the effective beginning of hostilities ...
> was a real "cause" of an armed conflict. (Trachtenberg 1990–1:
> 122)

Sagan uses the same sort of explanatory strategy of strong links to argue that because of the tight connection between Russian mobilization and German war decisions the Russian decision is a very important cause of the war:

> The German threat to Russia – that it would soon be forced to mobilize, which meant war, which meant the Schlieffen Plan's offensive, if Russia did not stop the *partial* mobilization against Austria–Hungary underscores the importance of the alliance commitment in Berlin's calculations.... This decision [Russian mobilization] was critical, for once the full mobilization of the Russian army began, Bethmann-Hollweg called off the attempt to avert war by having Austro-Hungarian forces "Halt in Belgrade." (Sagan 1986: 165–6)

In short, Russian mobilization led directly and almost inevitably to war.

Others in their analysis of World War I will stress the importance of the Schlieffen Plan and downplay the Russian decision: "But there was only one decision which turned the little Balkan conflict between Austria–Hungary and Serbia into a European war. That was the German decision to start general mobilization on 31st July, and that was in turn decisive because of the academic ingenuity with which Schlieffen, now in his grave, had attempted to solve the problem of a two-front war" (Taylor 1969: 101).[17] Levy (1986) makes a similar argument regarding the common hypothesis that rigid organizational routines in the form of military mobilization and war plans were an important cause of World War I (Tuchman 1962; A. Taylor 1969). He argues that such hypotheses often exaggerate the causal impact of organizational routines by neglecting the systemic variables that create a "military necessity" for developing such plans and for implementing them in a crisis: "The greater the extent to which military necessity influences both the development of contingency plans and their rigid implementation in a crisis, the less the causal weight that can be attributed to the nature of the plans themselves" (Levy 1986: 193). These kinds of debates are about the relative importance of the links in the chain.

Thus the strength of the linkage between events plays a key role in evaluating the importance of individual events and decisions. Another

---

[17] For recent scholarship on the Schlieffen Plan, which might affect some of these interpretations, see Zuber (2003) and Lieber (2006).

such example is the very close sufficiency link between the violation of Belgian neutrality and the British entry into the war: "The argument that British intervention in the war was made inevitable by the violation of Belgian neutrality has been repeated by historians ever since [Lloyd George]" (Ferguson 1999a: 231). Because of the strong character of the sufficiency link blame is often given to the earlier factor. Hence, World War I it is not the fault of the British but rather the Germans.[18]

In causal chains of this sort often one considers the factors at the beginning of the chain as more important than those at the end as we have seen with Sagan's argument. One can see this at work in Bennett's analysis of learning and Soviet–Russian interventionism during and after the Cold War. Initially he argues that there is a very close correlation between beliefs and actions on the part of Soviet leaders.

> There was a high degree of consistency in every case study be-
> tween the stated beliefs of Soviet and Russian leaders and their
> subsequent behavior. During periods in which beliefs were inter-
> ventionist – 1973 to 1979 and 1992 to 1994 – the Soviet Union
> and Russia did not fail to intervene when opportunities arose....
> During periods of noninterventionist beliefs – 1989–90 and to a
> less extent 1980 to 1989 – there were no new major interventions
> ... Even though the evidence is strong that stated beliefs corre-
> lated with subsequent behavior, it remains to be shown that ideas
> were not mere ephiphenoma of domestic politics or systematic
> pressures. (Bennett 1999: 351–2)

As we have seen above, constant conjunction (i.e., very high correlations) typify a sufficiency-like argument in analyses of particular historical events. However, one must be attentive to the possibility that beliefs were the result of more fundamental factors, e.g., systematic structures, and thus less important in the final causal explanation.

Turning points and critical junctures

The strength or weakness of the bonds between links is intimately related to the concepts of "critical junctures" or "turning points." We think that turning points are just those links that are weak in the causal chain. We would define turning points as those decision nodes where it would have been relatively easy to move onto a different path. In the terms of this section those are links that have weak bonds to the next link on the road to war (World War I) or peace (end of the Cold War).

---

[18]Shaver (1985) and Honoré and Hart (1985) provide extensive discussions of the close link between causal explanations and the attribution of blame.

Geiss's account (1966) of the German decisions leading to war illustrates a number of common and central characteristics of narrative accounts focusing on key choices. Geiss stresses two decision points that were critical in the German move towards war.[19] The first was the Kaiser deciding between two factions within the German government: "After Sarajevo Germany could not at once make up her mind which course to follow. The Auswärtiges Amt clearly saw the danger involved in Russia's trying to protect Serbia if Austria made war, namely, that a world war might result.... The German General Staff, on the other hand, was ready to welcome Sarajevo as the golden opportunity for risking a preventive war. In this situation it was the Kaiser's word that proved decisive" (Geiss 1966: 82–3). The second was when Bethmann-Hollweg suppressed the Kaiser's instructions (which would have helped avoid war) in despatches to Tschirschky on the evening of 28 July after he had learned that Austria had declared war on Serbia: "[Bethmann-Hollweg] stifled the only initiative from the German side which might have saved the general peace" (Geiss 1966: 86).

These key decisions appear to have two core, and correlated, characteristics. They were necessary links in the chain of German decisions that led to war or that could have led to peace. Second, they were possible "turning points" that could have led away from war. For the purposes of the present section the idea of a turning point means that there was a weak bond between the turning point and the decision taken.

The idea of a turning point is very closely related to the influence idea of "critical junctures": "Not all choice points represent critical junctures. Critical junctures are specifically those choice points that put countries (or other units) onto paths of development that track certain outcomes – as opposed to others – that cannot be easily broken or reversed.

Before a critical juncture, a broad range of outcomes is possible; after a critical juncture, enduring institutions and structures are created, and the range of possible outcomes is narrowed considerably" (Mahoney 2001: 7; see also Collier and Collier 1991).[20]

Hermann and Lebow (2001) have made turning points a central part of their analysis of the end of the Cold War. They define turning points as events where major new directions were taken that could not easily be undone:

---

[19]The turning points identified by Geiss (1966) are consistent with the causal chain posited by Levy (in this volume), and in fact occur within it.

[20]Clearly, concepts such as critical juncture and turning points are closely related to theories of path dependence (Mahoney 2000; Pierson 2004; Bennett and Elman 2006).

> We define a turning point in terms of two properties. First, it must
> be a change of significant magnitude, not an incremental adjust-
> ment but a substantial departure from previous practice. Second,
> it must be a change that would be difficult to undo. (Herrmann
> and Lebow 2004: 10)

Our conceptualization of turning points is different in that we think of
them as decision nodes (forks in the road) where one can or perhaps
did take a new direction. In our conceptualization, one can reaching
a turning point and *not turn*. In Herrmann and Lebow's take turning
points are only those nodes where a decision to turn was made.[21]

A turning point implies that the alternative was a "real possibility"
(obviously a counterfactual proposition) and hence a weak bond in
the causal chain. A strong bond is illustrated by Sagan's argument
(see above) about the intimate bond between Russian and German
mobilization decisions, whereby Russian mobilization entailed almost
automatically German mobilization; it involved a decision, of course,
but a decision that was very hard for the Germans not to make. The
nature of the bonds, weak or strong, between key decisions plays an
absolutely essential role in determining the relative importance that we
attribute to decisions in a causal chain.

In the context of the debate about the end of the Cold War one can
see, as we noted above, those that stress the importance of ideas argue
that there was significant indeterminacy in Soviet policy in the mid- to
late 1980s. One can formulate counterfactuals regarding the likelihood
of other leaders taking power in the mid-1980s. It is a turning point in
part because we can make plausible counterfactuals that lead to very
different outcomes.

The key point is that there were necessary condition decisions
and events along the road to World War I and the end of the Cold
War. Many of these decisions were also turning points where leaders
and governments could have taken the road away from war or toward
continued confrontation. These two ideas, necessary conditions and
turning points, are logically separate but nevertheless appear frequently
together. Both necessary conditions and turning point hypotheses imply
strong counterfactuals. Taking the path to crisis deescalation was very
possible; the decision actually taken was necessary on the road to war.

---

[21] Critical junctures also often have this property: "Thus, the concept of a critical
juncture contains three components: the claim that a significant change occurred within
each case, the claim that this change took place in distinct ways in different cases, and
explanatory hypothesis about its consequences. If the explanatory hypothesis proves to
be false – that is, the hypothesized critical juncture did not produce the legacy – then
one would assert that it was not, in fact, a critical juncture" (Collier and Collier 1991:
30).

The importance of individuals in historical causal explanations

Diplomatic history is just as much about narratives as about causal explanation. Hi(story) is often about the actions of key individuals. Not surprisingly then, counterfactuals about individuals are quite common. The most obvious example of this in our two cases is the importance (or lack thereof) of Gorbachev in the end of the Cold War.

While we have not conducted a formal survey, we think that many historians and political scientists believe that Gorbachev was an essential part of the explanation for why the Cold War ended. This view easily takes a necessary condition counterfactual form: "[F]or it is nearly impossible to imagine any of Gorbachev's competitors for the general secretaryship even undertaking, much less carrying through, his bold domestic and foreign reforms" (English 2000: 3; see also p. 192).

Here the counterfactual methodology is easier than in other situations. To support the necessary condition counterfactual one needs to go through the list of people, usually a relatively small number, who might have taken power instead of Gorbachev in the mid-1980s. One can then assess the likelihood of any of these players doing something as radical as Gorbachev did.[22]

In analyzing the likelihood that other possible Soviet leaders might have acted as Gorbachev did, we need to be very careful in the selection of the set of possible individuals for analysis. Ideally, we should be able to imagine that leader coming to power with a minimal change in international or particularly domestic political conditions. Otherwise, the inference that other leaders would have behaved differently (e.g., continued the Cold War) might be explained either by the importance of individuals or by other factors that changed. This is the logic underlying what Tetlock and Belkin (1996: 23–5) call a "minimal rewrite counterfactual."

One can find claims about the centrality of leaders in the World War I case as well. For example, "Absent the Iron Chancellor [Bismarck], it is hard to imagine a defeated Austria aligning with Prussia after the humiliations of Sadowa and Königgrätz. Similarly, it is equally hard to imagine a leader other than Wilhelm II repeatedly antagonizing Britain for so little purpose" (Byman and Pollack 2001: 134). Lebow's argument (in this volume) that the outbreak of World War I was contingent upon

---

[22]Similarly, some have gone beyond the rather common argument that Adolph Hitler was an important cause of World War II in Europe to make the stronger claim that Hitler was a necessary cause of the war, and have explained why other individuals who might conceivably have been in the role of German Chancellor would have behaved differently (Mueller 1989).

the assassination of Archduke Ferdinand (and other factors) is based on the use of a minimal rewrite counterfactual. One can easily imagine a failed assassination attempt without assuming a change in other key variables. One could use a similar logic in a counterfactual analysis of whether individual differences would have led Al Gore to pursue a different policy toward Iraq than George W. Bush. One needs to change virtually nothing to imagine Gore rather than Bush becoming president in 2000. We must recognize, however, that other variables would quickly change as the causal result of this individual-level change (e.g., the president's advisors and his political constituency), and we would have to consider their independent causal impact.

Structural explanations almost by definition downplay the importance of individuals. In the most extreme position the international or structural constraints are so strong that the leadership *has no choice*:

> We would be prepared to sustain the counterfactual claim that given the material distribution of power of the 1980s, a rapidly declining Soviet Union would have most likely sued for peace in the Cold War even if led by old thinkers. (Schweller and Wohlforth 2000: 100)

One of the rules of social science – as opposed to history – is to avoid proper names in giving causal explanations (Przeworski and Teune 1970). Instead one should give the properties or characteristics of the individual event or object that are casually relevant. This avoidance of proper names is closely linked to the desire for general theories. By giving the property of the individual that was casually relevant we assume that in other similar circumstances this property will also play a causal role. For example, Evangelista has argued that it was Gorbachev's skill in packaging his ideas [heresthetics] that accounts in large for his success:

> But only a skillful heresthetician such as Mikhail Gorbachev could have made controversial accommodations to material forces seem natural; only a skillful heresthetician could have ensured that enlightened ideas held by an elite few would seem universal. (Evangelista 2001: 32)

Of course, we can see the same set of issues at work in the literature on the causes of World War I. Here it is the assassination of Archduke Ferdinand that plays the role analogous to Gorbachev. Once again the structuralists argue that many crises could have just as well started World War I, just as the realists argue that many (new or old) thinkers would have ended the Cold War. Lebow's analysis of the assassination also focuses on its properties that were casually relevant to the outbreak of World War I, just as Evangelista does for Gorbachev.

In many, if not most, causal analyses of specific events, key actions or individuals will seem essential to the outcome. At the same time there are almost always structural accounts that will downplay the importance of individuals in favor of larger historical or structural forces.

Windows of opportunity

Without a doubt the image and metaphor of a window of opportunity plays a key role in explanations of World War I and the end of the Cold War. We shall argue that powder kegs, windows of opportunity, preconditions, (pre)requisites, permissive causes, and the like are all variations on the same causal theme. One reason that all these terms refer to the same causal explanation is that they are all seen as necessary conditions. We shall focus most of our attention on the window of opportunity metaphor and causal explanation, but our arguments apply directly to these other causal metaphors as well.

In spite of the popularity of the window metaphor we have found little in the way of a rigorous analysis of what this means in terms of causal explanations. Kingdon's classic work (1984) on agenda-setting is the most extensive analysis of the window of opportunity concept in the literature. Since it is about policy it is substantively quite relevant to government decisions about war or peace. Kingdon is quite explicit about the original use of the window of opportunity metaphor and what it means in a policy framework:

> In space shots, the window presents the opportunity for a launch. The target planets are in proper alignment, but will not stay that way for long. Thus the launch must take place when the window is open, lest the opportunity slip away. Once lost, the opportunity may recur, but in the interim, astronauts and space engineers must wait until the window reopens. Similarly, windows open in policy systems. These policy windows, the opportunities for action on given initiatives, present themselves and stay open for only short periods. If the participants cannot or do not take advantage of these opportunities, they must bide their time until the next opportunity comes along. (Kingdon 1995: 166)

Two of Kingdon's "streams" constitute windows of opportunity for agenda-setting. The "political stream" consists of the larger political context such as the mood of the public, but also exogenous events like crises. The "problem" stream is the specific problem that the policy is meant to address and solve. Each of these two streams must be present for something to make it onto the agenda. The final stream is the solution(s) proposed by policy entrepreneurs.

> If one of the three elements [streams] is missing – if a solution is not available, a problem cannot be found or is not sufficiently compelling, or support is not forthcoming from the policy stream [context] – then the subject's place on the decision agenda is fleeting. (Kingdon 1984: 187)

In short, nothing can happen when a window is closed, it must be open: it is a necessary condition for an item to make it onto the agenda.

The window metaphor has been quite popular among those in the end of the Cold War who stress the importance of ideas. Checkel (1997) and Evangelista (1999; see also Larson and Shevchenko 2003) have been the most consistent users of this explanatory framework:

> These resources, idiosyncratic in nature, are necessary but not sufficient conditions for successful entrepreneurship. Two situational factors are also essential. Are there problems whose resolution would be assisted by the implementation of the entrepreneur's ideas? Are there leaders in power who recognize that resolution would be assisted by the implementation of the entrepreneur's ideas? Are there leaders in power who recognize that such problems exist? Taken together, these two factors create an opportunity – a policy window – for the aspiring entrepreneur to sell a particular idea, intellectual outlook, or policy. (Checkel 1997: 9–10)

> Nevertheless, they [transnational actors] succeeded in implementing some major initiatives, thanks to the peculiar nation of the Soviet domestic structure and the confluence of several policy windows – the severity of the economic crisis, the challenges of the Reagan administration, and, most important, the advent of a strong reformist leader. (Evangelista 1995: 36)

Beyond this Checkel (1997) has chapter titles stressing the centrality of the window of opportunity idea: "Entrepreneurs looking for a window" (chapter 3), "Windows opening" (chapter 4) and "Open windows, new ideas, and the end of the Cold War" (chapter 5).

It is important to note that it is the material factors emphasized by the realists like Brooks and Wohlforth that tend to define the presence of an open window. When those that stress the importance of individuals or ideas include factors like material decline into their explanations it is most often via something like the window of opportunity.

In the context of World War I we see this same sort of idea expounded by well-known scholars:

> Germany and Austria pursued bellicose policies in 1914 partly to shut the looming "windows" of vulnerability which they envisioned

> lying ahead, and partly to exploit the brief window of opportunity
> which they thought the summer crisis opened. This window logic,
> in turn, grew partly from the cult of the offensive, since it depended
> upon the implicit assumption that the offense was strong. (Van
> Evera 1984: 79)

Van Evera (1984) constantly uses the window of opportunity idea to
explain how the cult of the offensive was an important cause of World
War I, and in a subsequent book he generalizes the argument about the
importance of windows and extends it to other cases (Van Evera 1999).
Also, domestic politics (in both Austria–Hungary and Russia) play a
key role in two key causal streams in Lebow's model of open windows.
Open windows, prerequisites, permissive causes, and the like set the
stage for the event to happen. Without these favorable circumstances,
the catalyst can have no effect. Specifically, "possible" often refers
to necessary conditions while "probable" invokes sufficiency. Open
windows make the event possible: the occurrence of other contributing
factors can make the event quite likely.

Powder keg explanations

> The figure of exploding powder is probably the most common of those
> employed by historians who try to account for the occurrence of
> events; and therefore it is well to have in mind the logical structure of
> this constantly used scientific model or metaphor, to say nothing of
> that other favorite, the fertile soil that flowers when seeded.
>
> *Morton White*

The situation in Europe pre-1914 has often been described as a powder
keg that was set off by the catalyst in the form of the assassination of
Archduke Ferdinand. Almost as frequent is the idea that there were
windows of opportunity opening and closing during this period that
explain the actions of various governments.

Window of opportunity causal explanations are very often coupled
with a catalyst or spark causal factor. To use Aristotle's language,
the catalyst is the proximate cause of the event while the window
of opportunity is the prerequisite condition that gives the catalyst
its causal efficacy. The title of Lebow's 1984 article – "Windows-of-
opportunity: do states jump through them?" – illustrates how the
window of opportunity and catalyst metaphors often go together to
form a sufficiency-like explanation.

Individually, window or catalyst arguments form univariate explanatory strategies. Together they form a multivariate explanation of events

like World War I. Because the window must be open when governments jump through it we call these "synchronic" multivariate necessary condition explanations. This presents a contrast with the diachronic, chain of necessary or sufficient conditions discussed above.

If windows of opportunity are typically background causal factors then catalysts are usually about the action, events, and decisions of individual people or governments. Windows of opportunity are usually structure; catalysts are agents.

In Kingdon's model we see this quite clearly. The political and problem streams form the window of opportunity, the actions of policy entrepreneurs are the catalyst that gets the item onto the agenda. Similarly in World War I the catalyst will be a crisis such as the one provoked by the assassination of Archduke Ferdinand. Because Lebow has been the most vigorous recent promoter of the importance of this catalyst it is useful to see how he thinks of catalysts in necessary condition terms:

> In the absence of a catalyst, several more years of peace could have altered the strategic and domestic contexts of the great powers and made war less likely. There was a two-year window when the leaders of at least two great powers thought their national or dynastic interests were better served by war than peace. (Lebow this volume, p. 86)

> To recapitulate, the Sarajevo assassinations changed the political and psychological environment in Vienna and Berlin in six important ways, all of which were probably necessary for the decisions that led to war. (Lebow this volume, p. 99)

Of course, those who focus on the chain of decisions leading to World War I will also see the catalyst event or decisions as important. What these scholars are missing is the emphasis on the structural, window factors that give the catalyst its causal efficacy. For example, Schroeder criticizes Remak for this sort of thing when he says that Remak argues that "Only the particular events of 1914 caused this particular quarrel and this diplomatic gamble to end in world war" (Schroeder 1972: 319).

Powder kegs go along with sparks to form a multivariate explanation of World War I. It is when both factors are simultaneously present that the event occurs. A key part of the causal explanation is that both necessary conditions must occur at the same time: it is the *conjunction* of the two that explains the outcome. Not surprisingly, Kingdon too uses the same explanatory framework:

> [T]he rise of an item [on the agenda] is due to the joint effect of several factors coming together at a given point in time, not to the

effect of one or another of them singly ... It was their *joint* effects
that were so powerful. (Kingdon 1984: 188)

It is the requirement that the two necessary conditions occur at the
same time which gives these window–catalyst explanations the characteristic of *contingency*. Just as Kingdon talks about "streams" coming
together, Lebow talks about the confluence of causes: "A confluence
envisages a multiple stream of independent causes that come together
to produce an outcome" (this volume, p. 90). He sees World War I as
the result of a contingent confluence of multiple causal chains:

> World War I is probably best understood as a nonlinear confluence
> in which multiple, interrelated causes had unanticipated conse-
> quences. Three causal chains were critically important. First and
> foremost was Germany's security dilemma, caused by the prospect
> of a two-front war ... The second causal chain consisted of all
> the Balkan developments that threatened the external security and
> internal stability of Austria-Hungary ... The third chain centered
> on St. Petersburg and was itself a confluence of external setbacks
> (defeat in [the] Russo–Japanese War of 1904-5, ...) and internal
> weaknesses (the revolution of 1905, ...). (Lebow this volume, p. 91)

The same powder keg appears in the end of the Cold War literature.
In fact, we think that it is the dominant multivariate explanatory framework for those who stress the importance of ideas. As we have seen
above, the ideas scholars stress that materialist explanations are not
sufficient to explain the end of the Cold War. They all recognize the
importance of material decline as a powder keg situation. To achieve
something like a sufficiency explanation, however, one needs to include
other factors, notably those related to new thinking. It is the coming
together of these new thinking policy entrepreneurs with an open policy
window that gives a relatively complete explanation of the end of the
Cold War.

The powder keg or window of opportunity-policy entrepreneur
explanatory framework has a number of key characteristics:

1. The explanatory model is conjunctural. Necessary condition hypotheses virtually always imply conjunctural theories.

2. The model is very nonlinear since the outcome is *not the sum* of
   the individual effects.

3. The process is often contingent in nature: only when the necessary
   conditions happen to be present together does the outcome occur.

4. Most applications of this model have two kinds of variables: (1) structural, background, contextual and (2) catalysts such as individual agency, decisions, events.

The relative importance of necessary conditions in multivariate causal explanations

> "Newman, I shouldn't be surprised if my brother were dead." "I don't think you would, "said Newman quietly. "Why not, sir?" demanded Mr. Nickelby. "You never are surprised," replied Newman, "that's all."
>
> Charles Dickens in *Nicholas Nickelby*

While historians and political scientists may agree that X_1 and X_2 are (necessary condition) causes of World War I, they may still do battle over the relative importance of the two. In this section we analyze the kinds of arguments that scholars have used to say that X_1 is more important than X_2, or to say that X_2 is not important in some absolute sense.

Specifically, with regard to necessary conditions, one way of downplaying the causal weight of a factor X_2 is to claim that the factor is a trivial necessary condition. One concedes the necessity of X_2 but argues that it is nevertheless trivial.[23]

But what is a trivial necessary condition? Downs illustrates the most common view:

> The search for necessary conditions is problematic because the utility of a necessary condition is contingent and poorly understood. There are an infinite number of necessary conditions for any phenomenon. For example, it is true that all armies require water and gravity to operate, but the contribution of such universals is modest. (Downs 1989: 234)

To make explicit Downs's criterion for trivialness we can say that X is a trivial necessary condition because the condition is always present. In Downs's view armies are a necessary condition for war, but trivial because virtually all states have had armies. In statistical terms, trivial necessary conditions are those where the independent variable is constant for all cases. A variation on this would be events, e.g., crises, that occur with great frequency.

The issue of "relative frequency" is key in the weighting of individual factors even in single case studies. In the examples above the trivial

---

[23] As Braumoeller and Goertz (2000) stress, the question of the necessity of a factor is distinct theoretically and methodology from questions about its trivialness.

necessary conditions are ones which always are present, hence they have a very high relative frequency. This will be true beyond the limited context of necessary conditions. The following principle is key for most arguments in case studies that give more weight to one cause than another:

> The rarer the necessary condition cause, relatively, the more important it is.

Hence a necessary condition for war like "has an army" is trivial given that this factor is extremely common.

Take the powder keg metaphor, one might say that since both the spark and the keg are necessary they have equal causal weight: how can X_1 and X_2, which are after all both necessary, have unequal causal weights? Since the window–catalyst model is conjunctural – i.e., involves interaction terms – we can ask the same question of "$2 * 3 = 6$." Which is more important in producing 6, the 2 or the 3?

The answer to these two questions is the relative frequency with which X_1 and X_2 occur. Thus if 2's are rarer than 3's then 2 is a more important cause of 6. We take the least common factor to be the more important cause. To see this intuition take some powder keg scenarios which vary the relative frequency of the spark and the keg. A smoker lights up and there is a gas leak in his house; the result is the explosion of his house. Lighting a match and the presence of gas due to the leak (like 2 and 3 in the production of 6) are both causes of the explosion. Yet when asked for *the* cause of the explosion people will say it was a gas leak. Gas leaks are relatively rare while the smoker has lit thousands of matches. On an oil rig, where gas is often present, the cause of an explosion will be the careless worker who lights a cigarette.

Honoré and Hart (1985) show how this principle is embodied in most Western legal systems. Courts have to decide in many individual cases that are causally complex. While it is not the only causal principle used, the relative frequency rule plays a key role. Normal events, situations, and occurrences are not seen as important causes, rare and unusual actions much more often are seized upon as the main cause.[24]

As the reader has already realized, this is the sort of argument that has been used in the World War I case to deny importance to the assassination as a key cause. Everyone agrees that the assassination was a link in the causal chain leading to World War I, but not everyone thinks it was an important link. Before 1914 there were many crises

---

[24]The result is supported by two related propositions about the availability of counterfactual alternatives: (1) exceptions tend to evoke contrasting normal alternatives, but not vice versa, and (2) an event is more likely to be undone by altering exceptional than routine aspects of the causal chain that led to it (Kahneman and Miller 1986: 143).

and wars, if the July 1914 crisis had not produced the war then another of the crises that would have inevitably arisen could have done the job. Notice how this argument invokes frequency notions, the argument is that there were and would have been many crises like that of July 1914, hence one should not give too much causal weight to the specific crisis that actually did set off the war.

Lebow has been in the forefront of recent attempts to argue that the assassination was an important cause of World War I. What kind of explanatory strategies does he employ to make his argument? He too uses relative frequency tactics. His first relative frequency argument disagrees with the proposition that there were many possible sparks. Not just any crisis will do, it needs to be a special kind of crisis with a variety of distinctive characteristics. The appropriate spark is thus a rare event, so its actual occurrence makes it an important cause of World War I:

> To recapitulate, the Sarajevo assassinations changed the political and psychological environment in Vienna and Berlin in six impor-
> tant ways, all of which were probably necessary for the decisions that led to war. (Lebow this volume, p. 99)

War needed a crisis with at least six key characteristics, which all were important (even necessary) to make it the sort of crisis that would lead to world war (see Lebow's chapter in this volume for a discussion of these six characteristics). Thus, it is unlikely that more crises with the required characteristics would arise. Clearly, Lebow is following the relative frequency strategy in making his case.

A second strategy employed by Lebow is to decrease the temporal duration of the window variable. For many analysts the keg is ready to explode during an extended period, say, 1912–18. Lebow says that the window for the war was much shorter, only a couple of years. This makes it much harder for a spark to occur because it must do so in a much shorter time. Again this reduces the frequency of potential matches that set off the world-wide fire.

In short, Lebow exploits two variants of the relative frequency principle in making his case for Sarajevo as an important cause of World War I. The first variant says that only special – and by implication rare – crises can do the job. The second variant reduces the duration of the window, again reducing the population of crises that can start the war.

The same issue comes up in terms of how one views individual decision-making. If a leader is doing what any rational leader would do, his decisions are often seen as less important causes. For example, in the end of the Cold War if leaders are merely doing adaptive learning in response to structural change then one would place little weight on the learning variable. If, on the other hand, leaders' idiosyncratic beliefs lead them to interpret a changing environment in different ways, then we would give more causal weight to learning (see Bennett 1999 for an extensive discussion of this point). Similarly, in the case of World War I, Levy (this volume) argues that although political leaders had choices, they had very little room to maneuver, so that the probability of avoiding a war, while not nonexistent, was very slim. Typically, as Honoré and Hart (1985) analyze in detail, we do not attribute blame if the person had no choice. While we recognize that the decision did lead to the outcome we tend to minimize its importance.

Schroeder quite explicitly refers to Hexter's essay on galloping gertie in his discussion of Fischer's views on World War I. The example of gertie is that of a bridge that collapsed once oscillations got out of control and became self-reinforcing. Schroeder thinks that this is a good metaphor for what happened in World War I. It makes sense because it is no longer the confluence of *independent* chains à la Lebow but rather a series of self-reinforcing chains. Because these chains are self-reinforcing, the events like the assassination are no longer separate catalysts but rather are endogenously produced by the structural, system factors. Levy (this volume) makes a similar argument. The rise of Russian power in the context of a two-front war gave Germany an incentive for preventive war and consequently an incentive to create or provoke an event that provided a convenient justification for war.

The galloping gertie framework illustrates another kind of critique that one can make when several factors, e.g., streams, come together to cause an event. "Endogeneity" is a good, if two-bit, name for this criticism. Instead of assuming that each causal chain or stream is independent, one might argue that one chain is an *effect* of the other. This is typical of structural explanations. We can see this strategy used both in the World War I and end of the Cold War cases. Thompson takes this as a core part of his explanation of World War I. One effect of the the intersection of several serious major power rivalries is severe crises. The assassination of Archduke Ferdinand is thus the result of more basic causal factors. Similarly, the realists suggest that leadership and policy change was a result of more basic structural and resource constraint problems. It is the endogeneity position that is vividly expressed by the famous streetcar (not of desire) aphorism: "Pleikus are streetcars. If you are waiting for one, it will come along." (Bundy as cited in Halberstam, 1972: 646).

In summary, there are various strategies for trying to evaluate the relative importance of causal factors in case studies. We have seen that in the explanation of individual events involving multiple necessary conditions relative frequency considerations play a key role in assessing causal importance. Of course, these relative frequency ideas are closely tied to counterfactuals since the event only occurs once. Nevertheless, they are useful and valid considerations when trying to understand or explain individual historical events. A second kind of strategy endogenizes factors the causal importance of which one is trying to minimize. This can work across streams or chains of events or within them. Recall that the issue of relative importance within sufficiency-like chains says that the effects (e.g., British declaration of war) are less important when there are strongly linked causes (e.g., German invasion of Belgium).

Conclusion

> The disaster of 1914 did not derive therefore from a failure by industrialists to understand the political logic and requirements of economic integration or even the failure or refusal of politicians, military men, various interest groups, and broad publics to appreciate the long-range advantages of peaceful international cooperation over unrestrained competition and conflict. It lay rather in the structure of international politics – the fact that its component individual states would not and could not, either separately or together, leap from a power-based competitive international system to a rule-based one. For governments and peoples effectively to realize that an international system dominated by power-political competition is in the long run incompatible with real, durable international economic integration and its benefits, and for them genuinely to opt for the latter rather than merely wish for it, they must first be convinced that the power-political game has become intolerably expensive and dangerous and must be abandoned and also persuaded that another more cooperative system is available, or at least possible and that the other important players will try it as well or, if not, that some other player or players will protect them and their interests if they alone defect from the competition. None of these essential conditions prevailed before 1914.
>
> *Paul Schroeder*

Schroeder's language – "must first be convinced," "must be abandoned," and "essential conditions" – is typical of much of the literature on the explanation of historical events. Necessary conditions along with their related counterfactuals provide an essential theoretical tool for explaining individual events. We have surveyed some of the theoretical and methodological dimensions of such explanations, both at the univariate and multivariate levels.

Necessary conditions imply major counterfactual claims as we have seen in the literature about the causes of World War I and the end of the Cold War. However, the converse is not true: not all counterfactuals imply a necessary condition explanatory framework. One reason why counterfactuals remain an important topic for historians is because they often make necessary condition claims: so in this respect the importance of counterfactuals is an *effect* of a particular kind of explanatory strategy.

In both the causal chain and window–catalyst frameworks we have a situation where multiple necessary conditions are jointly sufficient for the outcome. If the study in question is really a univariate one, then we see the claim that X is necessary but certainly not sufficient for the outcome.

Before moving on to more complex dynamic explanations à la galloping gertie, historians and political scientists need to be more conscious of the theoretical and methodological issues that appear in virtually any causal explanation of a single case.

Fischer (1970: 186) finds the following as the main kinds of causal explanation given by historians:

1. All antecedents

2. Regularistic antecedents

3. Controllable antecedents

4. Rational and/or motivational antecedents

5. Abnormal antecedents

6. Structural antecedents

7. Contingent-series antecedents

8. Precipitant antecedents

From our point of view necessary antecedents are notably absent from the list. On the other hand, we have found important links between necessary condition explanations and (5) abnormal antecedents, (6) structural antecedents, (7) contingent-series antecedents, and (8) precipitant antecedents. We suggest that the underlying logic of these kinds of antecedents uses a counterfactual necessary condition form.

We have used the end of the Cold War and World War I as our main examples. Many influential scholars have made an appearance as an example in our discussion. We hope that our methodological and theoretical analysis provides insights into these causal claims and also suggests ways that they can be evaluated. Our goal has been to elucidate the structure and implications of arguments about World War I and the end of the Cold War, not to adjudicate between conflicting perspectives on the war. Having summarized the causal logic underlying statements of necessity and sufficiency, and noted the different ways in which those statements are expressed, we now turn to more detailed analyses of the outbreak of World War I and the end of the Cold War.

Chapter 3

The role of necessary conditions in the outbreak of World War I

Jack S. Levy

Over a decade ago I used some basic concepts of rational choice theory to guide an analysis of decision-making and strategic interaction in the July 1914 crisis (Levy, 1990–1). My aim was to assess whether the outbreak of World War I was better explained by the interests of political leaders and the international and domestic constraints on their choices, or by their mismanagement of the crisis. I concluded that given the structure of power and alliances, the interests of state leaders, and the domestic problems in each state, the probability of war was already high at the time of the assassination. Decision-makers had some room to maneuver, but not much, and the constraints on their actions intensified as the crisis progressed, further increasing the probability of war and leaving fewer and fewer opportunities for leaders to manage the crisis without risking significant harm to their interests.

In retrospect, it is striking how much my analysis of the July crisis relied on the language of necessary conditions and the use of counterfactual logic to support my arguments. The same is true for some of my other historical case studies. Perhaps this should not have been surprising, because the nature of case studies is quite conducive to the use of the concepts of necessary and sufficient conditions. This is due in part to the fact that many case study researchers aim to provide a "complete" explanation of a particular outcome, one conceived in deterministic terms rather than the probabilistic terms generally associated with statistical analysis, and to the fact that we usually think of necessary conditions as referring to deterministic or quasi-deterministic relationships.

The task of providing a complete explanation of individual events through an historical narrative is more likely to lead to the use of the

language of necessary conditions than is the task of explaining variation
over outcomes in a large number of cases. This relates to the fact that
we have few if any theoretical generalizations about international relations that approach law-like status and involve empirically confirmed,
deterministic propositions. There may be strong patterns, as captured
by "probabilistic laws," but there is enough complexity and contingency
in the social world that there are extraordinarily few if any relationships
for which it can be said that an outcome never or even almost never
occurs in the absence of a particular condition. The argument that the
democratic peace "comes as close as anything we have to an empirical
law in international relations" (Levy 1988: 662) – which implies that
the presence of a non-democratic regime is a necessary condition for
an interstate war – is a comment not only about the strength of democratic peace proposition, but also about the absence of empirical laws
in international relations.

With this enhanced sensitivity to the role of necessary conditions
in case study analysis, I rework my earlier treatment of the July crisis.
I highlight my use of necessary conditions, note how my analysis of
necessary conditions in the World War I case differs from those in the
other chapters in this section, and conclude with a summary of my
primary arguments that invoke necessary conditions.

Conceptual framework

Did World War I occur primarily because of the structure of the international system and the conflicting interests of the European great
powers in 1914 or was it the result of the misperceptions, miscalculations, overreactions, and loss of control by political leaders?[1] Could
statesmen have acted to avoid war while preserving their vital interests,
or did significant conciliatory actions carry unacceptable risks? Did
political leaders mismanage the crisis or did they perceive no interest
in managing the crisis to avoid war in the first place? These questions
are still critical. World War I is the most frequently cited illustration of
"inadvertent war" (Tuchman 1962), the primary source of many hypotheses on the subject, and a common historical and strategic metaphor
in the nuclear age (Bracken 1983: 2–3, 65, 222–3; Lebow 1987: chaps.
2–4; Trachtenberg 1990–1). Thus it is essential that we understand
precisely in which respects (if any) World War I was inadvert. This is
especially important in light of the ongoing debate over Fritz Fischer's
(1967; 1974; 1975) argument that German elites provoked a great power

---

[1]This is closely related to the question of the relative importance of structure and
individuals in the processes leading to World War I (Kennedy 1982).

war in 1914 in order to secure Germany's position on the continent, establish its status as a world power, and solve its domestic political crisis (Koch 1972a; Moses 1975; Kaiser 1983).

Previous attempts to answer these questions have failed, in part because of a lack of rigor in their formulations of the problem and the failure to use a theoretical framework adequate to the task. Crisis management frameworks (Williams 1976; George 1991a) generally do not acknowledge that some crises are structured in such a way – in terms of the preferences of the actors and the military/diplomatic and domestic constraints on their actions – that give political leaders few incentives to attempt to manage the crisis to avoid war. Hypotheses of inadvertent war are plagued by several ambiguities. Assertions that actors "did not want war" are meaningless without the precise specification of the full range of policy alternatives and the perceived costs of each, and the simple war/nonwar dichotomy is not analytically useful. Psychological and other actor-oriented explanations (Holsti 1972) usually neglect structural constraints; analyses of power distributions, alliance patterns, and the structural instability of the international system (Schroeder 1972; Waltz 1979; Mearsheimer 2001) rarely consider the motivations of individual actors; and neither acknowledges the importance of domestic politics (Mayer 1967; Fischer 1975; Snyder 1991).[2]

Neither an actor-based nor a structure-based explanation is complete without the other (Morrow 1988; Lake and Powell 1999), and it has become increasingly evident that neither actor preferences nor the constraints on their choices can be fully specified in the absence of domestic variables. With these considerations in mind, I use a rational-choice framework based on preferences, constraints, informational environments, and choices to organize an analysis of the outbreak of World War I. I do not assume unitary nation-state actors, however, and I define constraints to include internal bureaucratic, organizational, and domestic variables as well as military and diplomatic factors.[3] I reformulate my initial question as follows: To what extent was the outbreak of World War I determined by the foreign policy preferences of the great powers and by the strategic, domestic, and informational constraints on their choices?

I begin by specifying four possible outcomes of the July crisis and the *preferences* of each of the great powers over these outcomes.[4] I then

---

[2] For explanations of World War I that include both internal and external variables, see Choucri and North (1975), Lebow (1981), and J. Snyder (1984).

[3] Prior to the 1990s most applications of rational-actor models of international politics assumed unitary national actors (Allison 1971, chap. 1; Bueno de Mesquita 1981)

[4] The concept of preferences refers (in the formal decision-theoretic sense) to preferences over possible outcomes of the crisis, not preferences over alternative strategies

identify a number of *critical decision points* in the processes leading to war. At each of these points I specify the options available, the external and internal *constraints* on political leaders, and decision-makers' *expectations*, based on available information, regarding the intentions of their adversaries and the likely consequences of various courses of action. I analyze the extent to which the strategic choices of political leaders were compelled by their perceived interests, expectations, and the constraints under which they operated, and the extent to which those actions can be better explained by theories of flawed information processing, decision-making pathologies, and crisis mismanagement. I also examine whether the expectations and probability assessments of political leaders were reasonable in light of the information available at the time.[5] I consider as well whether any key choices were contingent upon the presence or absence of any particular necessary conditions. I utilize counterfactual reasoning to analyze whether more timely actions, or different actions, might have had more favorable consequences, and whether more creative statecraft might have generated new options and changed the structure of incentives in a way which could have led to a less costly outcome.[6]

I conclude that the image of World War I as inadvertent and the image of World War I as the intended product of Germany's drive for world power are both exaggerated. Germany wanted war, but a local war, and neither Germany nor any other great power wanted a general European war with British involvement. Although there were several points at which political leaders could have done more to manage the crisis so as to secure their vital interests without the costs of a general war, their ranges of choices were extremely limited. The primary causes of World War I were the underlying international and domestic forces which shaped the preferences of the great powers, the strategic and political constraints on their actions, and informational asymmetries. The mismanagement of the crisis by political leaders was at most a secondary factor contributing to the outbreak of the war.

---

to achieve those outcomes. Preferences are not always uniform among leading political and military decision-makers, and I note important differences among key factions within each state.

[5]Because my primary concern is to evaluate whether the combination of interests and constraints precluded political leaders from acting in ways that might have avoided a major war, and to do so within a reasonably parsimonious framework, I will not give much attention to individual-level variables that may have influenced foreign policy preferences and choices.

[6]For recent work on the methodology of counterfactual analysis, see Tetlock and Belkin (1996), and Lebow (2000). For the use of counterfactual analysis to explore whether World War I was structurally determined or contingent, see Ferguson (1999a, 1999c), and the Lebow, Schroeder, and Thompson essays in this volume.

The interests, preferences, and expectations of the actors

In the aftermath of the assassination of Archduke Franz Ferdinand, political leaders throughout Europe expected that Austria–Hungary would seek some form of compensation from Serbia and that significant Serbian concessions would be forthcoming and be sufficient to maintain the peace. Few feared war or even a major crisis, but this changed abruptly on July 23–24 with the news of the extreme demands of the Austrian ultimatum to Serbia (Butterfield 1965: 7–8; Fay 1966 [1928] vol. 2: 286–91; Fischer 1967: 51, 66; Joll 1984: 9). Interlocking alliance agreements increased the fear that an Austro-Serbian war might draw in Russia in support of Serbia, Germany in support of Austria-Hungary, and France in support of Russia, along with the Balkan allies of each of the great powers (Sagan 1986; Christensen and Snyder 1990). Such a continental war could expand further into a general European or world war through the intervention of Great Britain on the side of the Entente.

Thus most leading European decision-makers in July 1914 recognized four possible outcomes of the crisis:

1. a peaceful but one-sided negotiated settlement based on extensive but not unconditional Serbian concessions to Austria

2. a localized Austro-Serbian war in the Balkans

3. the expansion of the Austro–Serbian conflict into a continental war involving Russia, Germany, and France as well as Austria–Hungary and Serbia

4. the expansion of the continental war into a world war through the intervention of Britain.[7]

These four possibilities constitute the set of feasible outcomes of the crisis in the decision-theoretic framework that guides this study. Next, I explain how each key state defined its interests and preferences.

---

[7] Additional outcomes might have included an unconditional Serbian acceptance of all terms of the Austrian ultimatum, an early punitive strike by Austria against Serbia, or a limited Austro-Hungarian invasion of Serbia based on the "Halt in Belgrade" plan. I will argue that the first would have been too great a violation of their sovereignty for Serbian leaders to tolerate; the second would not have eliminated the perceived Serbian threat to the domestic problems facing the Dual Monarchy; and the third was not seriously considered until much later in the crisis, after German leaders realized that the world war they feared might be a serious possibility after all.

Austria–Hungary

Faced with increases in the strength and hostility of Serbia, internal decay in Austria–Hungary's multinational empire, and the decline of its position among the great powers, Austro–Hungarian leaders believed that they must break Serbia's hold on the loyalties of the Serbian and Croatian minorities of the Dual Monarchy, and that this required war.[8] Austrian leaders preferred a local war over a riskier continental war, but preferred the latter over a negotiated peace that failed to eliminate Serbian influence.[9] Although they were willing to risk a continental war, Austrian decision-makers believed they could minimize the risk of Russian intervention by a fait accompli against Serbia backed by firm assurances of German support, at a time when the assassination provided a cover of legitimacy for military action and when Russia and France were not yet ready for war (Joll 1984: 10–11; Williamson 1988: 610). They also believed that a preventive war against Serbia to arrest both external and internal decline was necessary while the military and diplomatic contexts were still favorable (Ritter 1969–73, vol. 2: 227–39; Kennedy 1987: 215–19).

Vienna's preference for a local war over a negotiated settlement based on Serbian concessions was not unconditional, but for both strategic and domestic political reasons was clearly contingent on German support, which was forthcoming in the "blank check" of July 5–6.[10] Luigi Albertini concludes that if Germany had not wanted Austria to

---

[8]Since 1867, Austria and Hungary had shared a common monarch. They also shared a Ministry of Foreign Policy and Ministry of War, which were dominated by Austrian officials, particularly during the July crisis. Austrian leaders believed that without the reconstruction of the Balkans under Austrian domination, the Dual Monarchy would collapse. They would have accepted an unconditional capitulation by Serbia, but recognized that would be politically impossible for any Serbian regime. They constructed a humiliating ultimatum that would certainly be rejected and that they hoped would provide a rationale for Austrian military action. When Serbia unexpectedly accepted nearly all of the terms of the ultimatum, Austria–Hungary still proceeded with a declaration of war (Farrar 1972: 10; Albertini 1980 vol. 2: 168–9, 286–9).

[9]The worst case for Vienna involved British intervention, for that would put more pressure on Germany in the west, delay Berlin's ability to divert its armies to the east, and therefore leave Austria–Hungary in a very vulnerable position with respect to Russia. But Austrian leaders dismissed this possibility as being extremely unlikely.

[10]Both Foreign Minister Leopold Berchtold and Chief of Staff Conrad von Hötzendorf feared abandonment by Germany and preferred a negotiated settlement to fighting a two-front war with Russia and Serbia without German support. They also believed that their decaying monarchy could embark on war only if it was united internally. But Hungarian Prime Minister István Tisza opposed war and Emperor Franz Joseph wanted to wait until the official investigation of the assassination proved Serbian complicity. The "blank check" satisfied von Hötzendorf and the political opposition within Austria–Hungary (Fischer 1967: 52, 56; Ritter 1969–73,vol. 2: 236; Taylor 1971: 527).

move against Serbia, "neither [Emperor] Francis Joseph, nor [Austro-Hungarian Foreign Minister] Berchtold, nor even [Chief of the General Staff] Conrad would have gone ahead with the venture" (1980, vol. 2: 162). Thus German support was a necessary condition for an Austro-Hungarian war against Serbia.[11] This is the first of several necessary conditions in the causal chain leading to war in 1914.

Serbia

Serbia preferred peace to war with Austria and was willing to make significant concessions in order to preserve it, but only up to a point. Prime Minister Nikola Pasic was determined not to accept any Habsburg demands that infringed on Serbian sovereignty, and while his uncompromising position predated both the ultimatum and Russian pressures for firmness against Austria, his confidence in Russian support undoubtedly strengthened his resolve. Pasic was further constrained by a severe domestic political crisis and by tensions between the army and his civilian government, and in fact he was away campaigning for the general elections when the ultimatum was received (Albertini 1980, vol. 2: 352-62; Joll 1984: 73; Williamson 1988: 811-13).

Pasic accepted most of the terms of the Austrian ultimatum and thereby won the sympathies of Europe. But he carefully evaded the demands that representatives of the Austro-Hungarian government be allowed to participate in the Serbian inquiry into the origins of the assassination plot (for Pasic knew where such an inquiry could lead) and in the suppression of subversive activities directed against the Austro-Hungarian state.[12] The conciliatory but brilliantly evasive Serbian reply represented Serbia's maximum concessions, but they still fell short of Austria's minimum demands.[13]

---

[11] German support might not have been necessary for a limited Austrian punitive strike against Serbia or for an Austrian decision for war after Vienna declared war on July 28 (Williamson 1988: 807). Note that a declaration of war was not equivalent to war.

[12] The Austrian ultimatum also demanded that Serbia suppress anti-Austrian propaganda in Serbia in general and in its public schools in particular, remove all army officers and civilian officials who had engaged in such propaganda, arrest two named officials suspected in the assassination, dissolve the Serbian nationalist association Narodna Obrana and prevent the formation of similar societies in the future, and eliminate the traffic in arms across the border between Serbia and Austria-Hungary. For the text of the ultimatum, Serbia's reply, and Austria's line-by-line response, see Albertini (1980, vol. 2: 286-9, 364-71).

[13] Serbia preferred a continental war with Russian support (and therefore also a world war with British intervention) to a localized war with Austria-Hungary, but its role in the expansion of the war is negligible.

Russia

Russian decision-makers believed that their strategic and economic interests in the Turkish Straits depended on maintaining Serbia and Romania as buffer states, and that Russian influence in the Balkans and indeed its great power status depended on maintaining its influence among the southern Slavs and its patronage of Serbia. But Tsar Nicholas II was appalled by the royal assassination and could not risk alienating Britain by giving unconditional support to Serbia. On balance, he was willing to allow Serbia to be chastised severely as long as Austria removed from the ultimatum "those points which infringe on Serbia's sovereign rights."

Although Russian leaders preferred peace based on some Serbian concessions to a Austro-Serbian war, for both diplomatic and domestic political reasons they preferred a continental war, and therefore a world war with British intervention on their side, over a local war in the Balkans in which Serbia would undoubtedly be crushed by Austria. Sensitive to Russia's humiliating defeats in the 1904–5 Russo–Japanese War and the 1908–9 Bosnian crisis, Russian leaders feared that another retreat would permanently undermine Russian influence in the Balkans and reduce Russia (in Foreign Minister Sazonov's words) to "second place among the powers" (Lieven 1983: 141–7; Joll 1984: 55). Russian leaders also believed that domestic stability and their own political interests required an assertive foreign policy.[14]

Britain

Although British Foreign Secretary Edward Grey, like most others in England, preferred a negotiated settlement to any war, he was more concerned to localize the conflict and prevent a great power war than to avoid Austrian action per se. Grey strongly preferred a local war to a continental war as long as Austrian actions were limited (Butterfield 1965: 7; Fischer 1967: 66), but he recognized that the best way to avoid a continental war was to prevent a local war, and to that end he undertook several diplomatic initiatives. These included his July 26 proposal for a four-power conference in London and his July 29 proposal that Austria halt its military advance in Belgrade. But if the war were to escalate to a general continental war, Grey and his political allies recognized that British interests in the integrity of France and

---

[14]There was a strong pro-Serbian reaction by public opinion and the press in Russia (Geiss 1967: nos. 90, 100, 141a; Albertini 1980, vol. 2: 403–5). The Russian incentive for diversionary action was offset by the fear that war could lead to revolution (Lieven 1983: 121, 153).

the balance of power in Europe required British intervention, and Grey thus preferred a world war to a continental war. But significant factions in the Cabinet, Parliament, the financial community, and elsewhere preferred neutrality,[15] and it took the German violation of Belgian neutrality to sway the idealists on the left (Wilson 1975; Steiner 1977, chaps. 7-10; Kennedy 1981: 136-9). Thus British preferences between a continental war and a world war were context-dependent and unstable, and emerged with clarity only by the end of the crisis.

France

France had no direct strategic or reputational interests in the Balkans, but the French alliance with Russia was the cornerstone of French security policy. French leaders feared entrapment in a Russo–German dispute involving Austria and the Balkans, but not as much as they feared abandonment in a Franco–German conflict. They had to support Russia in any war with Germany,[16] but could not behave so provocatively as to alienate Britain, whose military support would be essential. President Raymond Poincaré and Premier René Viviani hoped that Austria would not push too hard and that Russia could tolerate some Serbian concessions, and their first preference was thus a negotiated peace, their second a local war. They attempted to restrain Russia without alienating her and to support plans for the localization of any Austro–Serbian war (including the "Halt in Belgrade" Plan), but their absence from France during much of the crisis limited their role.[17] Thus France preferred a negotiated peace to a local war, and the latter to a continental war. But if Russia insisted on war, French leaders knew that they had to follow rather than risk the disintegration of the alliance, and in that case preferred a world war with Britain on their side.[18]

---

[15] The financial community's preference for neutrality derived from high levels of economic interdependence between Britain and Germany and the belief that war would interfere with trade and generate substantial economic costs. Thus the economic interdependence that liberals generally associate with peace actually made war more likely by helping to keep Britain from issuing an explicit deterrent threat to Germany (Papayoanou 1999). Note, however, that economic variables had a rather different impact at earlier stages of the Anglo–German rivalry, because an economic rivalry was the fundamental dynamic driving increasing Anglo–German hostilities (Kennedy 1982).

[16] For domestic reasons, however, it was highly desirable that French public opinion perceive that the issue over which the war was fought involved a direct threat to France, and that Russia not initiate the war (Taylor 1971: 486-88; Joll 1984: 99).

[17] Poincaré's and Viviani's absence also increased the influence of Maurice Paleologue, the revanchist ambassador to Russia (Keiger 1983, chap. 7).

[18] Some early revisionists claimed that France wanted a world war to recover Alsace-Lorraine, and that Russia wanted such a war to seize the Turkish Straits (Barnes 1926).

Germany

Germany is the critical actor, because key Austrian and particularly Hungarian decision-makers were unwilling to move against Serbia without German support. I argue that German officials preferred a local war in the Balkans to even a one-sided negotiated settlement, and that while they preferred a local war to a continental war, they were willing to risk the latter if necessary to achieve these goals. All of this was conditional, however, upon German confidence that they could avoid their worst-case scenario, a world war resulting from British intervention.

There is substantial evidence that the "blank check" granted by Germany went beyond giving Austrian leaders a free hand and actually encouraged them to take military action against Serbia.[19] Many German leaders doubted Vienna's resolve, repeatedly urged Vienna to move as quickly as possible, and subsequently did their best to sabotage the crisis management efforts and mediation proposals of Grey and Russian Foreign Minister Sergei Sazonov (Fischer 1967: 53–64; Jarausch 1969: 56; Röhl 1973). While willing to risk a continental war and acknowledging that those risks were real, German decision-makers hoped and expected that an Austrian fait accompli against Serbia in the immediate aftermath of the royal assassination, backed by German warnings to Russia, would minimize the likelihood of Russian intervention (Jagow to Licknowsky, July 18, in Geiss 1967: 122–4; see also, Fischer 1967: 60; Albertini 1980, vol. 2: 159–64; Van Evera 1984: 83). Austria would almost certainly defeat Serbia in a local war, increase its relative strength, and reduce the Slavic threat in the Balkans. Moreover, German Chancellor Theobald von Bethmann-Hollweg believed that if France were economically and militarily unable or unwilling to come to the aid of Russia, the Entente might very well split apart and give way to a new diplomatic realignment, which was Germany's primary foreign policy objective (Fischer 1967: 60).[20]

---

[19]The revisionist view in the 1920s held that Germany did not want war of any kind but needed to maintain Austria–Hungary as Germany's only great power ally, and that in spite of its best efforts to restrain Vienna, Germany was ultimately dragged into a world war by its weaker ally (Fay 1966 [1928], vol. 2). This hypothesis has been discredited by the path-breaking work of Fischer (1967; 1975), but I differ from Fischer's conclusion that Germany preferred a continental war to a local war.

[20]On July 8 Bethmann-Hollweg said that the assassination provided the opportunity for victorious war or for a crisis in which "we still certainly have the prospect of maneuvering the Entente apart" (Van Evera 1984: 80n). See also Bethmann-Hollweg to Roedern (secretary of state for Alsace-Lorraine), July 16 (Geiss 1967: 118). Similarly, Jarausch (1969: 58) argues that "a local Balkan war would bring a diplomatic triumph, a realignment of the south-eastern states and the break-up of the Entente." It is not clear, however, exactly how confident Bethmann-Hollweg was that a local war would split the Entente or why he believed it. He may have assumed that France would support

There is little doubt that world war was seen as the worst case by all German leaders. As Konrad Jarausch concludes, "Bethmann-Hollweg clearly preferred local war, was willing to gamble on continental war, but he abhorred world war" (1969: 58, 61, 75; see also Berghahn 1973: 192, 196; Van Evera 1984: 83; Lynn-Jones 1986: 142–3; Sagan 1986: 168). Even Fritz Fischer (1967) and Imanuel Geiss (1967: 84–8), the strongest supporters of the German war guilt hypothesis, argue strongly that Bethmann-Hollweg sought the neutrality of Britain. It would be much easier to handle Britain after the defeat of France and Russia, or after Austria smashed Serbia, leaving the Entente in shambles.[21]

The question of German preferences between a continental war and a local war are more difficult to establish. Fischer (1967; 1975) and his associates argue that German political and military elites preferred a continental war because they wanted a preventive war against Russia before Russia completed its "Great Program" and the modernization of its railroad system, expected by 1917.[22] A military victory would bolster the German elites' domestic political support, and give them added time to deal with internal crises generated by industrialization and the rise of social democracy (Berghahn 1973; Mommsen 1973; Gordon 1974; Fischer 1975; Kaiser 1983). I argue that the fear of Germany's decline as a great power and the need for a dramatic foreign policy victory for domestic purposes led German political leaders to prefer a continental war over the status quo, but that their expectations that a localized Austro–Serbian war would split the Entente led them to prefer a local war over a continental war as a less costly and less risky means of achieving Germany's larger security interests (Stevenson 1997: 149).[23] That is, German leaders preferred a local war to a continental war, and

---

Russia if and only if Russia were directly threatened by Germany (as stipulated by the terms of the Franco-Russian alliance) and that the absence of French support would not only prevent Russia from coming to Serbia's aid but also lead it to drop France as an unreliable ally. I have argued that, although France preferred to stay out of a local war and might have tried to convince Russia that it was in Russia's interests to do the same, France would follow its ally if necessary and give whatever support Russia needed.

[21] It is more difficult to establish the intensity of the preferences for a continental war or a negotiated peace over a world war among various German decision-makers. This is critical, because it affects the level of perceived risk of British intervention that German leaders were willing to tolerate in their pursuit of a local or even a continental war. The German military were most willing to take this risk; unlike their civilian counterparts, many expected British intervention.

[22] The Russian program called for a 40 percent increase in the size of the army and a 29 percent increase in the officer corps over the next four years (Geiss 1966: 79, 86; Schmitt 1966 [1930], vol. 1: 321–5; Fischer 1975: 480, 515; Lieven 1983: 111; Van Evera 1984: 79, 86;). On preventive war see Levy (1987) and also Copeland (2000), who emphasizes the decline of relative power as the fundamental cause of most major wars.

[23] Thus Bethmann-Hollweg hoped to avoid a preventive war against Russia (Mommsen 1966: 60).

TABLE 3.1:   The preferences of the great powers (plus Serbia) in 1914

Country	Preference structure
Austria–Hungary	LW > CW > NP > WW
Germany	LW > CW > NP > WW
Russia	NP > WW > CW > LW
France	NP > LW > WW > CW
Great Britain	NP > LW > WW ? CW
Serbia	NP > WW > CW > LW
Assessments of German preferences	
"Inadvertent war" school	NP > LW > CW > WW
	LW > NP > CW > WW
Fischer school	CW > LW > NP > WW
Levy	LW > CW > NP > WW

Note: These are the preferences of the central decision-makers in each state;
there were significant differences within each state, as noted in the text.
Key:
NP = negotiated peace with significant but not unconditional Serbian concessions
LW = localized Austro–Serbian war in the Balkans
CW = contiznental war, Germany with Austria, Russia; France with Serbia
WW = general European war or world war, Britain joining against the Central Powers
> = "was preferred to"
? = a definitive preference cannot be established

the latter to a negotiated settlement, but they were willing to risk a
continental war in order to avoid an unfavorable status quo.

Table 3.1 summarizes the preferences of the five leading great
powers plus Serbia over the set of the four most likely outcomes of
the crisis. Each of the European great powers and Serbia preferred
a negotiated settlement to a world war, yet they found themselves
entrapped in a world war that involved enormous human and economic
costs, led to the collapse of three empires, settled little, and set the stage
for another cataclysmic world war only two decades later. An analysis
of the calculus of choice at each of a series of critical decision points
demonstrates that this unwanted outcome resulted primarily from
the diplomatic, military, bureaucratic/ organizational, and domestic
constraints on the choices of political elites, and only secondarily from
their mismanagement of the crisis.

This view of great power preferences in July 1914 differs from the implicit preference order inherent in other interpretations of the origins of World War I. In fact, differences in preference orderings for Germany are one useful way to differentiate among the alternative interpretations of the origins of the war advanced by the inadvertent war school (Tuchman 1962), the Fischer school (1967; 1975), and myself.[24]

Critical decision points

Political leaders were confronted not with a single decision of whether to go to war in 1914, but instead with a series of decisions at a succession of critical decision points as the crisis unfolded over time. Their preferences as to outcomes were stable over time, but their international and domestic constraints, available information and expectations, and policy options and strategies were constantly changing. Each decision altered the constraints existing at the next critical juncture and further narrowed political leaders' freedom of maneuver.[25]

The choices made at several of these critical points follow directly from the preferences of leading decision-makers, along with their expectations regarding the probabilities of various actions and the consequences of those actions. This was certainly true for the German decision to support Austria, given German assumptions of British neutrality; for Serbia's refusal to accept unconditionally all Austrian demands; for the Austrian decision to attack Serbia rather than accept negotiated Serbian concessions, given Austrian confidence in German support; for the Russian decision to intervene in support of Serbia rather than allow it to be crushed by Austria; and for the German decision to come to the aid of Austria once Russia made its intentions clear.[26]

I argue that the German decision to support Austria-Hungary was a necessary condition for a local war and thus for any larger war; Russian intervention was a necessary and sufficient condition for a continental war, but not sufficient for a world war. (Many of those who argue that Germany preferred a continental war to a local war in the Balkans would argue that Russian intervention in an Austro–Serbian war was not a necessary condition for a continental war, because Germany would have probably moved against Russia in any case.) The Serbian refusal to

---

[24]Jarausch (1969: 75) and Van Evera (1984: 100) share my preference order for Germany, but not my overall interpretation of the causes of war.

[25]Thus the attempt to model the 1914 case as a 2×2 game in normal form (Snyder and Diesing 1977: 207) is flawed on several counts: the situation cannot be reduced to two homogeneous coalitions, to two strategic options for each actor, to the simple dichotomy between war and peace, or to a single set of interactive choices, each uninformed by the other.

[26]In terms of the discussion in chapter 1 of this volume, each of these links in the causal chain is a sufficient condition for the next, and hence involves strong bonds.

unconditionally accept all of the Austrian demands was probably not necessary for war. Austrian leaders had designed the ultimatum to make its acceptance unlikely and might have created another pretext for war even in the event of a total Serbian capitulation. Each of these choices hinged on the German assumption of British neutrality, which was the critical link in the escalation of all stages of the crisis.

The German assumption of British neutrality

My argument is that Bethmann-Hollweg and other key German political leaders were quite confident of British neutrality and that they based their policy on that expectation, to the point that the German assumption of British neutrality was a necessary condition for Germany's blank check to Austria and therefore for the Austrian decision for war. Only with the shattering of this assumption on July 29 did Bethmann-Hollweg reverse his policy and attempt, briefly, to manage the crisis to avoid war. I will explain why German leaders clung to this erroneous assumption for so long, focusing both on the British failure to give a clear commitment and on the German failure to recognize warnings that did exist. I then return to three other sets of critical decisions in the July crisis: Austria's failure to move immediately after the assassination; the failure of the Halt in Belgrade proposal; and the interlocking sequence of mobilization decisions.

Kaiser Wilhelm II and Foreign Secretary Jagow were convinced from the beginning of the crisis that Britain would stand aside from a European conflict,[27] though the Kaiser abandoned that assumption in late July, two days earlier than Bethmann-Hollweg did. Although Bethmann-Hollweg recognized the uncertainties involved and sometimes wavered in his estimates of British intentions (Steiner 1977: 126), the bulk of the evidence suggests that he was generally confident of British neutrality (Fischer 1967: 50–92; 1988; Lynn-Jones 1986: 142–5). He based his entire policy on this assumption and undertook several diplomatic initiatives to secure a formal commitment of nonintervention from Grey.

While German leaders believed that Britain would stand aside in a continental war, they also believed that British neutrality was contingent on the British perception that Germany was fighting a defensive war in response to Russian aggression.[28] Thus Bethmann-Hollweg went to

[27] Jagow said on July 26, "We are sure of English neutrality" (Albertini 1980, vol. 2: 429). Later in the war, the Kaiser exclaimed, "If only someone had told me beforehand that England would take up arms against us!" (Tuchman 1962: 143).

[28] As early as winter 1912–13, Bethmann-Hollweg expressed confidence that Britain would stand aside "if the provocation appeared to come directly from Russia and

great lengths to ensure that Germany did not mobilize before Russia, in an attempt to shift the onus for starting the conflict onto Russia (Fischer 1988: 373–5, 380, 382). He believed that by blaming Russia he could also secure the support of the Social Democrats at home, which he thought was vital.[29] The military was generally less confident of British neutrality in a protracted war,[30] but given their assumption that war would be short, they were confident that any intervention by Britain would come too late to influence the outcome of the war against France (Ritter 1958: 71, 161–2; Fischer 1967: 49; Farrar 1973).[31] There is no doubt that Bethmann-Hollweg, even in his most pessimistic moods, accepted this minimum assumption."[32]

France," and Moltke insisted that "the attack must come from the Slavs" (Fischer 1967: 27, 31–3). The German bid for British neutrality failed because it required that German *involvement* in war be sufficient for British neutrality, whereas Britain insisted that it could offer neutrality only in the event of an unprovoked attack on Germany (Fischer 1967: 63, 70–85; Geiss 1967: 269, 350; Jarausch 1969: 63–8; Albertini 1980, vol. 2: 502; Joll 1984: 20–9, 116; Fischer 1988: 373–82).

[29]Bethmann-Hollweg believed that it was essential to maintain a united front at home and was uncertain of the intentions of the Social Democrats, who had vacillated between socialist-internationalist and social-patriot positions supporting the Army Bill in 1913 (see Geiss 1967: 269; Jarausch 1969: 67–8; Fischer 1975: 494). I thank Daniel Garst for ideas on this point.

[30]Tirpitz and some others wanted to do everything possible to delay British entry, which reinforced German determination not to mobilize first (Sagan 1986: 170–1). Military views were not crucial, however, for they had limited influence on German foreign policy decisions prior to July 30, and by that time civilian expectations had shifted (Kaiser 1983: 469; Lynn-Jones 1986: 144; Stevenson 1997; Trachtenberg 1990–1, 137–44).

[31]Moltke's comment to Conrad in May 1914 (explaining why Germany had not yet initiated a preventive war against Russia) confirms civilian expectations of British neutrality but at the same time demonstrates his own doubts: "Our people unfortunately still expect a declaration from Britain that it will not join in. This declaration Britain will never make" (cited in Fischer 1975: 400). Moltke had argued in a 1913 memo that Britain would intervene in a Franco–German war "because she fears German hegemony, and true to her policy of maintaining a balance of power will do all she can to check the increase of German power" (Tuchman 1962: 144; see also Woodward 1967: 19–20; Wilson 1986, chap. 1).

[32]Bethmann-Hollweg's statement to the Kaiser (July 23), that "it was improbable that England would immediately enter the fray" implies that the expected delay was critical (Jarausch 1969: 62). Bethmann-Hollweg stated that "England's interest in the preservation of a European balance of power will not allow a complete crushing of France," assumed this was the British threshold for intervention, and was confident that intervention could be avoided by promising that Germany would "demand no territorial concessions from France" (Fischer 1988: 382). Germany's primary war aims, after all, were to support Austria and defeat Russia. Thus, civilian and military leaders shared the assumption that if the British intervened at all, it would not be until it was clear that France was about to be crushed, and that this would be too late to influence the outcome of the war in the west. Civilian and, to a lesser extent, military leaders in Germany believed that they could influence the British decision by providing guarantees that it sought no territorial annexations from France. Bethmann-Hollweg would not

The importance of the German assumption of British neutrality is demonstrated by the reaction in Berlin to reports (beginning July 25) from Prince Lichnowsky, German ambassador to Britain, that Grey had changed his position toward opposition to Germany. The Kaiser was the first to take these warnings seriously (July 27) and within a day made his compromise Halt in Belgrade proposal, which was delivered to Austria on the morning of July 29 (Albertini 1980, vol. 2: 431–5; Lebow 1981: 131–2, 140–1). There was enough ambiguity in the July 27 message, however, to leave Bethmann-Hollweg unmoved.

On July 29, however, Lichnowsky sent another telegram, this time with an unequivocal warning from Grey that Britain could not stand aside in a continental war involving France (Kautsky 1924, no. 178).[33] The response in Berlin was immediate and quite revealing. As Fischer (1967: 78–82; 1988) argues, Bethmann-Hollweg and other German political leaders were "shattered" by the telegram, for "the foundation of their policy during the crisis had collapsed." Bethmann-Hollweg responded with a flurry of increasingly urgent telegrams that night. He proposed that Vienna accept mediation and the Halt in Belgrade proposal and warned that Germany would not allow itself "to be drawn wantonly into a world conflagration by Vienna," hinting that Germany might abandon its ally rather than be drawn into a world war that it had always feared (Bethmann-Hollweg to Tschirschky, 2:55 A.M. and 3:00 A.M., July 30, 1914, in Kautsky 1924, nos. 192, 193; see also Schmitt 1966 [1930], vol. 2: 156–72; Fischer 1967: 78–82; Jarausch 1969: 65–8; Albertini 1980, vol. 2: 504–27; Lynn-Jones 1986: 143–4).[34]

Thus in a desperate attempt to avoid the one outcome that he had always feared – but only on the 29th had recognized was likely – Bethmann-Hollweg suddenly reversed the policy that had guided Germany throughout the July crisis. This evidence that German policy

---

risk a continental war in the absence of these assumptions. Thus in my argument that the German assumption of British neutrality was a necessary condition for war of any kind, by "neutrality" I mean the absence of British intervention in the early stages of a German invasion of France.

[33]Grey gave the impression that Britain could remain neutral if France were not involved.

[34]Fischer (1967: 79–82) and to a lesser extent Geiss (1967: 269) argue that Bethmann-Hollweg's policy shift on July 29–30 was genuine but temporary and that "peace moves" later that day were simply tactical expedients to deceive Britain and ensure that the blame for the conflict could be shifted onto Russia. Lebow (1981: 135–9) emphasizes the importance of psychological stress, emotional turmoil, exaggerated confidence and pessimistic fatalism, and hypervigilant coping behavior in Bethmann-Hollweg's shifts in policy on July 29–31. Copeland (2000) argues that Bethmann-Hollweg's last-minute pleading for Austrian restraint was all a charade. In his view Bethmann-Hollweg was bent on war but wanted to create the impression that he had done everything possible to avoid war.

reversed course with the change in German expectations of British behavior provides strong support for my argument that the German assumption of British neutrality (in the early stages of a war) was a necessary condition for the German blank check to Austria–Hungary and thus for war in 1914.[35]

Trachtenberg (1990–1) argues that the German policy reversal was a response to news on July 29 of the imminent Russian partial mobilization, not to messages from London of Britain's likely entry in the war. A careful analysis of the content, timing, and sequence of telegrams, however, provides convincing evidence that it was the news of likely British entry rather than the news of the Russian partial mobilization that led Bethmann-Hollweg to reverse course and attempt to restrain Austria–Hungary on the night of July 29–30.

The shift in the tone in Bethmann-Hollweg's telegrams was much more striking in the first telegram that mentioned British intervention than in the first telegram that mentioned the Russian mobilization, which Bethmann-Hollweg described as "far from meaning war." Moreover, it was only after the news from London, but not after the earlier news of the imminent Russian mobilization, that Bethmann-Hollweg dropped his concern about shifting the blame for any conflict onto Russia (which had been a standard phrase in many of his telegrams to Vienna) and spoke only about avoiding a world war. It was also only after the news from London that Bethmann-Hollweg hinted that Germany might prefer to abandon its ally than be dragged into a world war.

This takes us back to the question of why German political leaders were so confident of British neutrality. It is easy to say that Germany should have known that Britain would intervene in any continental war involving its French and Russian allies, particularly if Belgian neutrality were violated. A German victory in a two-front war would give it a position of dominance on the continent and control of the critical Channel ports, leave Britain without strong allies on the continent, and provide Germany with a strategic and industrial base from which to mount a global challenge to Britain.[36] Moreover, there had been

---

[35] The critical impact of British intentions is also demonstrated by the German response to Lichnowsky's August 1 report of Grey's offer that if Germany "were not to attack France, England would remain neutral and guarantee the passivity of France" (Albertini 1980, vol. 3: 380–1). With the Chancellor's eager support, the Kaiser announced, "[N]ow we can go to war against Russia only. We simply march the whole of our army to the East" (Tuchman 1962: 98). Moltke objected but was overruled, and Germany telegraphed its acceptance of what was thought to be the British proposal, only to learn that Lichnowsky's report had been erroneous (Albertini 1980, vol. 3: 380–6).

[36] Naval agreements with France, of which the Germans had some knowledge, created an additional British obligation. Moreover, British policies in the two Moroccan crises

numerous warnings that Britain would not be able to stay neutral in a
continental war.

Although the German political leaders' dismissal of these warnings
and their failure to appreciate Britain's strategic interests can be explained in part by motivated psychological biases and wishful thinking
(Lebow 1981: 130–1), their assumption of British neutrality was not
entirely unreasonable. Not all of the signals coming out of London
were consistent with the warnings from Lichnowsky, and the fact that
Lichnowsky was out of favor in Berlin may have led to his early warnings being discounted (Lebow 1981: 129). Though Grey repeatedly
refused to give Berlin an unconditional commitment of neutrality, he
also refused to give France and Russia a commitment to come to their
defense. That German "misperceptions" derived as much from the inherent uncertainty of the incoming signals as from any motivated biases
is suggested by the fact that officials in France and Russia, whose motivated biases would have led in the opposite direction from Germany's
and who had constantly pressured Britain for a clear commitment, were
also uncertain of British intentions.[37] Indeed, the British themselves
were unclear as to what they would do. Cabinet members David Lloyd
George and Winston Churchill were both skeptical regarding whether
the government would intervene on the continent, and Grey himself
was uncertain.[38]

Britain's failure to give a clear and timely commitment in support
of her allies was a critical step in the processes leading to an Austro-
Serbian war and its expansion into a world war, for it eliminated the
one threat that would have led German political decision-makers to
restrain their counterparts in Vienna. Yet British leaders were faced
with serious diplomatic and domestic political constraints, and it is
not clear that they could easily have acted differently. Their strategic
dilemma was that while a clear commitment would reinforce deterrence
against Germany, it might at the same time encourage Russia to pursue

---

indicated that no British government was likely to stand aside while Germany increased
its influence at the expense of France.

[37]French Chief of Staff General Joffre was so uncertain of British intervention that he
did not assume it in forming the French army's war plan. Sazonov warned the Russian
Council of Ministers on July 24 that any escalation of war would be dangerous "since it
is not known what attitude Great Britain would take in the matter" (Williamson 1979:
146; see also Sagan 1986: 169–70).

[38]On July 29, Grey told French Ambassador to Berlin Jules Cambon that "if Germany
became involved and France became involved, we had not made up our minds what we
should do." On August 1 the British Cabinet rejected a proposal to dispatch the British
Expeditionary Force to the continent and forbade Churchill to order the full mobilization
of the navy (British Documents, vol. 11, no. 283: 180; Joll 1984: 19–20; Wilson 1986:
149–50). On the difficulty of identifying misperceptions and the usefulness of the "third
party" criterion, see Jervis (1976: 7), Levy (1983: 76–89) and Sagan (1986: 170).

a riskier course against Austria–Hungary in the Balkans. Many British leaders assumed that by leaving their commitment ambiguous they could maximize the likelihood of restraining Russia without alienating her and deterring Germany without provoking her.[39]

Grey's policy of diluting and delaying Britain's deterrent threat against Germany was reinforced by his perception that Anglo–German relations had improved over the previous three years and his belief that a more accommodative strategy toward Germany might induce a cooperative solution to the July crisis, as it had in the Balkan Wars (Lynn-Jones 1986: 125–40).[40] The fear of provoking Germany was undoubtedly less compelling after July 27–28, however, for the German rejection of Grey's proposal for a four-power conference and the Austrian declaration of war greatly reduced any remaining doubt regarding the intentions of the Central Powers.

By July 27, if not before, the primary factor preventing Grey from issuing a clear warning to Germany was cabinet politics in England. About three-quarters of Liberal cabinet members were opposed to British involvement in war, and Grey knew that it would be difficult to secure any commitment from them.[41] Grey's objectives were to prevent a continental war if at all possible, but to bring Britain into the war united if war occurred. An early warning to Germany might advance the first aim but generate a domestic reaction that threatened the second. With regard to warning Germany that Britain would declare war if Germany attacked France or violated Belgian territory, Churchill (1931: 204) later wrote: "I am certain that if Sir Edward Grey had sent the kind of ultimatum suggested, the Cabinet would have broken up." Churchill went on to say that "up till Wednesday [29th] or Thursday

---

[39] Grey's attempted balancing act has been described as a "straddle strategy" (G. Snyder 1984). This strategy was based on the assumption that uncertainty would induce caution in both Russia and Germany, but the assumption that states are always risk averse is questionable. Prospect theory, for example, suggests that people tend to be risk acceptant when they are faced with choices involving negative outcomes (Kahneman and Tversky 1979).

[40] This argument is reinforced by evidence suggesting that Grey perceived that Berlin was divided between a peace party (headed by Bethmann-Hollweg) and a war party (associated with the military), feared that pressure against Germany would only strengthen hard-line elements in Berlin, and believed that conciliatory actions might strengthen Bethmann-Hollweg in his internal political struggles with the military (Eckstein 1971: 121–31).

[41] At a meeting of the Cabinet on July 27, Grey asked if Britain would intervene were France attacked by Germany. Five ministers warned that they would resign if such a decision were taken. On July 29 the Cabinet refused to specify the conditions under which it would decide for war. On August 1 Grey stated that "we could not propose to Parliament at this moment to send an expeditionary military force to the continent" (British Documents vol. 11, no. 426; see also Woodward 1967: 21–2; Wilson 1975: 148–59; Steiner 1977, chap. 9).

[30th] at least, the House of Commons would have repudiated his action. Nothing less than the deeds of Germany would have converted the British nation to war."

It is significant that Churchill refers to *German* deeds. Austrian action against Serbia was not sufficient to bring Britain in, for if a settlement were not possible, Britain preferred a localized war in the Balkans, whatever its outcome, to a continental or world war. But what specific German deeds would be necessary or sufficient to bring Britain into the war?[42] Although one cannot know for sure how the cabinet would have acted under various contingencies, it appears that the critical trigger for cabinet approval of British intervention in the early stages of the war was the German violation of Belgian neutrality, which was an integral part of the German Schlieffen Plan (Ritter 1958; J. Snyder 1984, chaps. 4–5).[43] For years the radicals had refused to be swayed by balance-of-power arguments, and in the end they needed the moral justification provided by the 1839 guarantee of Belgian neutrality (Steiner 1977: 237).[44]

Grey's domestic political constraints still permitted him some ways of influencing Germany. A formal threat to Berlin was probably precluded by cabinet politics but an informal warning was not. Although Grey's warning of July 29 had not been approved by the cabinet, it had a tremendous impact on Germany, and a similar informal warning could have been issued much earlier. Had a warning been issued prior

---

[42]To Grey, any Franco–German war sufficiently threatened British interests that it required intervention. For the Cabinet, severe military setbacks to France and the threat of German continental hegemony were probably prerequisites to intervention; this was the German "weak neutrality assumption," described above. Grey was also worried about parliamentary support (Mayer 1967: 298–9).

[43]Without the German violation of Belgian neutrality, British intervention in a continental war would have been considerably less likely, or at least delayed, because British radicals probably would not have been convinced of the strategic necessity for military action short of severe military setbacks to France. Thus the significance of Belgium, particularly for the radicals in the Cabinet, was more political than strategic; the balance-of-power on the continent and the future of Belgium and its Channel ports would ultimately depend upon the outcome of a Franco–German war, regardless of whether Belgian neutrality was violated at its onset. In this way, the Schlieffen Plan and the envelopment of France through Belgium not only precluded the effective management of the crisis by Germany to avoid the world war they feared but also ensured that the British would enter the war at an early stage and thus maximize their impact. Thus part of the explanation for the erroneous assumption of British neutrality by political decision-makers must be traced to their miscalculation of the consequences of the Schlieffen Plan, to which I return below.

[44]While either the German violation of Belgian neutrality or the near-defeat of France significantly increased the probability that the radicals in the Cabinet would lend their support to war, it probably goes too far to say that one of these was a necessary condition for British intervention in the war. Grey might have been able to persuade the radicals to go along, or he may have decided to take the country into war despite internal divisions.

to the Austrian ultimatum on the 23rd, or perhaps even as late as the 27th, it would have been sufficient to alarm Germany and to provoke successful German pressure against Austria–Hungary, and war could have been averted, at least for a time. At that time, however, Grey was constrained by strategic considerations. Although we now know that Germany was more in need of restraint than was Russia and that earlier British pressure against Berlin probably would have averted war, it is more difficult to say that Grey should have known this in July 1914.

Although the erroneous assumption of British neutrality was a necessary condition for German support of an Austrian invasion of Serbia and consequently for a continental or world war (at least until the Austrian declaration of war on July 28), it was not a sufficient condition for war. It is conceivable that a continental war could have been avoided if Austro-Hungarian leaders had undertaken military action immediately following the assassination, if they had agreed to the Halt in Belgrade plan for limited military action against Serbia or if diplomatic efforts to force them to accept this plan and manage the crisis had been given more time to work. Below I consider each of these "roads not taken" and identify the strategic and domestic constraints that made these options too costly in the eyes of statesmen.

The delay of Austro–Hungarian military action

Austria pursued a fait accompli strategy (George 1991a, chap. 5), but delayed military action against Serbia for a month after the assassination of the Archduke. The timing was critical, because the combination of universal outrage against Serbia, the widespread belief that a limited Austrian response in defense of its honor would be legitimate, the fear of a wider war, and German threats against Russia might have been sufficient to localize the war. A. J. P. Taylor concludes that "the one chance of success for Austria-Hungary would have been rapid action" (1971: 522–3).[45]

Most German political and military leaders assumed that a larger war might be avoided if Austrian leaders would take immediate action, and this was a primary factor underlying their pressure on Vienna to move as quickly as possible.[46] The greater the delay, the more the punishment of Serbia would be decoupled from the assassination that might have provided it some legitimacy, and the more the Tsar would

---

[45] Similarly, Ritter (1969–73, vol. 2: 236) concludes that "swift action would have been politically much more effective and less dangerous to the peace of Europe than the endless delay that did take place." Williamson (1979b: 151–3) writes that "what had appeared in early July to be a calculated, acceptable risk – a local war with Serbia – would loom more dangerous and provocative two weeks later."

[46] Grey also accepted this assumption (Butterfield 1965: 10–11; Fischer 1967: 53–61).

shift his concerns from the principle of monarchial solidarity to his strategic and reputational interests in the Balkans. A major consequence of the delay was to transform the possibility of an early punitive strike into a larger local war that was more likely to escalate.

How do we explain the delay? Nothing could be done before the blank check from Germany July 5–6, because strong assurance of German support was a necessary condition for a major military action by Austria. One reason for the extensive delay after this was military. Berchtold, who initially wanted to attack Serbia without first mobilizing, was distressed to learn from Conrad on July 6 that an invasion could not begin until two weeks after mobilization (Albertini 1980, vol. 2: 455).[47] The delay was exacerbated by domestic structural and political constraints. The goal of a unified monarchy precluded any further action (including an ultimatum or declaration of war) until July 14, when Hungarian Prime Minister Tisza retreated from his earlier opposition to war in return for the willingness of the Austro–Hungarian Council of Ministers to accept his demand for the renunciation of territorial annexations (excepting minor frontier "adjustments") at Serbia's expense.[48]

Two additional factors explain the nine-day delay in the ultimatum after July 14. Organizational constraints imposed by the timetable of the harvest furloughs for the army complicated the recall of troops before their scheduled return on July 21–22, because that might disrupt the harvests and possibly the railroad-based mobilization plans and eliminate the possible benefits of surprise (Williamson 1979a: 152–3; Levy 1986: 202). In addition, Austrian decision-makers did not want to deliver the ultimatum to Serbia until after the state visit of Poincaré and Viviani to St. Petersburg on July 23, fearing that the French leaders might encourage a stronger Russian response (Geiss 1967: 114–15).

---

[47]The critical questions are whether Austria could have taken limited military operations (a punitive strike) against Serbia, independent of a general invasion; whether contingency plans for this option existed in early July (or later, with the Halt in Belgrade proposal); and whether such an action would have interfered with a subsequent mobilization against Serbia or Russia (Renouvin 1928: 128; Holsti 1972: 157, 216; Levy 1986: 200). Taylor (1974: 445) argues that Serbia had decided not to defend Belgrade. If so, Austria could easily have occupied Belgrade without substantially interfering with later operations.

[48]Tisza wanted to reassure the Tsar and minimize the likelihood of Russian intervention. This renunciation of territorial annexations may have come too late, however, and in any case it is not certain that Austria–Hungary planned to fulfill this promise (Schmitt 1966 [1930], vol. 1: 345–57; Stone 1966; Albertini 1980, vol. 2: 175; Williamson 1988: 810). For an argument that Tisza's opposition to war was politically motivated, driven by a fear that a successful war (including the annexation of Slavic territories) would further centralize power in Vienna and shift the balance of power in the Dual Monarchy further away from the Hungarians, see Levy and Mabe (2004).

By this time, however, the cloak of legitimacy for an Austrian military action resulting from the royal assassination would have dissipated. Moreover, once the unprecedented terms of the ultimatum became known, European political leaders began to see Austria, not Serbia, as the primary violator of international norms. At this point, it is more likely that the best hope for peace lay in a *delay* of the Austrian declaration of war.

Conrad wanted to delay a declaration of war and a crushing fait accompli against Serbia until August 12, when military operations could begin. Berchtold insisted (July 26) on an early declaration of war (July 28), which he thought would pacify Germany and an increasingly vocal press and domestic public (Turner 1970: 98; Albertini 1980, vol. 2: 453–8). Berchtold now welcomed the lapse between the declaration of war and the invasion and hoped it would provide time for additional coercive pressure to secure Serbia's "unconditional submission."

Thus Berchtold apparently shifted his preferred strategy from military victory over Serbia to coercive diplomacy. After designing the ultimatum so that its inevitable rejection would provide a justification for the war that he wanted, and then recognizing that Austria lacked the means for an immediate fait accompli, Berchtold switched to a coercive strategy but did not combine it with the diplomatic measures that might have made it effective. He did not soften the degrading terms of the ultimatum to provide Serbia with a face-saving way out of the crisis, and he compounded matters further with a premature declaration of war that only strengthened the resolve of Serbia and the Entente and contributed to the further escalation of the crisis.[49]

The timing of Austrian moves was critical, first, because the Austrian declaration of war and concurrent mobilization against Serbia led directly to the partial Russian mobilization, which initiated a rapid and nearly irreversible sequence of threats and mobilizations over the next four days. Second, it made it much more difficult for Vienna to give in to German pressures for restraint, which began during the night of July 29–30 after Lichnowsky's warning from Grey.

It is important to recognize that Vienna's declaration of war and military mobilization were driven by political rather than military considerations, as a brief examination of Austria's mobilization plans and its strategic dilemma suggests. Facing the prospect of a two-front war against both Russia and Serbia, Austrian military planners incorporated a degree of flexibility into their mobilization and war plans. They allowed for partial mobilization against either Serbia or Russia and for offensive action against one and defensive action against the

---

[49]I thank Alexander George for suggesting this line of argument.

other, depending on the specific threat. But once a partial mobilization was initiated against Serbia, the troops involved could not easily be shifted back to the Galician front to meet a major Russian attack.[50] Although this created an incentive for Vienna to speed up the flow of events rather than slow them down once mobilization had begun, it also created a military incentive to delay mobilization as long as possible, until Russian intentions became more certain. Mobilization was, for Berchtold, an essential element of a strategy to force Serbia's submission by coercive diplomacy if possible and by war if necessary. But mobilization was not essential to Conrad's preparation for war, and in fact was damaging to it.[51]

In retrospect, a delay in the declaration of war until the onset of military operations, as Conrad preferred, may have increased the probability of a peaceful settlement, but not by much. Russian interests were threatened far more by the Austrian mobilization than by the declaration of war per se. Given the acceleration of events unleashed by the Russian mobilization, it is unlikely that a delay in the Austrian declaration of war would have bought much time for crisis management.

On the other hand, Russian leaders might have been somewhat less certain of Austrian intentions in the absence of the declaration of war and therefore slightly less inclined to mobilize, which would have provided a little more time for efforts to manage the crisis through the Halt in Belgrade proposal.[52] In addition, the Austrian declaration of war may have been more difficult to reverse, in the eyes of its decision-makers, than was mobilization.[53] A delay in the declaration of war alone would therefore have reduced the reputational, domestic political, and

---

[50]This rigidity was due to the inherent difficulties of fighting a two-front war, the poor quality of the Austro–Hungarian railway system, and the inability and unwillingness of the Germans to provide significant help against Russia in the early stages of a war because of the requirements of the Schlieffen Plan. Conrad's defense plan called for minimal defense forces in both Galicia (A-Staffel, 30 divisions) and the Balkans (Minimalgruppe Balkan, 10 divisions). An additional 12 divisions (B-Staffel) could be sent either to the Balkans (where they would add sufficient strength to destroy Serbia) or to Galicia (where they would combine with A-Staffel to provide for a powerful offensive against Russia). But once committed, B-Staffel could not be shifted to the other front easily or quickly (Stone 1979: 225–6, 243–4).

[51]Conrad insisted that he had to know by the fifth day of mobilization whether the Russians were planning to intervene or else his plans would go awry. He described a delayed Russian intervention as "[t]he most difficult yet most probable case." Moltke concurred (Fischer 1967: 74; Turner 1970: 92–3; Stone 1979: 228–35; Turner 1979a: 258; Albertini 1980, vol. 2: 482).

[52]This is particularly true had the Russians understood the opportunities created by technical rigidities in Austrian mobilization plans, as I argue below.

[53]The Austrians, unlike the Germans, did not perceive that mobilization necessarily meant war (Schmitt 1966 [1930], vol. 2: 215).

psychological costs to Austrian leaders of reversing course and thus increased somewhat the likelihood that they might have accepted the Halt in Belgrade proposal under German pressure.[54] But it is impossible to say whether the magnitude of these changes would have been large enough to delay, even temporarily, a world war that none of the great powers wanted.

The "Halt in Belgrade" proposal

After hearing of Austria's ultimatum on July 24, Russian leaders concluded that it was designed to provoke war. The next day the Tsar authorized preparatory military actions (short of mobilization) in order to deter an Austrian move against Serbia, and, if that failed, to facilitate military intervention in Serbia's defense.[55] Grey began exploring the possibility of British mediation on the same day, and on July 26 he invited France, Germany, and Italy to send their ambassadors to a conference in London. Austria refused; so did Germany, which was still confident of British neutrality and continued to press for immediate military action as a means of localizing the war.

By July 27–28 the Kaiser began to fear British intervention and at the same time believed that after the conciliatory Serbian reply, "every cause for war has vanished." He instructed Jagow to request that Vienna accept a "temporary military occupation" of Belgrade pending successful great power mediation (Kautsky 1924, nos. 273–4). This "Halt in Belgrade" proposal aimed to manage the escalating crisis and to localize it in the Balkans, by allowing Austria to gain a significant diplomatic victory and demonstrate its military prowess and prestige without damaging Russia's reputation.[56]

Bethmann-Hollweg's pressure on Austria for restraint, induced by his changed perceptions of British intentions, came less than a day after the Kaiser's Halt in Belgrade proposal was delivered to Austria.

---

[54]This assumes that Grey would have seen the combination of the ultimatum, Bethmann-Hollweg's rejection of the proposal for a four-power conference, and Russia's early preparations for war as threatening enough – even in the absence of Austrian declaration of war – to issue a strong warning to Germany. Nothing less than such a warning would have induced Germany to pressure Austria for restraint. That is, a strong British warning to Germany was a necessary condition for German efforts to restrain Austria and therefore for peace.

[55]Russia's initiation of "the Period Preparatory to War" on July 26 is best seen as the first stage of mobilization (Schilling 1925: 62–6; Turner 1979a: 261–2; Albertini 1980, vol. 2: 565–72; J. Snyder 1984, chaps. 6–7; Van Evera 1984: 72–9; Stevenson 1997).

[56]Grey made a similar proposal the next day. He requested that Russia suspend military operations against Serbia, while Austria "hold the occupied territory until she had complete satisfaction from Servia ... [but] not advance further" (British Documents, no. 286, 182).

Although Berchtold's formal response was delayed and deliberately evasive, he immediately told German Ambassador Heinrich Tschirschky that it was too late to change course. Strategically, Berchtold believed that the temporary occupation of Belgrade would not be sufficient to achieve Austria's initial objective of eliminating the threat from Serbia and the southern Slavs. He feared that although a temporary occupation of Belgrade would provide leverage against Serbia, it would also generate diplomatic pressure on Vienna to soften its demands. Moreover, even if Russia were willing to tolerate an Austrian occupation of Belgrade, it would be "mere tinsel," for the Serbian army would remain intact and see Russia as its savior, and Serbia would provoke another crisis in two or three years under conditions much less favorable to Austria.[57]

Berchtold was also concerned about the reputational and domestic political costs of reversing course after an earlier declaration of war. After considerable pressure from Germany to move quickly against Serbia, Austro–Hungarian leaders had taken the politically difficult decisions to issue the ultimatum, declare war, and begin mobilization. Once taken, these actions were very difficult to modify and redirect. This would have undermined Austrian credibility, upset a coalition of domestic political interests that had been very difficult to construct, and broken a serious psychological commitment. As Lebow argues, "[H]aving finally crossed their psychological Rubicon, the Austrian leaders obviously felt a tremendous sense of psychological release and were hardly about to turn back willingly" (1981: 136).

This episode demonstrates the importance of the timing of actions designed to reinforce crisis management. Had Germany initiated this pressure against Austria *prior* to the declaration of war on the 28th, it would have been far more difficult for Vienna to resist. Austria would have been even more likely to acquiesce had the German pressure come before the ultimatum was delivered on July 23, and there is every reason to believe that an earlier warning from Grey would have been sufficient to trigger a German warning to Vienna. Albertini concludes "[I]f Grey had spoken before 23 July, or even after the 23rd but not later than the afternoon of the 27th, as he spoke on the 29th, Germany would very likely have restrained Austria from declaring war on Serbia and the European war, at least for the time being, would have been averted" (1980, vol. 2: 514, vol. 3: 643; see also Kaiser 1983: 471; Lynn-Jones

---

[57]Austro–German negotiations were also complicated by disagreements over how much to concede to their Italian ally to keep it in line (Schmitt 1966 [1930], vol. 2: 217–22; Fischer 1967: 73; Albertini 1980, vol. 2: 656–7). It has also been argued that Vienna was constrained because it had no contingency plans for the occupation of Belgrade (Renouvin 1928: 128; Holsti 1972: 157, 216).

1986: 139, 144).[58] This reinforces my argument that German support for Austria–Hungary was a necessary condition for Austrian military action and therefore for a world war.

Even as late as July 30, however, it is still conceivable that war could have been avoided, though the margin for maneuver was admittedly thin. Berchtold continued to delay a response to Bethmann-Hollweg's proposal, and Bethmann-Hollweg continued his pleas for peace but without increasing the pressure against his Austrian ally.[59] This was critical, because stronger German pressure, including an explicit threat to withdraw support from Austria, probably would have been sufficient to compel Vienna to accept the Halt in Belgrade plan and thus avoid more extensive military action, at least for the time being. Despite the costs of reversing course after a declaration of war, the prospect of being left to fight Russia and Serbia alone was even less desirable. In addition, Hungarian Prime Minister Tisza might have seized on German pressure as an excuse to back out of a decision that he had undertaken only with the greatest reluctance, and his defection would have undermined the internal unity necessary for a successful war effort. Thus David Kaiser argues, "[T]he Vienna government could not possibly have held out against united pressure to accept some variant of the Halt in Belgrade plan" (1983: 471).[60]

But German pressure on Vienna was only moderate in intensity, accompanied by mixed signals, and withdrawn early. The Kaiser's proposal was ready for delivery early on July 28, before the declaration of war, but Bethmann-Hollweg delayed sending it to Ambassador Tschirschky in Vienna for 12 hours and distorted its content in significant ways to reduce its impact.[61] Tschirschky delayed further and

---

[58]In terms of the theme of this volume, the absence of a clear warning from Grey (or other credible British leaders) was a necessary condition for Germany to push Austria toward war against Serbia.

[59]Lebow (1981: 136–47) emphasizes Bethmann-Hollweg's increasing fatalism and perception of narrowing options and loss of control, induced by psychological stress.

[60]Albertini concludes that "Berchtold was assailed by doubts and hesitations [about general mobilization on July 31], so that it remains an open question whether he would actually have put the order into execution if he had received further strong pressure from Berlin in favor of the Halt in Belgrade and mediation" (1980, vol. 2: 659, 669–73).

[61]Whereas the Kaiser insisted only that Austria had to have a "guaranty that the promises were carried out" (Fischer 1967: 72), the chancellor emphasized in his telegram to German Ambassador Tschirschky that the aim of the temporary occupation was "to force the Serbian Government to the complete fulfillment of her demands" (Kautsky 1924: 288–9). Bethmann-Hollweg also deleted the phrase about war no longer being necessary. He also told Tschirschky "[T]o avoid very carefully giving rise to the impression that we wish to hold Austria back ... [We must] find a way to realize Austria's desired aim ... without at the same time bringing on a world war, and, if the latter cannot be avoided in the end, of improving the conditions under which we shall have to wage it" (Kautsky 1924: 288–9).

in fact may have encouraged Austrian belligerency.[62] The ambiguous
signals from Berlin continued even after Bethmann-Hollweg reversed
course on July 29 and began pressing Vienna to accept Grey's Halt in
Belgrade proposal. At the same time Bethmann-Hollweg was urging
Berchtold to consider the proposal, Chief of the German General Staff
Moltke was urging Conrad, his Austrian counterpart, to press forward
with mobilization and warning that any further delay would be disastrous. This led Conrad to complain, "Who actually rules in Berlin,
Bethmann-Hollweg or Moltke?" (Albertini 1980, vol. 2: 673–4).[63]

Berlin's pressure, too weak to impress Austrian leaders with the
potentially serious consequences of their failure to accept the peace
proposal, was not sustained. Bethmann-Hollweg reversed his position
and effectively withdrew German support from the Halt in Belgrade
proposal on the evening of July 30, after fresh reports that Russia was
about to begin mobilization, that Belgium had begun preparations for
war, and that Austria was concentrating its forces against Serbia.[64]
These reports led to an abrupt shift in Moltke's position, an uneasiness
among the military, an increase in military influence in the political
decision-making process,[65] greater inclination toward a preventive war,
and intense pressure for the declaration of a "state of imminent war."[66]
The consequences were enormous. Albertini concludes "[I]f on the 30th
Bethmann-Hollweg had not let himself be overruled by Moltke, had
insisted with Berchtold, on pain of nonrecognition of the *casus foederis*,
that Austria should content herself with the Anglo–German proposals,
and had then waited for Sazonov to follow suit, the peace of the world
might have been saved" (1980, vol. 3: 32).

---

[62]Tschirschky also delayed notifying Berlin of the Austrian declaration of war. Albertini (1980, vol. 2: 653–61) concludes that Tschirschky and Berchtold "were in league" to
deceive Berlin and deflect German pressure for restraint.

[63]Moltke may have acted with the approval of the Kaiser (Schmitt 1966 [1930], vol. 2:
198; Albertini 1980, vol. 3: 11–13; Trachtenberg 1990–1: 139). Ritter (1969–73, vol. 2:
258) states that Moltke's telegram arrived on July 31, after the Austrian decision for
general mobilization.

[64]Belgian preparations might bottle up the German invasion of France, and therefore
disrupt the entire war effort based on the Schlieffen Plan (Trumpener 1976: 77). Austrian
concentration against Serbia would leave inadequate strength in Galicia for an offensive
against Russia (Turner 1979a: 215; Albertini 1980, vol. 2: 500).

[65]The military did not exert much pressure on Bethmann-Hollweg prior to July 30.
See footnote 33 above.

[66]At 9 P.M. on July 30 Bethmann-Hollweg sent Telegram 200 to Vienna, requesting
that Austria accept the Halt in Belgrade plan. But this request was not accompanied
by the coercive pressure that was necessary for its success, and in any event it was
followed in two hours by another telegram suspending the first. Albertini (1980, vol.
2: 21–4) interprets this as evidence of the increasing influence of the military, but
Trachtenberg (1990–1, 139) dissents.

The Russian mobilization

The Russian mobilization was particularly important in the shift in German policy toward war on July 30–31, because it changed both the strategic landscape and the mindsets of political and military leaders. The Russian mobilization led political and military decision-makers to believe that a continental war was inevitable and that they had lost control of events. These perceptions began to acquire a self-fulfilling character. Decision-makers became more willing to let events run their course, and efforts to deter war gave way to preparations for an unavoidable war (Lebow 1981: 134–9, 254–6; Joll 1984: 21, 107, 203).

Russian leaders hoped that mobilization, in conjunction with diplomatic pressure from the other powers, would deter Austria from an all-out military attack against Serbia, limit the concessions Serbia would have to make, and improve Russia's ability to defend Serbia in the event of war.[67] It is not clear, however, that Russia needed to mobilize in order to protect its vital interests and deter an Austrian move against Serbia. It only needed to *threaten* to do so. In fact, a careful examination of the structure of Russian mobilization plans, in conjunction with those of Austria–Hungary, reveals that there was an opportunity for Russian leaders to slow down the accelerating pace of events without threatening their vital interests.

The Austrian mobilization against Serbia posed no immediate military threat to Serbia, because an Austrian invasion could not begin until August 12. Neither did the Austrian mobilization plans threaten Russia. The longer Russia delayed, the more Austrian mobilization against Serbia would progress, and the more difficult it would be for Austria to mount a successful defense against any Russian offensive from the east, which would ultimately determine Austria's fate. As L. C. F. Turner concludes, "[I]t was very much to Russia's advantage to delay any mobilization until a substantial part of the Austrian Army was entangled in operations against Serbia" (1970: 92; see also Turner 1979b: 258, 266; Albertini 1980, vol. 2: 482, vol. 3: 31).

Thus Russia could have delayed a partial mobilization for several more days without harming Russian interests in the Balkans. Such a delay would presumably have delayed the alarm felt by Moltke and the German generals, eliminated the need for a German mobilization or even preparatory military action, and thus provided more time for Bethmann-Hollweg to continue to press Vienna to accept the Halt in Belgrade plan. The Russian decision to mobilize was taken in part

---

[67]Russian leaders also hoped that mobilization might help diffuse internal unrest (Fay 1966 [1928], vol. 2: 305; Rogger 1966: 229–53).

because "Sazonov and the Russian generals failed to grasp the immense diplomatic and military advantages conferred on them by the Austrian dilemma" (Turner 1970: 93; see also 1979b: 258, 266; Kennedy 1979: 15).[68]

The Russians' belief that mobilization against Austria was necessary had serious consequences, because for technical military reasons it would be costly to initiate a partial mobilization against Austria and then wait before mobilizing against Germany. A partial mobilization would disrupt railway transport and delay for months a systematic general mobilization against Germany. Russia would be dangerously exposed to a hostile and war-prone Germany and unable to come immediately to the aid of France. Thus Albertini concludes that the Russian choice was "either general mobilization or none at all" (1980, vol. 2: 543).

Russian leaders failed to recognize that constraints on the Austro–Hungarian mobilization created advantages for Russia by extending the window of opportunity for delay. They believed that speed was of the essence, that a few days' delay would put France in an increasingly precarious position, that war had become inevitable (Trachtenberg 1990-1, 125-6),[69] and consequently that they must mobilize as quickly as possible. Thus the Tsar, convinced that he lacked military options that would allow him to stand firm against Vienna without threatening Berlin and beset by increasing pressure from the Russian military and from Sazonov, decided to order general mobilization for July 31 rather than a partial mobilization against Austria–Hungary alone.[70] This was tragic, because the Russian mobilization was the decisive act leading to the war (Kennedy 1979: 15; Turner 1979b; Albertini 1980, vol. 3: 31; Levy 1986: 210), and because Russian leaders failed to appreciate the diplomatic advantages and time for maneuver they derived from technical rigidities in Austrian mobilization and war plans.

Russian political leaders' lack of comprehension of the meaning and consequences of mobilization also affected decision-making earlier in the crisis, though it is hard to assess its importance. Until fairly late in the crisis, Russian Foreign Minister Sazonov perceived partial mobilization as a usable and controllable instrument of coercion. He did not realize that it would precipitate a general mobilization by Austria, which would invoke the Austro–German alliance, trigger a general mobilization by Germany, and therefore lead to war. Nor did Sazonov

---

[68]Sazonov's original plan was to wait until Austria invaded Serbia before initiating partial mobilization (Albertini 1980, vol. 2: 538).

[69]This belief was reinforced by Russia's fear that Germany was looking for an opportunity to launch a preventive war against Russia (Van Evera 1984: 86-9).

[70]A general mobilization had been ordered and canceled on July 29, and a partial mobilization was ordered that day.

realize that Russian partial mobilization would seriously interfere with a subsequent general mobilization. His ignorance is explained in part by the fact that Janushkevich had been chief of staff for only five months, was not familiar with the details of mobilization, and therefore failed to warn Sazonov of the implications of partial mobilization. The situation was compounded further by Germany's failure to warn Russia of the risks involved. In fact, on July 27 Jagow had assured both the British and then the French ambassadors to Berlin that "if Russia only mobilized in the south, Germany would not mobilize."

Albertini concludes that if Sazonov had understood this, there is "no doubt" that he would have acted differently (that is, Sazonov's erroneous beliefs about the consequences of mobilization were a necessary condition for his strong support of mobilization). He would have attempted to delay mobilization, rather than press for it from July 24 or proclaim it on July 29, and the Tsar probably would have gone along (Turner 1979b: 260; Albertini 1980, vol. 2: 294, 480–2, 624, and vol. 3: 43; Van Evera 1984). This would have slowed down the momentum of events in Germany and provided additional time for political leaders to find a diplomatic solution to the crisis through the Halt in Belgrade plan. But whether this would have made a significant difference in the outbreak of war is open to question, because in the absence of an early partial mobilization by Russia it is unclear whether Grey would have issued the warning that induced Germany to restrain Austria.

The German mobilization

Because German political and military leaders believed strongly that for diplomatic and domestic political reasons it was essential that Russia be perceived as the aggressor, they had a strong incentive *not* to be the first to mobilize. Given this belief, some form of Russian mobilization was for all practical purposes a necessary condition for German mobilization. Russian *general* mobilization was a *sufficient* condition for German mobilization. But was a Russian *partial* mobilization a sufficient condition for German mobilization? Although Albertini and others may be correct that a partial mobilization by Russia "would have led to war no less surely than general mobilization" (Albertini 1980, vol. 2: 485n, 292–3; see also Turner 1970: 92, 104; Kennedy 1979: 16–17; J. Snyder 1984: 88; Van Evera 1984: 88; Levy 1986: 198), the causal linkage was delayed and indirect rather than immediate and direct: a Russian partial mobilization would eventually lead to a German mobilization because of the Russian threat to Austria, not because of the direct threat to Germany. In fact, the Russian threat to Germany would have been lessened somewhat as Russian partial mobilization measures against Austria progressed, because they would have delayed a subsequent Russian general mobilization.[71] If Russian leaders had known of these diplomatic and domestic political constraints on Germany and recognized that rigidities in the Russian mobilization plans gave Germany incentives to delay mobilization, Russia could have avoided its fateful mobilization without undermining its coercive pressure against either Austria or Germany.

This argument is supported by evidence that German military and political leaders were cautious in reacting to Russian military actions prior to the Russian general mobilization. Germany did not respond in kind to Russia's pre-mobilization measures, as evidenced by Moltke's refusal to support War Minister von Falkenhayn's July 29 proposal for a proclamation of *Kriegsgefahrzustand*, or "threatening danger of war."[72] Later that evening Bethmann-Hollweg refused to order an immediate German mobilization, on the grounds that Germany must wait for a state of war between Russia and Austria–Hungary, "because otherwise we should not have public opinion with us either at home or in England."[73] The German military began pressing hard for *Kriegsgefahrzustand* only at noon July 30, after receiving new information regarding the intensity of Russian military preparations, but Bethmann-Hollweg rejected this demand.[74] Only with the news of the Russian general mobilization at noon the following day did Bethmann-Hollweg agree to a German mobilization.[75]

Once both sides had mobilized, however, Germany had a strong incentive to strike first because of the demands of the Schlieffen Plan. Because the capture of Liège, with its vital forts and railroad lines, was necessary before the invasion of France could proceed, the Schlieffen Plan required that German armies cross the frontier and advance into Belgium as an integral part of mobilization. The perception that even small leads in mobilization would have significant military benefits

---

[71]An early partial Russian mobilization would also have allowed Austria to delay a partial mobilization against Serbia.

[72]Note that Falkenhayn did not believe that a preemptive mobilization by Germany was necessary (Albertini 1980, vol. 2: 496–7, 502; Trachtenberg 1990–1: 138).

[73]Moltke made only slight objections (Fischer 1967: 85; 1975: 495–6), and in fact he agreed with Bethmann-Hollweg that Austria must not appear as the aggressor. Late on July 29, Moltke, with unanimous support, instructed Conrad: "Do not declare war on Russia but wait for Russia's attack" (Fischer 1975: 496).

[74]*Kriegsgefahrzustand* would make mobilization more likely but not automatic (Albertini 1980, vol. 2: 491, 599; vol. 3: 6–18; Trachtenberg 1990–1: 138n). Bethmann-Hollweg promised the military a decision by noon on July 31.

[75]At this point Berlin sent a 12-hour ultimatum to St. Petersburg demanding that all military preparations be stopped. The Russian rejection of this demand was followed by the German declaration of war on August 1 (Fischer 1967: 85–6; Albertini 1980, vol. 2: 494–503; vol. 3: 6–18).

and that small delays could be catastrophic created additional military incentives to move as quickly as possible (Turner 1979a: 216; Van Evera 1984: 71–9; 1999; Levy 1986: 195–6).

Thus once Russia moved to a general mobilization, the German decision for war would immediately follow because of the structure of the alliance system and existing mobilization plans. Military require-ments of preparing for war took precedence over political requirements for avoiding one, and a continental war was inevitable. Because the Schlieffen Plan involved movement through Belgium, a world war was almost certain to follow (Taylor 1969: 25; Turner 1970: 63; Albertini 1980, vol. 2: 480; Levy 1986: 197–8).

The Schlieffen Plan made it inevitable that *any* war involving Ger-many would necessarily be a two-front war in which Britain would be forced to intervene, independently of the particular issues at stake or the political conditions under which it occurred.[76] This worst-case outcome for Germany derives in part from the separation of military planning in the previous decade from the political objectives which it was presumably designed to serve, and from the disproportionate emphasis given to *winning* a war, as opposed to avoiding war in the first place.[77] The Schlieffen Plan was constructed exclusively by the military, who consulted only minimally with civilian leaders and only on the basis of technical military considerations rather than political ones.[78] The sweep through Belgium, for example, did not take into account the political impact on England of the violation of Belgian neutrality.[79]

The narrow military orientation of the Schlieffen Plan and the rigidi-ties that made it difficult to modify by political leaders in response to changing political circumstances were compounded by the limits on political leaders' knowledge of the nature of mobilization and how existing plans might constrain their strategy of coercive diplomacy.[80] The mobilization plans, which they thought provided an instrument for

---

[76]For analyses of the feasibility of a German offensive in the East while Germany maintained a defensive holding action in the West, see J. Snyder (1984: 116–22).

[77]Technical military planning and military influence in political decision-making in the final stages of the July crisis are also evident in Russia, less so in France and Britain (Steiner 1977: 220; Kennedy 1979: 7; Keiger 1983, chap. 7; Lieven 1983: 63, 122).

[78]Thus Taylor argues that the mobilization plans "aimed at the best technical results without allowing for either the political conditions from which war might spring or the political consequences which might follow" (1974: 19; see also Ritter 1958: 1969–73, vol. 2, chap. 9; Kennedy 1979: 17; Turner 1979a: 205; J. Snyder 1984, chap. 4).

[79]Jagow's request in 1912 that the plan for violation of Belgian neutrality be re-evaluated was rejected by Moltke, and until 1913 there was not even an inquiry into the feasibility of alternative operational plans than might carry fewer political risks (Ritter 1969–73, vol. 2: 205; J. Snyder 1984: 121).

[80]Albertini argues, "[T]hey had no knowledge of what mobilization actually was, what demands it made on the country, what consequences it brought with it, to what risks it exposed the peace of Europe" (1980, vol. 2: 479; see also Levy 1986: 209–10).

an admittedly risky strategy of coercive diplomacy, had in fact been constructed as a strategy which was to be implemented only when war was perceived to be inevitable. Bethmann-Hollweg might very well have acted differently had he realized that his attempts to neutralize Britain would be defeated by the demands of the Schlieffen Plan (Albertini 1980, vol. 3: 249).[81]

These and related points have led numerous analysts to conclude that the mobilization plans of the European great powers were themselves one of the leading causes of World War I.[82] While the causal impact of the mobilization plans was hardly insignificant, it should not be exaggerated. These mobilization plans were part of the overall structure of constraints on the strategic choices of each of the great powers at several critical junctures in the July crisis, but we must keep in mind that these military mobilization and war plans were in place long before. They were the products of diplomatic alignments, strategic beliefs about the offensive nature of warfare, bureaucratic compromises among political and military leaders, and political and cultural assumptions about the interests of each of the great powers and the fundamental dynamics of international politics (Kennedy 1979: 18–19; Joll 1984, chap. 8; J. Snyder 1984; Van Evera 1984: 58–63; Levy 1986: 203–18; Sagan 1986). Although the mobilization plans, and the confusion surrounding them, clearly contributed to the spiral of escalation in the July crisis, the inference that the plans themselves were the primary cause of the war would be spurious.

Conclusion

I have argued that political leaders in each of the great powers in the July 1914 crisis preferred a peaceful settlement to a world war. The primary explanation for the outbreak of the world war – which none of the leading decision-makers of the European great powers wanted, expected, or deliberately sought – lies in the irreconcilable interests defined by state officials, the structure of international power and alliances

---

[81] Bethmann-Hollweg knew of plans to seize Liège, but he did not learn until July 31 that the invasion of Belgium must begin on the third day of mobilization (Turner 1970: 213). Jagow, Tirpitz, and the Kaiser had even less knowledge about the Schlieffen Plan.

[82] Ritter argues that "the outbreak of war in 1914 is the most tragic example of a government's helpless dependence on the planning of strategists that history has even seen" (1958: 90). Albertini concludes that the primary reason that Germany "set fire to the powder cask" lay in "the requirements of the Schlieffen Plan, which no doubt was a masterpiece of military science, but also a monument of that utter lack of political horse-sense which is the main cause of European disorders and upheavals" (1980, vol. 3: 253; see also Turner 1970; Taylor 1974: 19; Levy 1986: 209–10).

that created intractable strategic dilemmas, the particular plans for mobilization and war that were generated by these strategic constraints, decision-makers' critical assumptions regarding the likely behavior of their adversaries and the consequences of their own actions, and domestic political constraints on their freedom of action. Thus the causes of World War I are to be found primarily in the underlying economic, military, diplomatic, political, and social forces which existed prior to the onset of the crisis. These forces shaped the policy preferences of statesmen and the strategic and political constraints within which they had to make extraordinarily difficult decisions. Thus the probability of war was already quite high at the time of the assassination.[83]

To say that war was likely, however, is not to say that it was inevitable. At several critical points in the July crisis, political leaders took actions that increased the probability of war, and failed to take other actions that might have bought additional time for crisis management without seriously threatening their vital interests. No war would have occurred in the absence of the German assumption that Britain would stay neutral in the early stages of a continental war, but that assumption was not entirely unreasonable given the information available at the time. Britain's allies and in fact Grey himself were uncertain of what Britain would do. An earlier explicit warning from Grey might have been sufficient to maintain the peace, but Grey was faced with a strategic dilemma and severe domestic constraints that would have made it very costly for him to issue such a warning.

An earlier punitive strike by Austria might have avoided a larger war, but that was delayed by political pressures related to the domestic structure of the Dual Monarchy and by cumbersome mobilization plans that precluded immediate action. The ultimatum and the acute international crisis that followed transformed the minimum military option from a punitive strike to a more substantial invasion and therefore increased the likelihood of Russian intervention. The Halt in Belgrade plan was the only remaining hope for peace, but this required strong and perhaps highly coercive pressure on Vienna from Berlin, pressure that could not be forthcoming until Grey's actions induced a change in German expectations.

The Halt in Belgrade plan was undercut by Vienna's premature and politically motivated declaration of war, which increased the reputational and domestic costs to Austrian leaders if they subsequently reversed course, and by insufficient pressures on Vienna from Berlin.

---

[83] Thus while I focus on the July crisis, I conclude by giving causal priority to the underlying causes of the war. Schroeder and Thompson (in their respective chapters in this volume) each reach a similiar conclusion but through different lines of argument.

An opportunity to implement the Halt in Belgrade plan was also undercut by the Russian partial mobilization on July 29, which was the crucial
action of the escalating crisis. Russian leaders feared that war was
inevitable, failed to recognize German diplomatic and domestic incentives not to mobilize first, and failed to appreciate that the structure of
mobilizations gave them military incentives to refrain from responding
immediately to the Austrian mobilization against Serbia.

Some of these miscalculations and failures of judgment might have
been avoided, and some of the domestic and bureaucratic pressures
might have been finessed, but it is extraordinarily difficult to assess the
causal impact of these missteps and missed opportunities. Europe in
1914 was a highly interdependent system in which small changes could
have enormous and therefore unpredictable effects, and it is impossible
to validate counterfactual propositions with any degree of confidence.[84]
But my judgment is that the causal effects of these miscalculations
and oversights were modest relative to the structure of incentives and
constraints that were already in place. In fact, the miscalculations
were, in part, the product of those incentives and constraints and the
underlying strategic assumptions that helped shape them.

The windows of opportunity for the management of the July crisis
by political leaders were narrow and constantly changing, at different
rates and different times for each of the great powers in response to
its own political dynamics. This placed enormous demands on the
intellectual, diplomatic, and political skills of leading decision-makers.
It is certainly possible that the July crisis might have ended differently
if other individuals had been in positions of power at the beginning
of July 1914.[85] But even the most successful cases of crisis management are characterized by numerous misperceptions and perhaps some
good luck as well.[86] Thus, it is problematic to infer a causal relationship between war and misperceptions and missed opportunities, or to
validate the counterfactual proposition that better crisis management
would have resulted in a more peaceful outcome, particularly when the
strategic and political constraints on central decision-makers are this
severe.[87]

---

[84]It is perhaps not surprising that decision-makers in 1914, with limited information and under tremendous pressure, may have missed some opportunities for crisis
management. Indeed, after seven decades of research and reflection, scholars continue
to debate the consequences of the mobilization plans and of various conditions and
actions during the crisis.

[85]Of course, different individuals (a Bismarck, for example) might have attempted to
prevent the European state system from developing into a rigid two-bloc system prior
to 1914.

[86]The Cuban Missile Crisis would be one example.

[87]The crisis mismanagement hypothesis would be more compelling if it were validated
by some type of comparative research design that controlled for context. It would
be useful to identify other crises with equally incompatible preferences and equally

Moreover, even if Austria had agreed to the Halt in Belgrade proposal, and even if that bought enough time for the negotiation of a
peaceful settlement, it is far from certain that this settlement would
have been sufficiently stable to survive the next crisis that would inevitably arise in the next few months or the next few years – particularly
in light of German leaders' continued concerns about their ability to
prevail in a future war against an increasingly powerful Russia; the
likelihood of continued domestic political instability in the Austro-
Hungarian, Russian, and German empires; and the temptations for political leaders to attempt to deal with their domestic problems through
aggressive foreign policies.

Note that each of these factors plays an important role in Lebow's
(this volume) argument about the role of contingency in the outbreak
of war in 1914 (see chapter 4 in this volume). Lebow traces the war to
a confluence of three independent causal chains – Germany's security
dilemma arising from the growing power of Russia, Austria–Hungary's
domestic crisis, and Russia's domestic crisis and recent diplomatic
humiliations – which created a narrow window of opportunity for war
in 1914. If the assassination had not occurred, and if war could have
been avoided in 1914, Lebow argues, the pressure from each of these
sources would have diminished, and the likelihood of a later war would
have been significantly reduced. By 1916 or 1917, German military
advantages would have eroded to the point that it would not be possible
to mount sequential offensives against France and Russia. The German
military would be forced to abandon the Schlieffen Plan and adopt
instead a more defensively-oriented strategy. It would be too late for
a preventive war against Russia, and Germany would have to behave
much more cautiously in a crisis.

I find most of Lebow's analysis quite compelling, but I dissent from
Lebow's conclusion about the diminished likelihood of war after 1914.
Lebow is absolutely correct about German fears of the rising power
of Russia. These fears were reinforced by ongoing internal decay in
Austria–Hungary, which would further weaken Germany's only great
power ally and allow Russia to reinforce any offensive against Germany.
Lebow is also correct that the window for a German preventive war
would soon be closing as Russia completed its expanded armaments
program, army reforms, and reconstruction of its railroad system. In
fact, Moltke and other German military and political leaders in 1914
would have accepted Lebow's analysis, and that is precisely why it is
extremely unlikely that Lebow's world of 1917 could ever have come

---

constraining strategic and domestic pressures, but that turned out differently because
of skillful crisis management.

about. In the absence of war in 1914, German political leaders, pressured by their military, would have found another opportunity for a preventive war against Russia before their situation deteriorated to the point that they would run out of military options. Incentives for preventive war, advocated by the German military for decades but rejected by Bismarck and by subsequent German leaders, grew more and more intense as Germany approached the point that its leaders feared that they could no longer be confident of victory in a two-front war in Europe. This is probably the single most important factor explaining why a general war occurred in 1914 and not in response to any of the earlier crises of 1905, 1908, 1911, and 1912–13.

Analytic summary

Let me end by summarizing some of the primary arguments of this chapter regarding the role of necessary conditions in the escalation of the July crisis. Please refer to the body of the chapter for a more nuanced elaboration of each of these propositions.

1. The German assumption of British neutrality during the early stages of a continental war was a necessary condition for German support for Austria–Hungarian military action against Serbia, for Germany's willingness to risk a continental war against Russia, and therefore for the outbreak of a World War Involving all of the great powers.

2. German support for Austria–Hungary was a necessary condition for a major Austro–Hungarian military action against Serbia, and consequently a necessary condition for a war of any kind in 1914.

3. Russian intervention in an Austro–Serbian war was a necessary condition for a continental war and consequently for a world war.

4. Russian Foreign Minister Sazonov's belief that a partial mobilization against Austria–Hungary would not lead to a general European war was a necessary condition for his willingness to push for mobilization.

5. Some form of Russian mobilization was a necessary condition for German mobilization.

Chapter 4

Contingency, catalysts and nonlinear change: the origins of World War I

Richard Ned Lebow

Wars, revolutions and depressions change the world and the way in which we think about it. World War I was a seminal event in both respects. It ushered in a profound transformation of the international system, and is described by many historians as the crucible in which the 20th century was shaped. It has also been a critical case for the generation and testing of theories about conflict and international relations more generally.

Many historians contend that World War I – or something like it – would have been very hard, if not impossible, to avoid. The distinguished British historian F. H. Hinsley insisted that if the Sarajevo crisis had not precipitated a particular great war, some other crisis would have precipitated a great war at no distant date (Hinsley 1995: 4). Neorealists and power transition theorists make similar claims, albeit for different reasons (Organski 1968: 202–3; Organski and Kugler 1980; Gilpin 1981: 200–1; Schweller 1998: 2). I do not doubt that many, perhaps most, of the causes of war in 1914 that historians and political scientists have identified created a conflict-prone environment. But underlying causes, no matter how numerous or deep-seated, do not make an event inevitable. Their consequences may depend on fortuitous coincidences in timing and on the presence of catalysts that are independent of any of the underlying causes.

Seemingly overdetermined, World War I was actually highly contingent. It was contingent in both its underlying and immediate causes. Historians have proposed a variety of underlying causes for World War I, including social Darwinism, nationalism, the alliance structure and shifts in the balance of power. But what made Europe ripe for war was not the multitude of alleged causes, but the nature of the interactions among them. World War I is best understood as a nonlinear confluence of three largely independent chains of causation. These chains produced independent but more or less simultaneous *gestalt* shifts in Vienna and Berlin, and a slightly earlier one in Russia. Had the timing of the Austrian and German shifts been off by as little as two years, Austrian leaders would not have felt so intent on destroying Serbia or German leaders would not have been so willing to encourage them to do so. For this reason alone, World War I was overdetermined *and* highly contingent.

Theoretical explanations for war take catalysts for granted. If the right underlying conditions are present, some incident will sooner or later set armies on the march the way the twin assassinations at Sarajevo did in 1914. But Sarajevo was not just any provocation; it met a diverse set of political and psychological requirements that were essential for Austrian and German leaders to risk war. It is possible, but extremely unlikely, that some other provocation would have met these conditions, or that some other combination of great powers would have started a war for different reasons. In the absence of a catalyst, several more years of peace could have altered the strategic and domestic contexts of the great powers to have made war less likely. There was a two year window when the leaders of at least two great powers thought their national or dynastic interests were better served by war than peace. Social scientists often assume that major social and political developments are specific instances of strong, or even weak, regularities in social behavior. But these developments may be the result of accidental conjunctures. Conversely, events that seem highly likely may never happen. The concatenation of particular leaders with particular contexts, and of particular events with other events is always a matter of chance, never of necessity (Almond and Genco 1977).

My findings have important implications for the study of international system change – by which I mean a change in the polarity of the system or the rules by which it operates. They suggest that system transformations – and many other kinds of international events – are unpredictable because their underlying causes do nothing more than create the *possibility* of change. Actual change depends upon contingency, catalysts and actors. Neither contingency nor catalysts have been analyzed systematically by social scientists, and I offer some thoughts about how this might be done. There is a large literature on actors, most of it based on the premise that they are instrumentally rational. A striking finding of the World War I case, and of the two other system transformations of the 20th century – World War II and the end of the

Cold War – is the extent to which the behavior that brought about these transformations was based on extreme miscalculations of its likely consequences. Such behavior may not be the norm in everyday foreign policy decision-making, but it may be characteristic of the decisions that unwittingly usher in system transformations.

The first two stages of my inquiry make use of counterfactual thought experiments (Tetlock and Belkin 1996: 15–16; Lebow 2000). Counterfactuals are past conditionals, or more colloquially, what if statements about the past. They alter some aspect of the past (e.g., doing away with a person or event, changing a critical decision or outcome, inserting an event or development that never happened or making it take place sooner or later than it did), to set the stage for a what might have been argument. I use only minimal rewrite counterfactuals. They entail small, plausible changes in reality that do not violate our understanding of what was technologically, culturally, temporally or otherwise possible (Weber 1949 [1905]). A world in which Archduke Franz Ferdinand and his wife returned alive from their visit to Sarajevo is an example. Princip's accomplice missed the royals en route to city hall, and Princip was lamenting his failure in a bar when the touring car carrying Franz Ferdinand and his wife came to a stop in front to allow the cars at the head of the procession to back up because they had made a wrong turn. With only a minimal rewrite of history – the procession stays on the planned route – the assassination might have been averted. Such a rewrite does not strain our understanding of the world because most 20th century royal processions follow their intended routes. The Archduke's was an exception.

Case selection

Case studies are often described as ill-suited for testing propositions and theories. One confirming or infirming case – even if the latter meets the criteria of a critical case – permits no definitive conclusions. Unless the case can be shown to be representative of the phenomenon under study, there is always the possibility that it is an outlier. But the laws of statistics are not the sole criterion or justification for case selection. Interesting cases, especially anomalous ones, are a primary source of theory generation. Careful analysis of an infirming case can suggest reasons why the outcome was contrary to predictions and reveal more general problems with a theory. Infirming cases can also improve a theory. By demonstrating why it fails in a single case, a researcher may identity the scope conditions of the theory and the variables or

processes it must take into account to expand the domain in which it is
applicable (Lijphart 1971; Eckstein 1975).

I do not use the 1914 case to evaluate a proposition or theory, but
to critique a more general approach to understanding social phenomena
based on the determining role of so-called structures – e.g., system polarity, balance of power, alliances, regime types. I argue that structural
theories cannot adequately account for World War I, and identify the
reasons for this failure and the additional processes these theories must
take into account to offer a better account of international politics. I do
not claim that the 1914 case falsifies structural approaches; approaches,
like paradigms, cannot be falsified. Rather, I contend that structural
approaches, while valuable, provide only part of the analytical purchase
needed to understand key foreign policy decisions, especially those
responsible for system transformations.

There are two ways to generalize from a single case. The first
strategy is to add additional cases in the hope of making the finding
statistically significant. In this connection, I discuss two additional
cases of system transformations: World War II and the end of the Cold
War. I review the relevant literature on these cases which suggests the
presence of the same phenomena that confound structural explanations
in 1914. Three cases do not represent a large N, but they do constitute
the universe of 20th century system transformations and thereby lend
a certain weight to my findings. The second strategy is conceptual.
A researcher can argue that a problem, process or phenomenon that
confounds a theory in a single case is *prima facie* universal, or so
widespread, as to render the theory inadequate or invalid. I make two
such claims: that social systems are open and can be transformed
through their internal operation as well as through external stimuli, and
that all wars and system transformations require independent catalysts.

Statistical logic is not the only criterion of case selection. Not all
cases are equal. Some have greater visibility and impact because of
their real world or theoretical consequences. World War I is *nonpareil* in
both respects. Many historians contend that it was the crucible in which
the 20th century was formed. Its origins and consequences are also the
basis for many of our major theories in domains as diverse as political
psychology, war and peace, democratization and state structure. If
World War I can be shown to be highly contingent, with the corollary
that a very different 20th century was possible – in its absence, imagine
the gradual evolution of Wilhelminian Germany toward a constitutional
monarchy, no Russian revolution, or at least a noncommunist Russia,
no World War II and no Holocaust – then so too are the social realities

that structural theories not only attempt to explain but make appear foreordained.

Underlying causes of war

To use counterfactual experiments to explore alternative worlds, it helps to have as a starting point a generally accepted interpretation of why the world we live in has come about. Historians rarely agree about causes, but even for a contentious profession the degree of controversy surrounding the origins of World War I is extreme. Scholars disagree about the causes of war and the appropriate level of analysis at which to search for them. They also differ in their judgments of which state or states were most responsible for the war and the reasons why their leaders acted as they did. If the nature of the explanations and limitations of evidence make it difficult to discriminate among competing interpretations, limitations of space make it impossible to address all, or even most, of these interpretations.

Fortunately, something of a dominant interpretation has emerged in recent years. Historians associated with this interpretation disagree on specific points (e.g., Chancellor Theobald von Bethmann-Hollweg's motives for risking war, the relative responsibility of Austria and Germany), but agree that both powers set in motion the chain of events that led to war; Austria–Hungary exploited the assassination of Franz Ferdinand as the pretext for war with Serbia, and Germany encouraged – even pushed – Austria toward decisive action (Hillgruber 1966; Stern 1967; Jarausch 1969, 1973; Mommsen 1969, 1973; Williamson 1974, 1988, 1991; Zechlin 1979; Kaiser 1983; Erdmann 1984; Evans 1988; Herwig 1998, chap. 1; von Strandmann 1988; Röhl 1995). Students of Austria–Hungary argue that its leaders acted for a combination of closely related foreign and domestic concerns. Since the publication of the Riezler diaries, a near consensus has emerged among German historians that von Bethmann-Hollweg did not seek to provoke a European war but recognized that an Austrian conflict with Serbia would be difficult to contain. He was willing to run the risk of a continental war in the belief that such a war was sooner or later inevitable and that Germany's chance of winning it declined with every year that passed (Koch 1972b; Riezler 1972). Given the primary responsibility of Austria and Germany for initiating the chain of events that led to war, I will focus on their decisions, and secondarily on Russia's, but in full recognition that it is only part of the story.

Counterfactual experiments are a wonderful means of exploring relationships among hypothesized explanations. Even a superficial counterfactual examination of underlying causes of World War I reveals that many theorized causes are tightly coupled. Counterfactual experiments also help us probe contingency. The most straightforward way to do this would be to use minimal rewrite counterfactuals to remove putative causes of an outcome. To apply minimal rewrites at levels of analysis other than leaders it would be necessary to go back to a time and place where the structures, ideas or institutions in question were more malleable or still in the process of taking shape. The fewer counterfactuals necessary to remove the causes, the more counterfactuals that can accomplish this end, and the more proximate they are to the outcome, the more contingent it is. Limitations of space preclude such an exercise, and I employ a different strategy to address the problem of contingency. I look at the extent to which the underlying causes of war can be understood as a confluence, and use minimal rewrite counterfactuals to examine the implications of this causal metaphor for contingency.

A confluence envisages a multiple stream of independent causes that come together to produce an outcome. A house goes up in smoke. Investigation reveals that the fire spread from a lighted candle that was left unattended on a window sill. The window was not completely sealed, and a draft blew one of curtains close enough to the flame for it to catch fire. The smoke alarm, connected to the house security system, did not function because its battery was dead, and the fire department failed to receive the timely warning that might have permitted it to save the dwelling. What caused the house to burn down? The insurance investigator pointed to the candle, but it would not have been lit or placed on the window sill if it had not been the holiday season and had its owners not been following a neighborhood custom. If the window had not been warped, or the insulation around it had provided a better seal, the candle would not have started a fire. If the owners had been home, or if the smoke alarm had a charged battery, the house would not have burned down. No single factor was responsible for this disaster; it took a combination of them interacting in a particular way (Harré and Secord 1972; Mackie 1976; Bhaskar 1979; Patomäki 1996).

An outcome that requires the confluence of many independent causes, but could be prevented by removing any one of them with a minimal rewrite – like the fire in the house – is highly contingent. An equifinal outcome to which multiple pathways lead, any one of which could bring it about requires multiple interventions to prevent. Its contingency would depend on how many minimal rewrites were necessary to halt or deflect each possible pathway. Some outcomes might be so highly redundant as to make them all but inevitable. Sooner or later, we will all die no matter how careful our diet, how much we exercise or how many diseases modern medicine is able to prevent or cure.

World War I is probably best understood as a nonlinear confluence in which multiple, interrelated causes had unanticipated interactions and unpredictable consequences. Three causal chains were critically important. First and foremost was Germany's security dilemma, caused by the prospect of a two-front war in which the general staff believed it would soon no longer be possible to defeat one adversary at a time. The second causal chain consisted of all the Balkan developments that threatened the external security and internal stability of Austria-Hungary, and encouraged influential opinion in Vienna to consider war with Serbia as a possible solution to these threats. The third chain centered on St. Petersburg, and was itself a confluence of external setbacks (e.g., defeat in Russo–Japanese War of 1904-5, humiliation in the Bosnian Annexation crisis of 1909) and internal weaknesses (e.g., the revolution of 1905, growing alienation of the middle classes, rise of a powerful revolutionary movement) that made Russian leaders fearful of the foreign and domestic costs of another foreign policy defeat.

Each of these three chains of causation was contingent; they were the result of decisions, bad and generally avoidable ones, that had the unintended consequence of dividing Europe into two armed and hostile camps. If Bismarck had been able to dissuade Wilhelm I from annexing Alsace-Lorraine, there might have been no enduring Franco-German rivalry. If Bismarck's successors had managed relations with Russia better, St. Petersburg would have had no incentive to ally with France. The Anglo–French *Entente* might have been prevented by a Kaiser who knew how to keep his mouth shut and recognized the unnecessary expense and counterproductive nature of a naval race with England.

The point of no-return in Austro–Serb relations was the Empire's annexation of Bosnia and Herzogovina in 1908. Austrian chief-of-staff, Conrad von Hötzendorff, had been pushing for annexation for some time, and convinced Alois Lexa von Aehrenthal, who became foreign minister in 1906, to do this as part of a new, assertive policy in the Balkans. Aehrenthal's poorly conceived initiative provoked a war-threatening crisis, humiliated Russia and deeply embittered the Serbs. The annexation crisis destroyed a decade of Austro-Russian cooperation and put the two empires on a collision course. With more far-sighted foreign ministers in Vienna and St. Petersburg, this clash could have been avoided and Austro-Russian rivalry managed more effectively. In this environment, Russia would have been more restrained, and probably would not have violated the tacit agreement between the empires that neither would support dissident groups within the other's empire. If St. Petersburg had not encouraged anti-Habsburg factions in Belgrade or stoked the fires of Romanian nationalism in Transylvania, the Austrian foreign office would have been much less threatened by the likely defection of Romania from its secret alliance with Austria. In the long run, Slavic nationalism would almost certainly have asserted itself, but that threat could have been managed for some time; as late as 1914 there were relatively few voices for independence within the Habsburg empire. The division of Europe into two militarily powerful but insecure alliance systems contributed to the outbreak of war, but did not make it inevitable.

Even more important than these chains of causation was the synergistic interaction among them. Two features of nonlinear systems came into play here. The first is that the effect of one variable (or cause) often depends on the state of another variable (or cause). In such cases, the consequences of either cannot be predicted or understood independently (Jervis 1997). This phenomenon is well-illustrated by the relationship between Russian armaments and railway construction and the Schlieffen Plan. German generals planned to solve the problem of a two-front war by committing most of their forces to a invasion of France in the expectation that they could occupy Paris before Russian forces penetrated too deeply into eastern Prussia. The general staff worried that Russian mobilization and railway reforms would render the Schlieffen Plan obsolete, and this fear shaped the response of Germany's political leaders to Austria's request for support in its confrontation with Serbia. They reasoned that it was better to fight a war while there was still a chance to win. France had underwritten the expense of the Russian railways in the hope of restraining Germany; French leaders reasoned that Berlin would become more cautious in proportion to its fear of the consequences of a two-front war. The French strategy of deterrence actually encouraged the German invasion it had been intended to prevent. Something similar occurred during the July crisis when Russia mobilized in the hope that it might restrain Germany, not prove a *casus belli*. In each instance, the intensity and effect of particular actions or policies were determined by other actions and policies. In their absence, the leaders in question might have made very different choices, or the same choices might have had different consequences.

Game theorists who model strategic interactions have long recognized the need for actors to share a common framework, or at the very least to agree on the kind of game they are playing. They assume that actors use a Bayesian process to update estimates of one another's preferences and that such learning will allow them to establish a common framework (Brams 1985: 48–85; Nalebuff 1986; Powell 1987, 1988). In practice, new information is commonly assimilated to existing frameworks, and actors can continue to communicate for prolonged periods of time without realizing that they are playing different games. Signals may be missed, or their intended import only grasped after it is too late to respond appropriately. Frameworks also change in the course of interactions, and these changes can have profound consequences for behavior. The ability of actors to transform themselves and their understandings of their strategic interactions in the course of those interactions is a second fundamental characteristic of nonlinear, open systems, and central to understanding the events of July and August 1914.

Key Austrian and German leaders underwent independent *gestalt* shifts in 1913–14 that prompted dramatic reversals in their foreign policy preferences. Moltke and Bethmann-Hollweg had been troubled by Russia's seemingly growing military and mobilization capability for some time, but only in 1914 – and probably as a result of the assassination of Franz Ferdinand – did the Chancellor's concern reach the level where he was willing to do something he had consistently rejected in the past: risk war in the hope of achieving a diplomatic triumph that might break up the *Franco-Russe*. Austrian leaders worried about a Balkan League directed against them that would constitute an external threat and fan the fissiparous tendencies within their empire. Conrad wanted to exploit the assassination of Franz Ferdinand as a pretext to attack Serbia, Berchtold and Franz Josef saw no alternatives and Berlin was now willing to offer its support. Serbs and Russians knew nothing about these *gestalt* shifts, and behaved in ways that exacerbated Austro–German insecurities and provoked a war that neither country wanted. Wilhelm, Bethmann-Hollweg and Foreign Secretary, Gottlieb von Jagow were in turn victims of a Russian *gestalt* shift. They deluded themselves into thinking that they might repeat the success of 1909 and compel Russia to remain on the sidelines of an Austro–Serb war. But that humiliation had led to a commitment not to back down again, something the Russians believed would undermine their status as a great power. This commitment was strengthened by cabinet shifts in 1914. These several *gestalt* shifts entirely changed the nature and outcome of great power interactions.

One of the most remarkable features of 1914 was the coincidental timing of Germany and Austria's security problems and *gestalt* shifts. Although Russia was a common threat, each ally's security problems had largely independent causes, and there was no particular reason why they should have become acute at the same time. Germany's security dilemma was the result of its geographic position and prior policies that had encouraged its two most powerful neighbors to ally against it. Russia's improved military and mobilization capability, the development that drove Germany to brinkmanship in 1914, was the result of Russian industrialization and access to French capital markets. German willingness to risk war was also the result of the perceived decline in capability and will of Austria–Hungary, Germany's principal military ally. German political and military authorities worried that failure to support Austria in 1914 would accelerate its decline and leave Germany at the mercy of Russia and France.

Austria–Hungary's insecurity was the consequence of a precipitous decline in Ottoman power. That decline had many internal causes, but it was dramatically hastened by the Italian occupation of Tripoli in September 1911 and the war this unexpectedly triggered with the Ottoman Empire. The war provided the opportunity for Serbia, Bulgaria and Greece to take up arms, and to almost everyone's surprise, they succeeded in all but expelling Turkey from Europe. Serbia doubled its population and territory, and backed by Russia, sought to organize an anti-Austrian alliance in the Balkans and to incite national unrest within the Dual Monarchy.

German leaders did not feel so threatened before 1914; German Chancellors rejected military demands for war in 1905 and 1912, and supported diplomatic resolutions to the 1912 and 1913 crises that threatened war between Austria and Serbia and Austria and Montenegro. If Italy had not occupied Tripoli – and there had been considerable opposition to this ill-conceived venture – no Balkan Wars would have started in its wake, and Serbia would not have constituted a threat, if it did at all, until some later date. Alternatively, if the Balkan events that Austria-Hungary found so threatening had occurred a few years earlier, the German Kaiser and Chancellor would probably not have encouraged Austria to draw its sword. Timing was everything in 1914, and that timing, so to speak, was fortuitous, if that is the right word. For this reason alone, World War I was highly contingent.

Immediate causes of war

Wars, like fires, need catalysts. Most structural theories assume an unproblematic relationship between underlying and immediate causes. If the underlying causes are present, an appropriate catalyst will come along – or it will be manufactured by leaders (Lebow 1981, chap. 2). In

February 1965, in the aftermath of a Vietcong attack on the American advisors' barracks at Pleiku, National Security Advisor McGeorge Bundy wrote a memorandum to President Lyndon Johnson urging the sustained bombing of North Vietnam in response. Bundy later acknowledged that he conceived of Pleikus as streetcars. He could count on repeated Viet Cong attacks against South Vietnamese forces or their American advisors to provide him with the pretext he needed at the opportune moment to sell escalation to the president (Hoopes 1969: 30; Senator Gravel Edition 1971, vol. 3: 687–91).

Pretexts do not always resemble streetcars. They may be infrequent, inappropriate, or may fail to materialize, and without a catalyst, the predicted or intended behavior may not occur. In a matter of months or years, the underlying conditions may evolve so as to make war less likely even if an otherwise appropriate catalyst ultimately comes along. The window of opportunity for war may be temporally narrow or broad, depending on the nature and rate of underlying changes, leadership, security conceptions, and domestic and international structure. War, like many other kinds of events, requires a *conjunction* of underlying pressures and appropriate catalysts.

One of the most common metaphors used to describe Europe in 1914 is that of dry kindling waiting for a spark to set it alight. As sparks are frequent in acute international conflicts, this metaphor is well-chosen by structuralists because it emphasizes the underlying causes of war. Metaphors are no substitute for careful analysis, and historians and political scientists need to develop more precise conceptions of catalysts. We can begin by asking what about Sarajevo made it a successful catalyst, and what other provocations or events might have served the same end? Answers to these questions will provide a second perspective from which to estimate the contingency of war in 1914.

Joachim Remak insists that Sarajevo was more than an excuse for war, it was one of its major causes (Remak 1971). Although he does not elaborate on his claim, many reasons can be adduced in support. Arguably the most important was the assassination itself and the political challenge it constituted for Austria–Hungary. In June 1914, Berchtold, with Franz Josef's support, began a diplomatic offensive to arrest the decline of the Empire's position in the Balkans, and to frustrate Entente efforts to build a new Balkan League. There was no talk of war (Bridge 1972: 334–5). The assassination transformed the situation. Not only Conrad pushed for war, but other officials in the foreign office and military argued that failure to respond forcibly to this provocation would undermine, if not destroy, the Empire's standing as a great power and embolden its domestic and foreign enemies (Remak

1971; Bridge 1972: 335-7; Herwig 1998: 8-18). For Franz Josef there was an additional, personal dimension to Sarajevo; he was outraged by the assassination of a member of the royal family. Kaiser Wilhelm also grieved over the loss of Franz Ferdinand, whom he considered a friend, and had spent time with only two weeks before (Samuel R. Williamson to the author, 22 January 1999). He wanted Austria to take action against Serbia to show that actions against legitimate rulers would not be tolerated (Albertini 1980, vol. 2: 129-30; Williamson 1991: 85).

Sarajevo shifted the balance of power in Vienna. Franz Ferdinand's views on defense matters were almost as important as the Emperor. His influence derived from his official status as successor to the throne (*Thronfolger*), from his interest and knowledge about military affairs and the extensive network of contacts he had cultivated throughout the armed forces. His decidedly peaceful orientation evolved during the course of the Balkan wars (Williamson 1991: 51). The *Thronfolger* was intent on extending Austrian influence in the Balkans, but not at the risk of war with Russia. He warned that a war between Austria and Russia would end either with the overthrow of the Romanovs or with the overthrow of the Habsburgs – or perhaps the overthrow of both (Spitzmüller-Harmersbach 1955: 103).[1] He cherished the unrealistic idea of monarchial unity in the form of some revival of the Holy Alliance, and had made a point of cultivating good relations with Nicolas II. On a more practical level, he took Russian military capability more seriously than either the war minister or chief-of-staff, and was convinced that war against Serbia would draw in Russia. He did not believe that the Austro–Hungarian army was ready for war, worried that Italy would defect from the Triple Alliance and that Germany would find some reason to stand aside. More fundamentally, Franz Ferdinand opposed war because it would make it impossible for him to impose fundamental changes in the structure of the empire upon his accession to the throne (Williamson 1974).

Samuel R. Williamson offers an intriguing counterfactual: If Governor General of Bosnia–Herzogovina, Oskar Potiorek, had been killed at Sarajevo instead of Franz Ferdinand, Vienna would have responded differently (Williamson 1991: 434).[2] Like Conrad, Potiorek was a charter member of the war party and his death would have removed another supporter of military action from the scene. More importantly, Franz Ferdinand would have been influential in shaping Austria's response. His opposition to war, combined with that of Hungarian Prime Minister, István Tisza, the senior voice against war in June and early July 1914,

---

[1] Franz (1943: 107) quotes a similar statement Franz Ferdinand made to his wife in 1913.

[2] Stevenson (1988: 14) believes war much less likely in general if Franz Ferdinand had remained alive and continued to exercise restraint in Vienna.

would have carried considerable weight because the two men were otherwise always at odds. Tisza was the great defender of Hungary, and Franz Ferdinand made no secret of his dislike of Tisza and Hungarians more generally (Williamson 1974; Vermes 1985: 230–1; Galántai 1989: 100–18). With Franz Ferdinand and Tisza urging moderation, Berchtold, a weak personality, would also have pursued a cautious line, and Franz Josef, cross-pressured in 1914, would probably have sided with them instead of Conrad. If so, there would have been no Hoyos mission; Germany would have been consulted with a diplomatic end in mind. The channel for communication with Germany would not have been the hawks in the foreign office but Franz Ferdinand, who had close personal relations with Kaiser Wilhelm and had been used in the past to sound out Berlin's intentions in the Balkans. Merely changing the victims of the terrorist attack in Sarajevo might have been enough to alter in a fundamental way Austria–Hungary's response.

Sarajevo provided a necessary incentive and opportunity for Germany. Moltke had pushed for war almost from the moment he became chief of staff because he wanted to fight Russia and France while Germany still had a chance of victory. Although the German general staff had a low regard for the military prowess of their Austrian ally, they were horrified at the prospect of an Austrian decline because it would leave Russia free to concentrate all of its forces against Germany in East Prussia. In Berlin, the assassination was perceived to threaten Austria's standing as a great power if it exposed Austria's lack of will to act like one. This additional consideration, when weighed in the balance along with the general concern for the deteriorating military balance, made Chancellor Bethmann-Hollweg more receptive to Moltke's pleas for action at the height of the crisis. The assassination may well have been the catalyst for Bethmann-Hollweg's *gestalt* shift described in the previous section (Konrad Jarausch, email to the author, 4 January 1999).

Bethmann-Hollweg was more prescient than most of his contemporaries in recognizing, as he put it, that a European war was likely to topple more thrones than it would prop up. He accordingly deemed the backing of the Social Democrats, the largest and best organized working class organization in Europe, the *sine qua non* of military action. Without it, the Chancellor would not have taken his leap into the dark. Moltke knew this, and in February 1913 had discouraged Conrad from attacking Serbia on the grounds that the German people would not support a war that Austria provoked against a seemingly conciliatory adversary (Conrad von Hötzendorff 1921–25, vol. 3: 144ff; Moltke to Conrad, Mendelsohn-Bartholdy, Lepsius, and Thimme 1922–6, no. 12,824).

Sarajevo was a tailor-made provocation for Bethmann-Hollweg. The assassination aroused considerable sympathy for Austria throughout Europe, and not the least among the German working class. Although the Austrian ultimatum was widely regarded as heavy-handed by the politically sophisticated, German opinion perceived their country as a bystander to a Balkan conflict and the innocent target of Russian aggression. The Chancellor played up this interpretation, and benefitted from the general fear and dislike of Russia by Social Democrats, who regarded the Tsarist regime as barbaric because of its treatment of labor, dissident intellectuals and minorities. The result was the *Burgfrieden* of 4 August in which the Social Democrats voted for war credits.

Sarajevo created the necessary psychological environment for the Kaiser and the Chancellor to overcome their inhibitions about war. Admiral Tirpitz observed that when the Emperor did not consider the peace to be threatened he liked to give full play to his reminiscences of famous ancestors, [but] in moments which he realized to be critical he proceeded with extraordinary caution (von Tirpitz 1924–26, vol. 1: 242). To his contemporaries, the Chancellor came across as a fatalist, as a man who had a deep revulsion of war, but felt powerless to oppose the prevalent view that it was necessary. Kaiser and Chancellor were caught on the horns of a dilemma: Germany's vital interests seemed to require war, or a diplomatic triumph that would break up the *Franco–Russe*, and the latter could only be achieved at the risk of war, but they were not prepared to accept responsibility for starting such a confrontation. Until July 1914, they procrastinated. By deferring a decision that was too difficult for them to make, Kaiser and Chancellor preserved their psychological equilibrium. The July crises offered them a way out of their decisional dilemma.

When Hoyos met Wilhelm and Bethmann-Hollweg on 4 July in Potsdam to secure their support, he did not confront them with a choice between peace and war but only with a request to back Austria *if* Russia threatened intervention in support of Serbia. Kaiser and Chancellor both expected Russia to back down as it had in 1909, and this was also the view of their ambassador in St. Petersburg.[3] They doubted that France would come to Russia's assistance, or that Britain would intervene if the Balkan conflict provoked a continental war. Their support for Austria precipitated its ultimatum and declaration of war against Serbia, Russia's subsequent mobilization against Austria, German ultimatums to Russia, Belgium and France and German mobilization, which was the equivalent of war. When Kaiser and Chancellor confronted Russian

---

[3] See Lebow (1981: 122–9) on the hold of the Bosnian precedent on German leaders in 1914.

mobilization, or more accurately, premature and exaggerated reports of Russian mobilization that flooded through the channels of German military intelligence, they convinced themselves that they were only reacting to Russian initiatives, and that St. Petersburg, not they, bore the brunt of responsibility for the war they were about to unleash (Janis and Mann 1977: 59–60, 205; Lebow 1981: 135–45).

To recapitulate, the Sarajevo assassinations changed the political and psychological environment in Vienna and Berlin in six important ways, all of which were probably necessary for the decisions that led to war. First, they constituted a political challenge to which Austrian leaders believed they had to respond forcefully; anything less was expected to encourage further challenges by domestic and foreign enemies. Second, they shocked and offended Franz Josef and Kaiser Wilhelm and made both Emperors more receptive to calls for decisive measures. Third, they changed the policymaking context in Vienna by removing the principal spokesman for peace. Fourth, they may have been the catalyst for Bethmann-Hollweg's *gestalt* shift. Fifth, they made it possible for Bethmann-Hollweg to win the support of the socialists, without which he never would have risked war. Sixth, they created a psychological environment in which Wilhelm and Bethmann-Hollweg could proceed in incremental steps toward war, convincing themselves at the outset that their actions were unlikely to provoke a European war, and at the end, that others were responsible for war.

A striking feature of the July crisis was the tremendous psychological difficulty German leaders had in making a decision for war. Given their unwillingness to accept responsibility for starting a great power war, it is certainly difficult to imagine how Kaiser, Chancellor, foreign office could have taken this step if they had been compelled to recognize their share of responsibility for it from the outset. If the Archduke had not been assassinated, giving rise to this unusual opportunity, Germany might have reached the fateful year of 1917 still at peace with its neighbors. If so, its leaders might have discovered that their fears of a window of vulnerability were greatly exaggerated; their adversaries were constrained from attacking Germany for many of the same reasons that had prevented Germany from exploiting its military window of opportunity in the decade before 1914.

The double assassination was critical in its nature and timing, but it could easily have been avoided. Reports reached Vienna that Sarajevo was seething with discontent and a dangerous venue for a royal visit. Franz Ferdinand explored the possibility of postponing his trip and seems to have been encouraged by the Emperor to do so. The High Command nevertheless decided to proceed with its great maneuvers, and the Archduke, who was Inspector General of the armed forces, decided that he had no choice but to attend. Duchess Sophie had come to Bosnia with dark misgivings that something dreadful was about to happen to her husband. She was aware that Dr. Josip Sunari, one of the leaders of the *Sabor*, the Bosnian parliament, had urged General Potiorek to cancel their impending visit because of the hostility of the local population to the regime. The evening before the assassination, Karl von Rumerskirch, the Archduke's chamberlain, urged him to cancel the next day's visit to Sarajevo. General Potiorek's aide-de-camp, Lt.-Col. Eric von Merizzi, interceded and convinced Franz Ferdinand to proceed because cancellation would be a rebuke to his superior. The next morning the Archduke and his wife were met at the Sarajevo train station by General Potiorek and the Lord Mayor, and ushered into an open touring car to go to a nearby military camp for a quick inspection before going on to the city hall. The lead car in the procession was supposed to carry six specially trained security officers, but their chief departed with three local policeman instead. On Appel Quay, a long street with houses on one side and an embankment on the other, a young man in a black coat asked a policeman which car carried the Archduke and then stepped out into the street to throw a grenade at it. Franz Ferdinand's Czech driver saw the object coming and accelerated. The bomb fell on the folded roof, rolled off into the pavement and exploded under the rear wheel of the next car in the procession. The would-be assassin jumped over the embankment into the river (Dedijer 1966: 10–12, 408–9).

Lt.-Col. von Merizzi and another officer, both in the car behind the Archduke, were hit by bomb fragments and were rushed to a military hospital. Franz Ferdinand dismissed the attack as madness and insisted on preceding to the city hall. Following the ceremony there, the Archduke asked General Potiorek if there were likely to be any more attacks. Potiorek advised taking a different route and skipping the planned visit to the museum. Other members of the Archduke's party urged him to leave Sarajevo immediately, but he insisted on visiting Lt.-Col. von Merizzi in the military hospital and then going on to the museum. The cars drove up Appel Quay, this time at high speed, but the lead car turned by mistake into Franz Josef Street and the second car with the police guard followed. Franz Ferdinand's driver, in the third car, was turning to follow when he was ordered to stop by General Potiorek, back up and continue down Appel Quay. At that moment, Princip, standing at the intersection, took a revolver out of his coat, and a nearby policeman reached out to grab his hand. An accomplice struck the policeman, and Princip fired twice at point blank range into the car containing Franz Ferdinand and Sophie (Dedijer 1966: 13–15).

Numerous minimal rewrites could prevent the assassinations: Princip might have obeyed the order to abort the assassination sent to him by the military conspirators in Belgrade, Austrian authorities in Bosnia might have taken security as seriously as they did the menu and music for the banquets they planned in the Archduke's honor, Franz Ferdinand might have canceled his trip in response to multiple warnings and his wife's fears, he might have followed the advice of his advisors and left Sarajevo directly after the ceremony at city hall, or his cavalcade could have adhered to the planned route and raced down Appel Quay past Princip. None of these changes strain our understanding of the world because most royal processions do not stray from their intended routes and most security details would have rushed the Archduke and his wife to safety at the first sign of violence.

Without the assassinations there would have been no war in the summer of 1914. Could some other country, or combination of countries, have found a reason to start a war? Britain was committed to the status quo and was consumed with its Irish problem. France coveted Alsace-Lorraine, but had been on the defensive in Europe since 1871, and perceived itself increasingly weaker militarily vis-à-vis Germany. The lynchpin of French security was the *Franco-Russe*, and France supported Russia in 1914 to preserve this alliance. France had also drawn closer to Britain, and relied on British military assistance in case of a war with Germany, but the French knew this would only be forthcoming if they were attacked by Germany. Italy pursued an aggressive colonial policy that led to war with the Ottoman Empire, and aspired to those parts of Austria–Hungary inhabited by Italian speakers. But before 1914, Italy was constrained by its alliance with Austria and Germany. The Ottoman Empire was everywhere on the defensive and not about to challenge any major power or provide it with a pretext to intervene in support of any of its neighbors. Russia was more or less recovered from its defeat in the Russo–Japanese War and intent on expanding its influence in the Balkans. But Russian leaders did not want war; they mobilized reluctantly in 1914, and in the hope that it would deter Austria from attacking Serbia. Serbia had long-term aspirations to acquire Bosnia–Herzogovina but its energies were fully consumed with overcoming the resistance of its newly acquired subjects in Macedonia. In 1910, German foreign minister Alfred von Kiderlen-Wächter rightly observed that "If we do not conjure up a war into being, no one else certainly will do so" (Kantorowicz 1931: 360; Geiss 1976: 126).

A failed assassination attempt could have had beneficial consequences for Europe. Serbia's diplomatic humiliation in 1909 encouraged the formation of secret societies aimed at undermining Austrian
rule in Bosnia–Herzogovina. Apis was at the center of many of these
conspiracies, and supplied arms and other assistance to the Archduke's
assassins. Pašlić was hostile to the conspirators and knew of their
preparations, but felt constrained to provide only veiled warnings to
the Austrian ambassador. Ironically, neither Apis nor the other conspirators wanted war with Austria, and Apis did not expect the assassination
to provoke one. Apis hoped to strengthen his hand vis-à-vis civilian
authorities, and sought to call off the assassination when he became
convinced that it would not buttress his authority. From the perspective of those who mattered in Belgrade, the war was an unintended
and largely undesired consequence of an unwanted assassination. An
abortive assassination attempt might have allowed Pašlić to rein in Apis,
which he did in the summer of 1915. Apis was arrested a year later,
tried and executed in 1917.

Historians who contend that a European war was inevitable root
their argument in the deeper trends they see pushing the powers toward
war. Would these trends have become more or less pronounced in the
years after 1914? Structural determinists assume they would have
intensified, although they offer no reasons why. We can conjure up
scenarios of more acute Austro–Russian competition in the Balkans,
British–German naval and economic competition and the breakup of the
Triple Alliance due to Italy's defection. With no more imagination, we
can identify developments that would have muted underlying tensions
and made war less likely.

The principal difference between the Balkan crises of 1908–9 and
1914 was Russian willingness to go to war in support of Serbia in
1914. Some historians maintain that Russia was ripe for revolution
in 1914 and that World War I postponed the upheaval for three years
(Rogger 1966; Mayer 1967). If revolution had broken out in the absence
of war, Russia might have been consumed by domestic turmoil for
several years afterwards and not have been in any position to pursue
an aggressive policy in the Balkans. This could also have happened to
Austria. Franz Josef died in 1916 and was succeeded by Prince Karl.
If Franz Ferdinand had lived, he would have ascended to the throne.
Motivated by hatred of Hungarians and the *Ausgleich* of 1867, Franz
Ferdinand would have sought to reduce the power of Hungary, and had
considered several strategies toward this end including trialism and
a looser form of federalism. The documents he had prepared for the
transition indicate that he probably would have introduced universal

suffrage in Hungary at the outset of his reign in the hope of increasing the power of minorities at the expense of the Magyars. This would have provoked a strong reaction from Budapest, and further attempts by Franz Ferdinand to undercut the *Ausgleich* would have raised the prospect of civil war. Vienna would not have been in any position to start a war with Serbia (Dedijer 1966, chap. 7; Zeman 1988: 24).

One of the principal causes of war in 1914 was the German military's belief that war was inevitable and had to be fought before 1916 or 1917 when improved Russian mobilization and armaments made the Schlieffen Plan unworkable. The most obvious alternative, a direct onslaught on France across the Meuse and Moselle, had little chance of success because of the mountainous terrain and French fortifications. Schlieffen contemplated such a campaign in 1894, but quickly gave the idea up as unrealistic (Ritter 1969–73, vol. 2: 196). Could Germany have conducted an offensive in the East? Russian railway and fortress construction made an Austro–German offensive in Poland difficult, but not impossible. It could not produce the kind of decisive victory Moltke sought. If the Germans broached the Narew River line, the Russians could withdraw with relative ease into their vast hinterland.

If offensives against Russia or France were unrealistic, the most sensible strategy was a defensive posture on both fronts; German generals knew that France and Russia planned to march against Germany at the outbreak of war. With no German invasion of Belgium, Britain would have remained neutral. The French army would have exhausted itself, as it began to do in 1914, in a series of unsuccessful and costly assaults against the strong German defensive position in Alsace. In the East, the Russian offensive into Prussia was blunted by the meager forces Germany had left in the region and forced to withdraw in great disorder. Reserve forces could have conducted a limited counter-offensive, after which Germany could have called for a restoration of peace on the basis of the *status quo ante bellum*. It seems improbable that there would have been much support in France or Russia for continuing the war after a series of disheartening defeats. Nor could these powers have resisted British, and perhaps, American, pressures to lay down their arms and accept a reasonable peace. Austria–Hungary would have been preserved, although the Russian empire might have succumbed to revolution. German preeminence on the continent would not only have been maintained but immeasurably strengthened.

Moltke was willing to tinker with details of the Schlieffen Plan but reluctant to consider alternatives. Some members of the general staff doubted the likelihood of victory in 1914, but clung to the Schlieffen Plan because of their collective commitment to the offensive (Förster

1995: 61–95). By 1917, according to the calculations of the general staff, Germany would have had no hope of waging successful, sequential offensives against France and Russia. If war had been avoided in 1914, the contradiction between Germany's strategy and military reality would have become more pronounced. Moltke, or more likely, his successor, would have been compelled to abandon the Schlieffen Plan. As funds for additional troops were out of the question, and the concept and technology of the *Blitzkrieg* had not yet been developed, there were no viable alternatives to the defensive. The German general staff might have been compelled to adopt such a strategy, or variant of it. If so, they would no longer have had the same incentive to launch a preventive war or preempt in a crisis, and to the extent that they became fearful of Russian military capabilities, they might even have become a force for preserving the peace.

I have asked if a European war could have been delayed in the absence of an appropriate catalyst. Could it have come *sooner*? I am inclined to discount the prospect of an earlier war. Austria considered and rejected going to war with Serbia in December 1912, April-May 1913 and October 1913. Between 1905 and 1914, German leaders spurned Moltke's several pleas to exploit great power crises as pretexts for war. Austrian and Germans swords remained sheathed because political leaders in Berlin and Vienna saw war as politically and militarily risky and did not feel threatened enough to take these risks.

If war had come earlier, there is no structural reason to suppose a different outcome. The biggest military change between 1909 and 1914 was the Russian railway construction that so worried the Germans. The German general staff would have felt more confident about war in 1910–12, but whether their confidence would have kept Moltke from panicking, as he did in 1914, and given him the courage to adhere to the original invasion plan, are open questions. Gerhard Ritter does not think it would have made any difference; the Schlieffen Plan, he insists, left too much to chance (Ritter 1958: 92). Gordon Craig believes that Germany sorely misjudged the military capability of its adversaries and even if the Schlieffen Plan had achieved a battlefield success it would not necessarily have been decisive for the outcome of the war. I have made a similar argument elsewhere (Craig 1964: 280, 1978: 343; Lebow 1985: 45–78).

Alternative Europes

How different would Europe and the world have been if the major powers had avoided war in the first two decades of the 20th century? The

Great War accelerated the relative political and economic decline of Europe (Holborn 1951). It sapped the continent's strength demographically by killing off so many men and leaving its generally undernourished population vulnerable to the great influenza pandemic of 1919; undermined French and British will to fight another war; created the conditions for Hitler's rise to power and the vastly more destructive war he and Stalin would unleash; led to the Russian revolution, the Bolshevik coup, civil war and communist triumph that kept Europe divided for seventy years; hastened the emergence of the United States as the world's leading economic and military power; and accelerated demands for independence by Europe's colonies. Could any or all of these outcomes have been averted?

Let me edge towards a conclusion by identifying two of many possible futures for Europe. I do not want to make an argument for the contingency of World War I and then insist that some alternative world was structurally determined.[4] In the optimistic scenario, Europe avoids a First World War and enjoys decades of sustained economic development. Eastern Europe, not held back by two world wars and communism, pulls abreast of the West sooner rather than later. Russia undergoes a revolution, loses most of its empire and is governed by a quasi-authoritarian but avowedly capitalist regime. Like the countries of the Pacific rim in the late 20th century, Russia and most of its successor states gradually evolve more stable and democratic regimes as the result of economic prosperity and the emergence of a large, educated middle class and export-oriented business elite. Austria–Hungary survives, but under pressure from dissident nationalities and a democratic Germany concerned about the consequences of unrest along its southern border, adopts a looser, federal structure despite Magyar opposition. Later in the century, European powers confront demands for independence in Africa and Asia, but decolonization works itself out in relatively peaceful ways, and in the absence of a Cold War and ideological competition, most newly independent countries maintain reasonably amicable relations with their former metropoles. Europe remains the political and economic center of the world but confronts stiff economic competition from the United States and Japan. In response,

---

[4]Niall Ferguson (1999c), contends that if Britain had not intervened, or intervened too late in 1914, Germany would have won the war and created a benign suzerainty over continental Europe. Michael Howard (1998) rightly takes him to task for using contingency to establish a determined alternative world. Victory might just as easily have encouraged instead of restrained German militarism. The 1914 "September Program" might be cited in evidence, as it indicates the kinds of far-reaching territorial and economic demands German industrialists were willing to press on their willing government at the moment when hopes for victory were high.

the continent evolves various forms of supranational cooperation and organization, a development facilitated by nearly universal knowledge of German by the region's political, business and intellectual elites.

The pessimistic scenario also starts from the premise that there was no war. But Russia is consumed by a revolution that leads to prolonged civil war, and these events destabilize Austria–Hungary, leading Vienna and Budapest to rely on increasingly repressive measures to retain their empire and hegemony in the Balkans. Germany remains the preeminent military and economic power, consolidates its economic hold on Eastern Europe and achieves something akin to superpower status. Within Germany, democratic reforms at the national level are frustrated, and during a period of sharp economic downturn — a version of the Great Depression — an authoritarian regime comes to power in France and develops a "special relationship" with its German counterpart. Great Britain is increasingly isolated from "illiberal" Europe and moves closer to the United States. Two power blocs emerge — Anglo-America and a German dominated continent — and the ideological and interest-based divisions between them lead to a prolonged Cold War, made more threatening by their mutual acquisition of nuclear weapons. An authoritarian Japan holds the balance, and exploits this situation to expand its territorial and economic influence throughout the Pacific Rim. As the century ends, the millennium is greeted with great pessimism throughout the developed world. The number one book on the best-seller list, Paul Kennedy's *The decline of the great powers,* argues that war is inevitable.

Either future, or others we have not described, could have come to pass — just as World War I could have been averted. Social scientists and historians of a deterministic persuasion err in thinking that major social and political developments are invariably specific instances of strong, or even weak, regularities in social behavior. These developments are sometimes the result of accidental conjunctions; they are events that might have had a low subjective probability. Conversely, events that seem highly likely may never happen. The concatenation of particular leaders with particular contexts, and of particular events with other events is always a matter of chance, never of necessity (Almond and Genco 1977).

Contingency and causation

The origins of World War I are best understood as a confluence of three largely independent chains of causation that came together in 1914. Their interaction has the characteristics of a complex, nonlinear system.

The value of important variables was not independent, but depended on the presence and value of other key variables. And they in turn depended on the changing understandings actors had of their strategic interactions.

A linear model that specified the presence of A (the set of variables associated with the German security dilemma), B (the set of variables relevant for Austria's security dilemma) and C (Russian willingness to risk war to support Serbia) would only capture part of the strategic picture. The values of A, B and C were determined by *gestalt* shifts that took place in 1909 in Russia and in 1914 in Austria–Hungary and Germany. The presence of A*B*C prior to these *gestalt* shifts would not have produced a war. Nor, I have argued, would their coincidence have been likely to do so after 1916 or 1917 if the political alignment in the Balkans had changed, if Russia's domestic situation had become more acute or if the Schlieffen Plan had been replaced by a more defense-oriented alternative. War required the coincidence of A*B*C *after* the *gestalt* shifts and *before* important underlying conditions changed to produce further shifts. The catalyst for the C *gestalt* shift was Russia's perception of its humiliation in the 1908–9 Bosnian Annexation Crisis, and for the A and B shifts, the twin assassinations at Sarajevo.

World War I is not unique in its nonlinearity. World War II, which brought about the next transformation of the international system, was also the product of a highly contingent set of conditions. Aggressive as Hitler was, it is more difficult to imagine Germany starting a war in a less fortuitous context. In the 1930s, France was divided internally, and Britain and France were loath to collaborate with the Soviet Union. Because his imperial policy in Africa had run afoul of Britain, Mussolini abandoned his opposition to German expansion and entered into an alliance with Hitler. In the Far East, Japan attacked China, and posed a serious security threat to the Soviet Union and the Western powers. Isolationism guaranteed that the United States, whose intervention had determined the outcome of World War I, was no longer a player in the European balance of power. Hitler could attack his enemies piecemeal, while counting on the support of Italy and the neutrality of the Soviet Union and the United States. The end of the Cold War – which brought about the third system transformation of the century – can also be described as the result of complex, path dependent, nonlinear interactions (Lebow and Stein 1994).

International relations theory needs to consider multiple paths of causation and their possible interaction. Current theories of international relations almost invariably focus on one chain of causation. Power transition theory, for example, attempts to explain the outbreak of wars responsible for system transformations in terms of the changing power balance between hegemons and challengers (Doran and Parsons 1980; Organski and Kugler 1980; Gilpin 1981). Some power transition theorists, notably, Robert Gilpin, identify responses other than war for declining hegemons (Gilpin 1981: 191-2, 197). Power transition theories that acknowledge choice are indeterminate, and attempts to use them to account for the end of the Cold War elicit the criticism that they are being used to explain *ex post facto* what they did not and could not possibly have predicted. The indeterminacy problem arises because factors, independent of the power balance, shape actors' responses to an actual or anticipated decline in their power (Wohlforth 1994/1995; Lebow 1994).

In 1914 power was only part of the story; shifts in the political and military balance may have made German and Austrian leaders more willing to consider the use of force but were insufficient cause for them to draw their swords. Power transition theory – or any other monocausal explanation for system transformation – may be a useful analytical starting point, but it is unlikely to offer much analytical purchase in and of itself. Other causal chains inevitably need to be considered as well as their interaction.

Contingencies in the form of random events and conjunctures of multiple chains of causation are difficult to deal with theoretically. Random events, by definition, lie outside our theories, as do conjunctures, which in turn may be caused by random events. For this reason alone prediction in individual cases is an unrealistic goal. Conditional forecasting may be a more appropriate strategy for attempting to cope with the manifold uncertainties associated with open ended, complex systems. Conditional forecasts use existing theories and behavioral regularities as a starting point to develop alternate scenarios of likely future developments, or of a system transformation. They consider multiple chains of causation and look at some of the possible interactions that might take place among them, as well as the paths that might lead from one scenario to another. They also stipulate the kind of information or events that will used to determine the extent to which events track according to the expectations of any of the scenarios. As events unfold, researchers repeatedly revise their scenarios and expectations in light of the new information. Such a process is messy and time consuming, but it is the only reasonable way of taking into account coincidence and random events. At the very least, it can provide early warning of major changes in a system or of the faulty expectations of those who are tracking its performance (Weber 1997; Stein et al. 1998; Bernstein et al. 2000).

Catalysts

In many physical processes catalysts are unproblematic. Chain reactions are triggered by the decay of atomic nuclei. Some of the neutrons they emit strike other nuclei prompting them to fission and emit more neutrons, which strike still more nuclei. Physicists can calculate how many kilograms of uranium 235 or plutonium at given pressures are necessary to produce a chain reaction. They can take it for granted that if a critical mass is achieved, a chain reaction will follow. This is because trillions of atoms are present, and at any given moment enough of them will decay to provide the neutrons needed to start the reaction. Wars and accommodations, and the system transformations they may bring about, involve relatively few actors. And unlike the weak force responsible for nuclear decay, political catalysts are not inherent properties of the interacting units. For both these reasons, we can never know if or when an appropriate political catalyst will occur.

Political catalysts differ from their physical counterparts in another important respect. They are often causes in their own right, as was Sarajevo. The twin assassinations caused the Austrian leadership to reframe the problem of Serbia. Risks that had been unacceptable in the past now became tolerable, even necessary. The independent role of catalysts creates another problem for theories and attempts to evaluate them. All the relevant underlying causes for an outcome may be present but absent a catalyst it will not occur. The uncertain and evolving relationship between underlying and immediate causes not only renders point prediction impossible, it renders problematic more general statements about the causes of war and system transformations – and many other international phenomena – because we have no way of knowing which of these events would have occurred in the presence of appropriate catalysts, and we cannot assume that their presence or absence can be treated as random. It is thus impossible to define the universe of such events or to construct a representative sample of them.

The independent role of catalysts in some classes of events also renders statistical tests meaningless because of the impossibility of coding outcomes. If war is the dependent variable, researchers will distinguish between cases or interactions that ended in war and those that did not, and will look for association between these outcomes and their independent variables. Their results will be misleading if war would have occurred in the presence of their variables if a suitable catalyst had been present. Meaningful statistical studies would require two stage data sets that accounted for this variation.

Theorizing about catalysts is difficult because they are so often situation specific. It is nevertheless useful to distinguish between situations in which actors are actively looking for an excuse for war, and those in which the catalyst reshapes the way the think about the situation, making them more willing than they were previously to consider high-risk options because of the greater perceived costs of inaction. Classic examples of the former include Hitler in 1939 and Lyndon Johnson in 1964; both leaders invented pretexts to go to war when their adversaries failed to provide them. Sarajevo may be the paradigmatic case of the situation in which catalysts play important, independent roles.

Once again, the best way to address the problem of catalysts in specific contexts is likely to be through some form of scenario generation. Analysts can reason forward and ask themselves what kind of event(s) would be required to prompt behavior likely to bring about war, accommodation and system change. Or, they can reason backwards by identifying the kind of events most likely to occur and ask themselves if any of these would serve as effective triggers.

Actors

Most models of political behavior assume instrumental rationality, and this may be the norm in everyday decision-making. The evidence from both world wars and from the end of the Cold War suggest that this is not true for the series of decisions responsible for system transformations. In all these cases, the behavior in question led to results diametrically opposed to those intended by key actors, and there was ample information available at the time to suggest that this would occur.

The pathology of German decision-making in the two world wars has been extensively documented. The Austrian case in 1914 is less well-known, and provides another striking example of deviance from instrumental rationality. In a seeming fit of emotion, Austrian leaders went to war to uphold the honor of the royal family, crush Serbia and remove the domestic and foreign threats to the security of their empire. They had no appropriate mobilization plan for coping simultaneously with Serbia and Russia, and could not fight the short war they deemed essential. In a longer war, they recognized they would become increasingly dependent upon Germany, and end up losing the very independence they were fighting to maintain. More enigmatic still, was their crisis policy that maximized the likelihood that Russia would intervene and confront them with the two-front war they knew they were unprepared to wage.

Unintended consequences have been described as emergent properties of systems (Waltz 1979; Cederman 1997; Jervis 1997). As presently used in the international relations literature, the concept of emergent properties elides two significantly different consequences. The first, and most common, are the unanticipated outcomes we would expect in a stable system. Examples include arms races, runs on banks or the 1990s Asian financial crisis. These phenomena are the aggregated, unintended and counterproductive result of individual behavior based on instrumentally rational calculations of self-interest. The second kind of consequence, and the one relevant to my argument, are those that are *doubly* unintended. Here, behavior has unintended consequences for the actors and their strategic interaction, and also for the system as a whole. It sets in motion a chain of events that lead to the system's transformation. None of our theories, as presently constituted, can account for this outcome.

Niklas Luhmann suggests that systems are repertories of codes, and that outside influences must be translated by the logic of the system to have an effect upon its operation (Luhmann 1997, vol. 1, chap. 2). Outside influences in economics, for example, are translated into prices. Simple structural theories like that of Kenneth Waltz completely ignore outside effects. Waltz acknowledges that an international system can change, but says nothing about how such change might come about. More evolutionary approaches to system – Robert Jervis makes the case for them in his book – acknowledge that the structure and operating principles of systems undergo fundamental shifts in response to *outside* stimuli. World War I and the end of the Cold War indicate that systems can also be transformed through their *internal* operations. These cases point to the existence of a self-referential loop by which actors change their understanding of themselves, the system and how it operates.

The possibility of system change through actor learning has important implications for the study of international relations. It suggests that structural change may be the *product*, not the cause, of behavior – the opposite of what most realist theories contend. It also directs our attention to the understandings actors have of each other and of their environments, and how these understandings evolve and become shared, an underlying premise of constructivism. Finally, it constitutes a possible conceptual bridge between scholars in the neo-positivist tradition who privilege structures and those in the constructivist tradition who privilege ideas.

Chapter 5

Powderkegs, sparks and World War I

William R. Thompson

Richard Ned Lebow (this volume chapter 4) has recently invoked what might be called a streetcar interpretation of systemic war and change.[1] According to him, all our structural theories in world politics both overdetermine and underdetermine the explanation of the most important events – such as World War I, World War II, or the end of the Cold War. Not only do structural theories tend to fixate on one cause or stream of causation, they are inherently incomplete because the influence of structural causes cannot be known without also identifying the necessary role of catalysts. As long as we ignore the precipitants that actually encourage actors to act, we cannot make accurate generalizations about the relationships between more remote causation and the outcomes that we are trying to explain. Nor can we test the accuracy of such generalizations without accompanying data on the presence or absence of catalysts. In the absence of an appropriate catalyst (or a "streetcar" that failed to arrive), wars might never have happened. Concrete information on their presence ("streetcars" that did arrive) might alter our understanding of the explanatory significance of other variables. But since catalysts and contingencies are so difficult to handle theoretically and empirically, perhaps we should be extremely cautious in attempting to test ostensibly nonlinear processes with existing data sets.

Lebow's challenge to the normal industry of explaining the Big Bang events of world politics contains a mixture of points, with some of which it is hard to disagree. Yet there are other parts of the argument with which it is very hard to agree. More importantly, though, Lebow almost makes an argument about explaining World War I that

[1]My thanks for comments on earlier versions from Mike Colaresi, Ned Lebow, Karen Rasler, Jo Rennstich, Paul Schroeder, and John Vasquez.

seems more compelling than the possible role of catalysts and contingency. By arguing that World War I was a "nonlinear confluence of three largely interdependent chains of causation which produced independent but simultaneous gestalt shifts in St. Petersburg, Vienna, and Berlin," Lebow highlights an interpretation of World War I that contains considerable potential for synthesizing other interpretations, overcoming the tendency to promote one causal factor over others, and developing a general structural interpretation that may prove useful in helping to explain other systemic wars. Drawing out this alternative argument about systemic wars which is underdeveloped in Lebow's challenge is the main focus of the present essay. Along the way, some ancillary observations will need to be made about other aspects of the streetcar explanation and causal arguments in general. When all is said or done, and regardless of whether streetcars arrive on time, theoretical generalization and empirical testing about structural change remain viable enterprises.

The streetcar challenge

Lebow's many specific points about World War I include the contention that we do not give sufficient credit to the assassination of Archduke Ferdinand at Sarajevo as a major cause. Instead, the tendency is to focus on German blank checks and Austrian pretexts for war. But if Ferdinand had not been killed in 1914, Lebow believes, it is possible that war might have been avoided altogether and that the underlying conditions promoting war could have dissipated in the absence of a catalyst at just the right time to provoke Austrian, German, and Russian bellicosity. More generally, though, his assertions about war explanations can be summarized in the following condensed form:

1. Current theories of international relations almost invariably focus on one chain of causation; multiple paths of causation (including international and domestic structures, domestic politics, and leaders) and their possible interaction (in linear or nonlinear ways) need to be considered.

2. Theoretical explanations for war take catalysts for granted, assuming that as long as the right underlying conditions are present, some incident will sooner or later set armies on the march. But, just as streetcars do not always come, underlying causes do not make events inevitable; they only create the possibility of change. Fortuitous contingencies or catalysts that are independent of the causes may be necessary in the sense that the outbreak of war

requires the conjunction of underlying pressures and appropriate catalysts. Without an appropriate catalyst, the underlying causes may evolve in such a way that the pressure for change is weakened or eliminated.

3. If a war could have been prevented by avoiding the catalytic event, the war outcome must be regarded as highly contingent. Contingencies and catalysts in the form of random acts or conjunctures of multiple chains of causation are difficult to deal with theoretically. Not only are they difficult to theorize about, they also render theory construction and empirical testing of theories problematic. If catalysts are necessary conditions, we cannot make generalizations about the relationships between underlying conditions and the probability of war outbreak unless we also assume the presence of any appropriate catalyst. Nor can one test general theories of war if it is impossible to control for the mediating role of catalysts between independent and dependent variables.

Lebow's first statement about monocausal propensities is virtually unassailable. Without a doubt, theories of international relations tend to privilege some factor or small set of factors over others. In some respects, that is precisely what theories are supposed to do. The problem is that it is usually easier to focus on one element and/or level of analysis – polarity distribution, power transition, alliance bipolarization, democratic dyads, arms races, crisis behavior – than it is to develop a fully specified set of statement about how some of these elements combine to increase the probability of war. This monocausal penchant is an old problem of international relations theory, one that has long been recognized, yet also one that has not received adequate attention for we continue to prefer monocausal "solutions" to our international relations puzzles. We know better but the path of less resistance continues to be highly tempting.

The second group of statements on the role of catalysts is more debatable. Yes, precipitants do tend to be taken for granted. Structural theories are about piles of firewood that are viewed as becoming either exceptionally dry or impregnated with starter fuel. The general nature of such arguments is that given this highly combustible set of ingredients (whatever they may be), the probability of a conflagration is higher than if the firewood is wet or unsoaked in kerosene. No structural theorist says that a possibly ensuing conflagration is due to spontaneous combustion. Someone still has to light a match or spark a flint. Nor do most structural theorists say that the presence of the appropriate sort of underlying conditions makes some outcome inevitable – only that it is more probable.[2] If no one lights a match, then it is possible that the primed firewood will not catch on fire.

Yet the very ability to say empirically that there is a greater probability of fire if the wood is dry than if it is wet implies that dry firewood, historically, has ignited more often than wet firewood. The presence or absence of a lit match does not vitiate the ability to generalize about the circumstances that make lighting the match more successful. This is one place in which the Lebow argument goes astray. Specific wars may well be highly contingent on the specific event(s) that precipitate them. British entry into the 1739 War of Jenkins' Ear against Spain was precipitated in part by the alleged mistreatment of a British ship captain.[3] Yet can one really feel comfortable in saying that the British would never have entered the war if the damage to Jenkins' ear had not occurred? British decision-makers, or some of them at least, presumably were looking for an opportunity to improve their Caribbean position. It is not hard to imagine another streetcar coming along to serve the purpose of precipitating further gains in the penetration of the Spanish colonial empire.

More generally, though, the question is whether wars in general tend to break out given some set of underlying conditions? If they do, it suggests that the catalytic role may not be as critical to either a theory's construction or evaluation as Lebow thinks. Either some type of precipitant is present or it is not. If it is frequently absent and one still finds a strong relationship between the development of underlying conditions and the outbreaks of war, the catalyst can hardly be a major or necessary causal factor. If the catalyst is frequently present when the appropriate underlying set of conditions is also present, assuming again the strong relationship between the structural causes and war outcomes, the assumption that "some incident will sooner or later set armies on the march" may in fact be appropriate.

At the same time it is not inconceivable that a theory's explanatory power or its pre- or post-dictive utility might be enhanced by knowing something about certain types of precipitants. It could be that the interaction of some types of precipitants and underlying causes makes

---

[2]Some power transition language may verge on statements about the inevitable. But even in these cases the emphasis is usually on the apparent inevitability of the power transition, not on how decision-makers will respond to the transition (see, for example, the discussion about the possibility of a Chinese ascendancy in the twenty-first century in Tammen et al. (2000).

[3]Spanish coast guards in the Caribbean were confiscating ships believed to be engaged in illegal trade with Spanish colonies. While the British government had negotiated successfully a settlement of grievances with Spain in 1739, opposition to the arrangement pressed for a more coercive response in both the press and Parliament. Captain Jenkins brought his severed ear to Parliament in a pickle jar as evidence of Spanish atrocities and as part of a factional campaign to provoke a war in the face of governmental reluctance (Jones 1980: 199).

war outbreaks much more probable. For instance, if a precipitant or catalyst removes barriers to war participation that might otherwise have been difficult to overcome, the catalytic factor begins to take on more significance than simply a randomly lit match. The alleged attack on Captain Jenkins is one such example. It galvanized popular and legislative support for British entry into a war that might otherwise have been more difficult to justify. It also weakened the governmental inclination to avoid war in this instance. Lebow's interpretation of Sarajevo is similar in spirit. Whatever else it may have done, it removed an influential decision-maker who was reluctant to see Austria–Hungary go to war in 1914, thereby facilitating a 1914 Viennese hawkish decision in conjunction with other factors.[4]

Yet it is difficult to know how far to push the relative significance of such factors if we examine cases one by one. One is limited in what can be said about the significance of polarity distributions or democratic dyads when the case N is only one or two; so, too, for the role of catalysts and, for that matter, alternative historical scenarios in which we can probe the significance of various factors in a speculative vein.[5] We would need to look at an array of cases (and, preferably, a simultaneous array of noncases) if we wish to assess the importance of catalytic factors. In other words, Lebow may be right to suggest that we are missing out on an important clue by slighting the role of catalysts. It remains to be seen whether slighting catalysts precludes theorizing or testing theories. The odds are that it does not but that certainly does not mean that no one should bother to check whether understanding catalysts strengthens our overall explanatory capabilities.

But there is a second argument embedded in Lebow's challenge that is far more intriguing. Sarajevo is so important to Lebow because he argues that it helped change the way decision-makers in three countries regarded the prospective costs and benefits of war. Prior to 1914, German decision-makers were reluctant to encourage Austrian action in the Balkans, especially in view of the prospects for being forced to deal with Russian and French threats on two fronts. Yet they also were worried about future Russian military improvements. Austrian decision-makers disagreed about how best to cope with Southeast European threats to their interests and imperial integrity. Russian decision-makers had to deal with a string of foreign policy failures ranging from the Russo-Japanese war outcome to the 1908 Bosnian crisis and the threat of

---

[4]Others have made this argument as well without turning the assassination into a major causal factor (e.g., Ferguson 1999c: 148).

[5]While there are a number of roles that counterfactual analysis can play in the analysis of interstate politics, including exploring, probing, or reinforcing more general analyses, it seems improbable that such analysis could ever supplant the complementary need for systematic analysis. For a review of the uses of counterfactual analysis in world politics, see Tetlock and Belkin (1996).

revolution. Another failure had to be avoided. Sarajevo helped stim-
ulate decision-makers into action in all three capitals. The Germans
encouraged the Austrians to do something fairly risky. The Austrians
were encouraged to take the offensive against Serbia. The Russians felt
they had to avoid another foreign policy embarrassment. The interaction of these shifts toward greater risk-taking perspectives, according
to Lebow, made an Austro–German-Russian escalation of hostilities
much more likely than had hitherto been the case.

So far we are still in the realm of the catalytic event's significance.
Lebow makes the argument even more interesting by suggesting that
each of these three shifts in perspective were strongly influenced by a
variety of earlier developments. If Wilhelm I had not annexed Alsace–
Lorraine after the Franco–Prussian War, there might have been no
Franco–German rivalry. If the German statesmen who followed Bismarck's ouster from control over German foreign policy had been able
to handle Russia as well as Bismarck had, the Russians might have
been less likely to ally with France. If Germany had not provoked an
unproductive naval race with Britain, there might not have been an
Anglo–French entente. If these three chains of causation had worked
out differently, Europe might not have been bipolarized into two hostile
camps.

Lebow further contends that it was the interaction among these
chains of causation that was more important than any of the individual
chains themselves. That is to say, no single chain could have produced
a war. It took the interaction of all three to generate World War I. Moreover, while it is clear that Lebow is arguing for the coming together
of multiple streams of causation, it is not clear that he is content to
limit the argument to three chains (and their interaction effects). He
also notes that Austria's annexation of Bosnia in 1908 precluded the
possibility of cooperation between Austria and Serbia. By humiliating
Russia shortly after Japan had done something similar, the Austrian annexation also meant that Russia would look for opportunities to return
the favor. Three years later, the Italian movement into Libya encouraged
Serbia, Bulgaria, and Greece to attack what remained of the Ottoman
Empire in southeastern Europe. Serbia emerged from the Balkan Wars
ending in 1913 even more inclined to encourage Slav unrest in the Austrian empire at a time when Germany was becoming more inclined to
support an Austrian preemptive strike on one of the southern sources
of threat to the maintenance of its empire. This interpretation sounds
more like at least five chains of interactive causation.

We need to take a step back from these specific arguments to recognize what is being said more generally. Lebow can be viewed as
arguing that Austria, Germany and Russia became likely to go to war in

1914 thanks in part to a structural background of developments in the Franco-German, Russo-German, Anglo-German, Anglo-French, Austro-Serbian, Austro-Russian, Russo-Japanese, Serbian-Turkish, Greco-Turkish, and Bulgarian-Turkish rivalries. Implicit to these fairly explicit arguments are references that might have been made about still other rivalries. The Anglo-French entente emerged from the British decision to better confront the main threat of Germany by deescalating its rivalries with not only France, but also the United States and Russia. France, Russia, and the United States had all also elevated the threat perceived to be posed by Germany. Italy attacked Turkish territory in North Africa in part because Italy was unable to do much about pursuing directly its rivalries with Austria or France and was therefore safer seeking territorial expansion and great power glory on another continent altogether. A residual Franco-Austrian rivalry persisted as well (Schroeder 1999). Austro-German cooperation after the 1870s presumed the termination of their old rivalry. So, too, did Russo-French cooperation after 1890. The Balkan Wars further weakened Russia's Bulgarian client to the profit of Bulgaria's Greek and Serbian rivals. The number of relevant causation chains multiplies rather quickly.

Discussion of rivalries has been with us at least since Thucydides. Perhaps because they seem so familiar in the conflict landscape, we have long taken them for granted. Only recently have we begun to focus on them explicitly as structured relationships that are not all that common in frequency but which are uncommonly related to conflict propensities. In other words, rivalries offer exceptional clues to who is more likely to fight whom because rivals have already pre-selected one another as their most likely enemies and sources of threat.[6] What is most remarkable about the above paragraphs is that 16 of the 38 existing rivalries in 1913, identified in table 5.1, are mentioned explicitly. If we limit the geographical focus to rivalries involving at least one European actor, the proportion is 15 of 22, excluding three or four important rivalries that were terminated prior to the outbreak of World War I.[7]

Even so, one of the more interesting dimensions of the European rivalry structure is not merely that so many of the extant rivalries were active at the same time. Rivalries tend to blow hot and cold over time, although, admittedly, finding 15 proximate hot ones at the same time seems more than coincidental. More critically, a large number had

---

[6]One way (Thompson 2001a) to identify rivalries is to define them as the relationships that form when decision-makers identify competitive enemies that are posing strategic or military threats. The more common quantitative approach, however, involves establishing minimal threshold criteria for the number of militarized interstate disputes dyads participate in within specific periods of time. See, among others, Diehl and Goertz (2000).

[7]This group includes Austria-Prussia/Germany, Britain-United States, Britain-France, and France-Russia.

also escalated to tension and hostility levels at which war was at least conceivable. As is well known, the main great powers were engaged heavily in various types of arms races in attempts to gain edges over their competitors, or at least not to fall too far behind.[8] They had also gravitated toward a bipolarized alignment. Neither the arms races nor the alliance structures necessarily meant that war was more likely, but these structural and behavioral processes certainly underscored the tensions and concerns about positional losses – whether it be located in Austria's unstable, southeastern European bailiwick, Anglo–German industrial/commercial/colonial/naval competition, or German fears that it was falling behind Russian military improvements. In their strategies to try and catch up or keep up with their rivals, an unusually large number of adversaries had become "ripe" or riper for resorting to martial policy alternatives by 1914.[9]

None the less, one of the more frustrating aspects of World War I analyses is that practically every explanation for conflict seems to find some resonance in the events leading to war in 1914. This is the flip side of Lebow's argument about tendencies to focus on only one chain of causation. Authors can construct plausible explanations of what happened without seeking to be fully comprehensive in circumstances in which a good number of the explanatory foci in international relations seemed to be at work. The question should not be whether we can add a ripe rivalry structure to the broad inventory of World War I explanations. Rather, can a ripe rivalry structure help to unify some of the partial explanations for the 1914 onset of war? And, if that should be the case, just what does a "ripe" rivalry structure mean?

---

[8]David Herrmann (1996: 227–8) argues that arms races facilitated the perception of a closing window of opportunity for Germany to be able to deal with its rivals on the battlefield. Stevenson (1996: 418) credits European arms races on land with bestowing the perception of a Franco–Russian ascending power curve while encouraging the Austrians and Germans, and their rivals, to see the Austro–German power curve as a descending one. In this respect, arms races encouraged both sides to contemplate war as a desirable option, albeit for different reasons.

[9]Other analysts have drawn attention to the idea of multiple rivalries influencing the severity and spread of war. John Vasquez's (1993) "steps-to-war" model suggests that war diffusion may be a function of territorial contiguity, rivalry, and alliances. The presence of any one of the trio should have a positive impact on the spread of war, but the combination of two or more could greatly increase the probability of war joining. Vasquez (1993: 247) also notes that these variables tend to interact with each other. For example, a territorial dispute between two proximate actors can lead to a dyadic rivalry that, in turn, can lead to the search for allies in an attempt to gain an advantage on the adversary. The question then becomes one of whether allies can restrain their own and other states' rivalries or whether they become ensnared in other peoples' conflicts. Diehl and Goertz (2000: 241–62) argue and find some empirical support for the idea that close ties between rivalries reinforce rivalry duration and increase the potential for rivalry escalation and conflict severity.

0

TABLE 5.1:   Strategic rivalries existing in 1913

Rivals among European actors	Rivalries with only non-European actors
Albania-Greece	Afghanistan-Iran
Austria-France	Argentina-Brazil
Austria-Italy	Argentina-Chile
Austria-Turkey	Bolivia-Paraguay
Austria-Russia	Bolivia-Peru
Austria-Serbia	Chile-Peru
Britain-Germany	China-Japan
Britain-Russia	Colombia-Ecuador
Bulgaria-Greece	Colombia-Peru
Bulgaria-Romania	Colombia-Venezuela
Bulgaria-Turkey	Ecuador-Peru
Bulgaria-Serbia	El Salvador-Guatemala
Ethiopia-Italy	El Salvador-Honduras
France-Germany	Guatemala-Honduras
France-Italy	Iran-Turkey
Germany-Russia	Japan-United States
Germany-United States	
Greece-Turkey	
Greece-Serbia	
Japan-Russia	
Russia-Turkey	
Turkey-Serbia	

Note: Rivalries identified in italics in the left hand column are discussed in the text.
Source: Extracted from information reported in Thompson (2001a).

The nature of the First World War also seems to facilitate allocating blame for the outbreak of war to almost every conceivable actor, and not without some claim to credibility. Can a ripe rivalry structure shed any light on this question which, after all, is not that far removed from more neutral inquiries into more abstract causes? If we know (or think we know) which explanations are most powerful, there are usually implicit or explicit links to which set of decision-makers were most at fault. For instance, if one emphasizes the German challenge of Britain's political-economic preeminence, accusatory fingers are apt to point in the German direction. If one emphasizes the Sarajevo precipitant, the primary but not exclusive finger of blame points to Austria–Hungary. If the British had been less ambiguous about their intentions, or if the Russians had been even slower to mobilize, or if the French had been willing to settle for second place position on the continent, the war might have been avoided. As will be demonstrated, there seems a considerable amount of blame to be allocated and a number of directions in which to point. Rather than play the blame game in the traditional sense, it should be more useful to look for a framework that is capable of spreading the blame around for the onset of a regional war that became a global war in a way that no one quite anticipated. Among other things, after all, World War I is supposed to have been the global war that no one really wanted.

At the same time, there may also be some profit in shifting the focus on catalysts or precipitants that may seem accidental in whether they occur or not to "system accidents." System accidents are situations in which machine failures compound their malfunctions in unanticipated fashions and nonlinear interactions to bring about catastrophic breakdowns. International politics do not work like machines but world wars certainly do resemble catastrophic breakdowns of normal processes of world politics. The question is whether the system accident analogy can be employed in a concrete way to illuminate the nature of interaction among multiple rivalries.

System accidents

How is it possible for wars that no one really wants to become truly global affairs? One metaphor for such a phenomenon is offered by Charles Perrow's (1984) study of "systemic accidents." Focusing on disasters such as nuclear reactor breaches, Perrow first breaks down complicated machinery into four levels: each individual part, units that represent collections of parts, subsystemic arrays of units, and systems in which the various subsystemic arrays come together. Of

TABLE 5.2:   Attributes of complex and linear processes

Complex	Linear
Proximity	Spatial segregation
Feedback loops	Few feedback loops
Limited understanding	Extensive understanding

Source: based on Perrow (1984: 88).

least concern are the breakdowns or failures of parts and units, termed "incidents" that have no impact beyond the part or unit level. Machine failures that disrupt the subsystemic or systemic level ("accidents") are more serious, especially if they entail multiple and unanticipated failures at several levels (part, unit, subsystem, and system).

One of the prime ways in which a system accident can occur is attributed to the complex interactions of the various machine components. Linear interactions represent the programmed or designed functioning of the machinery. For instance, we are all familiar with freeway driving. A large number of automobiles, trucks, and motorcycles occupy a fairly small space yet move, some of the time anyway, at high speed without problems. Something unexpected happens – a tire goes flat, a driver falls asleep at the wheel, a deer attempts to cross the road. The unprogrammed event initiates a chain reaction in which one car hits another, and then several more are affected by the initial impact. The outcome can be quite messy with a large number of vehicles damaged and lives lost.

The disaster described above involves a single, initial failure and multiple, unexpected interactions among the components of the freeway system. When components begin interacting in ways not intended by a programmer, the interactions can be described as "nonlinear" and "complex." Table 5.2 elaborates the distinction by summarizing the situations in which interactions may stay linear or become more complex. The problem reduces in many respects to physical insulation. If all the components can be kept apart in ways that do not permit their interaction, linearity or an anticipated outcome is more probable. But machinery is not set up to work that way very often. The parts are often proximate and interconnected in order to make the machinery work the way it is programmed. When failures occur, feedback loops aggravate the level of complexity by creating unanticipated interactions that may not even be recognized at the time – let alone understood in time to do anything about the problem(s).

Perrow makes one more distinction of some utility in analyzing complex interactions. "Tightly coupled" systems allow for no buffer between different parts, units and subsystems. "Loosely coupled" systems provide some amount of insulation, if only in the form of slack, between components. Consequently, the tightly coupled systems respond very quickly to disturbances and, therefore, are more vulnerable to disasters while loosely coupled systems can absorb some level of failure without the entire system being disrupted.

Disaster in a freeway system is one thing; disasters in nuclear reactors or shuttle launches are entirely different matters. So, too, are disasters in international systems. Yet even though individual decision-makers (parts), decision-making groups (units), states (subsystems), and international systems (systems of subsystems) can be equated with Perrow's four level distinctions without much of a stretch, it could be argued that international systems are not the same entities as man-made machinery. Metaphors about machinery failures may be interesting but not transferrable to international relations in which the components are not designed to run as if political interactions were linearly programmed to produce products of peace and stability. No doubt there are limits in applying machine failure metaphors to world politics. However, the utility of the metaphor lies not so much in the machinery imagery as it does in distinguishing between linear and complex interactions and applying them to rivalry structures.[10] The basic point is that dense and proximate rivalry fields are highly susceptible to producing complex and unanticipated interactions. What takes place in one rivalry can have implications for the course of several other rivalries. If they are also tightly coupled, "failures" in one or more rivalry to manage their levels of conflict can spread throughout the system.

For instance, a war breaking out between rival states A and B requires A's rival, state C, to come to the aid of B. State C's assistance to B motivates state D, also a rival to C, to support A. State D proceeds to attack state C and its main ally state E (also D's rival), which, in turn, encourages state F (still another D rival) to enter on the side of states C and E. States C, E, and F had once been rivals to each other but had deescalated their conflicts to better deal with the implications of D's ascendancy in the region and global systems. State F is allied to states A and D but believes it can profit more by switching to the CEF side, in part because states A and F are rivals over territory that A controls

---

[10]Although he does not apply his argument to rivalry structures, Jervis (1997: 17) also displays no reluctance to endorse Perrow's perspective on densely interconnected systems to the analysis of international systems. Lebow (1987) is also quite comfortable with the implications of Perrow's perspective.

and F covets. States G and C are also rivals but G is allied to state F and also stands to gain more in its own region by joining the CEF side. After CEFG and AD become deadlocked on the battlefield, state H becomes motivated to intervene on the CEFG side. The point here is that states A and B (or D and E) were unlikely to foresee that their actions would lead to an eventual CEFGH versus AD showdown in which CEFGH would triumph over the AD combination.[11] A "system accident" can thus become a "system disaster," without anyone fully intending to bring about the actual outcome that eventually emerges. Decision-makers do not plan on global wars when they start smaller-scale wars that sometimes escalate via multiple hostilities, tight coupling, and complex interactions into much wider affairs than anyone initially foresaw.

Who should we blame then for these occasional system meltdowns? If no one can foresee the full scale of hostilities that emerges, is no one responsible? Did the "system" make them do it? Or, is it more accurate to spread the blame throughout the system? As hinted at earlier, assessing blame in complex interaction circumstances is not really all that profitable an endeavor. Variable levels of culpability can be identified, just as various interpretations that center on different actors in the system as the principal culprits can be acknowledged as at least partially accurate. That is to say, it can make sense to focus on German fears of falling behind, Austrian fears of losing imperial control, Russian fears of further humiliation, French desires for revenge, or British reluctance to make explicit their commitments simultaneously if it can be demonstrated that these attributes existed and contributed to priming various rivalries for conflict escalation. The same can be said of analyses that stress Anglo–German power transition or Austro–German–Russian competitions in the Balkans and elsewhere. Neither emphasis need be mutually exclusive forcing us to pick one over the other – unless it can be demonstrated that one or the other genuinely deserves greater explanatory weight. We err by not confronting these alternatives in preference for more single-minded arguments about one factor being the key to explaining World War I.

To pursue this argument further, a sampling of recent arguments about World War I can be examined, albeit only very briefly. The point of such an exercise is not to confront or evaluate the fundamental disagreements about interpretation that they exemplify. We will continue to debate who did what to whom and why in the period leading up to 1914 because the evidence and the statements made by the decision-makers

---

[11] The point here is not that decision-makers on both sides failed to foresee the possibility of defections from one side to the other, but that no one in early 1914 could be expected to predict very well the alignments and war participants of 1917.

themselves can be interpreted in different ways. Rather, the sample reviewed here is meant to reinforce the argument that, in marked contrast to the views advanced in the sample, we would be better off constructing our explanations in the context of the interaction of multiple rivalries or antagonisms that led to what approximates a "system accident" in world politics. Calling the outcome a system accident does not rule out the possibility that some decision-makers actively sought a war – only that no one fully realized just what scale of warfare would actually ensue.

Nor does the occurrence of system accidents rule out the possible utility of giving greater emphasis to catalysts as Lebow argues. Yet an appreciation for ripe rivalry structures – multiple, proximate rivalries many of which are operating at heightened levels of tension and hostility and are also tightly coupled – does tilt us away from the expectation that precipitants will prove to be all that significant. The match that ignites a fire somewhere in a field that is only occasionally prone to either ignition or spreading widely (due to structural causes – e.g., power transitions, arms races, conflicts over spheres of influence, tightly coupled rivalries and so forth) must take on a relatively diminished significance. Streetcars (precipitants) may not always arrive on schedule but their probability of appearance in some form, given the appropriate structural context, is likely to be greater than average.[12]

Multiple rivalries

Recent arguments about the origins of World War I can be translated readily into rivalry interpretations. Dale Copeland (2000) argues that German decision-makers felt that they were militarily preponderant in the first decade of the 20th century but expected to lose this status to a rapidly rebuilding Russia by 1916–17. Crisis diplomacy was attempted up to 1912 when the decision was finally made that a preventive war was the only viable option to stave off the anticipated relative decline. Moreover, there was only a limited window of opportunity to fight such a war before Russian military improvements made it too dangerous to contemplate. War might have broken out that year but was postponed to improve Germany's naval position vis-à-vis Britain.

---

[12]Another way of looking at this issue is to ask whether Franz Ferdinand's assassination would have or could have served as a catalyst to World War I in the absence of a structural context predisposed toward major power warfare? Lebow maintains that we cannot understand the significance of the structural arguments without translating them in terms of the catalyst. But we can turn the logic around just as easily and suggest that the catalyst may have little meaning in the absence of an appropriate structural context.

Niall Ferguson (1999c) blames Germany for forcing a continental war on a reluctant France and a more eager Russia and Britain for transforming a continental war in to a world war unnecessarily. The British behavior was based in part on what is called a "Napoleonic Neurosis." The idea that Germany was the main threat for Britain was couched in language that portrayed Germans seeking full control of Europe via coercive tactics. Once this control was achieved, European resources would be placed at German disposal and would allow Germany to mount a formidable challenge against Britain in the world at large.

Ferguson's complaint is that there was little evidence to support the Napoleonic ambitions attributed to German decision-makers and that, furthermore, British decision-makers were aware that Germany was not in a position to mount such a campaign prior to 1914. He also contends that British decision-makers were not really alarmed by German colonial ambitions and that no one in London felt threatened by the possibility that the Germans might achieve parity with British naval superiority. This interpretation leads Ferguson to suggest that British decision-makers consciously chose to exaggerate the level of German threat in order to justify a commitment to France. Left unclear is why a desired commitment to France preceded an exaggeration of German threat unless, of course, the French connection was considered essential to meeting an emerging German threat.

Paul Schroeder (2006) contends that the primary cause of World War I was the breakdown of the relationships among the Austro-German–Russian triangle, linking the three major powers of the European core. For the most part, two of the triangle's dyads (Austria and Russia and Prussia/Germany and Russia) had managed to avoid fighting one another. Prussia/Germany and Austria had been intense rivals and had fought, but only rarely and not for extended periods of time. In general, the modal relationship within the triangle had been one of cautious cooperation and even alliance, creating a type of long peace at the European epicenter. The long peace prevailed as long as the three did not seek to exclude one of the three by force from the sub-regions in which they were engaged in positional competitions or, more seriously, to destroy any of the members of the triangle. The long peace broke down when Russia began seeking the elimination of Austria after 1908–9. The European region then became involved in a general war that could only have begun in southeastern Europe.

Edward McCullough (1999) emphasizes French attacks on the post-1871 European status quo. Alliance with Russia in 1894 threatened German predominance which was further aided by the French enlistment of the British in its anti-German coalition. Its confidence boosted by its external support, France proceeded to challenge Germany over Morocco in the first decade of the 20th century, even though its ultimate goal was to secure the return of Alsace-Lorraine. World War I thus reduces to a Germany on the defensive ultimately deciding on war to preserve the existence of its Austrian ally which was also acting in the Balkans on grounds of self-preservation.

These four arguments intersect in some places and diverge extremely in others. Copeland (2000) stresses the Russo–German rivalry as central. Ferguson (1999c) emphasizes the Anglo–German rivalry. Schroeder (2006) argues that World War I stemmed from a breakdown in the Austro–German–Russian triangle, with particular emphasis on the Austro–Russian rivalry. McCullough (1999) accentuates the Franco–Germany rivalry. In his own argument, Lebow (this volume) notes the significance of the Franco–German, Russo–German, and Anglo–German rivalries, among several others. This is not the place to sort out the evidence for their various specific interpretations. One need not accept all of their claims as equally plausible in noting, however, that they are all engaged in implicit and explicit forms of rivalry analysis – even if they never even use the word "rivalry." Nor does it require much of a stretch of the imagination to suggest that all of the named rivalries probably had something to do with the initiation of World War I. Rather than privilege one or two of the rivalries as the main culprits, why not implicate all or almost all of them in a nonlinear interaction of multiple adversarial relationships?

This is not the same thing as saying that all of the rivalries were equally important to the war onset. Some played relatively minor or secondary roles. The rivalries among France, Italy, and Austria were probably not major factors. The course of the Serbian–Turkish rivalry (and those involving Greece, Bulgaria, and Turkey as well) seems to have indirectly escalated tensions in the Austro–Serbian rivalry. War in the Russo–Japanese rivalry definitely weakened Russia; consequent attempts to rebuild the Russian military machine alarmed the Germans. Somewhat secondarily, the preliminary negotiations first between Germany and Austria and later between Britain and France, the United States, and Russia to either terminate or deescalate temporarily (in the Anglo–Russian case) their rivalries made the bipolarization of the great powers possible. One could also relegate the German–U.S. rivalry to the secondary category as far as the 1914 onset was concerned; the entry of the United States into the war in 1917 would be a different matter.

According secondary or minor status to eight rivalries still leaves five major ones. Austria–Russia, Austria–Serbia, Britain–Germany, France–Germany, Germany–Russia all seem significant to the initial outbreak of war, and its subsequent escalation to continental and world scale. All five rivalries experienced increases in hostility and tension in the decades leading up to 1914. In that sense, all five were primed toward exchanging greater conflict, not less. Of the five, only the Anglo-German one may have been moving away from an upward spiral of greater animosity just before 1914.

Two sets of rivalries were tightly coupled in Perrow's language. The rivalries linking Austria, Serbia, and Russia formed one triangular set. Anything Austria did to Serbia reverberated in the Austro-Russian rivalry. The rivalries linking Germany to France, Russia, and Britain formed a quadrilateral set. What Germany did to France reverberated in the Anglo-German and Russo-German rivalries even if Germany's attack on France was only a prelude to an attack on Russia. But the Franco-Russian alliance meant that the triangular and quadrilateral sets were also coupled fairly tightly. Thus, action beginning in the Austro-Russian-Serbian triangle was highly likely to affect the other cluster of rivalries no matter who lit the match. However, neither Serbia nor Russia, thanks to their relative weaknesses, were likely to attack Austria prior to 1914 even though their rivalries had escalated in animosity and tension levels. Austria, on the other hand, had the incentive and capability to attack Serbia. All it seemed to require was a reason and encouragement from its German ally. Once these prerequisites were satisfied and Austria was prepared to attack, Russia became the next link in the chain reaction. If it made no move to come to the aid of Serbia, the ensuing war could have been a brief dyadic affair between Austria and Serbia. If Russia mobilized against both Austria and Germany, Germany would probably have been in the fray, regardless of whether German decision-makers desired an opportunity for a preemptive strike against Russia. If Germany was in that meant France would probably be attacked according to the Schlieffen Plan. An attack on France increased the probability that Britain would enter the war. None of these outcomes was inevitable but the structure of multiple and interactive rivalries made the outcomes more probable once certain preconditions were met. For instance, the Serbian response to the Austrian ultimatum did not seem to matter much. But the extent of Russian mobilization did matter. The German continuing commitment to the Schlieffen Plan was also critical to stimulating the full interaction across the rivalry structure. Arguably, the German naval challenge and the related conflicts over colonies and markets were critical to maintaining the British connections to the Britain-France-Germany-Russia quadrilateral. Arms race on land, it has been argued, at least contributed to the perception of various states catching up and others falling behind. Moreover, war breaking out almost anywhere among the main five rivalries, again given the impressive potential for coupled, nonlinear interaction, might have led to the same or similar outcome.

Generalizing the argument

Writing essays about events that occurred some 90 years ago, of course, is one thing. The social science problem is to develop some generalized appreciation of how ripening rivalry fields may explode into a world war that was not fully intended by anyone. Can we develop some way of detecting a ripening rivalry field before it explodes? The main problem at this juncture is that we do not have a strong understanding of individual rivalry dynamics. Why do rivalries begin, escalate, deescalate, and terminate? If we fully understood what drives rivalries, we could probably aggregate this understanding to a field of rivalries. But, we are just beginning to work on these questions after long ignoring the explanatory potential of rivalries. Excuses aside, we do have some strong analytical clues with which to work. These clues probably will not enable us to incorporate Schlieffen Plans, German obsessions about Russian military reform, or Russian hostility toward Austria. That is to say, it is not likely that we can bring all of the 1914 details into a model at this time. Yet we can make a start in modeling why rivalry fields escalate nonlinearly.

Generalizing nonlinear rivalry ripeness

The question is can a more general argument be developed that links multiple rivalries to nonlinear war expansion? We can start with some clues about conflict escalation in rivalry contexts. We know that serial conflict within rivalries increases the probability of war within the concerned dyads (Leng 1983; Colaresi and Thompson 2002). That is, the first clash in a rivalry has X probability of escalating into warfare. The second clash has $X + n$ probability, and so on. Multiple clashes in a relatively short period of time do not make warfare inevitable but they do enhance the likelihood of warfare. Within a field of rivalries, a pattern of increasing serial clashes within multiple rivalries should be indicative of a "ripening" rivalry field. Such a field would be ripening because more and more rivalries within the field are experiencing a greater probability of escalating to warfare.

A second clue involves the oft-invoked argument about the bipolarization of the principal disputants. This structural feature speaks explicitly to Perrow's coupling distinction. More tightly coupled situations are more likely to lead to nonlinear breakdowns than less tightly coupled circumstances. Accordingly, the bipolarization of contending rivals, the ultimate form of a tightly coupled structure, should increase the probability of a nonlinear breakdown of relationships.

A third clue speaks to the structural background of rivalries such as the Anglo-German and Franco-German antagonisms. Both represented transitional processes in which one state was being overtaken by another. "Power transitions" represent a structural dynamic that are thought to be especially dangerous. They are also a more specific instance of rivalries that are ripe for conflict escalation. On the one hand, the overtaking actor is optimistic about its chances of defeating a declining leader. On the other, the actor being overtaken is anxious about its loss of a long held position and the political-economic implications for the future. As they approach some semblance of parity, they are thought to become increasingly likely to fight (Organski and Kugler 1980; Tammen et al. 2000). The Anglo-German transitional case is well known. We may argue about the extent to which Germany had overtaken Britain and why Britain was more alarmed about German positional improvements than it was U.S. positional gains, but there is little debate about whether global structural transition was at work.[13]

The Franco-German case is more ambiguous. Observers often focus on Alsace-Lorraine or Moroccan territorial disputes that certainly existed but overlook a more persistent problem. Since the mid-17th century, France had been the largest and most powerful actor in the West European region. The defeats suffered by Louis XIV and Napoleon had not entirely altered that fact. The defeat experienced in the 1870-1 Franco-Prussian War did seriously damage France's claim to being the leading regional power on the European continent but it did not fully resolve the issue. Germany became the leading European military and economic power after 1871, but French decision-makers were not yet fully convinced of their loss of the regional lead. Hence, Alsace-Lorraine might be the more obtrusive index of regional discontent, but there was also an underlying and lingering structural question of regional hierarchy at stake. As long as the German lead over France was not too insurmountable, French decision-makers might hope to regain their regional lead, especially if allies could be mobilized to support the effort.

---

[13] See, for instance, the arguments found in Tammen et al. (2000), Ingram (2001) and Thompson (1999, 2001a).

Power transitions can be strictly dyadic in character. But those power transitions that are most central to global and regional pecking orders are the ones that are least likely to remain dyadic.[14] Their outcomes are important to too many other actors and their own hierarchical positions. This is another example of coupling at work. A Russian–Japanese struggle in then-peripheral East Asia, particularly one that is waged less than conclusively, is less likely to entice third party participation than is a similar positional struggle involving the world's main region and the constitution of global order. Even the United States ultimately could not stay aloof from the European combat that began in 1914.[15]

These more general arguments about serial conflict sequences, bipolarization, and structural transitions give us four different reasons to anticipate a stronger likelihood of nonlinear conflict expansion. It would be ideal if we could also incorporate Schroeder's insights on the course of Austro-Russian relations or Copeland's argument that Germany was most concerned about being unable to deal with Russia in the future. However, Schroeder's perspective does not lend itself readily to the sort of generalization that we might actually put to the test unless we could measure abrupt changes in Austrian perceptions about Russia over a period of time. Copeland's argument is operationable but, not unlike Schroeder's emphasis on the Austro-Russian-German triangle, it requires some acceptance of the assumption that the German–Russian rivalry was the principal concern of German decision-makers. The evidence for such an assumption remains debatable. The assumption also runs counter to the argument currently being explored on the interaction of multiple rivalries. None of these factors are reasons for ignoring arguments about fluctuations in the "temperatures" of specific rivalries but they do go beyond our current ability to tap into and monitor rivalry temperatures. Until we can improve on this ability, it seems preferable to put such concerns aside in the interim.

---

[14]Rasler and Thompson (1994) argue and find empirical support for the idea that, between 1494 and 1945, global wars represented situations in which declining global leaders were challenged by European regional leaders.

[15]We have historical myths that U.S. intervention in World War I was "to save democracy" or because of German interference with U.S. shipping and there is, as usual, some substance to these myths. But the most succinct explanation for U.S. involvement is that it could not afford to stay on the sidelines given the world order issues at stake, especially if its involvement could decide the outcome. A little more than a month before the U.S entry into the war, President Wilson told a group of pacifists visiting the White House that war was inevitable and that as the leader of a war participant he could expect to be a part of the post-war negotiations. But if he was the leader of a neutral country, he could only "call through a crack in the door" (Knock 1992: 120). This anecdote hardly nails down the U.S. motivation(s) for war joining. It does suggest that this particular motivation was not alien to the incumbent president.

Thus, we have at least three hypotheses about nonlinear conflict escalation in world politics:

> H1: As an increasing number of adjacent rivalries experience serial clashes, the probability of nonlinear conflict expansion increases.

> H2: As the major actors in world politics become increasingly bipolarized, the probability of nonlinear conflict expansion increases.

> H3: As central power transitions take place, the probability of nonlinear conflict expansion increases.

To these three, we can add a fourth:

> H4: As more of these structural changes associated with conflict escalation occur simultaneously, the probability of nonlinear conflict expansion (and interaction among the main variables) increases even more so.

Each of the independent variables can be operationalized for the period leading up to the outbreak of war in 1914. Assuming that the 1914-1918 combat can be equated with a nonlinear expansion of conflict, the empirical question becomes whether these processes take sharp upward turns immediately prior to 1914, and only prior to 1914. With only one instance of the dependent variable, there are rather major limitations on imputing causality.[16] Yet if we were to examine the nearly 100 years between the end of the Napoleonic Wars and the outbreak of World War I and find that the additive effects of rivalry disputatiousness, bipolarization, and central power transitions came together in a unique conjuncture in the years preceding 1914, we would have evidence that at least supports the notion that such factors are linked to "systemic accidents."

---

[16]World War I is not the only instance of nonlinear expansion conceivable. World War II and the Cold War also are worth examining in this context but space considerations preclude dealing with their complexities in a single examination. Earlier global wars, such as the 1792 outbreak, could also be examined but not necessarily with the same empirical rigor. With more variance in the dependent variable, it could be profitable to elaborate this theory with additional considerations that work towards and away from a global war outcome. Arms races, polarity, economic interdependence, democratic peace, and nuclear weapons come to mind as possible extensions. Another type of coupling worth examining more closely is the extent to which rivalries overlap. One could also test empirically for interaction effects among the variables.

Measurement

Three types of indicators – for multiple, serial disputes within rivalry fields, bipolarization, and central power transitions – need to be fashioned. They also need to encompass a long, pre-World War I era so that we can assess the extent to which structural circumstances changed just prior to 1914. The end of the Napoleonic warfare in 1815 seems as good a place to start as any. We would not want to go before 1815 because the 1792–1815 fighting has nonlinear connotations of its own and, of course, there are major data availability problems. Any other starting point between 1816 and 1914 would be arbitrary and might miss something of interest.

Identifying serial disputes within rivalries is a fairly straightforward proposition although it does require some explicit rules. All rivalries involving two European actors or two major powers that were operative between 1816 and 1913 were first isolated. Next, the beginning dates of any militarized interstate disputes (MIDs), the one standardized indicator of conflict (Jones, Bremer and Singer 1996) other than wars currently available for the 19th century, in which the pertinent dyads were involved were listed. Each successive dispute receives a successively higher number as long as the next dispute in the sequence took place within ten years of the one that preceded it. For instance, the Austrian–French dyad had MIDs in 1840, 1848, and 1888. The 1840 dispute received a score of one as the first dispute in the sequence. The 1848 dispute, occurring within ten years of 1840, received a score of two (as the second dispute). The third dispute in 1888 is not considered part of the earlier sequence and thus reverts to a score of one as the "first" dispute in a later sequence that failed to evolve.

Each of these differentially weighted dispute events are then assigned to the year in which they began. Each year's scores are aggregated and then multiplied by the number of rivalries engaged in a dispute in that year. The assumption here is that some mechanism needs to be in place to distinguish between circumstances in which one rivalry is very disputatious in a short period of time and those in which several rivalries are actively conflictual.[17]

This approach is quite conservative in most respects. Ten years may be too restrictive for decision-makers and populations with longer memories. A second or third dispute may deserve a higher score than one or two more points than the first dispute. Yet some coding rules

---

[17] A year in which one rivalry engaged in its fifth dispute in a sequence would generate the same score as a year in which five different rivalries participated in their first dispute in a sequence. The problem here is to avoid giving too much weight to the fifth dispute in a sequence and too much to multiple rivalries just beginning sequences.

are obviously needed. Disputes that are separated by too many years should not be regarded as belonging to the same sequence. Or, put another way, as more and more years intervene between disputes, it becomes less clear whether participants are likely to view themselves as sliding into a dispute sequence. Where exactly we should draw the lines between the start and ending of one sequence and a following one is not self-evident. Nor is the precise weighting formula for disputes within a sequence obvious either. As we start to think of disputes and crises more as serial phenomena, better mousetraps for capturing their sequential quality, no doubt, will be forthcoming.[18]

Bipolarization is not as easy to measure as one might think. Analysts need to know the identity of the poles are around which the mutual exclusive clustering takes place.[19] Yet knowing who the poles are after the war has been fought is one thing. Knowing who to tap as the structured interaction begins to take place is quite another. An additional problem is that the poles around which bipolarization may or may not take place are not necessarily the same poles that might be identified by polarity standards. For instance, in retrospect, the poles of attraction in the pre-World War I setting were Germany and France. One could not have foreseen this development in 1816 or 1848. Nor were Germany and France so powerful that they could be said to have constituted the two poles in a bipolar power structure outside of western Europe.

To avoid using information about the bipolarization that emerged most obviously between 1915 and 1917, Wayman's (1985) alliance polarization index is employed as a bipolarization indicator. Wayman counts the number of major powers that form blocs by possessing defense pacts with each other.[20] He then counts the number of "poles" (the number of blocs plus the number of nonbloc major powers) and calculates the ratio of actual poles to potential poles (or the total number of major powers). An index score that approaches 1.0 indicates

---

[18]A case in point is the Correlates of War research program on dispute density sometimes referred to as "enduring rivalry" analysis. Over the past 20 years, a number of different criteria have been put forward to measure how "dense" dispute activity is. At one point it was hoped that Diehl and Goertz's (2000) conventions about three classes (isolated, proto, and enduring rivalries) of density, which seem to be the most widely accepted stipulations, could be utilized for the construction of this index. It turned out, however, that their categorizations depended too much on disputes assigned to the 1914–18 interval to be of much use for the 1816–1913 era.

[19]A distinction is being made here between polarity which addresses the distribution of power and polarization which taps into the extent to which behavior clusters around the poles (see, among others, Rapkin, Thompson, and Christopherson 1979).

[20]Looking only at defense pacts underestimates the degree of bipolarization in general but especially in the pre-1914 setting in which ententes figured prominently. Thus, the Wayman score is also conservative.

multipolarization while a score that approaches 0.0 is most likely to signify bipolarization. For present purposes, the Wayman score is subtracted from 1.0 so that bipolarized settings have high scores as opposed to low ones.

Power transitions are often measured in terms of a diminishing gap between a once dominant state and an overtaking challenger (see, for instance, Organski and Kugler 1980). However, to do so in this context would again require knowing who fought whom in World War I. Rather than measure the diminishing gaps between Britain and Germany and France and Germany, indexes tapping into the relative positions of the global and regional leaders are used instead. The global leader in the 1816-1913 period was Britain. Its relative position is measured in terms of its share of major power leading sector production (Thompson 1988: 140). To index increasing structural dangers, the share is subtracted from 1.0, with a higher score indicating a stronger probability of global structural transition. France is viewed as the European regional leader between 1816 and 1871 with Germany replacing it after 1871. Regional leadership is measured in terms of share of European major power armies (Rasler and Thompson 1994: 197-98). Since these scores tend to be low after a defeat in global war (as in the Napoleonic Wars), rising scores are viewed as more troublesome. In this case, then, there is no need to reverse the scale.

Table 5.3 summarizes the data measurement outcomes. Conceivably, the measurement could have been carried out on an annual basis but Wayman's alliance polarization and Rasler and Thompson's army data are available in five-year intervals while Thompson's (1988) leading sector position information was published in ten-year intervals. Accordingly, the second column provides a normalized measure of sequential disputatiousness within the European/major power rivalry field.[21] The propensity for sequential conflicts was low in the first half of the 19th century, increased briefly in the middle of the century, and then remained relatively low until the turn of the century. Sequential disputatiousness did not ramp linearly upward in the early part of the 20th century. Instead, there was something of a lull between 1895-1905 before the explosion after 1910.

Part of the problem was an increase in the sheer number of rivalries. Table 5.4 indicates that the number of pertinent rivalries doubled after 1873. Many of these new rivalries were concentrated in southeastern Europe and increased their disputatiousness in the two decades leading

---

[21] The sequential disputatiousness numbers are recast setting the highest score to 1.00 and then recalculating every other interval's score as a proportion of the highest original score.

TABLE 5.3: Indicators for nonlinear conflict expansion

Years	Rivalry density	Alliance bipol.	Global leader decline	Reg. leader ascent	Aver. score
1815–19	.011	.60	.451	.050	.278
1820–24	.011	.80	.451	.230	.373
1825–29	.114	.20	.451	.188	.238
1830–34	.125	.20	.357	.192	.219
1835–39	.015	.40	.357	.213	.246
1840–44	.162	.60	.417	.150	.332
1845–49	.140	.40	.417	.191	.287
1850–54	.324	.20	.454	.204	.296
1855–59	.430	.20	.454	.245	.332
1860–64	.051	.17	.500	.187	.227
1865–69	.143	.17	.500	.159	.243
1870–74	.162	.00	.481	.156	.200
1875–79	.254	.17	.481	.176	.270
1880–84	.081	.17	.570	.178	.250
1885–89	.283	.33	.570	.192	.344
1890–94	.007	.33	.667	.182	.297
1895–99	.577	.44	.667	.167	.463
1900–04	.463	.38	.755	.159	.439
1905–09	.452	.50	.755	.172	.470
1910–13	1.000	.50	.854	.304	.665

up to the outbreak of global war, as demonstrated most dramatically in the two Balkan wars. But other rivalries also exhibited tendencies toward escalation of various kinds. As many as ten rivalries had three or more MIDs in the two decades immediately prior to World War I. Half involved Turkey as one of the rivals but the other half included Britain–Germany, Austria–Serbia, Japan–Russia, Britain–France, and Britain–United States. Of this group, the last three were deescalated intentionally, along with others, in order to concentrate, in part, on the first two.

The third column in table 5.3 lists Wayman's alliance polarization scores. Aside from a few early anomalies due primarily to the initial but gradually eroding nature of the consensus on French containment, the polarization scores begin to creep upward after the early 1880s. The fourth column, global leadership decline, also indicates an acceleration

TABLE 5.4:   Rivalries and the number and timing of militarized disputes, 1816–1913

Rivalry	1816–1833	1834–1853	1854–1873	1874–1893	1894–1913
Austria–France		2		1	
Austria–Italy		3	2	1	2
Austria–Prussia		1	3		
Austria–Russia			4		1
Austria–Serbia					4
Austria–Turkey		1		2	2
Britain–France	1	1		3	4
Britain–Germany					3
Britain–Russia	1	3	4	4	
Britain–U.S.A.					5
Bulgaria–Turkey					4
France–Germany	4	2	6	3	1
France–Italy				1	1
France–Russia	2	3	3		
Germany–U.S.A.				1	2
Greece–Serbia					1
Greece–Turkey				6	6
Italy–Turkey				2	6
Japan–Russia			3		7
Russia–Turkey	8	1		5	4
Serbia–Turkey					3
Number of Disputes	16	17	25	29	56
Number of Rivalries	11	12	13	22	25
Disputes/Rivalries	1.46	1.42	1.92	1.32	2.24

Note: Disputes that occurred either when a dyad was not in a rivalry relationship or when a non-European major power was not a major power are omitted.

of British decline from at least the 1880s on. Only the fifth column, regional leadership, contributes little to the general suggestion of incipient structural problems. There is little genuine fluctuation prior to the very end of the 1816–1913 period suggesting that neither France nor Germany, in contrast to Philip II, Louis XIV, or Napoleon, created armies that were meant to dominate the region prior to 1914 based largely on their numerical size.[22]

The sixth column in table 5.3 lists the average of columns two through five. As illustrated in figure 5.1, combining the different sources of structural change leads to an outcome that fluctuated roughly around the 0.25–0.30 level from 1816 through the early 1890s. After 1895, the average scores nearly doubled and in the few years just before 1914, the mean structural change index more than doubled what had been the norm throughout most of the 19th century after 1815. The conjunction of these structural changes did not mean that a world war had to break out in 1914. But their conjunction apparently made a violent reaction of some kind more likely because we know that historically some of these types of structural change have been associated with intense conflict. France and Spain fought repeatedly over European regional leadership between the end of the 15th and the middle of the 17th centuries. No global leadership transition has yet managed to avoid a prolonged period of intensive combat.[23] We also know that serial clashes within rivalries tend to lead to escalation and war. It stands to reason that the more rivalries that are in this situation, the greater are the chances for the expansion of the wars that do break out. We also know that bipolarization need not lead to war but that it does tend to align and couple potential combatants in a head-to-head confrontational array. Alliance commitments can be ignored when it comes time to fight but the commitments also tell us something about whose interests are deemed most and least compatible. When all or most major powers have aligned themselves on one side or the other, there is less room for compromise and negotiation. There is also more room for suspicion and misperception concerning the other side's motivations and intentions.

---

[22]Different measurement emphases on regional leadership would lead to different conclusions. For example, the regional shares are suppressed somewhat by the inclusion of Russian army sizes which grew increasingly large but not necessarily as powerful as the numbers suggest. Alternatively, an emphasis on the distribution of economic innovation would show Germany in a much stronger position than its continental rivals and one that came to approximate the British position. A stress on the quality of military force would also improve Germany's relative position.

[23]Consider, for example, the fighting in 1494–1516, 1580–1608, 1688–1713, 1792–1815, and 1914–1945.

FIGURE 5.1:   Structural change and nonlinear potential

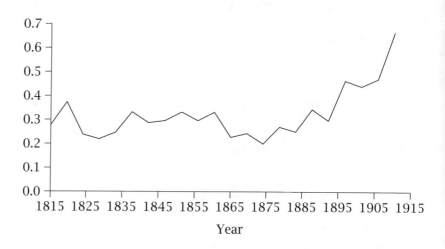

Any one of the four types of structural change could be anticipated to increase the probability of conflict. When all four, or some combination of the four, come together at one time, we should be able to anticipate a compounded additive effect and an increased probability of conflict. In the 1914 case, the probability of conflict appears to have been increased tremendously. This is why structural arguments invoke the metaphor of a dry stack of firewood ready for combustion and awaiting a precipitant of some sort. Sarajevo provided that spark in 1914. If Sarajevo had not occurred, something else might have (not would have) led to the same outcome because structural conditions were acutely ready for some type of combustion. Both the confluence of multiple processes of structural stress and the outbreak of war in the Austro-Serbian rivalry combined to make a nonlinear expansion of the conflict more likely - or so the data would suggest.

Conclusion

In 1923, George P. Gooch published his Creighton Lecture in which he (Gooch 1923: 3) argued that World War I was the outcome of "three separate but simultaneous antagonisms": the Franco-German conflict over Alsace-Lorraine, the Austro-Russian conflict over southeastern

Europe, and the Anglo–German conflict over sea power.[24] He was on the right track back then, even if he did not follow up on his own lead. Somehow, we have collectively been diverted down countless analytical tangents since then. It is high time that we return to the theme of separate but simultaneous and overlapping antagonisms as a general, synthesizing explanation of major power warfare. Lebow's argument about catalysts almost returned attention to this theme but his presentation was essentially sidetracked by an emphasis on catalysts and contingency. Contingencies surely happen but if we become too seduced by their presence, it becomes all too easy to be diverted from more comprehensive theory construction and empirical analysis efforts. Catalysts may prove to be more important than we realize but the burden of evidence is still out on that question. Even if catalysts should be promoted from minor to major cause status, the elevation in their status need not alter the way we go about crafting explanations.

Yet it is not just a field of multiple proximate rivalries that should receive more attention. It is the potential for unanticipated, nonlinear interactions between the ones that are most strongly coupled, and the systemic contexts in which they emerge, that should be of most interest. We may not yet know why some rivalries escalate to war while others do not, but we do have some strong clues about how sets of rivalries can make war escalation even more probable than the circumstances driving any of the individual rivalries. At the risk of relying on still another metaphor, one could say that the whole is more dangerous than the sum of its parts. These nonlinear interactions across multiple rivalries can probably be found in other major power war onsets. They certainly need not be restricted to major power wars.[25] Minor powers are capable of creating complicated rivalry structures, although it seems likely that the potential for minor power rivalry fields to explode in nonlinear ways is more limited than situations involving major powers. None the less, the empirical verdict on the dangers of nonlinear interactions remains open-ended. An examination of the 1816–1913 era is only a suggestive beginning – not the conclusive solution.

---

[24] As the title of his book indicates, Gooch chose to concentrate exclusively on only one of the three rivalries in his book. Interestingly, he argued that Franco-German relations were relatively pacific as long as France pursued imperial expansion outside of Europe and clashed with Britain, at least until Morocco. Nevertheless, France would always have been receptive to Russia as long as France had some possibility of resolving its old German quarrel to its own satisfaction. In other words, this structural proclivity did not require an intense interest in the fate of Alsace–Lorraine. It only required that the issue remain open-ended.

[25] Lebow (this volume) counts the end of the Cold War, a case of rivalry termination among other things, as an instance of nonlinear effects.

Yet the nonlinear potential for making dangerous situations even more dangerous should also alert us to the possibilities inherent in any future major power war onset – assuming that some potential for that kind of problem still exists. We have something new to look for – a field of interconnected rivalries (or their absence) – and perhaps an even more subtle problem – nonlinear interactions among rivalries – instead of malign expansionists, decision-makers frightened for their declining state's future, territorial irredentism, or statesmen reluctant to make explicit commitments. What we may have to worry most about, as Lebow suggests, are their interaction effects. Given our tendencies to focus on monocausal arguments, it should not be surprising that we do not have much practice either looking for them or dealing with them analytically. Until we gain more experience of this sort, it is difficult to estimate just how significant nonlinear interaction effects may prove to be in explaining the spread of war beyond what was anticipated by decision-makers. But, even if it is a very rare phenomenon, it seems worthy of our further attention.

Yet where does this argument fit vis-à-vis causal explanations in general, and this volume in particular? There are at least five areas of overlap. The most obvious area of overlap pertains to the call for more explicit and self-conscious attention to the nature of our causal arguments. As Gary Goertz and Jack S. Levy put it in their introduction "by being more self-conscious we hope to contribute to the clarification of existing arguments and the formulation of better ones." It is most difficult to argue with calls for clarification and improved formulations. Too often, we authors allow our arguments to become either too complex or too vague to be of optimal use. We should be prepared to discuss whether the causal claims that are being advanced are "necessary" (*Y* would not have occurred in the absence of *X*), "sufficient" (*Y* occurred because *X* occurred), or "contributing" (*X* made *Y* more probable in some way). We should not leave it to readers to guess which of the three best applies because we only facilitate our arguments being misinterpreted. Thus, by all means, we all should strive for more self-consciousness, more clarification, and improved causal formulations. Along the way, authors may even learn something overlooked in our own arguments.

The second area of overlap follows from the first one. Goertz and Levy would probably describe the argument between Lebow and myself as one of powder keg versus spark. Lebow is stressing the catalytic significance of the Archduke's assassination while I am emphasizing the environmental context of structural deconcentration, multiple rivalries, and polarization. Both of us seem to accept the "necessity" for both powder keg and spark. Neither one of us is arguing that either the powder keg or the spark is sufficient. Metaphorically speaking, neither one of us would deny the need for both powder keg and spark to create an explosion. But Lebow is saying that you cannot interpret the nature of the explosion in the absence of a strong appreciation for the spark. In contrast, I am not convinced that is the case. If sparks are substitutable and can take a variety of forms, one could argue that our theoretical attention would best be placed in delineating the nature of the powder keg. If sparks are unique and rare, then, by all means, we must improve our understanding of their interaction. However, I do not see how we can pick between these alternatives on the basis of a single case. Nor am I prepared to argue that the powder keg I outline and the spark Lebow emphasizes were sufficient to bring about World War I.[26] It is one thing to recognize the contribution and even the necessity of some factors. It is quite another to be confident that nothing more was needed to generate the 1914–18 outcome.

These considerations raise three more areas of contention. One has to do with the extreme causal awkwardness of spending as much time as we do with a single case such as World War I. This type of activity, of course, is much less awkward for historians than it is for social scientists. Historians are trained to value idiosyncratic events. But since I identify with the latter tribe more than I do with the former group, I find it exceedingly awkward to discuss necessary and sufficient causes of a single event. My interest in World War I relates to the 1914–18 fighting as an instance of global war or wars fought to determine which states will be privileged in influencing the postwar order, rules, and structure (e.g., Thompson 1988, 1992; Rasler and Thompson 1994, 2000, 2001). Therefore, my first priority lies not in attempting to explain why war broke out in the late summer of 1914. Rather, my first concern relates to explaining why and when global wars are more or less likely to occur. This type of prioritizing implies backing away in the causal funnel from the most immediate precipitants of any single instance of global war outbreak.[27] It should hardly be surprising, then, that I prefer to stress the causal significance of structural factors over catalytic factors. Archdukes, for better or worse, are not assassinated all that often. That the assassination of a specific Archduke served as a precipitant in 1914 cannot be denied. On the other hand, I do not know how to assess fully the claim that without that particular precipitant, global war would not have occurred. If I am right that the structural factors were most important in establishing a context in which various

---

[26]Obviously, I am not equating an Austro–Serbian war with World War I.

[27]Lebow, however, certainly disagrees.

sparks could lead to nonlinear outcomes, the ultimate significance of any given spark must be diminished (or dimmed?)

At the same time, it deserves to be emphasized that, not unlike roses, a spark is a spark. Yet powder kegs come in all sizes. Perhaps it should be made more explicit that I think the size of the 1914 powder keg was quite substantial. Moreover, the large size of the powder keg – the confluence of multiple rivalries, structural change, and polarization – is crucial to explaining not simply the outbreak of an Austrian–Serbian war, but rather the outbreak of a global war that eventually involved all of the major powers including the non-European ones. Sometimes, in assessing causal explanations, it makes a difference what one thinks is being explained. Many authors on the causes of World War I focus on explaining why war broke out when it did. That translates into accounting for the Austrian attack on Serbia and the subsequent entry of a number of other actors.[28] Frequently, this type of explanation takes the form of who did and said what to whom in the weeks leading up to the outbreak of war. There is certainly nothing inappropriate about this strategy. Yet an emphasis on decision-making tends to lead to explanations about war that assume that all wars are the same in an abstract sense.[29] What happened immediately prior to an outbreak can be critical to explaining the sub(con)sequent outcome which, in our case, happens to be war. My hunch is that such an approach may be more appropriate for some wars than for others. For relatively rare global wars involving all of the major powers in some sort of showdown conflagration, I doubt that focusing on the narrow end of the causal funnel will suffice to capture necessary and sufficient causes because the size and complexity of the powder keg is too easily forgotten.

Finally, I worry that a renewed emphasis on necessary and sufficient causes may detract from developing relative weights for multivariate explanations. Necessary and sufficient conceptualization tends to lead to dichotomous thinking and theorizing – as in, if X, then Y. We can hedge our bets by injecting some probability – if X, then the probability of Y is enhanced – but such arguments too often take on a binary form. One can certainly entertain ideas about multiple necessary and sufficient causes and perhaps even the notion that different mixes of necessary/sufficient variables can lead to similar outcomes. Yet that still falls short of being able to say that one factor is much more important than the other, or that the causal impact of a third variable

---

[28] Still, the perspective on war entrants tends to be restricted to the five European major powers that first entered the war in 1914.

[29] Levy (this volume) is a noteworthy exception to this tendency because he differentiates among local and wider war assessments.

may be significant but still relatively trivial in terms of its effect. These are the sort of outcomes that are more likely to emerge in empirical testing of theoretical arguments. Ideally, we might start with theories that go beyond telling us which factors are important by informing us which variables are more important. If indeed multivariate explanations are more persuasive in general than are univariate explanations, being self-conscious about what is causally "necessary" and "sufficient" may not be enough. We need to be equally self-conscious about the likely relative causal weights of various factors – whether they are thought to be necessary, sufficient, or merely contributing – if we wish to improve our causal formulations.

Chapter 6

Necessary conditions and World War I as an unavoidable war

Paul W. Schroeder

This essay[1] attempts to address the question of whether World War I was inevitable or not primarily through counterfactual argument rather than by directly asking whether necessary and sufficient conditions were present and whether these account for its outbreak. Its thesis and methodology, however, do bear on the issue of the necessary conditions for the outbreak of World War I for the following reasons. First, the beginning of any war obviously always means the termination of a state of peace. The two actions or events are coterminous and equivalent, two sides of the same coin. This is more than a truism; it applies particularly to World War I and contributes powerfully to its enormous significance. As everyone knows, the war terminated both the longest period of great-power peace in European history (no wars among European great power from 1871 to 1914) and, equally remarkable, a whole century of general peace, i.e., no general or systemic war among the powers since 1815. A fundamental assumption of this essay is that peace in history generally, but above all this remarkable long peace, did not just happen but was caused. The problematics of necessary and sufficient conditions apply as much to the active maintenance of peace as to its termination by acts or declarations of war. Without attempting systematically to pursue the question of what the necessary conditions were for the maintenance of general peace throughout most of the 19th century, my aim here will be to show that war at this juncture became unavoidable, not (or

---

[1] An earlier version entitled "Embedded counterfactuals and World War I as an un-avoidable war" was published in *Systems, stability, and statecraft: essays in international history by Paul W. Schroeder,* edited by David Wetzel, Robert Jervis, and Jack S. Levy (New York: Palgrave, 2004).

at least not necessarily) because necessary, sufficient, and compelling conditions at this moment in 1914 produced the particular acts and declarations of war, but rather because certain conditions and actions necessary to the further maintenance of peace were not taken; that these actions were not taken, moreover, not because they were objectively infeasible but because they had become subjectively unthinkable; and finally that the nonperformance of these actions constituted the absence of conditions necessary for the further maintenance of peace and thus rendered war unavoidable.

This line of reasoning has implications for both the necessary-conditions debate and that over contingency versus determinism – implications that (I hope) will become more clear in the concrete argument. Suffice it to say here that if my argument is determinist, as it appears and as most take it, it is so in a way different from other determinist arguments. It can, for example, accept that the particular events that led to a general crisis and war in 1914 were full of contingency and chance, as R. N. Lebow argues elsewhere in this volume, or that the particular actions taken by various governments in 1914 represented concrete decisions by statesmen who considered and rejected alternative courses of action, as David Stevenson and others contend. It even argues that in a certain objective sense the war remained avoidable up to its very outbreak. But the fact that some vital events in the causal chain could easily not have happened or that vital decisions could have been made differently does not in itself make the war avoidable, because it does not cancel the practical limits to the avoidability of outcomes in human affairs. To term an outcome inevitable often means no more than to say that the time when it could have been avoided is past – that the kinds of decisions, actions, or chance developments required to avert it, though possible earlier, have become so unlikely or unthinkable as to rule out any plausible scenario for avoiding it.[2] This is an obvious point, yet it is not easy or commonplace to apply it to particular developments

---

[2]An illustrative analogy: an attempt to drive an old automobile with faulty brakes and steering down a steep mountain road with no guard rails will not necessarily end in an accident. If the dangers of such an attempt are ignored and all the many decisions and moves necessary to avoid an accident are not taken, however, at some point a crash becomes inevitable. This kind of practical, commonsense reasoning is frequently used by historians. Orlando Figes (1998), for example, repeatedly points to junctures where the 1917 Russian Revolution could have been avoided, but also shows why the necessary steps were not taken or contrary ones were, and ascribes this failure above all to the thought and actions of the conservative forces ruling Russia and to the personality, character, and beliefs of Tsar Nicholas II. These are contingent factors; so was the occasion of the revolution in March 1917 – riots over bread shortages in Petrograd at a time when flour supplies were still available. Yet by this time a revolution had become inevitable.

in history, especially major ones like the outbreak of great wars or revolutions. My hope is to use a particular application of counterfactual reasoning to history to show a specific way in which World War I by 1914 had become unavoidable – that the determining factor or factors lie less in necessary, sufficient conditions impelling governments to war than in the absence of necessary and sufficient conditions for the active maintenance of peace.

I also broadly agree with the views of Philip Tetlock and Aaron Belkin on the necessity, unavoidability, and potential utility of counterfactual reasoning in historical study (Tetlock and Belkin 1996, chap. 1). Differing on the practical application rather than the theoretical analysis of the various types of counterfactual reasoning and the basic tests to use for them, I will suggest a different notion about how and where to apply counterfactual reasoning concretely to historical explanation, as a better way of showing historians the value of counterfactual reasoning for accomplishing their task. That task (here I agree with the historians who are skeptical about it) is not to speculate on what might have happened in history, but to shed light on what actually did happen, why it did, and what it means.

The case for "embedded" counterfactual reasoning

The Tetlock-Belkin theses seem to assume that the way for historians or other scholars to apply counterfactual reasoning to historical exposition and explanation is to pose the question, "What if?" – i.e., to imagine or conceive of a way in which a particular event or development could have unfolded differently, and to ask, "What if this had happened? What further changes would have resulted?" (Tetlock and Belkin 1996: 4, 8; 1997; Ferguson 1999c).

A working historian, however – even if, like me, he agrees that counterfactual elements are logically implied in all explanation, including historical explanation – may have serious qualms about this procedure. The reason is that though it is logically defensible to think up counterfactual questions with which to confront the historical record, the exercise seems pointless or at best of limited value from a practical standpoint because even so-called "easily imagined variations" introduced into the complex matrix of historical developments can change so many variables in so many unpredictable or incalculable ways, leading to so many varied and indeterminate consequences, that the procedure quickly becomes useless for helping us deduce or predict an alternative outcome. Tetlock and Belkin of course see the problem and deal with it in terms of abstract logic. Yet my feeling is that the procedure's practical limits and problems sensed by the working historian are not sufficiently grasped.

The difficulty, as noted, is that if the variation is really important, involving a central component or variable in the historical equation, introducing it will alter so much of the complex web of history that the results of omitting or altering that crucial variable become incalculable. If the variation introduced, however, is minor, sufficiently precise and limited enough that its immediate consequences can be calculated with confidence, its implications for general historical explanation or for suggesting any important alternative outcome are unlikely to be important. A major counterfactual, in other words, will change too much, and a minor one too little, to help us explain what really did happen and why, and why alternative scenarios failed to emerge, the only sound reasons for using counterfactual reasoning. Thus using this kind of "What if?" counterfactual procedure might well have the perverse and ironic effect of confirming ordinary historians in their resistance to counterfactual reasoning and strengthening their tendency to see history as the result of pure contingency and chance.

One might of course reply that if historians cannot or will not recognize the presuppositions and assumptions involved in the explanations they offer, other scholars will have to identify and analyze them, and subject them to various tests, including those of counterfactual reasoning. Again I agree, up to a point. The alternative kind of counterfactual reasoning I will suggest might help historians get over the tendency toward a naive pragmatic empiricism. Yet it would be rash of scholars in other fields to suppose that because a particular historian fails to give compelling theoretical grounds for being dissatisfied with a particular counterfactual procedure, his or her concerns can be safely ignored. Practitioners may well sense from experience and schooled intuition that a plausible idea or theory will not work in their field, even if they have difficulty articulating theoretical reasons why. Moreover, the principal contention here, that some major easily imagined counterfactual variations in particular sections of history change so much that the whole subsequent development becomes incalculable, while other variations, just as easily imagined, make no significant difference at all, can readily be illustrated in any period of history.[3]

[3]One such illustration comes from the War of the Second Coalition (1798–1801) in Napoleon's era. Suppose that Napoleon had been killed or captured during this war, either in battle or at sea on returning from Egypt or by conspirators after he seized power – all easily imagined variants in history. No amount of historical research and reasoning could enable us to tell what the consequences of his death would have been. But suppose that he had lost the final major battle of that war at Marengo in June 1800 – again something easily imagined, for it nearly happened and was only averted by the disobedience of his orders by a subordinate general. Here one can show by concrete

One can get round the difficulty, I suggest, by a different concept and method of counterfactual reasoning. It starts by conceiving of counterfactuals not as nonhistory (that is, imagined or virtual as opposed to real history, what might have happened rather than what did), but rather as *real* history, an integral part of history, embedded in history both in the actual experience of historical actors and in those constructions or reconstructions of history constantly made not only by scholars but also by everyone who reflects on the past. History, like life itself, is lived, acted, made, and relived and reconstructed in the face and presence of counterfactuals. Historical actors in all arenas of life constantly think, calculate, decide, and act in the face of uncertainty; they repeatedly ask the question, "What if?," try to answer it, and make decisions and act on that basis. Historians take this for granted. They know instinctively (or are quickly taught) that historical actors regularly face an uncertain, open future. Recognizing this, they must portray and analyze that situation and show why and how actors responded to the questions, choices and alternatives they faced as they did. If they are at all sophisticated, they also realize that carrying out this task requires not merely trying to discover and analyze the actors' thought worlds and the role played by their counterfactual questions and calculations, but also framing and posing their own counterfactual questions as to what might have happened had the actors answered their counterfactual questions differently. Thus in seeking to discover the real nature and results of the actual choices made by actors in the face of their uncertainty and their counterfactual questions, historians must use their advantages of hindsight and historical evidence to ask counterfactual questions of their own, such as: What other decisions and actions could the historical actors have made under the existing circumstances? To what extent did they recognize and consider these? What circumstances made these choices or alternative courses genuinely possible or merely specious and actually unreal? What might the alternative results of these choices have been? The real justification for the use of counterfactual reasoning in history and the best answer to those who reject it is the fact that historians cannot faithfully convey the real nature and results of historical decisions and actions simply by constructing a factual narrative of "what happened" without confronting the various counterfactuals, both those faced by the actors and those necessarily posed by the historian, integrally embedded in that story.[4]

---

evidence that reversing the outcome of this battle would not have changed the main outcome of the war, overthrown Napoleon's rule, or altered the course of history much at all.

[4]This argument agrees in part with Niall Ferguson's call (Introduction to Ferguson 1999b: 86–7) for historians to consider only plausible unrealized alternatives and to

This understanding of counterfactual reasoning not only justifies its use but also suggests how it ought to proceed. The first task is to discover and analyze the counterfactual questions actually seen and faced by the historical actors themselves. This part is so obvious, normal and ubiquitous an element of historical research that it needs no discussion here. The second step, less obvious but no less necessary, involves looking carefully at the reconstructions and explanations of historical events and outcomes offered by historians (especially oneself) with the specific aim of discovering and analyzing the implicit and explicit counterfactual questions and assumptions they contain. The next assignment is rigorously to test these counterfactual assumptions and scenarios that historians wittingly or unwittingly pose, by means of the kinds of tests and criteria Tetlock and Belkin suggest and the same types of historical evidence as are employed to construct the "factual" story. By ferreting out and analyzing the overt or concealed counterfactuals embedded in historians' reconstructions and explanations of history, I contend we can both better explain the actual course of historical events and better judge whether the counterfactual possibilities envisioned by the actors and those constructed and used by historians were sound or illusory. In short, it can help us better understand both what did happen in history and why this particular thing rather than some other possible thing occurred.[5]

This kind of counterfactual reasoning has other advantages as well. It represents something historians regularly do, whether or not they are fully aware of it, and thus is a method that, once understood, they can

examine these rigorously on the basis of valid evidence. He goes too far, however, in insisting that "We should consider as plausible or probable *only those alternatives which we can show on the basis of contemporary evidence that contemporaries actually considered* " (italics in original). This is too restrictive. As the discussion of World War I later will illustrate, the historian's purview includes both those possibilities and alternatives contemporaries saw and considered, and those they failed to see at all or to consider seriously.

[5]Once again this general principle can be illustrated by an example from the Napoleonic era, the object of much counterfactual speculation, the Battle of Waterloo and the possible results of a Napoleonic victory rather than defeat there. I think it can easily be shown that a French victory in this battle could not possibly have changed the fundamental balance of military forces, overwhelmingly favorable to the allies, or their willingness to prosecute the war to victory, and therefore it could not have significantly altered the ultimate outcome of the war, as many have supposed. However, a Napoleonic victory, by prolonging the war and making victory more costly for the allies, would almost certainly have destroyed the Vienna peace settlement concluded just before Waterloo and have resulted in a far harsher, less stable peace settlement resembling that of 1919, with many of the latter's unfortunate consequences. In other words, Wellington's victory was not critical for the ultimate outcome of the war but it was vital for saving the peace. The evidence is too extensive to discuss here, but is summarized in Schroeder (1994: 548–56).

hardly reject. Most important, it seems to me to fit the nature of history, recognizing its openness and uncertainty for the actors themselves while insisting at the same time that history's outcomes, though not predetermined, can and must be explained by causes. It thereby takes seriously both the contingent and the determinate character of the past; respects both the extent and the limits of its range of possibilities. It depicts history as unfolding in an indeterminate way, the product of unpredictable human conduct and material circumstances, but not as kaleidoscopic chaos. It offers a way of distinguishing between genuine and specious counterfactual scenarios, showing that while much could have happened differently, not everything, including many of the things historical actors and later historians have thought were possible, could have happened. It fits our sense, learned from life as well as history, that at some point some things once indeterminate do become inevitable.

Embedded counterfactuals and World War I as an unavoidable war

I now need to illustrate how a certain degree and kind of inevitability in history applies to the origins of World War I (not demonstrate it, which might be impossible and would certainly take too long).[6] The topic suits the purpose for several reasons. First, the story is very well known and does not need to be expounded in detail. Second, though the scholarly debate over the origins of the war has not completely died out, a clear consensus view has emerged which denies that the war was inevitable and ascribes its origins to specific avoidable choices and actions taken by particular actors. Hence it represents a good challenge. Third, it illustrates particularly well the potential value of detecting and analyzing embedded counterfactuals, the surprising results it can lead to, and the dangers of failing to do so.

My treatment of this huge subject must be brief and sketchy, little more than an outline, and is bound to seem dogmatic in some places and trite in others. It will start by discussing the current prevailing view of the origins of the war, analyze and criticize the counterfactuals embedded in it, and from this develop a divergent view.

---

[6]This is my reason or excuse for the paucity of footnotes and the fact that many will be expository notes rather than references to the enormous scholarly literature on this subject. Though I think I know the literature reasonably well (not exhaustively – no one does), this is not the place to prove it.

The standard explanation and its counterfactuals

By common agreement, the direct proximate cause of World War I was the German and Austro–Hungarian decision that Austria–Hungary issue an ultimatum to Serbia in July 1914 following the assassination of Archduke Franz Ferdinand by Bosnian nationalists with connections to Serbia. The German powers intended by this ultimatum to provoke a local war against Serbia and eliminate it as a political factor in the Balkans, thus shifting the balance there and in Europe generally in favor of themselves. Without necessarily intending to start a general war, the German powers consciously risked provoking one by this initiative, as actually happened.

Disagreement persists over the motives and attitudes prompting this go-for-broke gamble, with some historians emphasizing the fear and desperation felt by leaders in Germany and Austria–Hungary, others stressing their aggressive aims and their hopes that they could either get away with a successful local war or win a wider one. This disagreement makes little difference in deciding whether this war was avoidable, however, because everyone agrees that Germany and Austria–Hungary, whatever their reasons, *chose* to take this gamble; they were not forced into it. This belief implies a counterfactual: they had viable alternatives, could have chosen other ways to protect their interests without risking a great war. A similar consensus prevails that the other great powers, Russia, France, and Britain, reacted essentially defensively to the German-Austrian move and had little choice other than to do so in self-defense, given their vital interests and the unmistakable challenge presented them. The counterfactual scenario embedded in the consensus explanation thus ascribes to Germany and Austria–Hungary a choice of an alternate strategy or strategies by which they could reasonably have hoped to protect their vital interests by peaceful means, while denying that the other major actors had practical alternatives for saving peace once the Central Powers launched their initiative.

To be sure, few attribute the German–Austro-Hungarian gamble purely to aggressive expansionism, militarism, and paranoia, or deny that the international situation was becoming increasingly unfavorable and dangerous for the Dual Alliance in 1914. The consensus view, in fact, uses this to help explain the Austro–German action, while denying that this justifies it or renders it necessary, claiming among other things that Germany and Austria–Hungary had themselves largely created the dangers threatening them by failing to reform internally while pursuing unrealistic, aggressive policies abroad. Again this involves an implied or stated counterfactual: even as late as 1914 the Central Powers could have changed their policies and thereby made themselves more secure within the existing international system without overthrowing it.

Consensus historians recognize further that Germany, already in 1914 largely isolated diplomatically and threatened with encirclement by the Triple Entente, faced an imminent future threat, that once Russia had completed its announced plans for military expansion, scheduled for completion by 1917, the German army would be numerically as decisively inferior to those of its opponents as the German navy already was on the sea. But the consensus view claims that Germany had largely created this perilous situation for itself by the aggressive world policy it had followed ever since Bismarck's fall in 1890. Its naval race with Britain, its restless quest for colonies, bases, and spheres of influence around the globe, and its frequent resort to bullying and threats, all designed to give Germany hegemony over Europe and a world position competitive with those of Britain, Russia, and the United States, provoked the alliances, ententes, and armaments races, first at sea and then on land, by which Germany now felt encircled and threatened. Since these dangers arose primarily from Germany's policies and actions (here comes another important counterfactual), different German policies could over time have reduced or eliminated them. Even as late as 1914, had Germany realized that none of its neighbors intended to attack it or violate its rights and had it decided to give up its drive for world power, pursuing instead a sensible, moderate policy focused on economic expansion, it had good chances to enjoy a reasonably secure, prosperous, and honorable place in the European and world international system. In fact, prominent historians have argued that Germany's economic dynamism was so great that it needed only a prolonged period of peace to achieve mastery in Europe (some leading historians who maintain this are Martin Kitchen, A. J. P. Taylor, Volker Berghahn, and J. C. G. Röhl).

Almost everyone also recognizes that Austria–Hungary faced even graver dangers than Germany, and that these were less obviously the result of its own actions, at least in the international arena. The Habsburg Monarchy before 1914 was growing steadily more isolated politically and diplomatically and losing its great power status and reputation. Two allies, Italy and Romania, were unreliable and hostile, the latter to the point of open defection. Its most important ally, Germany, was the Monarchy's most serious economic rival, especially in the Balkans where Austro-Hungarian interests were concentrated, and the Germans tended both to dominate Austria–Hungary politically and strategically and to ignore its vital interests. Austria–Hungary's military security against a host of possible or probable enemies (Serbia, Russia, Italy, Russia's ally France, and even Romania) depended totally on receiving major, timely help from Germany in case of war. Yet given Germany's own threatened military position facing a likely two-front war, Germany's gambling offensive strategy for fighting it (the Schlieffen Plan), and the fact that the Dual Alliance lacked a military convention or an agreed and coordinated military strategy, how much actual military help Germany would provide its ally was anyone's guess. Meanwhile Austria–Hungary's long-standing security problem had been further worsened by the disastrous outcome of the two Balkan Wars in 1912–13. The Peace of Bucharest in August 1913 left Austria–Hungary with no reliable partner in the last region, the Balkans, where it still counted as a great power and had its most vital interests. The Ottoman Empire was virtually expelled from Europe, while Bulgaria, which the Austrians counted on to check Serbia, was defeated and exhausted, Romania alienated, the new Kingdom of Albania a basket case and albatross around Austria–Hungary's neck, and Italy an active rival in Albania and the Adriatic with irredentist claims on Austrian territory. Even Germany had not given its ally steady support during the prolonged crisis, but had held Austria–Hungary back in order to preserve general peace and pursue its own particular aims. Meanwhile Austria–Hungary's worst rivals and enemies, Russia, Serbia, and Montenegro, had emerged from the Balkan Wars stronger, more confident, and more hostile, and Russia, aided by its ally France, seemed poised to consolidate its dominance over the entire region by expanding the Balkan League it had earlier sponsored and thereby promoted the Balkan Wars in the first place. The decline in Austria–Hungary's strength and status, obvious to everyone, enabled other powers to ignore its interests, to exploit its internal problems, especially the nationalities conflicts, to raise irredentist claims on the Monarchy's territory, and in Serbia's case to wage a Cold War of propaganda and a guerrilla war of terrorist subversion against it. They further spurred dissatisfied nationalities and groups within Austria–Hungary to demand concessions from the Austrian and Hungarian governments, sometimes soliciting foreign support for them, thus exacerbating the already grave problems of governance in both halves of the Monarchy and inducing anger and hopelessness in those who remained *Habsburgtreu*. Most important, Austria–Hungary, far more than Germany, had fallen hopelessly behind in the land arms race then reaching a crucial stage among the great powers in Europe (only Italy was worse off, and Italy was only a would-be great power). Given Austria–Hungary's limited economic and fiscal resources and the restrictions imposed on its military exertions by the parliamentary system in both halves of the Monarchy and the autonomous position enjoyed by Hungary, there was simply no hope for it to catch up. It thus faced the prospect of fighting a great war against several foes with only doubtful German support and under conditions of hopeless inferiority.[7]

No historian to my knowledge denies the gravity of Austria–Hungary's situation; various factors in it are regularly invoked to explain its go-for-broke gamble in 1914. Yet many also contend, as they do with Germany, that Austria–Hungary had largely brought this on itself. For decades or generations it had failed or refused to solve its own internal problems, especially the nationalities conflicts, and thus exposed itself to irredentist subversion and external threats. It had made this worse by a stubborn, aggressive defense of outworn positions and untenable claims in foreign policy (its so-called Pig War against Serbia before 1908, its annexation of Bosnia in 1908, the subsequent humiliation of Russia in 1909, its refusal to reach reasonable compromises with Serbia, Montenegro, and Italy during the Balkan Wars of 1912-13, the hopeless attempt in 1913-14 to create a viable new Balkan satellite in Albania). Once more the consensus verdict, by implication more than explicitly, posits a major counterfactual: though by 1914 the hour was late, the Monarchy's one remaining chance to survive its crisis was not the use of force, either internal or external, but reform in the direction of federalism, turning itself into a more free and democratic union of peoples and recognizing the interests of the other nationalities besides those of the master races, the Germans, Hungarians, and Italians (examples of historians who argue along these lines are Solomon Wank, Vladimir Dedijer, Steven Beller, Alan Sked, and Leo Valiani).

Thus in both cases the supposedly counterproductive and dangerous foreign policies of Germany and Austria–Hungary culminating in their gamble in 1914 are linked to a wider problem and at least partly explained by it: the failure or refusal of their regimes to reform and modernize in order to meet their internal political and social problems. Instead these regimes chose to stay in power, preserve their existing social order and the interests of their respective elites, and manage their internal social and political divisions and problems through an assertive, expansionist foreign policy (a resort to so-called secondary integration and social imperialism).

These explanations, in assigning Germany and Austria–Hungary the primary responsibility for causing the threats against which they decided to act in 1914 and explaining their policies as directed as much against internal problems as external dangers, add (as noted) further counterfactuals to the original counterfactual thesis, that these two powers had means and choices for protecting their legitimate

---

[7] On the military situation, see Stone (1975), D. Herrmann (1996), and Stevenson (1996). For more general depictions of Austria-Hungary's critical position, see Bridge (1990) and Williamson (1991).

interests in 1914 other than aiming for a local war and risking a general one. To lay these out for Germany: (1) had Germany not conducted a reckless, aggressive pursuit of world power for decades before 1914, its general interests and position in world politics would not have been threatened as they were or were perceived to be in 1914; (2) had Germany pursued political reform and social integration rather than manipulated social imperialism and secondary integration at home, its government would not have needed to pursue a reckless, aggressive foreign policy for domestic-political reasons; (3) a more democratic, liberal, and well-integrated Germany using peaceful, normal ways of protecting its legitimate interests would not have encountered enmity and opposition from the other great powers, especially from Britain and France as fellow democracies, but would have been welcomed as a partner for peace and prosperity in Europe and the world.[8] Somewhat similar counterfactuals apply to Austria–Hungary. A reformed, more progressive and democratic Monarchy pursuing wiser policies toward its nationalities and a more conciliatory foreign policy could have solved or managed its internal and external problems to such an extent that it would have both been less vulnerable to pressures and threats from its opponents and have encountered fewer such threats, thus eliminating the need for the suicidal gamble of 1914.[9]

The counter-argument and its counterfactuals

First, a logical and methodological point: if, as I claim, these counterfactuals are embedded in the consensus scenario and logically implied by it, then those who advance this view have an obligation to back them up, showing by research, analysis, and evidence that these counterfactual propositions are at least reasonable, more probable than not. The burden of proof lies on them to do this, not on others to disprove them. By and large this has not been done. Historians have instead mostly given close attention first to determining the facts on the origins of the war, both immediate and long-term, and then to linking the outbreak of the war to the German–Austro–Hungarian initiative in July 1914, both by connecting that initiative to their particular situation and aims in 1914 and by trying to show how their general situation and aims derived from their previous foreign and domestic policies and actions.

---

[8]This view is expressed most clearly by Stone (1975), Bridge (1990), Williamson (1991), D. Herrmann (1996), Stevenson (1996), and in general by Fritz Fischer and his school; it is more nuanced but still present in Mommsen (1993) and Hildebrand (1995).

[9]Besides the historians mentioned above, this view still dominates the nationalistic historiography of the successor states, Serbia, Czechoslovakia, Romania, and to some extent Poland, as represented in Wandruszka and Urbanitsch (1993).

In other words, starting from a correct initial premise that the German powers' initiative was the immediate proximate cause of the war, they have then constructed a plausible case that this initiative derived from and was caused by a general situation which also primarily resulted from German and Austro-Hungarian actions and policies over a much longer term. The null hypothesis stated or implied in this argument, however, has not been systematically laid out and examined, nor have the counterfactuals embedded in it been analyzed and researched in detail. No serious attempt has been made to back up the (hidden, implied, unarticulated, but real and logically necessary) claim that absent those supposedly decisive German and Austro-Hungarian policies and actions, the general situation in 1914 would have been different in the ways the consensus view contends.

Whatever the reasons for this disparity, so long as the counterfactuals clearly, logically, and necessarily implied in the consensus argument have not been researched and analyzed with the same care as the other so-called facts in the case, both the argument making the German-Austro-Hungarian initiative the main cause rather than merely the occasion for war and thus making these powers primarily responsible for it, and the argument that the war was inherently avoidable, the result of particular decisions that could have been made differently, remain unproved. Absent this analysis of the embedded counterfactuals, we do not know whether in fact the leaders of Germany and Austria-Hungary had any real freedom to act otherwise than they did, or what difference it would have made (ex hypothesi) had they done so.

The argument could stop here, with a claim that the consensus case for World War I as an avoidable conflict remains unproved and a call for more research. While this might be prudent, it would be inconclusive and not very interesting or helpful. Instead I will attempt three things. The first is to show that the counterfactual assumptions and implications of the consensus view are not only largely unexamined and unproved, but also improbable and in some instances untenable. The second is to lay out an alternate set of counterfactual conditions and performances necessary if war were to be averted both in 1914 and for some indefinite but significant period thereafter. The last is to argue that this (counterfactual) set of conditions and actions required *ex hypothesi* for avoidance of a general war in that era not only was not recognized, accepted, or carried out by the various actors at this time, but also that the existing international system, i.e., the circumstances, political culture, and rules and practices which then prevailed in international power politics, worked to make it highly unlikely that these necessary steps would or could have been taken.

This makes it in turn almost impossible to construct any plausible counterfactual historical scenario by which the war could have been avoided, and thus justifies terming the war inevitable.[10]

Obviously this is a tall order. The counter-argument against the consensus view will have to be as bare-boned as the previous exposition of that view, or more so. It starts with conceding (in fact, insisting on) several points in the standard view concerning the immediate origins of the war. It is basically correct that the German–Austro–Hungarian initiative of July 1914 aimed at a local war and risked a general war with the aim of reversing the prevailing trends in international politics by violence, that this launched the great-power crisis resulting in general war, that during the July Crisis the other great powers were primarily reacting to the Central Powers' initiative, and that without this particular Austro–German initiative no local or general war would have developed *at this particular time.* But these points have long been obvious. The key question regarding both responsibility for the war and its avoidability is the counterfactual one implicit in the consensus case: the question of whether other choices were available to the Central Powers at that time which, under the existing rules and conditions of the game, offered them an opportunity to satisfy their security needs reasonably without risking a major war. If so, they chose war when it was avoidable – if not, then not.

The related question, whether they were also responsible for creating the insecurity that prompted them to gamble, is not strictly speaking

---

[10]An illustrative analogy, inevitably inexact, might help indicate where the argument is going. Suppose that one intends to challenge the verdict of an inquiry into a fatal accident in which an automobile carrying a number of passengers plunged off a cliff on a steep mountain road – that verdict being that the accident was caused by two passengers who had sent the car over the cliff in their efforts to seize the wheel by force. One might challenge that verdict in several ways: by arguing that the defects in the car's brakes and steering made it unlikely that it would make the trip safely in any case; by contending that the car was already out of control and heading toward the cliff when the two intervened; or by claiming that their attempt to seize the wheel was only part of an ongoing struggle over control of the car which made a crash likely at some point anyway. None of these claims, however, even if true, would prove that an accident was inevitable or disprove that their effort to seize the wheel was the proximate cause of the accident, and that they therefore bore the prime responsibility for it. If, however, one could do the following: first, show what kind of driving conduct would have been required for this car to make this trip without accident; second, show that none of the passengers who were struggling to control and steer the car displayed this kind of driving conduct; third, show that this was because for all of them the most important goal was not finishing the journey safely, but getting control of the car and determining its final destination against the wishes of some passengers; and finally, that the actual attempt to seize the wheel came when the two were convinced this was their last chance not to be kidnapped and possibly killed by the others; then, I think, one could argue that the verdict, even if technically correct, was substantively misleading, and moreover, that under these conditions an accident was unavoidable.

relevant to the question of inevitability of the war, though it is to that of ultimate responsibility for it. If they themselves largely created the general situation which made a desperate gamble their only hope for survival, one might argue that this made war in 1914 in a sense unavoidable – they were bound soon to do something desperate that would touch it off – but also that they were responsible for it even if they had no better choice at that time. Yet though this question of responsibility is less central for our purposes than the first, the two are so closely related that even a prima facie case against the consensus argument, to be coherent, must deal with both. Therefore I will deny both sets of counterfactuals. That is, in addition to denying that Germany and Austria–Hungary had viable alternatives in 1914, I will also briefly state some reasons why they were not chiefly responsible for creating the critical security challenges they faced in 1914, why different policies on their part would not have substantially changed their situation, and why the existing international system precluded other reasonable peaceful alternatives for meeting the threats they faced.

I start with an assertion that will sound deliberately provocative, even outrageous, but that in my view represents a reasonable, almost self-evident interpretation of historical evidence. In the whole period from about 1890 to 1914, the international *policies* and *actions* of Germany and Austria–Hungary, as distinct from their aims, attitudes, gestures, language, and ambitions (especially those of Germany) were actually more restrained and moderate than those of any other great power. One cannot point to specific German or Austro–Hungarian *actions* between 1890 and July 1914 that were as aggressive, expansionist, imperialist, law-and-precedent-breaking, and belligerent as many of those taken during this same period by every other major power – Russia in East Asia and Central Asia, Britain in East and South Africa, Southeast Asia, and Central Asia, France in West, Central, and North Africa and Southeast Asia, Italy in North and East Africa and the Eastern Mediterranean, the United States in Central America, the Caribbean and the Western Pacific, and Japan in East Asia. The same point holds, *mutatis mutandis*, for a number of small powers, notably Serbia, Greece, Bulgaria, and Montenegro.

This of course does not make Germany and Austria–Hungary, especially the former, peace-loving defensive status quo powers. Germany was as active a participant in the colonialist-imperialist scramble of the era as it could be, while Austria–Hungary would have liked to participate, tried to do so on an informal basis, and did join half-heartedly in the open imperialist scramble toward the end, but never had the means to pursue it seriously. Both powers had active foreign policies and pursued aims by no means limited to preserving the status quo. Germany in particular constantly sought gains and repeatedly made attempts at achieving them – seldom, however, pursuing its initiatives consistently or very far or succeeding in doing more than arouse fear, resentment, and opposition from other states. Behind its various restless impulses lay the overall goals of *Weltpolitik.* This meant for Germany essentially a policy of maintaining its security in continental Europe (which, given Germany's central location, required at least half-hegemony there) while simultaneously making gains in world power and position (colonies, bases, markets, a formidable navy, and alliances) that would make it competitive in the 20th century with Britain, Russia, and the United States. Both goals were to be achieved with the aid of Germany's military and economic power, but mainly by means of shrewd diplomacy and power politics – using Germany's key position in Europe and the free hand it supposedly gave her to exploit what Germans supposed were irreconcilable rivalries between Britain, Russia, and France, so that Germany could reach favorable deals and arrangements especially with Britain. Austria–Hungary's main aims were necessarily more defensive – to preserve its territorial integrity, independence, and great power status against many serious challenges and threats, particularly in the one area where it still had vital great-power interests and some imperialist ambitions, the Balkans and Near East. Its policies, toward the other great powers if not lesser ones, were correspondingly more conciliatory.

Yet to dwell, as most historians do in explaining the origins of World War I, on what the Central Powers wanted and tried to do is largely beside the point. The salient fact is that throughout 1890–1914 their various initiatives, regardless of their nature and intent, regularly failed – failed either relatively in the sense of yielding them only limited gains at high long-term costs (e.g., Austria–Hungary's annexation of Bosnia in 1908 or Germany's Berlin-to-Baghdad Railway project), or absolutely in the sense of ending in defeat and greater insecurity for one or both (e.g., the two Moroccan Crises and the two Balkan Wars).

Equally striking is the contrast between their experience in this regard and that of the other great powers. The latter were able to gamble, commit serious blunders, provoke wars, experience serious setbacks and defeats, and not only survive their gambles and failures but often reap long-term profit from them. The French, though they were humiliated by Britain at Fashoda, escaped unscathed from this foolish gamble and eventually gained the colonial deal and entente with Britain they wanted. Two overt, dangerous French challenges to Germany in Morocco launched serious crises, but ended by improving

France's colonial and European positions. Britain used the threat of war successfully to compel France to back down over the Sudan and Egypt, got away with an aggressive, badly-run war in South Africa, and forced the Germans to accept their terms in Persia and Mesopotamia. The Russian government pursued an especially reckless imperialist policy almost everywhere, especially in the Far East, and yet not only survived the disastrous war and the crippling revolution in 1904–5 its policies had brought upon it, but by 1914 was not only pursuing its old imperialist goals in the Balkans and the Turkish Straits more boldly than ever, but also exploiting its new accord with Britain to encroach on Persia, and even laying the foundations for a revival of Far Eastern expansion. Italy's reckless adventure in Ethiopia in 1896 led it to a humiliating defeat – and subsequently to a rapprochement with France that enabled Italy thereafter to play off both sides in the European alliance system for the benefit of Italian interests in Africa, the Mediterranean, and the Balkans. Eventually this policy emboldened Italy to commit what was arguably the most cynical and dangerous act of imperialist aggression in the whole prewar period, condemned by everyone – its attack on the Ottoman Empire in Libya and the Dodecanese in 1911–12, an act directly linked with the two Balkan Wars and World War I itself. Yet Italy emerged from this adventure with no concrete losses and handsome territorial gains. Japan's risky, all-out gamble in 1904–5 in launching a preventive war against Russia paid off handsomely. The United States' war against Spain in 1898, a war against a state that posed no threat to the United States and was thus surely avoidable even if in some respects justified, paid off even more handsomely at almost no risk.

This will doubtless be seen as an argument drawn from a familiar exculpatory tradition: the contention that Germany and Austria–Hungary were not as imperialist, reckless, or aggressive in the prewar era as other powers – to which the obvious answer is that they were imperialist, reckless, and aggressive where and when it really counted, in Europe in 1914. Let me emphasize (I have the impression that this is an instance where one must shout in order to be heard) that this is not my point. The argument has nothing whatever to do with the character of German and Austro-Hungarian policy as compared to those of other powers. It has to do with who was really controlling the system, making the rules, and running the show, and thereby directly challenges the consensus case making the German powers primarily responsible for the security threats they faced in 1914 and contending that they could have warded off these threats by peaceful means. For it establishes that Germany and Austria–Hungary were not in control of the international system, but being restrained and controlled by it. The initiative and leadership in European politics from 1890 to 1914 always lay with their opponents, increasingly so as time went on. The standard reply, that the Central Powers lost control because of their own blunders and provocative acts, breaks down in numerous ways. It is a circular argument; it begs the question; it smacks of the ethic of success; it ignores the patent evidence that Germany's and Austria–Hungary's policies and initiatives regularly failed regardless of their character, whether aggressive and provocative or moderate and conciliatory;[11] it fails to specify concretely what different policies could have led to success, or explain how and why they could have. In more theoretical terms, it ignores a fundamental argument advanced by realists in international relations theory, an argument not always valid but here supported by strong evidence: that systemic factors, the distribution of power, vulnerability, and opportunities within the system, account for the major power-political patterns and outcomes of international politics more than do the character and aims of the individual actors. Logically and methodologically it errs in applying its principle of the primacy of domestic influences and interests not only to explain *decisions* in foreign policy (which is always in principle legitimate), but also to account for *outcomes* in international relations, where systemic factors must be taken into account. Finally, it errs by applying this dubious principle of the primacy of domestic politics one-sidedly, to the Central Powers far more than to the Entente.

The moral of all this is simple: to understand international outcomes from 1890 to 1914, one must stop looking first and foremost at what Germany and Austria–Hungary were doing, and concentrate on the powers who held the initiative in world affairs, basically running the system and making it work for them. One must further assume, barring evidence to the contrary, that their policies were also mainly internally motivated, driven essentially by their own needs, purposes, and interests, and that Germany and Austria–Hungary, who could not and did not control events, were reacting to what the other powers were doing more than the other way round. Research on the policy of the various Entente powers done from this standpoint serves to confirm this judgment and produces a picture very different from the standard

---

[11]Good evidence for this is found in Rosenbach (1993) who shows that Germany's policy toward Britain on the important issue of South Africa regularly produced British hostility and counterproductive results no matter what the Germans were trying to do or how; and Canis (1997) who demonstrates the same point on a wide range of other issues. Other instances illustrate the point. German efforts to put pressure on France over Morocco or to work in partnership with France there both failed equally; so did German efforts to work with Britain in the Berlin-to-Baghdad railway scheme; so did Austro-Hungarian attempts either to conciliate and cooperate with Russia in the Balkans, or to put pressure on her.

one (Miège 1961; Poidevin 1969; Allain 1976; Keiger 1983; Wilson 1985; French 1986; Neilson 1995).

The distortions produced by focusing on Germany and Austria–Hungary as the prime movers in the international system are not remedied but made worse by stressing the domestic pressures and unsolved internal problems supposedly driving their foreign policies. Regardless of the extent to which this explanation may be justified (obviously their foreign and domestic policies were inextricably interwoven; in the case of Austria–Hungary, the distinction between foreign and domestic policy virtually breaks down), such a concentration on their internal problems in explaining their policies and motives simply reinforces the fundamental error of making these powers the prime movers within the system. The key to explaining the German powers' policies lies not in what their governments and their constituent interest groups and elites would have liked to do, but what they found themselves compelled to do. It makes better sense to analyze British, French, Russian, American, Italian, and Japanese policy in terms of domestic pressures and influences, for each of these governments had more effective choices and room to translate its desires into some kind of action.[12] It also bears remembering that the foreign policy/domestic politics nexus works both ways. Domestic pressures influence and shape foreign policy, but success or failure in international politics and foreign policy also strongly influence domestic politics. This was obviously the case in prewar Germany, where the government's perceived failures in foreign policy promoted dissatisfaction throughout the political spectrum, with right-radical groups and special interests especially calling for strong action to defend the country's interests (Eley 1980; Blackbourn and Eley 1984; Coetzee 1990). If the danger to the regime and governing elites arising from foreign policy failure was serious for Germany, it was life-threatening for Austria–Hungary. The steady erosion of the state's independence and international prestige not only encouraged dissident elements to press their claims and weakened the attachment of the loyal and dominant ones, but at the same time encouraged foreign governments to advance irredentist territorial claims and to promote internal discontent and subversion within Austria–Hungary

---

[12]It might well be that had Germany and Austria–Hungary been less constrained by prevailing circumstances, their prewar policies would have been more aggressive and dangerous than those of their opponents, at least Britain and France. I myself am inclined to believe this, given the German and Austro-Hungarian record during World War I, when some of the prewar restraints ceased to operate, and the joint German-Austrian record in 1933–45. But this does not apply to the period before 1914, when they were so constrained.

and, in the Serbian case, to support terrorist resistance within it,[13] and encouraged almost every government to ignore or oppose its interests in international crises. To contend that the internal problems allegedly motivating the Central Powers' aggressive, dangerous foreign policies should have been handled instead by internal reforms is to ignore the extent to which, especially for Austria–Hungary, developments in the international arena contributed to those internal problems and made them unmanageable without foreign policy success.

This is (to repeat) not an attempt to blame their opponents for the failure of German and Austro–Hungarian statecraft that terminated in their July 1914 gamble.[14] It is instead an attempt to get beyond the old, tired blame game by showing that the root cause lies deeper than the policies of either the Central Powers or their rivals. It derives from the overall character of the international game being waged and the fundamentally unfavorable geopolitical position Germany and Austria–Hungary occupied within it.

That game requires at least a thumb-nail description here. It comprised two simultaneous contests, inextricably intertwined and inter-dependent but with differing characteristics, stakes, and rules. The first was that of the old European balance of power. By 1914 this had evolved into an extremely competitive, zero-sum contest played for very high stakes (national survival) and at great risk (general war among populous industrialized states possessing mass armies); yet un-til just before 1914 certain minimal restraints or norms of international conduct left over from the Vienna era still prevailed. These norms, combined with prudence derived above all from fear of a general war, served to restrict the competition in Europe between individual powers and rival alliance systems to one waged for relative advantage rather than decisive victory; the powers aimed to ensure themselves victory in case of war and an upper hand in imperialist competition, but not to conquer or eliminate one's rivals. The notion of preserving a balance of power, still widely held as an ideal though each power defined the desired balance differently and pursued it in opposed, incompatible

---

[13]In Russia's case this was particularly true of its support of pro-Russian Ruthenian nationalism in East Galicia and the Bukovina and of some Russian official support and much public and press support of Czech and South Slav nationalism. On the Serbian anti-Habsburg program, see especially Behschnitt (1980) and Boeckh (1996).

[14]Once again, in anticipation of a plausible objection, let me make clear that just as I am not arguing that Germany and Austria–Hungary, had they not been under severe pressures in international politics before 1914, would have pursued moderate, peaceful policies abroad, so also I do not claim that had there been no outside pressures on them or interference in their domestic problems, they would have solved or managed them more successfully. The opposite is more likely. But this also is irrelevant to what happened before and in 1914.

ways, rested on a general recognition that even a victorious great war would be terribly risky and costly and might prove counterproductive, creating new international dangers by destroying the existing balance or eliminating essential actors. Thus the game resembled high-stakes poker played by heavily armed men bent on winning but reluctant to raise the stakes too high, both to avoid losing themselves and to avoid provoking others facing impending bankruptcy into kicking over the table and starting a gunfight. As a result, there was a certain unspoken, consensual limit on the size of the bets and a general assumption that over major issues some compromise involving a minimal level of satisfaction for everyone, or at least all the great powers, should emerge. This last remnant of the old European Concert principle remained alive, though barely so, in the two Moroccan Crises, the Bosnian Crisis, and the diplomacy of the Balkan Wars (Crampton 1979).

Another game was being played alongside European balance-of-power politics, however, called imperialism or world politics (different names for the same thing). Its stakes were shares in the economic, military, political, and territorial control and exploitation of the non-European world; its goals and rules resembled the board game Monopoly; and it evolved differently from its companion game. The 19th-century European balance game began in 1814–15 with conservative monarchical cooperation against war, revolution, and territorial change and gradually evolved by 1914 into almost unrestrained zero-sum competition. Imperialism, always present throughout the 19th century but only taking center stage after about 1870, started out then as an individualistic scramble, carried on initially more by individuals and firms than governments, for goods supposedly free for the taking. This made imperialism at first a win-win contest for governments, less dangerous and more cooperative than the European balance game, in some ways a safe outlet for drives and energies too dangerous to be employed in Europe. Hence late 19th and early 20th century imperialism sometimes led to confrontations but seldom to wars between European states (even the wars that occurred between European powers and the colonized peoples and states were usually small scale affairs (Pakenham 1991; Vandervort 1998) and often led to deals dividing the spoils between certain claimants.[15]

---

[15] The examples are almost too numerous to mention. The numerous Anglo–French contests over West and East Africa always ended in deals; even their dangerous confrontation at Fashoda led eventually to their colonial bargain of 1904. Franco–German confrontations over Morocco eventually led to a colonial bargain, though it left behind hostility on both sides. The Anglo–German contest of 1884–5 over Southwest Africa ended similarly; so did later ones over South Africa, though the Germans ended up with worthless paper concessions. The Anglo–Russian conflict over Persia and Central

Yet in the end European imperialism was more rapacious than ordinary balance-of-power politics, quite apart from the rapacity it showed to colonized peoples and territories. Unlike the European game, its primary aim was not security and relative advantage, but clear gains and acquisitions, which as time went on increasingly drove states to seek unchallenged control of particular areas, shutting others out. To be sure, sharing-out agreements continued to be made up to and through the Great War – consortia to build railways, carry on commercial activities, or exploit mineral resources in China or the Ottoman Empire, agreements to permit other powers commercial access to one's own colonies, international or bilateral deals over Egyptian, Ottoman, or Chinese customs, etc. Yet not only were these agreements often a *pis aller* necessary to avoid dangerous conflicts or to share prizes too expensive or troublesome to exploit exclusively, they were also usually monopolistic or semi-monopolistic in character, dividing up regions so as to exclude others and enable each partner to monopolize its own sphere. Moreover, even this element of cooperation tended increasingly to break down into confrontation or open conflict. New Imperialism, in short, tended inexorably toward exclusive paramountcy and control. Witness the aggressive extension of the American Monroe Doctrine in the Western Hemisphere (Cuba and the Caribbean, the Panama Canal, Venezuela, Brazil) and the Pacific, extending even to the Philippines; the British version of their own Monroe Doctrine, informal but effective, in much of Africa, India, and elsewhere; France's preemptive extension of its exclusive control from Algeria to Tunisia and Morocco; Russia's version of exclusive empire in Central Asia, tried less successfully in Manchuria, North China, and Korea, where Japan countered this with its own program. The Anglo–Russian Convention of 1907, which tried to avoid conflict and ensure cooperation by dividing Persia and Central and South Asia into clear-cut spheres, led to far more friction than cooperation between the two imperialist partners.

This points to further crucial differences. European balance-of-power politics before 1914, even at its most competitive as in its rival security alliances, was supposed to keep all the necessary players in the game and to last indefinitely with no decisive end-point. The players had established relatively fixed, legally recognized positions and well-known, comparable assets and opportunities, making the idea of regulating competition among them by an equilibrium of forces plausible, though not necessarily feasible. European imperialist politics, in contrast, was

---

Asia led to their Convention of 1907, though that did not end the rivalry; the Baghdad Railway dispute eventually led to an Anglo–German agreement. Even Russia and Japan ten years after going to war over East Asia came to an agreement for coordinating their imperialist aims in China.

designed to keep some players in the game while driving others out. Its conclusion, with final winners and losers, would come when all the available world spoils were divided up, promoting a dominant spirit of *Torschlusspanik* – panic at the closing of the gates – from early on. Finally, the players started from very different starting points with vastly different, almost incommensurable and noncomparable assets, liabilities, and opportunities. When the serious game began after 1870, Great Britain began with a vast empire and many opportunities for further expansion, but at the same time with a new formidable challenge facing it. Its vast, far-flung possessions and the informal character of its paramount position in much of Africa and Asia, both stemming from a period in which it had no serious rival in naval, industrial, and commercial terms, made the British Empire now vulnerable and hard to defend against new competitors at a time when Britain was gradually losing its industrial supremacy, and the efforts necessary to defend it might undermine the very commercial strength and prosperity on which the Empire ultimately depended and which it was supposed to promote. Two other powers, Russia and the United States, had extensive empires that were mainly continental and hence less vulnerable, giving them both considerable security and potential for further expansion. France had a substantial colonial empire and numerous opportunities for expansion, but relatively little power and capital to expend on them. Other actors (Spain, Portugal, and the Netherlands) had residual empires they were determined to retain and exploit but could not defend against serious challenge. Finally, new players having no prior stake and widely varying capacities nonetheless entered determined to play (Germany, Japan, Italy, the King of Belgium, and toward the end Austria–Hungary). Even this does not exhaust the roster of players. Those who became targets of imperialism – China, the Ottoman Empire, various African states and empires – did not simply react passively, but developed their own programs, sometimes expansionist-imperialist ones (Great Serbia, Great Bulgaria, the Greek *Megale Idea*, Pan-Turanianism, and the like.)

All this insured that the imperialist game, unlike the European one, could not be played according to more or less rational rules and calculations leading to some sort of balanced power and satisfactions, but would end in clear winners and losers. Moreover, while the high stakes of the European balance game, the fact that the survival of the nation was at risk in any general war, made for caution, the high stakes in imperialist politics, based on the general conviction that a nation's future survival and prosperity in the coming century depended on acquiring world power and position, had an opposite effect. Since the immediate danger of a great war breaking out over imperialist quarrels seemed small, imperialist competition encouraged strategic and tactical boldness, going for broke.

This relates to our main question, because in order to judge whether Germany and Austria–Hungary had alternative policies available by which they might have averted the threats they faced in 1914 and eliminated any need to gamble, one must appraise how much intrinsic chance they had to succeed in these two interlocking games, starting from an earlier point – say, 1890 – at which both games became more seriously competitive. In the European balance game, their basic starting positions, strengths, and liabilities gave neither much chance for significant gains and assured that Austria–Hungary in particular would have difficulty in holding its own regardless of what it did. The most fundamental miscalculation German leaders made was their expectation that Germany's central position in Europe would help it exploit rivalries between other powers and make itself indispensable to both sides, at a profit. That geographical position (as Bismarck had recognized – it gave him his nightmare of coalitions) was instead mainly a handicap, forcing both powers always to reckon with the likelihood of a two-front war (in Austria–Hungary's case a multifront one), increasing their vulnerability and limiting their freedom of maneuver and alliance capability. Centrally located as they were, they could make firm commitments only to each other or to weaker states needing their support, such as Italy and Romania. They also had an additional liability often ignored in the literature: unlike all the other important powers in Europe save the Ottoman Empire, they had territories other states and/or peoples coveted and in certain instances claimed by right. In Germany's case, this meant France (Alsace–Lorraine), Denmark (North Schleswig), and the Poles (Polish Prussia). Austria's case was far worse: Italian nationalists claimed the Veneto and Trentino, Istria, and parts of Dalmatia, Russian nationalists and leaders, including the Tsar, wanted to solve the Ukrainian problem by annexing East Galicia and the Bukovina, Serbia claimed all the Austro-Hungarian territories populated by Serbs or Croats, and Romania had its eyes on Transylvania.

To be sure, these claims and velléités did not immediately threaten Germany's and Austria–Hungary's territorial integrity. Like other notions some Russians entertained about the Turkish Straits, East Prussia, and Prussian Poland or some British and French had about Germany's colonies, these aims were likely to come into play, and did, once war broke out, but no one save radical Serbian nationalists and their backers in the Serbian military and in extreme Panslav circles in Russia wanted a war to achieve them. Throughout the prewar period the Central Powers, especially Germany, remained too strong for other powers to challenge them directly in Europe. In other words, their basic situation was unfavorable but not disastrous; it was likely that they would lose in terms of relative security and advantage, but unlikely that they would forfeit their positions as European great powers. This pretty much sums up the outcome of European great power politics from 1890 to 1910. Given their basic situation at the outset, the unfavorable course it took for them was natural and normal if not strictly predictable, readily understandable without invoking particular blunders or provocations on their part as explanations. Nor is there reason to suppose that other policies on their part would necessarily have changed this result very much.

The question of their basic chances for success in the imperialist-world politics game from about 1890 on could well be answered with the familiar bon mot about their wartime situations in 1917: in Berlin the prospects were serious but not hopeless, in Vienna hopeless but not serious. For success in imperialist expansion, almost everything in their geopolitical situation worked against them: no initial foundation in terms of colonies, overseas trade, bases, and readily projected naval or military power; an unfavorable geographic location with only limited access to one ocean, easily blocked by rivals in case of war; an exposed position in Europe which forced them to limit their commitments and be risk-averse in the world game, making them unattractive as imperialist partners and tempting as targets; and internal divisions and weaknesses hampering both, especially Austria–Hungary. Germany had only one of the requirements for success in the imperialist world game, a vibrant growing economy, and Austria–Hungary, though developing economically, did not enjoy even that.

Just as important as these liabilities in insuring their defeat were the rules of the imperialist game and the way the other powers played it. The dominant fact – obvious yet somehow frequently overlooked or, if noticed, not taken seriously – is that the other imperialist great powers, Britain above all, but also Russia, France, Italy, and to some extent the United States and later Japan, played the imperialist game so as to make Germany and Austria–Hungary lose, as part of their strategy to win. The common German charge that the Triple Entente deliberately encircled Germany in Europe was false, at least so far as Britain was concerned, but another charge, that Germany and Austria–Hungary were deliberately circled out of world politics as much as possible, is obviously true. The Anglo–French Entente Cordiale in 1904 was intended to keep Germany from interfering with exclusive British and French control in Egypt and Morocco. British efforts from 1890 on to reach an agreement with Russia over the Middle East, culminating in their 1907 convention on Persia and Central Asia, were designed to prevent German penetration of this region – an aim Russia shared. Much of British foreign policy on South Africa was directed at keeping Germany from interfering there at all, whether as a partner or as an opponent. France deliberately set out to do the same vis-à-vis Germany in both Moroccan Crises, violating international agreements of 1880, 1906, and 1909 in the process. The United States worked with Britain in Latin America, the South Seas, and the Far East to limit German influence. The British and Russians collaborated against Germany on the Baghdad Railway and fought especially hard against German influence at Constantinople and in Mesopotamia. Russia, encouraged by Britain and aided by France, worked from 1907 on to check Austro–Hungarian influence in the Balkans and especially after 1911 to eliminate that influence entirely. Russia, Britain, Japan, and the United States all tried to check German economic and political expansion in China and the Far East. In the prewar scramble for concessions in Asiatic Turkey, all the other powers, including Italy and Germany, worked against Austria–Hungary.

Of course this is not evidence of a sinister anti-German or anti-Austro–Hungarian conspiracy. These tactics broke no rules, because these *were* the rules, the way to play the imperialist game for fun and profit. One no more needs to invoke an anti-German or anti-Austro–Hungarian conspiracy to account for this pattern than one needs to talk of conspiracies to account for monopolistic and oligopolistic combinations and strategies in the business world, or to explain how these often target particular firms and sometimes drive them out of business. Everyone recognizes these tactics as part of the game.[16] The pattern, however, does further undermine the view that German and Austro–Hungarian policies were primarily responsible for the threats to their interests and security, and that Germany could have achieved its needed place in the sun had it followed less aggressive and provocative policies. This is like arguing that firms being deliberately driven out of business by others could have saved themselves by following less aggressive and provocative policies toward their competitors. It ignores both the concrete evidence to the contrary and the basic rules and nature of the game.

A similar unrealism afflicts the related argument that Germany, even if it lost the contest in power politics, would nonetheless have survived and prospered simply by continuing its current rate of economic

---

[16]It is somewhat surprising that historians and other international relations scholars, especially of the realist persuasion, do not automatically see this and apply it to the pre-1914 scenario, considering how commonly micro-economic competition between firms is used by realist theory as an analogy for the structure and operation of international politics.

growth, becoming in a few more years of peace an economic hegemon in Europe too powerful for the others to challenge. This argument, on the surface plausible, seems first of all to ignore certain elemental economic facts, such as the precarious nature of Germany's economic achievements and prosperity in an age of intense competition and frequent booms and busts (German economic growth was being surpassed by the United States at the same time and much the same rate as Germany was surpassing Great Britain, and Russia had the fastest rate of industrial growth before 1914); or the fact that the more German trade and exports grew, the more dependent the German economy became on external markets and imports for further growth and survival, and the more vulnerable it became to military threats to these. Given the fact that British leaders calculated that they could destroy German overseas commerce and ruin Germany's economy by a naval blockade and made this their primary strategy in case of war, it was reasonable for Germans to feel vulnerable to this threat regardless of how much economic power and wealth they amassed. Indeed, the more wealthy they became, the more that sense of threat would grow. Fear of loss, as psychologists have long established, is a more powerful motivator than hope of gain. But even apart from these considerations, obvious yet inexplicably widely ignored, the most important thing here is to understand the counterfactual question. It is not, "How would the European and world economies have developed had peace lasted for some years after 1914?" That question is both too loaded with indeterminate contingent variables to be answered, and not relevant here. The question is rather, "In the real world of 1914, could Germany's leaders and public reasonably have been expected to rely for their security, against foes already superior to Germany on the sea and expected shortly to achieve superiority also on land, on the prospect or possibility that if peace lasted long enough, Germany's economic dynamism would protect it against these strategic and military threats?"

The answer to this question seems self-evident to me, but it is apparently not so to others, and so one needs to look further at its underlying assumptions and implications. To rely on this expectation, German leaders would have had to be confident not merely that Germany would win the current economic competition, but also that a generally free, liberal world economic order with open access for everyone to international trade, especially overseas, would endure indefinitely, regardless of developments on the European and world strategic and military stage and regardless of whether Germany could if necessary support its economic interests with political and military weapons. This assumption simply flies in the face of the facts. It assumes that Smithian free-market liberalism had by 1914 decisively triumphed over neo-mercantilism, protectionism, and economic imperialism, when in fact all the major powers save Britain believed in protectionism and mercantilism rather than free trade, even Britain practiced a form of imperialist protectionism, and most states were more protectionist than Germany. It assumes that Germany's rivals would have peacefully come to terms with Germany's economic domination, when in fact they were already worried by Germany's economic progress and took active measures before the war, especially in Russia and France, to avoid becoming economically dependent on Germany.[17] It assumes that the prewar international economic system operated largely independently of European high politics and military strategy and would continue to do so, when in fact everyone believed that a strong state and a strong economy required each other and that it was the government's duty to bring the nation's political, military, and economic resources together to promote its national interests. Tariff wars, discrimination against foreign goods and enterprises, and attempts by governments to promote their nationals' economic interests or to use these interests to promote their political and strategic ends were central to the age of imperialism. Even the British, who still adhered to free trade principles, relied on their naval supremacy and empire as a hedge against dangerous competition or decline.

In other words, this counterfactual holds that the Germans, of all people, should have believed and trusted in the message of Norman Angell's prewar book *The Great Illusion*: that growing interdependence in the modern capitalist economy had rendered war obsolete, counterproductive, and irrational. Angell's criticism of the reigning neo-mercantilist, protectionist, and militarist doctrines of his day was sound enough, but not his ignoring of power political realities and their connection to economics then and since.[18]

The counterfactual argument that Germany could have broken up or loosened the alliances or quasi-alliances against it by more moderate,

---

[17]Fritz Fischer's well-known thesis (1964; 1969) of a continuity between Germany's prewar drive for world power and the imperialist war aims program it developed and pursued in 1914–18 may go too far in making Germany's wartime aims the actual motives for its prewar policy. Yet it is hard to deny that the aims Germany developed in wartime reflect what its elites were already thinking about before 1914 as to how Germany might solve its problems in case war arose. If we apply this same argument to the Allies, it tells us something important about their prewar attitudes toward Germany's economy. Prominent in the British, French, and Russian war aims programs were measures to break Germany's economic power while at the same time somehow preserving Germany as a market for their own economies (along with French (1986) and Neilson (1995), see especially Soutou (1970)).

[18]See the Forum in the *American Historical Review* 94(3), 1106–42, an exchange between Carl Strikwerda and Paul W. Schroeder on the former's article.

patient policies and conduct has similar problems. Granted, Germany's opponents genuinely perceived Germany as unpredictable and dangerous, and were acting partly to counter that threat. But this does not mean that Germany could have removed that perception and changed its opponents' policies simply by becoming somehow more moderate and conciliatory in its behavior. Germany posed a threat particularly to Russia and France mainly because of where it was located and the power it possessed rather than by its policies, and their alliances and ententes were intended to meet this objective, structural threat by giving the Entente powers a margin of military preponderance over Germany. Any signs of German restraint would and did serve as proof that these alignments were working and should be continued. Besides, as already noted, these combinations had important uses in world politics. Their central value for Britain was that good relations with France and Russia would curb both their colonial rivalries with Britain and German competition with Britain. Preserving the so-called balance of power in Europe was part and parcel of this policy. In other words, the anti-German alliances and ententes were too intrinsically valuable to the Entente powers for both their security in Europe and their world-imperialist purposes for German good behavior to have made them give them up, and that German attempts to undermine or loosen these combinations, or even join them, served as more proofs that Germany was treacherous and dangerous. The history of prewar politics repeatedly demonstrates this. The cognitive biases apparent in the consensus view – the ascription of more freedom of choice to one side (in this case Germany) than to the other, and the belief that it could easily have changed its policy and thereby have induced the other side to change its – are familiar to political psychologists.

All this concerns only the German side of the problem, on which most historians concentrate, ignoring thereby the more immediate and pressing half, the Austro–Hungarian problem.[19] The counterfactuals embedded in the consensus view involving Austria–Hungary are even stranger than those for Germany, and receive less scrutiny. But in a

---

[19]The problems this causes are illustrated by Niall Ferguson's recent revisionist and controversial book on World War I (1999b). Ferguson actually makes some sound and important, if not really new, points about the origins of the war, mostly directed against the prevailing German-war-guilt thesis. The trouble is, however, that because like most other historians he virtually ignores Austria–Hungary and Eastern Europe, he not only misunderstands the origins of the war but advances an unsound counterfactual argument that a German victory would not have been so bad for Europe or the British Empire – indeed, that it might have averted later disasters – and that Britain would have done better to stay out of it. Critics have generally ignored the sound points in his case and pounced on the unsound ones in reaffirming the conventional verdict about Germany as the main architect of the war.

way this is not surprising, for in regard to Austria–Hungary the consensus case with its embedded counterfactuals rests on assumptions so unwarranted as hardly to deserve discussion. A good example is the notion that internal reforms could have solved the nationalities disputes within Austria–Hungary and thus given it the needed power and cohesion to survive the ruthless competition of European and world politics. This assumes two things: that nationalities conflicts of the kind that have troubled the Habsburg Monarchy and other multinational states in modern times are genuinely soluble by any means,[20] and that internal reforms, if they succeed in promoting greater domestic harmony, also make a state stronger for foreign policy purposes. No support is offered in theory, argument, or evidence for either assumption, and none can be found. In fact, the Austrian government launched many reforms between 1867 and 1914 that helped make the Monarchy a progressive, modernizing state in important respects – a thriving culture, a growing economy, an advanced educational system, and a political system that, though riddled with conflict and tensions, respected civil rights and included democratic features. But these reforms also, inevitably, hampered rather than aided the Monarchy's efforts to conduct a strong foreign policy. The more freedom its many peoples, factions, and parties enjoyed to contend for their particular rights, status, and share of power within the Monarchy, and the more parliamentary (and thereby more chaotic) its politics became, the less chance there was to unite everyone on a single foreign policy agenda, or to raise the taxes needed to keep Austria–Hungary competitive in the European arms race, or to prevent foreign governments and groups from intervening in the Monarchy's nationalities conflicts, and the nationalities themselves from exploiting this.

Even more implausible is the suggestion that successful internal reforms, whatever these might have been, would have lessened the hostility or changed the aims of its opponents abroad. Russian nationalists and the Russian government were not interested in protecting the rights of Ukrainians (so-called Ruthenes) in East Galicia; their concern was to prevent Ukrainian nationalism from spreading from East Galicia and the Bukovina to Imperial Russia, and the ideal solution was to annex these territories to Russia. Much the same holds for Italian nationalists and their irredentist claims, as well as Romanian nationalists, to say nothing of the Serbs. This has nothing to do with the question of whether Austria–Hungary should have done something more or different to meet

---

[20] As Geoffrey Hosking notes (1997: 397), Tsarist Russia tried to solve its nationalities problems before World War I by repression and Russification; Austria–Hungary tried to solve its by concessions. Neither policy worked, and the problem may simply be insoluble.

its internal problems; it means only that meeting its internal problems would not have significantly changed the attitudes or actions of its opponents.

The central weakness in the counterfactual case on Austria-Hungary, however, parallels the one in regard to Germany: it ignores the basic rules and nature of the game. Austria-Hungary's competitors and opponents were acting in regard to the Monarchy essentially on behalf of their own interests and aims, not in reaction to what it did. Austria-Hungary could have prevented this only by changing the nature and stakes of the game to make this unprofitable – which was what it finally tried to do by its July 1914 gamble. One more feature of the standard counterfactual scenario deserves mention: that it leaves the two sides of its case, the German and Austro-Hungarian aspects, unconnected when they are in fact tightly interwoven. It suggests a counterfactual solution for Germany's security problem, namely, that it show greater restraint, moderation, and patience toward its opponents and accept some temporary military and strategic insecurity while seeking its future security through the relaxation of tensions in Europe and German economic growth. For Austria-Hungary it suggests domestic reforms to strengthen it politically and militarily so that it could better defend its interests against external challenges. Leave aside for the moment the inherent flaws in these proposals, already discussed, and ask simply how they fit and work together. The answer is, "They do not – they contradict each other." Suppose *per impossibile* that Austria-Hungary could before 1914 have achieved the internal cohesion and economic strength to keep up with the others in the arms race; how would that have fit with a simultaneous effort by Germany to try to cool the arms race? It would have been obviously and directly contrary to it – the main reason being that the fixed policy of all three Entente powers was to consider Austria-Hungary as simply Germany's subordinate ally, no matter how desperately the Austrians pleaded that they were pursuing an independent policy, so that a stronger, more confident and assertive Austria-Hungary automatically meant in St. Petersburg, Paris, and London a stronger, more dangerous Germany.[21] Or consider the impact that German efforts to conciliate its opponents had on Austria-Hungary's security problem. The historical evidence is clear: such efforts by Germany made Austria-Hungary's problems worse. What

---

[21] A good example of this is the Entente powers' reactions to the expansion of the Austro-Hungarian navy in the Adriatic before 1914. Entente leaders knew perfectly well that the Austrians were building solely against the Italians, their nominal ally, and had no thought of challenging Russia, France, or Britain on the sea. Never mind; Austria-Hungary was Germany's ally, and therefore its navy, like its army, must be regarded as simply part of the joint enemy forces in the coming war.

Russia wanted as proof of German moderation and cooperation, also demanded by Britain, was that Germany restrain Austria–Hungary in the Balkans. Germany's refusal in Russia's eyes to restrain Austria–Hungary in 1909 was the source of massive, permanent Russian resentment. When Germany did restrain its ally from 1910 to 1913, thereby helping prevent a general war and temporarily improving Russo–German and Anglo–German relations, that also contributed hugely to undermining Austria–Hungary's position and fuelling frustration and despair among its decision-makers. Or consider the suggestion that Germany should have relied on peaceful economic expansion for its future security. One of Germany's most important economic targets before 1914 was the Balkans and the Ottoman Empire. German economic expansion there directly threatened Austria–Hungary's trade, prosperity and independence more than those of any other state, serving to encourage Austria–Hungary's opponents, Serbia in particular, and push Austria–Hungary toward violent countermeasures.

These points are important not just as further instances of the internal contradictions in the consensus scenario and the ways it neglects the Austro–Hungarian problem, but as evidence of a profound misunderstanding of the German problem as well. Those who insist that Germany was mainly responsible for the Central Powers' gambling strategy in 1914, even though Austria–Hungary conceived that strategy, demanded German support for it, and finally launched it, argue that Austria–Hungary could not possibly have acted without German help, and that since Germany gave its ally a blank check, subsequently pressed Austria–Hungary forward, and never really tried to restrain it, Germany was chiefly responsible. Once again the embedded counterfactual assumptions demand examination. There are at least two, closely related: first, that the German government, if it genuinely wanted peace, could have rejected Vienna's demand for support, regardless of Austro–Hungarian warnings that a denial of support would critically affect the alliance, future Austrian policy, and the survival of the Monarchy as a great power; second, that Germany, in the interest of general peace, could and should have detached its security and great-power status from Austria–Hungary's survival as a great power – a survival that Germans, like everyone in Europe, including especially the Austrians, considered genuinely threatened.

It is hard to conceive how these assumptions could be defended. They seem to contradict everything known about the history of German and Austrian relations in Central Europe, the connection between this problem and the wider problems of relations with Russia over Eastern Europe and the Balkans, and the nature of European international politics, both political and military. Above all they strike one as an impossible way to promote durable European peace. In a more peaceful and stable earlier era, Bismarck recognized and acted upon an insight fully confirmed by history since 1914: that breaking up the Habsburg Monarchy or eliminating it as a great power, regardless of how this happened and whether or not Austria deserved it, would have revolutionary consequences for Germany and Europe as a whole. That insight is here ignored. The surprise is not that Germany recognized this community of fate in July 1914 and backed Austria–Hungary's desperate gamble; the decision to do so had essentially been taken earlier in 1914. The surprise is rather that the German government earlier tried for a long time to ignore its ally's problems or sweep them under the rug, even in various ways helping make them worse, and that only now it seriously reckoned with the consequences for Germany of Austria–Hungary's continued decline and potential collapse or defection as an ally.

The crowning anomaly in the consensus view and its counterfactuals lies thus in its ignoring precisely what the July Crisis most clearly proves: that Germany could not ignore the Austro-Hungarian problem even though it wished to, because the German and Austro-Hungarian problems were Siamese twins, and part of still wider and more complex Central and East European and Near Eastern problems, so that an attempt to solve or manage the German question and the question of European peace without seriously dealing with the Austro-Hungarian problem was an attempt to play Hamlet without the Prince of Denmark.

An account of the origins of the war with different embedded counterfactuals

The argument thus far seems to suggest that the war was inevitable for the following reasons:

1. The nature of the European power game and of Germany's and Austria–Hungary's respective positions within it made its actual outcome by 1914, namely, relative loss, frustration, and looming danger for Germany and even worse decline and immediate peril for Austria–Hungary, likely from the outset.

2. Similarly, the nature of the imperialist game and of Germany's and Austria's positions in it made its actual outcome, that Germany would lose relative to its rivals, but not absolutely or fatally, while Austria–Hungary risked losing completely, even more likely.

3. Yet these unfavorable outcomes and trends were probably not enough individually and by themselves to make the two powers risk a general war in order to reverse them. This is suggested by the fact that on several occasions previously (1904–5, 1908–9, and 1912–13) they passed up opportunities for war when their chances for success were better than they were in 1914. Nevertheless, given the facts that these two games were tied together both objectively and in their perception, and that the Central Powers, like others, believed that both contests were critical to their ultimate survival, security, and prosperity as great powers, their belief that they were losing and declining in both made it likely that at some point they would take some risky action to reverse the trend. Any immediate, overt challenge and threat to the independence, integrity, and great-power status of one or both of them, such as arose on June 28, 1914, would increase that likelihood dramatically.

4. Since their rivals shared their assumptions regarding the nature, rules, and stakes of the combined European-world politics game and were therefore equally determined to maintain their favorable positions or improve them, any German–Austro-Hungarian initiative to reverse the existing trends of the game was almost certain to meet strong resistance and produce a direct collision between the two sides. The tense, crisis-laden atmosphere of prewar politics, with many vital issues unresolved and major developments in flux, made it virtually certain that occasions for confrontations and clashes of interest would arise. These facts, plus the high stakes on both sides and the absence of any mutually acceptable compromise of their irreconcilable purposes, entitle one to consider a general war as inevitable sooner or later.

This view comes close, but it is too determinist or determinist in the wrong way. It makes the decisive element the nature, rules, and stakes of the prevailing game of international politics and the objective conditions under which the various actors entered it and played it out. The version I propose locates the determining element elsewhere – not in the international game itself, which still could conceivably have continued for some time without general war and without radical changes in its rules, but rather in the political culture of the era and in certain dominant beliefs about the prevailing game.

Let me try to show the subtle difference by an analogy, inevitably inexact but perhaps useful for illustration. Compare World War I to a train collision involving five trains, all in a race to reach the station first or at least to avoid coming in last. The strict determinist view just outlined holds that they collided because all five were on intersecting tracks, the only way to avoid an accident was for at least one or two of them to give way to the others and thereby lose the race, and all considered this action with its predictable outcome unacceptable. An indeterminist view would hold that the trains, though running on unsafe tracks at dangerously high speeds with obsolete equipment operated in certain instances by reckless engineers, were not running on intersecting tracks but parallel ones set dangerously close together. Hence a collision was not inevitable but could only arise by accident (say, if one of the trains left the tracks or swayed into another one) or by deliberate recklessness. My version holds that while all five trains involved in the race were running together closely enough that all would be involved in any accident, only three of the five were on a potential collision course. These three, however, had been in similar races over this same terrain a number of times before, and knew how an accident could be avoided – when to slow down, what signals to give, what switches or side-tracks to take, etc. – actions that involved some active coordination between themselves and at least passive cooperation from the other two trains in the race. What caused the collision in this instance was a refusal by the engineers on all five trains at critical moments to take the steps their experience told them were needed to avoid an accident. They failed to act out of a shared conviction that the game no longer allowed for such actions – that they had become futile and counterproductive, would cause them to lose the race, and were in any case not their particular responsibility. This collective mentality and fixed attitude made the collision unavoidable.

Notice that this last version shifts the focus from, "Who or what caused the train wreck?" to "Who or what caused the failure to avoid it?" Applied to World War I, the focus is changed from, "Who or what caused the outbreak of war?" to "Who or what caused the breakdown of peace?" For many reasons impossible to discuss here, I contend that explaining peace rather than war should be the prime emphasis in studying war and international politics in general. But regardless of this claim as a broad principle, the aim here is solely to show in a prima facie way that the distinction makes sense and that World War I is better explained as the breakdown of peace than the outbreak of war. The analysis intends to show how the war had become unavoidable not because the forces and impulses driving the different powers toward it had become irresistible, but because the actions needed to avoid it had become unthinkable. Once again the argument involves counterfactual reasoning.

The strict determinist argument sketched out earlier holds that under the circumstances prevailing by 1914 the German powers were virtually certain sooner or later to try to reverse the prevailing trends pointing toward an outcome unacceptable to them through violent means that would risk general war, and that the others were equally certain to resist this strongly, resulting in war. To see why this comes close but misses the target, one needs to ask two closely related counterfactual questions. First, what plausible circumstances might have led Germany and Austria–Hungary in 1914 to decide once again, as they had done several times before, to try other less provocative and dangerous ways of defending their security and vital interests? Second, what actions, plausible under the circumstances, might the other powers have decided to take before or during the July Crisis suitable to deter and/or dissuade the German powers from a course risking war?

These counterfactual questions seem to give the game away to the indeterminists, opening the door wide to many suggestions and alternative scenarios commonly encountered in the literature. Things would have been different had the assassination attempt failed, or had the Austro–Hungarians agreed to stop their attack on Serbia at Belgrade, or had Russia given the Serbian government different advice, or had Britain given Germany a clear warning that it would enter the war on France's side, etc. However, the argument made earlier, that all the major actors were fundamentally driven by long-term concerns based on shared assumptions about the nature, rules, and stakes of the game and a shared understanding of where that game was headed, closes the door against that kind of general speculation about contingencies. If one side by 1914 was determined to reverse the prevailing trend and avert the predicted ultimate outcome even at the grave risk of war, and the other side was equally ready to accept war rather than let that happen, then different individual events and actions at the time of the July Crisis would only have altered the occasion, timing, and form of the final collision, not averted it, *unless the different events and actions also changed these shared assumptions, beliefs, and expectations.* The real questions therefore are: first, was such a change in these reigning collective European mindsets and understandings about international politics possible at all before or during the July Crisis? Second, what alternative policies, decisions, and actions conceivable in terms of the minimal-rewrite rule regarding counterfactuals and compatible with historical evidence might have effected this change, i.e., might have altered the reigning perceptions of current and future trends sufficiently on both sides, especially on the Central Powers, to change their views of what could and must be done? The strong determinist position denies that any such shift in collective outlook was possible; the indeterminist one denies that any was necessary. The view advanced here is between and beyond both. It holds that, objectively and historically speaking, certain strategies and tactics still available to the great powers in 1914 might have averted an immediate collision and also had the effect of changing crucial prevailing mindsets in the longer term, but that subjectively, in terms of what the actors considered conceivable and feasible at the time, these strategies and tactics were not real choices – and therefore war was inevitable.

The first step in testing this is establishing just what needed to change in the mindsets of what particular actors. The consensus view holds that only German and Austro-Hungarian attitudes needed to change; that view, as we have seen, will not do. But did virtually everything in the whole situation have to change? The determinist view fits the common impression that Europe by 1914 was a tinderbox filled with explosive material waiting for a spark, so that war could have broken out over any one or any combination of many issues or causes. That picture is also misleading. Actually, Europe in June 1914 was near general war, as it had been repeatedly since 1908, but it was not yet at the brink or certain to go over it, and most of the conflicts which divided the great powers were not suited to set off a war. In fact (here again comes counterfactual reasoning) no convincing scenario can be constructed by which most of the issues in dispute could have caused a general war, either alone or even in combination. One could compile a long list of issues – Anglo-German naval rivalry, Alsace-Lorraine and other irredentist territorial claims, military threats, colonial and commercial rivalries, historic national hatreds, ethnic and racial animosities – that were serious, sufficient to create hostility and tension, but not matters over which any great power wanted or intended to fight, or for which it could plausibly start a war. Instead, only three great powers contemplated starting a general war under any circumstances – Russia, Germany, and Austria-Hungary – and their respective grounds for doing so were limited and specific. Russia was willing, though not eager, to fight for two reasons: to prevent any other power from gaining control of the Turkish Straits (witness its willingness to use force to prevent its own allies and associates, Bulgaria and Greece, from seizing Constantinople in the first Balkan War, and its strong stand over the Liman von Sanders affair in early 1914); and to prevent what the Russian government, driven by a nationalist press and so-called public opinion, viewed as another humiliation like that of 1908-9 in the Balkans at the hands of the German powers. Germany was willing to go to war rather than allow its army to become decisively inferior to those of its foes, either through Russia's successful completion of its armaments program or by Austria-Hungary's collapse or defection, or both. Austria–Hungary's will for war was the most desperate and dangerous of all. Although with good reason it feared general war more than any other great power, its leaders had already concluded by early 1914 that it could not tolerate any further deterioration of its great-power status and its Balkan position, particularly through more challenges and provocations from Serbia. These were the only issues that could have caused general war in 1914, and they did cause it. The question of the avoidability of war therefore rests neither on whether some impossible set of sweeping changes in the whole international situation occurred, nor on whether certain particular contingent events involved in the outbreak of war in July 1914 could have gone differently, but on the specific question of whether these particular great powers could have been deterred and/or dissuaded from risking general war for these particular reasons.

The answer is "Yes." It arises not from theory or speculation, but solid historical evidence. The first thing to recognize is that these problems were not new to these powers, but old and familiar, almost in fact standard; they had repeatedly caused wars or threatened to cause them before.[22] Twice in the previous century (1809 and 1859) Austria had gone to war rather than accept a further decline in its great-power status and position and more threats to its prestige and rights. In 1756 Prussia had deliberately launched a preventive war against Austria and Russia rather than wait for an overwhelming coalition to jell against it.[23] Russia had been ready in the Bulgarian Crisis of 1884–7 to fight Austria rather than accept another supposed humiliation at its hands. Not only were the essential dangers in 1914 familiar, almost commonplace; so were the theater, the terrain and the three players. Ever since 1763 at the end of the Seven Years War, when Russia and Prussia had fully emerged as recognized great powers, these three states had dominated Central and Eastern Europe, competing over territory, interests, influence, leadership, and security. This area, even during the Napoleonic Wars, had been constantly the main focus and center of European politics. The issues that dominated the Austro–German–Russian relationship and threatened the peace in 1914 had *mutatis mutandis* been vital for them the whole time.

But if the issues and dangers were familiar, so were the remedies. The astonishing fact (astonishing both in itself and in its being so widely

---

[22]This is the point, in the analogy of the train wreck, of noting that the engineers of the three trains had been over this terrain previously and knew what caused wrecks and how to avoid them.

[23]Lest one suppose that these historical examples counted for little in 1914, Johannes Burkhardt argues convincingly that analogies with Prussia's situation in 1756, 1813, and 1870 were very prominent in German thinking in 1914 (Burkhardt 1996).

ignored) is that the 150 years of Austro–German–Russian relations after 1763 represent a story not of constant rivalry, conflicts of interests, struggles for power and influence, and frequent tensions and crises leading to war, but of constant rivalry, conflicts of interests, struggles for power and influence, and frequent tensions and crises resulting in *peace.* Between 1740 and 1914, Austria and Russia, always rivals in the Balkans, often rivals elsewhere as well, frequently at swords' points, *never* fought each other, except for two occasions in 1809 and 1812 when they were dragged by Napoleon into half-hearted campaigns that they would never have entered on their own. The same is true between 1762 and 1914 for Prussia-Germany and Russia. Austria and Prussia fought two short wars over Germany, to be sure – one indecisive in 1778–9, the other decisive in 1866. Yet within 13 years of the latter they were again allies, as they had been most of the 50 years before 1866 – without ever ceasing to be rivals. In the same way Austria and Russia and Germany and Russia were frequently allies though always rivals.

Thus the central story in European international history from 1763 to 1914 is this remarkable Austro–German–Russian *peace.* 1914 must be seen first and foremost not simply and generically as the outbreak of general European war, but as the breakdown of that specific long peace. To explain the war, scholars must first explain it, understand what maintained and revived it so long, often against improbable odds, and then, having done this, ask themselves whether the measures and devices that had previously served to maintain this Austro–German–Russian peace no longer would work in 1914, or whether (as I believe) they simply were not tried.

To attempt any such serious analysis here would stretch the already elastic bounds of this essay beyond the breaking point. I will therefore merely make some general points, more by assertion than by argument. First, the procedures and principles of European diplomacy used for dealing with such problems as these, especially those of the European Concert, were well known. Where seriously tried, they still worked even in 1914. One vital issue capable of causing war in 1914, that of the Turkish Straits, was actually handled successfully in this way. Russia's warnings to Bulgaria and Greece to stay away from the Straits and its success (with British and French support and restraint) in inducing Germany and the Ottoman Empire to back down on the Liman affair under cover of a face-saving formula without using force against the Turks were examples, if risky ones, of traditional Concert diplomacy on the Eastern question. The underlying principles behind both were traditional: that Russia had special interests in the Straits and could not allow others besides Turkey to control them, but could rely on diplomacy and the Concert to defend its interests and would not be allowed to act unilaterally or by force. True, the other fighting issue for Russia, that it would not tolerate another humiliation in the Balkans at the hands of Austria–Hungary and Germany, and the corresponding fighting issue for Austria–Hungary, that it could not endure any further undermining of its great power position in the Balkans or challenges from Russia and its client Serbia, were far more difficult to handle, not merely because of the mutually incompatible perceptions and enflamed public opinion on all sides, but also because (in my view) Russian perceptions were one-sided and unjustified. The widespread belief that Russia's rights had repeatedly been violated, its prestige and honor challenged, and its security and historic mission in the Balkans threatened ever since 1908 by the German powers simply does not square with undeniable facts. In 1908–9, even more than in 1904–6, Russia had been lucky to escape dangers of its own making, that the Central Powers could have exploited but did not. Since then Russia had been mainly pursuing and getting away with a very bold offensive policy in the Balkans. Yet this was far from the first time that Russia had blamed difficulties largely of its own making on Germany and Austria (witness the Eastern Crisis of 1875–8 and the Bulgarian Crisis of 1884–7) or that Austria had seen Russian pressure as an alp that it had to shake off at almost any cost (the Crimean War). Historically, there were tested ways of handling such problems short of war.[24]

As for Germany's fear of Russia, here again one must distinguish between the irrational German fear of being overrun by barbarian hordes from the East or the concomitant belief in a great, inevitable Teuton-Slav struggle for mastery in Europe, and the concrete, rational German fear of being hopelessly outmanned by 1917 by the combined Russo-French armies and those of their allies. Diplomacy could not directly combat the former fear, but it could have done something to manage the latter, even within the existing alliance structure. For instance, there could have been some informal equivalent for Germany of Bismarck's Reinsurance Treaty with Russia in 1887, assuring Germany that France and Britain would not support a Russian attack on Germany, as Bismarck had reassured Russia that Germany would not support a British–Austrian offensive against it.

The other requirement for simultaneously deterring and reassuring Germany concerns Austria–Hungary, and brings us to the heart of the

---

[24]For example, France was held back from war over the Near East in 1840 and Russia from war with the Ottoman Empire over Greece in 1821–3 and with Austria over Bulgaria in 1885–7 by just such collective pressure.

problem. One can hardly overemphasize the destabilizing effect of the conviction among German leaders by 1914, one promoted by the Austrians themselves, that Germany must now use its ally or lose it – stand by it now at any risk and cost, or expect shortly to have to fight without it because of Austria–Hungary's defection, paralysis, or breakup. It is difficult enough to imagine a counterfactual scenario in which Germany with its powerful, irresponsible military, its erratic, impulsive monarch, and its semi-authoritarian, deeply divided government and society would have calmly stood by while Russia and France completed their efforts to achieve military superiority over it. It is quite impossible to imagine Germany doing so while it simultaneously was losing its last remaining useful ally. The implication is clear: one indispensable key to restraining Germany and in general to preventing a major war was stabilizing Austria–Hungary's international status by doing something serious about the Austro-Hungarian problem.

The common reply to this assertion, or rather, dismissal of it, is that Austria–Hungary's decline and eventual collapse were irreversible, the result of its internal decay and impossible to solve or arrest by international politics and diplomacy. As already indicated, I deny the premise, as do other scholars more expert on Austro-Hungarian internal affairs than I. Austria–Hungary's problems and weaknesses were real and would not go away or be cured, but they were not of themselves destroying it or even keeping it from being a working political entity, functioning far more soundly in most respects, for example, than Russia or its Balkan neighbors or Italy. It was the combination within the cauldron of European international competition of internal and external pressures on Austria–Hungary and the purposeful exploitation of these by other states that was ruining its international position. It is simply not true – in fact, it is nonsense – to say that European international politics could do nothing about this or about preventing a war that might arise out of it. Were this principle true, the Habsburg Monarchy would not have survived any number of crises in its long, crisis-riddled existence. It had repeatedly been saved in the past by support, usually passive but sometimes active, from various members of the European family of states including Russia who recognized that its disappearance would bring with it incalculable consequences and insoluble problems.

Yet making this simple historical observation, or citing the traditional balance of power principle of the need to preserve Austria–Hungary in order to maintain a viable international system, risks confusing the central issue to the advantage of those whose interest it is to confuse it. The question is not whether the Habsburg Monarchy could have been saved by international action in 1914, or should have been, or what other powers including its rivals could and should have done to save it. My own view, indicated earlier, is that the Monarchy did not

need active intervention by anyone in its internal problems in order
to survive and continue to muddle through, as it had done for most
of its existence with fair success. Quite the contrary – it needed less
intervention and pressure from outside. Regardless of this, the real
question is whether, in the face of mounting evidence of the possibility
or likelihood of the collapse or paralysis of so essential an actor as
Austria–Hungary, the members of the European international system
had reasons, incentives, precedents, and devices for taking some kind
of action to manage and control the process and international consequences of so momentous a change, or whether they were bound simply
to let it happen and see what emerged from the wreckage.

Thus correctly posed, the question answers itself, and not on the basis of any moral considerations, but on those of history and elementary
state self-interest. The Austro–Hungarian problem in its *international*
dimensions and repercussions was precisely the sort of question with
which the international system was supposed to deal, and could have
dealt. The European system in 1914 offered ample historical precedents for the management of the problems and dangers presented by
declining and threatened vital units. They varied widely, of course, from
brutal measures like planned partitions of the declining units with more
or less balanced compensations to the more powerful ones (Poland and
the German Empire in the late 18th and early 19th centuries) through
less brutal, more controlled management (the Ottoman Empire in the
Balkans and North Africa) through measures of joint guarantee and pro-
tection (Belgium, Switzerland, Denmark, and for a considerable period
the Papal State). What was unprecedented was what actually happened
before and during 1914 – the ignoring of this issue, the absence of any
collective European response to the prospective downfall or disappearance of a central actor like Austria–Hungary, a contingency long and
widely foreseen and predicted. That was a great, astonishing departure
from tradition.

What could and should have been done to manage the international
aspects and consequences of the Austro–Hungarian problem over the
longer term is of course controversial, as is whether any feasible international action would have been effective. But it is not hard to propose
measures, plausible on their face, for short-term action in 1914, i.e., for
a European intervention following the assassination of Franz Ferdinand
to stop the incident from escalating into a dangerous confrontation
and war. Something certainly could have been attempted to satisfy
Austria-Hungary's prestige and honor and to compel Serbia to conform
at least outwardly to its international commitments to act as a good

neighbor.[25] Since the particular steps Austria–Hungary demanded – a serious investigation of the ties between the assassination plot and Serbia's government, its nationalist organizations, and its military intelligence, followed by concrete measures to prevent future provocations, would not and probably could not be carried out by Serbia no matter what its government promised, and since Russia's attitude meant that such actions also could not be undertaken by Austria–Hungary without provoking an international crisis, the obvious conclusion, based on historical precedents, would be that Europe acting in concert would ask

---

[25]To be sure, there are historians, not merely Serb nationalists but others as well, who deny any Serbian responsibility for the assassination, arguing *inter alia* that Austria–Hungary had brought it on by the provocative character of the state visit to Sarajevo. Niall Ferguson (1999: 146, n. 3) quotes A. J. P. Taylor's remark that if British royalty had chosen to visit Dublin on St. Patrick's Day during the Troubles, they could also have expected to be shot at. Let me amend Taylor's analogy to make it conform better to Austria–Hungary's position:

> Suppose that the United Kingdom in 1914 was not separated from the continent by the English Channel, but had as its direct neighbor in the southeast, where the Low Countries are, an independent Kingdom of Ireland. This Kingdom of Ireland, though small and backward, was fiercely combative, violent and conspiratorial in its politics, and committed to an ethnic integral-nationalist hegemonic state ideology calling for it to unite all Irishmen under its rule. Its definition of "Irish" included other Celts in the UK (Scots, Welshmen) on the grounds that they were really Irish corrupted by an alien regime and religion, and it taught its children in school that large parts of the UK really belonged to the Kingdom of Ireland and should be liberated. To this end its nationalist press waged a propaganda war against the UK calling for its overthrow and dissolution, and its military intelligence arm, operating secretly and without control of the government, supported dissidents and revolutionary organizations in the UK, and trained and armed terrorists to operate there. This Kingdom of Ireland was allied with and supported by Germany. When the decision to send the Prince of Wales on a state visit to UK Ireland was made in London, the Irish royal government, knowing that some form of Irish terrorist action was being planned and being unready for a war but not daring for internal reasons to act decisively to prevent one, gave a vague warning to London that the visit might have bad results. But London also knew that a cancellation of the planned state visit, designed as a measure to support and encourage UK loyalists in British-ruled Ireland, would be exploited by the royal Irish press and nationalist organizations as more proof of British cowardice and weakness and a further spur to Irish rebellion. Would the UK government under these circumstances have cancelled the visit? Or, when the Prince was assassinated by a UK Irishman who had contacts with the royal Irish military intelligence and when the entire royal Irish press and public hailed this act as a glorious patriotic deed, would British leaders have shrugged their shoulders and said, "Well, we asked for it"? One need not know the actual British response to Irish acts of rebellion like the Phoenix Park murders or the Easter Rising to guess the answer.

Austria–Hungary to turn its cause and demands over to them, and then carry through seriously on an investigation of the terrorist attack and any required sanctions on Serbia. The 19th century provided ample precedent for international action to compel smaller states, however innocent they might claim to be and however righteous their cause, to stop challenging great powers and causing international crises, just as there were precedents for requiring great powers to act through the international community and not take the law into their own hands. Greece and other Balkan states, for example, had repeatedly been compelled by joint great-power intervention to stop irredentist campaigns against the Ottoman Empire, and the Ottomans prevented from taking revenge on their rebels and enemies. Russia was more than once required in the 19th century to turn its cause and national honor in the Balkans over to the European Concert to defend. The fact that this procedure did not always work or was not always tried makes no difference. It was there, it could and did sometimes work, and in some instances like this one it was the only thing that could have worked (the only means, for example, that could have prevented the Crimean War, and almost did).

Yet in a way this discussion too, however necessary it is to clear the ground, is irrelevant and distracting, for the obvious, overriding fact is that before and during 1914 no action of this sort was tried, seriously considered, or even entertained. The danger of war steadily increased, the European powers were quite aware of the crucial specific source of that danger in the Austro-Hungarian problem, they knew about the kinds of measures used in the past and still available to meet such dangers, and collectively they did nothing. This inaction is the most important development in prewar diplomacy and in the July Crisis. It also strikingly illustrates both how counterfactual reasoning can serve the vital historical purpose not of telling us what might have happened, but of illuminating what really did happen, and why one needs to see 1914 not as the outbreak of war but as the breakdown of peace. Every account of the July Crisis discusses the crucial delay between July 5, when Austria–Hungary received Germany's support for its ultimatum to Serbia, and July 23 when it actually delivered the ultimatum. Some have speculated that the delay was fateful in allowing the initial shock of the assassination to wear off (which is doubtful – the Serbian and Russian reactions, the decisive ones, would have been the same earlier). But another delay, far more fateful and inexplicable, is hardly mentioned or discussed in the vast literature. For a full month after the assassination, the powers did absolutely nothing in concert to prepare for or deal with the possible or likely consequences of this sensational event. Everyone knew that Austria–Hungary and Serbia were mortal enemies, that they had gone to the brink of war at least four times in the past five years, three of them in the past year, and that Russia was Serbia's ally and protector and Austria–Hungary's main enemy. Yet when something occurred that anyone could see might set off this long-envisioned war, the Entente powers averted their eyes, went about their other business, waited for whatever Austria–Hungary and Germany might do, and insofar as they thought about the incident at all, shrugged their shoulders and hoped for the best. Meanwhile Austria–Hungary and Germany took actions that set off the war.

This argument seems paradoxically to prove the precise opposite of what was promised and intended – to show that the war was not inevitable. For if the means for a serious attempt at avoiding it were known and available, as I have just argued, then the root cause of the war must have been contingent, have lain in a collective failure to apply them.

But of course that collective inaction in 1914 is neither inexplicable nor really contingent. Behind the failure to act lay precisely those shared assumptions and convictions about the nature, stakes, and reigning course of the international contest earlier cited as the reasons why determinists consider the war objectively unavoidable. I contend rather that the pressure of events did not make war objectively unavoidable by making peaceful choices impossible in the face of security threats, alliance commitments, and arms races, but made it subjectively unavoidable by fatally constricting what all the actors would entertain as a conceivable, rational course of action in the face of this crisis or any other like it. The particular reasons why the various powers did not even consider taking any of the steps mentioned above to anticipate a crisis and manage it collectively are familiar and obvious. Austria–Hungary and Germany were determined to reverse the existing trend in international politics they considered fatal to them, and saw in this crisis a final chance to do so. The Entente powers equally saw in this crisis a danger to the existing trend favorable to them and were equally determined not to allow it to be reversed. Russian policy, seen by Russians as a defense against German and Austro-Hungarian aggression, was resolutely bent on maintaining and extending Russia's control over the Balkans. French policy was rigidly fixed on maintaining the existing alliances and therefore doing nothing to weaken the Franco-Russian one (Keiger 1983; 1997). Britain's was fixed on maintaining its ententes, both in order to check Germany in Europe and avoid threats to the British Empire – the latter aim, the primary one, requiring maintaining the entente with Russia at all cost (French 1995). But behind these familiar positive reasons for failure to act collectively, there was a still more fundamental negative one. No one believed that a sane, rational foreign policy allowed any longer for this kind of collective response. Anyone who tried to suspend the rules of power politics, of "every man and every alliance for himself, and the devil take the hindmost," was a fool and would earn the fool's reward. Hence to ask any British, French, Russian, Italian, or even German leader to sacrifice or subordinate particular interests and opportunities of theirs for the sake of some sort of collective action to stabilize the international position of Austria–Hungary so as to lessen the chances of a general war was to ask the impossible and absurd – to ask them to commit political suicide at home and to be laughed at and swindled abroad. Stabilizing Austria–Hungary's position was really not anyone's business except that of Austrians and Hungarians, or perhaps Germans if they wished to do so for their own power-political reasons.

This profound practical indifference to the survival of a vital actor such as the Habsburg Monarchy was, to repeat, a break with a long European tradition. It did not represent normal Realpolitik, but constituted a different concrete definition of it, a different collective attitude toward international politics.[26] The power whose final break with the Concert principle proved decisive, Austria–Hungary, was also the last and most reluctant to abandon it, because it was the one most dependent on it and on collective international support and restraint to survive. This outlook was evident before 1914. One of Foreign Minister Aehrenthal's chief aims in 1908 had been to revive the old Three-Emperors' League and the moribund Austro-Russian entente in the Balkans by a deal with Russia over Bosnia and the Straits. Even in 1914 this idea was far from dead. The original Austrian proposal for reversing the current disastrous trends in the Balkans called for political rather than military

---

[26]The history of the politics of World War I illustrates this dramatically. Imperial Germany was the great threat and object of hatred for the Allies, especially in the West; Austria–Hungary was taken much less seriously. Yet these same Allies never intended to eliminate Germany as a state, or even take away enough territory to cripple it as a major power. All, in fact, hoped to have Germany as a junior political and economic partner in the postwar era. In contrast, the territorial aims of the Allies were directed overwhelmingly against Austria–Hungary in the interest of gaining and keeping lesser allies – Serbia, Italy, Romania, and ultimately the Czechs and the Poles. This went on until, in a marvelous instance of the irony of history, the western Allies decided in 1916-17, when faced with Russia's defeat and the possibility of a German victory, that it would be nice to get Austria–Hungary, by this time on its last legs and totally dependent on Germany, to defect, help defeat Germany now, and balance against Germany in the future. The only thing more astonishing than the notion that this absurd 18th century-style volte-face was possible is the fact that some able historians take it seriously as evidence that Britain and France never meant real harm to Austria–Hungary and always wanted to preserve it (Hanak 1962; Grigg 1985; French 1995).

action and was changed only in the wake of the assassination (though how much difference this would have made is debatable).[27] During the July Crisis itself Austro-Hungarian leaders hoped against hope that Russia might let it get away with a local war against Serbia, and if Russia did, they intended to use the opportunity to seek a fundamental rapprochement with Russia through negotiations for a joint solution to both the Balkan and the Ukrainian problems (Lloyd 1993; Kronenbitter 1996). There is a tragic appropriateness about Austria–Hungary's breaking at last with the Concert principle and thereby destroying itself and Europe with it, like the blinded Samson pulling down the pillars of the temple, just as there is about Tsarist Russia's acting upon the shibboleths of its honor and its alleged historic mission of protecting the Balkan Slavs rather than its true state interests and thereby signing its own death warrant.[28]

To argue for the inevitability of World War I on this ground is, to repeat, *not* to blame Britain, Russia, and France for it while exonerating Germany and Austria-Hungary, or to characterize the former as more blind and reckless than the latter. It is an attempt to root the disaster deep in a political culture which all shared, which all had helped to develop, and upon which all acted in 1914, Germany and Austria-Hungary precipitating the final descent into the maelstrom. It is to see the origins of the war as finally a tragedy more than a crime, though crimes were surely involved; to view it as inevitable by reason of wrong beliefs, hubris, and folly too broadly and deeply anchored in the reigning political culture to be recognized, much less examined and changed. The tragedy of its origins thus connects with the tragedy of the war itself in its hyperbolic protraction and destruction, evoking, like Shakespeare's *Romeo and Juliet*, the verdict, "All are punished."

---

[27] The Matscheko memorandum of June 1914, changed after the assassination to be used against Serbia, called for joint Austro-German pressure on Romania to commit itself publicly to the Austro-German alliance from which it had just defected. It has been interpreted by some, including F. R. Bridge (1990: 334–5) as showing that Austria-Hungary contemplated a political rather than military solution to its problems until after June 28. My view is that the original plan, a proposal to force Romania, now independent, to do what it was never willing to do even when it was a secret ally, would certainly not have solved Austria-Hungary's problem and was almost as likely to escalate into a general crisis as the actual Austro-German initiative did (Schroeder 1975).

[28] For a convincing argument that Russia had never had the kind of vital interest in the Balkans that its Orthodox and Pan-Slav publicists claimed, and that throughout the 19th century it had repeatedly become involved in costly complications there against its best interests, see Jelavich (1991).

Chapter 7

Power, globalization, and the end of the Cold War: reevaluating a landmark case for ideas

Stephen G. Brooks and William C. Wohlforth

The end of the Cold War has become a case study of major importance for scholars of international relations for numerous reasons. Not least among these is that it helped spark a renaissance in the study of ideas in the field and contributed to the rise of constructivism as a major theoretical school in the 1990s.[1] It has also proven to be a rich case for developing new arguments inspired by constructivist thinking, as well as for extending standard models concerning how ideas shape strategic behavior drawn from cognitive or social psychology and organization theory. The result of this scholarly effort is a rich and diverse literature that advances numerous models of how norms, culture, identity, trust, persuasion, learning, demonstration effects, transnational conceptual flows, intellectual entrepreneurship, socialization, and numerous other ideational processes influenced the dramatic ending of the superpower rivalry. Indeed, it is difficult to identify another case that has generated as large and varied a literature devoted to exploring how ideas influence international relations (Lebow 1994; Lebow and Stein 1994; Koslowski and Kratochwil 1994; Risse-Kappen 1994; Mueller 1995; Stein 1995; Herman 1996; Checkel 1997; Kolodziej 1997; Larson 1997; Lévesque

---

[1] As Alexander Wendt notes, "The revival of constructivist thinking about international politics was accelerated by the end of the Cold War.... Mainstream IR theory simply had difficulty explaining the end of the Cold War, or systemic change more generally. It seemed to many that these difficulties stemmed from IR's materialist and individualist orientation, such that a more ideational, and holistic view of international politics might do better" (Wendt 1999: 4; see also, for example, Katzenstein 1996: 2; Katzenstein, Keohane, and Krasner 1998: 670).

1997; Mendelson 1998; Snel 1998; Bennett 1999; Evangelista 1999; English 2000; Risse 2000).

The question is clearly no longer whether but rather how and how much ideas matter under different conditions – and how best to model their influence on strategic behavior. The problem is that ideational models depend on an implicit or explicit contrast to explanations rooted in changing material incentives. How and how much ideas matter naturally depend on how and how much material incentives matter. In the case of the Cold War's end, the objective of a more sophisticated approach to the study of ideas is currently hampered less by the quantity of plausible models than by deficiencies in our understanding of the material incentives facing decision-makers. Despite the fact that Soviet economic decline is often seen as a key reason why the Cold War ended, there are relatively few studies in the international relations literature that specify rigorously how constrained the Soviet Union was economically, and exactly how those constraints influenced strategic choices. The result is a striking asymmetry: dozens of complex models on ideational influences arrayed against a few bare-bones accounts that examine the economic or other material incentives facing the Soviet Union. And the few accounts that highlight material incentives are not as helpful for evaluating the effect of ideas as they might be because they either include both ideational and material shifts without trying to establish their interaction, or they fail to compare their analyses in any detail to explanations based on ideas (Deudney and Ikenberry 1991/92; Wohlforth 1994/95; Oye 1995; Copeland 1999/2000; Schweller and Wohlforth 2000). The result is a proliferation of plausible models and hypotheses but comparatively few truly probative empirical tests (Wohlforth 1998).

Our central purpose in this chapter is to provide a more complete understanding of the material pressures facing Soviet policymakers in the 1980s. We bring three new sources of evidence to bear. First, we broaden the analysis of material incentives. Scholars on all sides in the international relations literature on the end of Cold War typically treat the balance of capabilities as the only material change that needs to be taken into account. We bring a new factor into the discussion: the changing structure of global production. Thus far, scholars of international security, in general, and students of the Cold War's end, in particular, have largely ignored this critical shift in the material environment. Introducing the structure of global production not only changes how we comprehend the end of the Cold War, but has important implications for understanding the role of material incentives in international relations more generally.

Second, we explore how Soviet relative decline affected the course of the Cold War in its final years. In recent years, new primary and secondary sources have become available that dramatically alter our earlier understanding of the material pressures facing Soviet policymakers in the 1980s and the ways in which those pressures influenced decisions. We supply a fuller picture of the exact extent of Soviet relative decline, analyze how Moscow's experience of decline compares with that of other modern great powers, and draw on the most recent evidence concerning how perceptions of decline, new ideas, and new foreign policies were related.

Third, we explore evidence on the role and attitudes of conservative or hard-line Soviet officials, most of which has only recently become available. The absence of evidence concerning such "old thinkers" has severely limited our understanding of the end of the Cold War. Examining old thinkers is especially important because they were exposed to the increasing material pressures facing the Soviet Union in the 1980s but were insulated from or resistant to ideational sources of change.

A major dividend of this analysis is a more accurate portrayal of the material setting of the Cold War's end, and thus a better understanding of the seminal event that ushered in the current international era. At the same time, this analysis provides a better grasp of how material incentives present in this case relate to, and interact with, the ideational factors featured in the literature. Our general finding is that the material pressures on Soviet foreign policy during the 1980s were much more marked than earlier analyses have assumed. Moreover, the evidence indicates that many of the causal mechanisms in ideational models of this case are endogenous to these changing material incentives, that is, their effects are largely a reflection of a changing material environment.

Beyond moving us toward a better understanding of this case, we also derive two general theoretical implications. First, our study indicates that it is now critical for scholars who focus on the causal role of ideas to pay much more attention to the issue of endogeneity. Second, our analysis suggests, contrary to the conventional wisdom, that changes in the material environment may sometimes help explain how alterations in states' fundamental goals or "identities" occur.

We proceed in four sections. We begin by specifying our treatment of the case and its relation to ongoing theoretical controversies. In the second section, we provide new evidence and analysis of the effects of Soviet relative decline on Moscow's decision to retrench internationally in the 1980s. The third section establishes how changes in the structure of global production shifted the underlying terms of the Cold War rivalry and generated incentives for a Soviet policy of retrenchment and engagement with the West. In the fourth section, we bring these two material pressures together in the context of examining recent evidence on Soviet old thinkers. In the conclusion, we sum up the results of our analysis and outline the repercussions for future research.

The Cold War's end as a case study

International relations scholarship on the end of the Cold War has been hamstrung by lack of evidence as well as by poor specification of the relationship between case and theory.[2] In this section, we clarify our treatment of the case. We then turn to an examination of the evidence.

The ideational models

Dozens of scholars – some explicitly inspired by constructivism, others following psychological, institutional, or organizational approaches – have proposed numerous pathways through which various kinds of ideas affected the course of events. These models identify both a process by which ideas are generated and transmitted to decision-makers and a causal mechanism through which ideas affect choices.

Concerning the origins and transmission of ideas, two generic processes do most of the work. The first is intellectual entrepreneurship. A crisis creates a window of opportunity by discrediting old policies and the ideas associated with them. Idea entrepreneurs then fill the gap by showing how novel ideas resolve strategic dilemmas. These entrepreneurs may be intellectuals in the various bureaucracies who feed their ideas to leaders eager for new concepts, as many scholars argue was the case in the Soviet Union in the mid-1980s (e.g., Herman 1996; Checkel 1997; Mendelson 1998; English 2000). Or the true intellectual entrepreneurs may be the top leaders themselves, as many others contend was the case with Mikhail Gorbachev and the end of the Cold War (e.g., Wendt 1992; Koslowski and Kratochwil 1994; Brown 1996; Larson 1997, chap. 6; Breslauer and Lebow 2004). Either way, these scholars maintain that although the crisis that opens the policy window may be a necessary condition of change, the response is a creative, fundamentally intellectual act that switches history onto new rails and whose explanation requires specific models. Many accounts add an important transnational element to the entrepreneurship process. Here, the origins of the ideas lie in substate intellectual communities

---

[2]Part of the problem may be that much of the debate has concerned "grand theory," while the empirical work on the case concerns "middle-range" theories. In keeping with this diagnosis, our focus is on middle-range theory.

that transmit new concepts across national borders (e.g., Knopf 1993; Risse-Kappen 1994; Evangelista 1999).

The second generic process is learning. Actors alter their cognitive structures in response to experience. They may change their strategies, their beliefs about how the world works, or even their most basic preferences or identities. The actors concerned may be individual leaders, institutions, elites, or states. Some scholars employ cognitive theory to explain why actors draw particular lessons from their experiences (Lebow 1995; Stein 1995; Bennett 1999). For others, especially those inspired by constructivist thinking, the learning process takes a more social form, where the emphasis is less on lessons drawn from specific events than on elite socialization to new norms or other cultural, social, or intellectual changes in international society (Koslowski and Kratochwil 1994; Herman 1996; Kolodziej 1997).

The mechanisms by which ideas affect choices also take two basic forms. Many scholars argue that ideas reduce the uncertainty inherent in any strategic situation by providing new "road maps," which in turn lead to new policy initiatives. In this vein, some scholars argue that new ideas led to a different framing of the Soviets' security problem, thereby suggesting different policy responses; others maintain that new causal beliefs about how the world works affected Soviet cost–benefit calculations and helped generate new policies (Checkel 1997; Lévesque 1997; Mendelson 1998; Bennett 1999; Evangelista 1999; on ideas as road maps, see Goldstein and Keohane 1993). A second group of scholars highlight deeper changes in underlying preferences or identities that, they argue, have even more profound effects. Constructivists, in particular, argue that changes in the Soviet leadership's or elite's basic identity led to a reorientation of the country's most fundamental interest from opposing and competing with the liberal West to becoming a part of it (Wendt 1992; Koslowski and Kratochwil 1994; Herman 1996; Forsberg 1999; English 2000).

Material incentives and their relation to ideational models

We make two basic points regarding this literature. First, these ideational models are crucially dependent on a careful specification of the material incentives facing Soviet decision-makers. Second, scholars in this literature routinely counterpose their arguments against a spare and impoverished understanding of material incentives. As a result, it is impossible to refine or accurately evaluate these basic ideational models, thereby limiting our understanding of these factors and of the end of the Cold War more generally.

As the scholars who use the entrepreneurship model recognize, the "crisis" that opened up policy windows for Soviet intellectual entrepreneurs was in important respects a result of Soviet economic decline (Checkel 1997, chap. 1; Mendelson 1998, chap. 1). Critical to constructing and assessing their various models of ideas and international change is therefore a careful assessment of exactly *how* constraining the Soviet Union's economic problems were. The more economic constraints pointed to specific policy responses, the less the need for a particular entrepreneur to come up with a novel solution to the problem and, in turn, the less likely any given entrepreneur's solution would differ greatly in practice from another's. The same goes for learning models. Actors learn in part by interacting with their material environment. The importance of cognitive processes in promoting learning hinges on precisely how constraining this environment is.[3]

The point of departure of all recent work on ideas and international security is that material incentives are never determinate; there is always some uncertainty that ideas help resolve. We do not question that essential proposition; ideas and material incentives clearly work together in complex ways, and their interaction varies across cases. Our response is simply that it is important to specify how much uncertainty characterizes various strategic situations in order to further empirical analysis and theory development. Ultimately, each of the basic causal mechanisms by which ideas shape choice hinges on some estimate of the uncertainty facing decision-makers *given* material incentives. To model the ways in which new ideas shape behavior, it is therefore crucial to have some working estimate of how much room for debate over choices the material setting creates. Given that social science still lacks an adequate general language for discussing levels of uncertainty, we must frame the assessment of uncertainty in the terms of a given case. This is the task we perform with respect to the end of the Cold War.

All ideational models of the end of the Cold War stand in contrast to an alternative baseline hypothesis: that the Soviets reoriented their foreign policy in large part in response to changing material incentives.[4] This brings up our second major point concerning the ideas literature:

---

[3] As Andrew Bennett notes, "Learning theory is itself indeterminate unless it takes many material and political factors into account" (Bennett 1999: 7).

[4] The contrast with this material hypothesis is most clear for ideational analyses that are *causal* in nature, which comprise the overwhelming preponderance of empirical work in the end of Cold War literature. To a lesser degree, this is also the case for examinations of this case that highlight the *constitutive* role of ideas. On this distinction, see Wendt (1998). Koslowski and Kratochwil (1994) come closest to implementing a constitutive perspective, but even their account has a strong causal element and they also ultimately counterpose their analysis to a baseline material account.

it does not adequately confront the evidence supporting this basic hypothesis. Ideational explanations of the Cold War's end instead are counterposed against an impoverished understanding of the material pressures confronting the Soviet Union. There are two basic reasons for this, neither of which lies with the scholars responsible for the renaissance of ideas in international relations.

The first reason is empirical: much of the relevant evidence on how changing material incentives influenced the reorientation of Soviet foreign policy either has been lacking or is not easily accessible to international relations scholars. The second reason is theoretical. Scholars in this literature routinely use Kenneth Waltz's neorealist framework as the theoretical foil for their analyses, because neorealism is typically seen as providing the definitive theoretical word on material incentives in the international environment (Waltz 1979). Neorealism does not have a monopoly on thinking about these factors, however; the standard neorealist understanding of material incentives is actually far too narrow to provide a productive backdrop for developing and evaluating models of how ideas affect strategic behavior (Brooks 2001, chap. 3). In particular, to fully explore the potential of such models it is necessary to move beyond a restrictive focus on the balance of capabilities. It is also important to move beyond the standard neorealist conception of state preferences in which security trumps all other priorities, including economic capacity (Brooks 1997: 450–3). Indeed, in situations such as that faced by the Soviet Union in the 1980s, it may make little sense to draw distinctions between economic capacity and security as state objectives, because as we show, Moscow's changing material fortunes undermined both goals simultaneously.[5]

The analysis

The remainder of this chapter provides a fuller analysis of material incentives and their relation to changing Soviet ideas and policies. Our empirical focus is on the Soviet Union's fundamental shift in grand strategy in the latter half of the 1980s.[6] We seek answers to two critical questions. Most important, why did the Soviets choose a grand strategy of retrenchment instead of continuing with the foreign policy status quo? In turn, why did the Soviets engage in retrenchment and at the

---

[5] As William Odom notes, it is important to recognize the "symbiosis of economic policies and military considerations in the Soviet Union" (Odom 1990: 62).

[6] A clear argument for why the pre-1986 policy can be treated as a case of continuity is English, *The idea of the west.*

same time seek to pursue engagement, in particular by opening up to the global economy?

We frame our analysis at this broad level for three reasons. First, most studies of this case in the general international relations literature are centered on Moscow's decision to move away decisively from the foreign policy status quo. This grand strategic reorientation has attracted so much attention in part because it involved changing the essential core of Soviet foreign policy, including many of its fundamental ideological precepts. Second, as we show, the choice between the retrenchment/engagement strategy and maintaining the foreign policy status quo was the operative decision for Soviet policymakers. Third, all accounts of these events agree that the Soviets' eventual decision fundamentally to reorient their foreign policy was one of the most important elements of the end of the Cold War. Indeed, most analysts hold that the Soviet strategic realignment we treat here was *the* most important immediate cause of the transformation of world politics in the late 1980s (Garthoff 1994).

We restrict our analysis in two critical ways. First, we define material incentives solely in terms of the costs of maintaining the status quo. Second, we define material costs exclusively as *economic* costs. Clearly, increasing economic costs were not the only relevant factors in the material balance sheet facing Soviet policy makers.[7] We limit the analysis to economic costs partly for reasons of parsimony, partly so that our analysis is falsifiable, and partly to ensure that our examination stands clearly in contrast to the ideational explanations outlined above.

Soviet relative decline

Most analysts now agree that the Soviet Union was declining relative to its rivals in the 1980s. Scholars developing ideational models of the end of the Cold War argue, however, that decline by itself is woefully indeterminate: retrenchment was not the only way Moscow could have responded to decline. Moreover, they contend that Soviet decline was comparatively mild in the mid-1980s. They conclude, therefore, that "new thinking" ideas emerged largely independently and were far more directly connected to Gorbachev's foreign policy responses than relative decline.

---

[7]Nuclear weapons are also clearly important. See the discussions in Deudney and Ikenberry (1991–2) and Oye (1995). Although nothing appreciably changed regarding nuclear weapons during this period and they did not propel the new Soviet interest in retrenchment, they did provide a margin of safety that made adopting retrenchment at this time easier for many to swallow.

These objections raise three critical issues. First is the depth and timing of decline. Exactly when did it begin, and how bad was it? Second is the comparative systemic context of Soviet decline. Given the logic of its placement in the international system, are there deductive reasons that we would expect the Soviet Union to be more or less sensitive to decline than other modern great powers? Third is the issue of endogeneity, that is, the connection between changes in capabilities and changes in ideas. How did decline, new ideas, and new policies relate? How deep was the Soviets' uncertainty about the optimal policy response to decline? The following subsections address these issues.

The nature of Soviet relative decline

The root of the Soviet Union's problem was declining growth. War years excepted, the Soviet Union grew rapidly from the 1920s to the 1960s, registering especially impressive performance in the 1950s. Beginning in 1960 growth rates began to decline steadily. All data sets agree on this essential trend (figure 7.1).[8] Indeed the official data, though they overstate absolute levels of output, show a much steeper rate of decline in growth tempos than the Central Intelligence Agency's (CIA's) calculations. Extrapolating from the official data would thus generate more pessimistic expectations than the Western numbers. Depending on whose estimates one believed, from the vantage of 1985 the Soviet Union was either about to begin declining in absolute terms or it was doomed to stagnate in a slow-growth equilibrium – unless something was done to reverse a 20-year secular trend.

Although the Soviet growth rates declined steadily for 25 years after 1960, there is an important break-point beginning roughly in the mid-1970s when Soviet economic performance took a sudden turn for the worse (figure 7.1). Data on Soviet industrial production and productivity reveal this shift even more clearly (figure 7.2).[9] More discrete indicators also moved precipitously downward in this period. Rates of return on capital investment and expenditures on research and development (R&D) and, critically, the rate of technological innovation

---

[8]Analysts agree that official data vastly overstated Soviet economic performance. The CIA's estimates, which were based on a complex reworking of official data, have also been widely criticized for overstating Soviet output. Russian economist G.I. Khanin's data, included in figure 7.1, reconcile many of the fundamental accounting contradictions in the official and CIA series, and thus capture many economists' best estimation of Soviet reality. Economists remain divided over Khanin's methodology, however. For discussions of these issues, see Harrison (1993), Khanin (1993, chap. 3), Becker (1994), and Schroeder (1995).

[9]In the aggregate statistics, the shift is somewhat obscured by weather-induced gyrations in agricultural production.

FIGURE 7.1:   The Soviet economic decline: average annual growth rate in total output

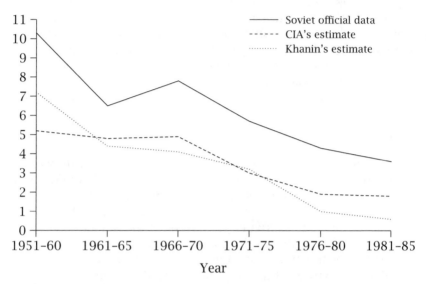

Source: Joint Economic Committee, U.S. Congress, *Measures of Soviet gross national product in 1982 prices.* G. I. Khanin, "Ekonomicheskiy rost: alternativnaia otsenka" [Economic growth: an alternative estimate] *Kommunist* No. 17 (November, 1988): 83–90. *Notes:* Output measurement for Soviet official data and Khanin is material product (NMP); for CIA it is gross national product (GNP). The 1950s are treated as one interval because Khanin does not divide the 1950s data.

all slowed measurably in these years.[10] Indicative of this slowdown, the number of foreign patents granted to Soviet scientists declined by almost 11 percent between 1981 and 1985, despite the fact that the Soviets devoted a growing share of national income to R&D (Kontorovich 1990).

The raw numbers on output and productivity highlight quantity rather than quality and thus understate the severity of Soviet decline. For example, few economists believe that a 3 percent Soviet growth rate was equivalent to a 3 percent U.S. growth rate, and most suspect that a Soviet-type economy growing at that rate was effectively treading water. The reason is that Soviet-type economies were especially dependent on high growth rates because the low quality of goods and negligent

---

[10] A good overview of data concerning the late 1970s decline is Kotz with Weir (1997, chap. 3). Additional data on the trends noted in this sentence are reported in Pitzer and Baukol (1991), Kontorovich (1992), Kontorovich (1990), and Gomulka and Nove (1984: 44). We provide a further analysis in Brooks and Wohlforth (2003).

FIGURE 7.2: The late 1970s decline: average annual percentage growth rate

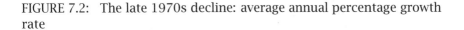

Sources: Gertrude E. Schroeder, "The slowdown in Soviet industry, 1976–1982" *Soviet Economy,* vol. 1, no. 1 (January-March 1985), 42–74; and G. I. Khanin "Ekonomicheskiy rost: alternativnaia otsenka" [Economic growth: an alternative estimate], *Kommunist* no. 17 (November, 1988): 83–90.

maintenance led to a very high turnover rate for all products in the economy (Winiecki 1986: 335). At the extreme, many goods that were produced and were counted as part of Soviet growth and productivity statistics were simply useless (Marer 1986: 86). For these reasons, slow growth created severe problems for Soviet policymakers. Backlogs, bottlenecks, chronic shortages, increased waste due to deteriorating infrastructure – these and many similar problems began to multiply as soon as growth moderated. For a given decline in growth rates, the negative effect on Soviet living standards and on the country's ability to compete was proportionally much greater than for a market-based economy.

Moreover, numerous noneconomic indicators also began to indicate systemic decline precisely in the mid-to-late 1970s. In particular, this was the period in which significant declines occurred in various demographic and public health indicators, with the Soviet Union making history as the first industrialized country to register peacetime declines in life expectancy and infant mortality (Feshbach and Friendly Jr. 1992, chap. 1: 273–4). Data on social and political problems of alienation and

disaffection – alcoholism, absenteeism, draft avoidance, and the like –
also accumulated in these years.[11]

The connections among all these various indicators are complex
and controversial. What matters is that so many quantitative and qualitative indicators concur on a fundamental downward shift in the Soviet
Union's trajectory beginning in roughly the mid-to-late 1970s. The key
point here is that stagnation is not a constant; it is a variable, every year
it continues is another piece of evidence that the problem is systemic
rather than cyclical. States can undergo temporary economic slow-
downs without considering major policy departures or international
retrenchment. But the Soviet slowdown was not temporary. By the early
1980s, all the indications were that a structural shift – for the worse –
had occurred in the country's material fortunes.

The new decline in Soviet growth rates – and the fact that this
decline was systemic – was devastating for the country's prospects.
Even in absolute terms, the new phase of decline was bound to be a
problem for a country that had become accustomed to rapid growth
for two generations. What made the Soviet decline truly salient, however, was the international context. Between 1960 and 1989, Soviet
growth performance was the worst in the world, controlling for levels of investment and education, and its performance relative to the
rest of the world was declining over time (Easterly and Fischer 1995:
347–71). In other words, the Soviet Union was becoming progressively
less competitive, even if competitiveness is defined solely in terms of
growth in gross production – a benchmark that, as discussed above,
greatly overstated the Soviet Union's economic capacity. Due to declining economic growth, the Soviet share of major powers' GDP began to
drop – the mid-1970s again being the transition point.[12] What mattered
most to Soviet policymakers, however, was the direct comparison between their country's economic performance and that of their main
rival, the United States. As figure 7.3 shows, the early 1980s marked the
beginning of the longest period in the post-World War II era in which
average Soviet growth rates fell behind those of the United States. For
the first time in the Cold War era it was now clear that barring some
dramatic turnaround the Soviet Union would never close the gap in

---

[11] The best general overview of the Soviet and Russian sociological research on this
period is Shubin (1997b). On rising rates of draft avoidance, see Nelson (1989: 312–45).
Nelson reports that the proportion of draft-age cohorts trying to avoid service increased
from 27 percent in the 1964–73 period to 38 percent between 1974 and 1978. After the
invasion of Afghanistan, the rate escalated further.

[12] Calculated from data in Maddison (1995). Major powers defined as the United States,
the Soviet Union, West Germany, France, Great Britain, Japan, and China.

FIGURE 7.3: Soviet and U.S. growth rates: annual average percentage growth in total output

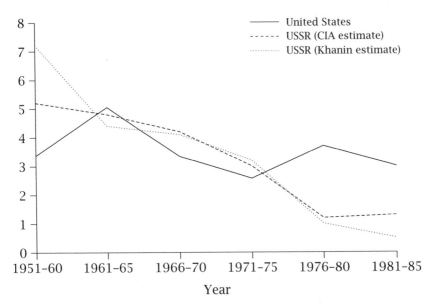

Sources: Joint Economic Committee, U.S. Congress, *Measures of Soviet gross national product in 1982 prices* (Washington, D.C., Government Printing Office, 1990); and Angus Maddison, *Monitoring the world economy, 1820-1991* (Paris: Organization for Economic Cooperation and Development, 1995). G. I. Khanin, "Ekonomicheskiy rost: alternativnaia otsenka" [Economic growth: an alternative estimate] *Kommunist* No. 17 (November, 1988): 83-90.
Note: Maddison data (for U.S.) is gross domestic product (GDP), CIA is GNP, and Khanin is NMP.

brute economic output with United States, to say nothing of closing the gap in technology.

While relative decline of this magnitude would be unsettling for any country, it was disastrous for a state in the Soviet Union's international position. When Gorbachev became general secretary in 1985, the United States had on average grown 1 percent per year faster then the Soviet Union over the preceding decade (based on CIA estimates that probably overstate Soviet performance). By contrast, between 1893 and 1913 Britain's economic growth lagged Germany's by an average of just 0.8 percent per year – a change sufficient to produce "an orgy of self-doubt and recrimination among British politicians and industrialists" (D'Lugo and Rogowski 1993: 72-3). Compounded over time, such marginal differences in growth rates become strategically significant, which is why few historians are surprised at the British elite's reaction to their country's declining economic fortunes. For example, over the 1893–1913 interval, Britain's economy grew by 56 percent while Germany's grew by 90 percent, with all the attendant consequences for Britain's security and prestige. Britain's relative decline produced a major reorientation in grand strategy that combined retrenchment and engagement with growing rivals, notably Germany.[13] And the clash between expectations and actual performance was much greater for the Soviet Union because it was coming down from a formative period of extremely rapid growth. Consequently Soviet decline was also unusually rapid, with growth rates dropping by half just between 1975 and 1980. Britain, by contrast, took a generation to travel a comparable path.

Thus, when Gorbachev announced a few months before taking office that restoring growth was a necessary condition of preserving the Soviet Union's status as a great power, there is no reason to believe that he was exaggerating.[14]

Placing Soviet decline in context

The British example is a reminder that the Soviet Union was hardly the only great power over the past two centuries to have suffered relative decline. The logical question then becomes: are there deductive reasons to expect that the Soviet Union would reorient its foreign policy more strongly in response to relative decline than other great powers had done in the modern era? This question has largely been absent from the end of the Cold War debate, perhaps because of the widespread (and misleading) view that Soviet relative decline was not especially rapid or marked. In fact, four overlapping aspects of the Soviet Union's international position – a combination that was unique in modern international history – made Moscow far more sensitive to decline than other great powers.

First of all, the bipolar distribution of power meant that the Soviet elite had a single, unambiguous "reference group" for measuring its relative position: the United States. In a multipolar setting such as that faced by Britain and all other declining great powers over the two centuries before 1945, relative gains calculations are indeterminate. London could (and did) take comfort in the fact that increments of power it "lost" to other states would be absorbed by their mutual

---

[13]On Anglo–German détente, see Lynn-Jones (1986). On the connection between Britain's decline and change in its grand strategy, see Friedberg (1988).

[14]As Gorbachev stressed, "Only an intensive acceleration of the economy ... will allow our country to enter the new millennium as a great and flourishing power" (speech delivered on December 10, 1984, in Gorbachev 1987: 86).

rivalries. For Moscow, any relative loss to the United States redounded unambiguously to its disadvantage. Moreover, bipolarity fostered a stable alliance system in which all of the world's largest and most advanced economies were arrayed against Moscow. When the Soviet Union's share of the great powers' GDP dropped, it was clear that the resultant advantage would accrue to rival states.

The second reason is that the Soviet Union was a declining challenger to U.S. primacy (Wohlforth 1994/95: 98–9). Moreover, it was a challenger that had never come close to rivaling the economic size of the U.S. hegemon, let alone the United States combined with its major allies. According to the most recent CIA estimate, the Soviet economy reached an all-time peak of 57 percent of U.S. gross national product in 1970. And this is the estimate most widely and intensely criticized – even by agency economists themselves – as massively overstating Soviet economic achievements.[15] The Soviet elite's basic reference point was one in which Moscow was gaining rapidly vis-à-vis the United States. Anything short of that was devastating: the Soviet Union could challenge the United Sates only if its relative capabilities were increasing. Once a challenger begins to decline steadily, it will eventually have to change its role – especially in a bipolar system in which the challenger is nowhere near to catching up to the hegemon. And that role shift may well be accompanied by considerable intellectual change and even anguish on the part of an elite that may have defined itself in terms of opposition to the status quo (Kupchan 1994). A leading state, by contrast, can suffer prolonged decline without such a role reversal as long as it clearly remains number one. The United States, for example, declined substantially relative to its allies and the Soviet Union as they recovered from the war in the first 15 years after 1945. But it remained number one by a large margin, and because its relative position stabilized after 1960, it never faced the anguishing reappraisal that the rise of a true peer competitor would have occasioned.

The outer limits of a state's capabilities are determined by its economic output. Once the Soviet economy began to decline vis-à-vis the United States, Moscow could maintain a challenge only by extracting ever more capabilities from its economy. And that brings up the third reason relative decline placed more pressure on Soviet grand strategy than on earlier declining powers: the Soviet Union was a challenger with a far more acute case of imperial overstretch than the reigning hegemon. Typically, the dominant power is encumbered by rising imperial burdens, not the rising challenger (Gilpin 1981; Kennedy 1987). In the Cold War, this situation was reversed: the relative costs of

---

[15] The estimate is in Becker (1994: 309), who also discusses criticisms of it.

FIGURE 7.4:   Soviet defense expenditures as a percentage of GNP

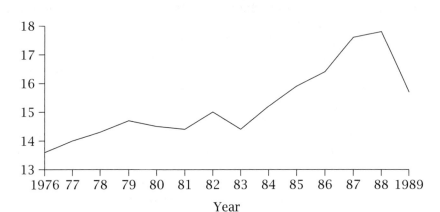

Source: Noel E. Firth and James H. Noren, *Soviet Defense Spending: A History of CIA Estimates, 1950-1990*. College Station: Texan A&M University Press, 1998.
Note: Based on current prices. Data points for 1977-78 and 1980 are extrapolations.

the United States' "empire by invitation" (Lundestad 1986) were not nearly as large as the imperial costs faced by the Soviets, who arguably confronted modern history's worst case of imperial overstretch.

Defense claimed a staggeringly large proportion of Soviet resources. Despite daunting measurement problems, different sources converge around an estimate of roughly 40 percent of the budget and 15–20 percent of GDP in the early 1980s, or at least four times the U.S. level.[16] By any comparative standard, this is a punishingly high peacetime commitment to military power. And not only was the defense burden high, but it was rising in the early and mid-1980s (figure 7.4). Moscow's international position imposed other costs that were also increasing in this period. The CIA estimated that the costs of the Soviet Union's "global position" more than doubled between 1970 and 1982 (Firth and Noren 1998: 134). At the beginning of the 1980s, the Central Committee estimated Soviet spending on foreign aid alone at 2 percent of GDP (Ellman and Kontorovich 1998: 293).

Perhaps most important, the economic burden of the Soviet position in Eastern Europe was also rapidly escalating at this time. The best-researched account of Soviet–Warsaw Pact economic relations concludes that by the mid-1980s, "Soviet subsidies to the region were becoming

---

[16]See Firth and Noren (1998) for the CIA estimate of around 15 percent in 1980. Using a different methodology (percentage of the workforce in the defense sector), Clifford Gaddy (1997, chap. 1) estimates 20 percent.

an intolerable burden.... What had been a serious problem in the early 1970s had grown into a crisis of threatening proportions by the mid-1980s (Stone 1996: 134)."[17] This imperial crisis stemmed from a variety of factors. Following the rise of Solidarity in Poland and the imposition of martial law in 1981, Moscow bankrolled a huge outflow of subsidized loans in the early 1980s to Poland, East Germany, and Bulgaria (Brown 1988: 138). The goods that the allies shipped to the Soviets were falling further and further behind world standards, and most were of much lower quality than the Soviets could have obtained on the open world market in exchange for the energy and raw materials they sent to Eastern Europe.[18] At the same time, the Soviets' marginal cost of extracting the energy and raw materials they supplied to Eastern Europe was progressively increasing because most of the easily exploitable sources in the Soviet Union had already been exhausted (Stone 1996: 37). Finally, the East European countries suffered a marked slowdown at this time in both technological competitiveness and economic growth – declining from an average real GDP growth rate of 3.23 percent in 1971–80, to 0.9 percent in 1981–5, and eventually reaching an average growth rate of –1.16 percent in 1989.[19] For these and other reasons, by the mid-1980s the Soviets felt "increasingly exploited by the East Europeans," and there was growing Soviet "exasperation at what they considered the self-seeking behavior of their East European liabilities" (Brown 1988: 155). This led Soviet leaders to take the uncomfortable step of publicly castigating their allies in the Council for Mutual Economic Assistance (CMEA). The most notable public expression of this growing frustration was at the 1984 CMEA summit, where General Secretary Konstantin Chernenko issued a stern warning to the East European countries to start living up to their economic "responsibilities," (Brown 1988: 154) and the summit's final document bluntly directed them to start "supplying the USSR with the products it needs."[20]

---

[17]More evidence for Stone's central conclusion is presented in Adomeit (1998). For an analysis based on earlier data that reaches this same general conclusion, see Bunce (1985).

[18]See, for example, Kramer (1996: 112) who reports that most of these East European exports to the Soviet Union were of such poor quality that they "would have been unmarketable, or saleable only at highly disadvantageous prices, outside the Soviet bloc."

[19]Clark (1993) is a good source on declining technological competitiveness. Growth figures are calculated from data in Stone (1996: 170).

[20]As Brown points out, "The directness of the above-quoted passage, which was, after all, part of an *agreed* document, gives some idea of what the debates over the issue must have been like and of what the Soviets' *original* suggestions might have been" (Brown 1988: 155, emphasis in original).

The fourth reason that relative decline placed more pressure on Soviet grand strategy than on that of earlier declining powers was the particular nature of the Soviet Union's technological lag with its rivals. By the late 1970s, it was becoming increasingly evident to Soviet analysts that the world's most advanced economies – all of which were arrayed against the Soviet Union – were undergoing an important transformation involving the rapid development of high-technology. The Soviets dubbed this the "scientific and technological revolution," and there was little doubt that it was leaving them behind (Hoffmann and Laird 1982). As Gorbachev's Chief of Staff Valery Boldin (a hardliner who later joined the August 1991 anti-Gorbachev putsch) acknowledged, "In the U.S. a truly colossal development took place in the electronic industry and aerospace production – in a word, the USA's development had entered the stage of the real technological revolution."[21]

Concerns about the technological lag became much more acute in the early 1980s, as evidence began to accumulate that the revolution in information technology and electronics would have profound implications for the competitiveness of the Soviet military sector. As William Odom recounts, "It was becoming clear to Soviet military leaders that they were facing a third wave of new military technologies. The developments in microelectronics, the semiconductor revolution and its impact on computers, distributed processing, and digital communications were affecting many aspects of military equipment and weaponry.... [The] new revolution in military affairs was demanding forces and weapons that the Soviet scientific-technological and industrial bases could not provide" (Odom 1990: 52–3, 63–4).

To be sure, many Soviet policymakers retained confidence in the competitiveness of the current generation of Soviet conventional weaponry. Of key concern, however, was the greatly increasing difficulty of keeping up in military technology. As Thomas Nichols reports, the Soviet military foresaw "a steepening of the curve of technological progress that was both unprecedented and dangerous," and "military writers then began an all-out campaign of alarmism on the issue of conventional technologies in the early 1980s" (Nichols 1993: 115, 116). Soviet policymakers were acutely aware of their lag in information processing technology. In 1987, for example, the Soviets produced 51,000 personal computers, compared to the Americans' 8,668,000 (Cooper 1991: 41). Soviet officials – including many in the military – were greatly concerned about what would happen when the Americans deployed the

---

[21]Interview with Valery I. Boldin, Feb. 24, 1999, conducted by Oleg Skvortsov, head of the Cold War Oral History Project at the Institute of General History, Moscow (on file at the Institute of General History and the Mershon Center at Ohio State University) (hereinafter cited as "Skvortsov interviews").

next generation of high-technology conventional weapons being developed in the 1980s that truly took advantage of the microelectronics revolution (Fitzgerald 1987: 9–10; Herspring 1990, chap. 6; Trulock III 1990: 37–47; Nichols 1993: 115–20; Odom 1998). Indeed, by the early 1980s, high-level military officials were arguing for another Soviet crash program – on the scale of the Herculean effort to match U.S. thermonuclear and missile capabilities in the 1950s – to develop new critical technologies.[22]

Of course, other declining great powers in the modern era had experienced periods of reduced military technological competitiveness vis-à-vis their main competitors. But as discussed above, the Soviet Union was in a unique position because it was a declining challenger in a bipolar system, and hence was especially sensitive to any trends that had negative consequences for its ability to keep up with the leading power. Furthermore, the cost, scale and, most important, the pace of technological change in the late 1970s and 1980s appear to have been more marked than in previous eras. As a result, the technological lag with the West promised not only to grow rapidly, but also to be extremely costly and difficult for the Soviets to redress. Of key importance here is that Moscow's quantitative decline sapped its ability to overcome the growing quality gap with the United States by the time-honored Soviet method of concentrating resources on the development of militarily significant technology. The Soviets' last massive effort to overcome technological backwardness (to develop missile and thermonuclear-weapon capabilities) occurred in the 1950s – precisely when the economy registered its best relative growth. Contemplating a new and massive campaign to develop a microelectronic base sufficient to meet the challenge from the West with a stalled or declining economy was far more challenging.

In sum, the logic of the Soviet Union's international position made its grand strategy more sensitive to relative decline than other modern great powers. And by the mid-1980s, the Soviet Union was clearly in a state of prolonged systemic decline. In the next section, we examine the link between these initial conditions and the Soviet elite's actual response.

---

[22] According to former Deputy Chief of Staff, General M. A. Gareev, "We even came up with the following plan. At one time the USSR had thrown all its resources at developing nuclear weapons. Similarly it was now necessary to develop a strong microelectronic base. We needed a big leap. We needed to merge our research facilities and set up new ones; to invest a lot of resources and put the best scientists to work in the area of microelectronics." Interview, excerpted in Ellman and Kontorovich (1998: 63).

Decline and change

The starting point of most models of ideas and foreign policy is the existence of a causal gap between material incentives and the behavioral response – a gap that only ideas can fill. In the case of the Soviet Union and the end of the Cold War, how big is this gap? In other words, how closely does the evidence on decline match up with Soviet perceptions and policy? The preponderance of evidence – especially the information that has come to light only recently – suggests that this gap was small. And that finding calls into question ideational models of the reorientation of Soviet foreign policy.

Consider first the relationship between decline and elite perceptions of decline. For material change to affect policy, it must be perceived. The connection between material change and perceptions of that change cannot be instantaneous, however: observers can only know that they are living through a "trend" if the phenomenon has been under way for several years. Therefore, *some* lag between a material change that we now know occurred and actors' contemporary perception of that change is inevitable. The question that is inadequately addressed in the current literature is how large that lag must be to present a "puzzle" for models based on material incentives. In the case of Soviet decline and the end of the Cold War, we would expect that Soviet policymakers would have been cognizant of some profound, systemic shift for the worse only after numerous indicators had steadily confirmed impressionistic evidence over a period of years. Based just on the aggregate data, therefore, we would expect the new phase of Soviet decline to have become an issue for policymakers some time in the late 1970s or early 1980s.[23] Because the quantitative indicators kept trending down, and because the evidence of the growing significance of the Soviets' qualitative lag accumulated rapidly in the 1980s, we would therefore expect that perceptions of decline would grow steadily in the first half of the decade.

The most recent evidence confirms these expectations. As Mark Kramer notes, "declassified transcripts of CPSU Politburo meetings from 1980, 1981 and 1982 ... are full of apprehensive comments about the Soviet Union's [declining] relative power. Similar comments can be found in Politburo transcripts from 1983 and 1984" (Kramer 1999: 566). Soviet policymakers at the national and local levels confronted

---

[23]The larger expectation based on that data would be: (1) great optimism in the 1950s; (2) greater circumspection in the 1960s and 1970s; and (3) serious concern in the early 1980s. With the exception of the optimism occasioned by Moscow's achievement of overall military parity in 1970, this corresponds to the evidence on perceptions reported in Wohlforth (1993).

more and more tangible indicators of decline that created increasing problems for them, including inflation, pressure on the budget, goods shortages, and production backlogs (Kontorovich 1992; Sinel'nikov 1995; Ellman and Kontorovich 1998;). Internal assessments hovered precisely in the range suggested by the CIA's estimates and G.I. Khanin's more pessimistic calculations (figure 7.1). As Politburo member Vadim Medvedev recalled, "We proceeded from the assumption that in the beginning of the 1980s, the growth of industrial production had stopped, and the real income of the population had actually declined" (quoted in Ellman and Kontorovich 1998: 95).[24]

Thus, when Gorbachev became general secretary in 1985 the problem of relative decline had been under discussion for a half-decade. It is hardly surprising, therefore, to discover that he was even more concerned about decline than his predecessors. Nor is it surprising that he focused so intently on the new technological challenges to the Soviet Union. Recently released internal documents show that the perception of decline was much more alarmist than the Soviets acknowledged publicly. They reveal a Gorbachev who seems well informed of the economic situation making ever more insistent arguments for the necessity of international retrenchment. Gorbachev's statements on the size of the Soviet military burden; the costs of the military sector's priority claims on scarce scientific, technical, and R&D resources; the other costs of the Soviet Union's international position; and the underlying trends in technology all match up very closely with experts' best assessment of the real material conditions he faced in power.[25] In one Politburo session, for example, Gorbachev stressed: "Our goal is to prevent the next round of the arms race. If we do not accomplish it, the threat to us will only grow. We will be pulled into another round of the arms race that is beyond our capabilities, and we will lose it, because we are already at the limit of our capabilities. Moreover, we can expect that Japan and the FRG could very soon join the American potential.... If the new round begins, the pressure on our economy will be unbelievable."[26]

Soviet perceptions, in short, closely track our best estimate of Soviet material decline. How do these perceptions relate to changing ideas

[24]Gorbachev's (1996: 216) own recollection is similar. For compilations of evidence on contemporary Soviet assessments, see Shubin (1997a, vol. 1; Adomeit 1998; Gaidar 1999: 23–5).

[25]Compare, for example, Gorbachev's assessment (1996: 315) with Firth and Noren (1998, chap. 5) and Gaddy (1997, chap. 1). Their estimates of defense spending all range from 15–20 percent of GDP, and all agree that the burden was rising in the 1980s.

[26]Politburo session of October 4, 1986, in National Security Archive Briefing Book, *Understanding the End of the Cold War: the Reagan/Gorbachev Years* (Providence, RI: Brown University, 1998, hereinafter cited as NSA 1998), doc. no. 32. See also docs. nos. 19, 25, 40, 52.

and policies? Once again, there is always likely to be some lag between perceptions of a material shift and a major behavioral response. For one thing, individual leaders are bounded in their ability to obtain and process information. On top of this, overcoming path dependency and instituting radical policy change is never a task to be taken lightly. Actors are first likely to try solutions within the old intellectual and institutional frameworks before turning to drastic reforms. And again, an unsettled question in the literature is how long the lag between perceived material change and the behavioral response must be to constitute a "puzzle" for models based on material incentives.

In the case of the Soviet Union and the Cold War's end, the newer evidence is strongly consistent with the proposition that the intellectual changes that accompanied the reorientation of Soviet foreign policy were largely endogenous to the country's relative decline. In particular, the mounting material costs of the policies associated with the old Soviet foreign policy created pressure to move toward retrenchment. There was actually more pressure to shift policy toward retrenchment before 1985 than standard accounts allow. It was Leonid Brezhnev who first gathered together his military leaders in 1982 to lecture them about keeping defense expenditures under control (*Pravda*, October 28, 1982: 1). It was Brezhnev, Yuri Andropov and Konstantin Chernenko who actually capped the growth in Soviet military spending (Firth and Noren 1998 report military spending restraint in the 1973–83 period). And it was Brezhnev, Andropov, and Ideology Czar Mikhail Suslov who privately revoked the Brezhnev Doctrine in 1980–1 when they ruled out direct intervention in Poland as beyond Soviet capabilities.[27] But these leaders were understandably reluctant to move away from the old precepts of Soviet foreign policy. Instead, the evidence suggests that they tried to cling to the status quo while struggling to contain its escalating costs.

The evidence regarding Gorbachev similarly suggests an early reluctance to face the tough trade-offs implicit in major change – a reluctance that was only overcome by mounting evidence of further decline. Gorbachev's initial policy response did not challenge system fundamentals. Newly released Politburo notes from 1985–7 show a Gorbachev who

---

[27]In reviewing the classified documents of the politburo commission on the Polish crisis, Georgy Shakhnazarov (1993: 115) notes that there was "total unanimity ... that the use of our military contingent in Poland should be excluded from our arsenal." According to KGB veteran Nikolai Leonov, Yuri Andropov opined in 1980 that "The quota for our interventions abroad has been exhausted: ... The Soviet Union already lacked the power for such operations" (Leonov 1994: 281). Available documents on the Polish crisis reveal a politburo deeply reluctant to enforce the Brezhnev Doctrine and acutely aware of the punishing costs of doing so (Mastny 1998).

wanted to shift the Cold War into a framework more favorable to the Soviet Union, and who believed he would have the resources to do this without placing traditional Soviet interests at risk (NSA 1998, docs. nos. 44, 52). Gorbachev began by reversing Brezhnev's policy of capping the military budget and programmed into the 1986–90 five-year plan an increase in military outlays; he approved an effort to end the Afghan war by military escalation; and he agreed to increase arms transfers to third world clients to magnify Moscow's bargaining leverage in talks on regional issues.[28] All of these expensive policies appeared to reflect the assumption that an "accelerated" Soviet economy would deliver the necessary funds – and that the country's vaunted military-industrial sector was the key to increased productivity.[29]

By 1988, however, it became apparent that this policy of "acceleration" [*uskoreniie*] was doomed to failure. As figure 7.1 shows, Gorbachev's effort to jump-start the economy had no effect on its relative macroeconomic performance (the upsurge in growth in 1986 resulted from a lucky harvest), while producing a budget deficit, inflation (suppressed through most of this period), a ballooning internal debt, a growing foreign exchange shortage, and a rising defense burden as a share of GDP. These fiscal and financial imbalances on top of the underlying systemic decline propelled the economy into a tailspin. And that led to dramatically increased pressure on the Soviets' traditional foreign policy. Only in this period did Gorbachev's foreign policy proposals truly begin to move in a more radical direction. And only in this later period did he begin privately to rely on the more radical intellectual proponents of new thinking and publicly to start a serious effort to radically redefine Soviet foreign policy practices and the country's international role.

As Gorbachev began the wrenching process of making unilateral reductions in 1988, resource constraints came to the fore at each key moment (Cherniaev 1993; Savelev, Detinov, and Varhall 1995; Vorotnikov 1995; Brooks and Wohlforth 2003). After Gorbachev announced a unilateral reduction of a half-million troops at the United Nations in

---

[28]Rhetoric aside, Gorbachev made no effort to increase outlays for consumer welfare in this period (Sinel'nikov 1995: 36; Lyakhovsky 1995 documents the early escalatory policy on Afghanistan).

[29]Gaddy (1997) documents the central role of the military industrial sector in the initial reform (see also Odom 1998, chap. 11, and with Skvortsov interviews with Egor K. Ligachev, December 17, 1998; Oleg D. Baklanov n.d.). Gorbachev (1996, chap. 11) claims that he expected the initial reforms to generate a sufficient upsurge in growth to permit more thoroughgoing changes in 1990. He anticipated a boost in quantitative output that would generate a surplus sufficient to address the more fundamental qualitative challenge. This expectation would explain a lot, including his support for military spending increases until 1988.

December 1988, the Politburo pondered whether to publicize the defense burden to defuse potential criticism at home. Gorbachev rejected the idea, arguing that if people at home and abroad knew how much defense drained from the Soviet economy, they would view the proposed unilateral cuts as absurdly small (NSA 1998, doc. no. 16). Again and again, in context after context, former Soviet policymakers repeat the argument that the Soviet Union simply could not bear the costs of its international position (Ellman and Kontorovich 1997: 259–79). This is true even of many within the Soviet military. Odom finds, "In interviews and in their memoirs senior former Soviet military officers uniformly cited the burden of military spending as more than the Soviet economy could bear" (Odom 1998: 225).

If the country's capabilities were in danger of falling behind, then they had to be augmented, or those against which they were arrayed had to be diminished. The great attraction of foreign policy retrenchment lay in its promise to tackle both problems at once. By scaling back Soviet claims on the international system, Gorbachev and other Soviet strategists hoped, both the cohesion and the commitment of the opposing coalition of states could be reduced. Moreover, retrenchment would directly contribute to increasing Soviet relative capabilities in the long run by easing resource constraints in the short run. As a result, a solid consensus emerged in the political leadership on the need for downsizing the military and scaling back the costs of empire. It is not surprising, therefore, that the two main economic reform alternatives to Gorbachev's course – the strategy of "optimizing the planning mechanism" favored by conservative officials such as Nikolai Ryzhkov and Yegor Ligachev, and the strategy of rapid marketization pushed by liberals like Yegor Gaidar and Grigory Yavlinsky – were both weighted even *more* heavily towards cutting back the imperial burden.[30] Even many elements in the military leadership and the defense-industrial sector agreed on the general need to reduce the imperial burden (Skvortsov interviews with Dmitry T. Yavov, December 16, 1998, and March 11, 1999 in Savelev, Detinov, and Varhall 1995; Odom 1998: 225; Nichols 1993: 212–14, 216–18).[31] Not all were in favor, of course, but given the extent of relative decline, the odds were heavily stacked against those who stood for the status quo.

As resource constraints mounted, the Soviet approach shifted from a competitive retrenchment on favorable terms to the far riskier strategy of graduated unilateral concessions in the hope of reciprocation. And

---

[30] On the "Ligachev/Ryzhkov alternative," see Hough (1997). On the liberal-market option, see Gaidar (1999).

[31] Evangelista (1999) is skeptical of military support for the initiation of reform but agrees that mounting resource constraints helped defuse opposition to change.

even after they switched to this riskier strategy, the new thinkers' strategic aim was still to end the Cold War by defusing the arms race and breaking up the two alliances, leaving the Soviet Union as one of two superpowers in a depolarized world (Lévesque 1997). The transition from this robust vision of successful retrenchment to accepting defeat on Western terms with the West's military alliance and all its Cold War institutions intact only occurred in 1989–91, by which time resource constraints were overpowering the policy process on all fronts (see figure 7.1).

The above evidence indicates that decline, perceptions of decline, new ideas and new policies were closely related. Of course, perceptions of decline lagged our best estimates of real material changes – though the lag does not appear particularly large. The evidence shows that politburo concern with decline become acute just as the Soviet Union's performance relative to its obvious reference group – the United States – reached new lows. There was a more notable lag between perceived decline and a major behavioral response. Gorbachev and his predecessors displayed a predictable reluctance to plunge immediately into radical new policies in response to clear evidence of decline. Based on existing ideational models, it is unclear whether these lags constitute significant explanatory puzzles. Before addressing this issue, however, we need to fill in our portrayal of the material pressures affecting Soviet policymakers in this period.

The changing structure of global production

Although Soviet relative decline goes a long way toward explaining the reorientation of Soviet foreign policy, it leaves a great deal unexplained. In particular, it cannot account for the integrative thrust of Soviet policy at this time. To many scholars, this move toward greater integration with the West strongly reflects a "Westernizing" intellectual shift on the part of Soviet elites (Herman 1996; English 2000;). This interpretation fails to note that the structure of global production was rapidly shifting at this time, greatly increasing the opportunity cost of being isolated from the world economy. In this section, we describe this change in the global economy, establish its link to the Cold War, and show how it affected the reorientation of Soviet foreign policy in the late 1980s.

The changing structure of global production and the Cold War

Three shifts in the structure of global production are particularly relevant to the superpower rivalry during the Cold War's last years: (1) the upswing in the number and importance of interfirm alliances; (2) the increased geographic dispersion of production; and (3) the growing opportunity cost of being isolated from foreign direct investment (FDI) (Brooks 1999, 2001). Each of these global production changes accelerated in the late 1970s and 1980s in large part due to two underlying and interrelated technological shifts: the greatly increased cost, risk, complexity, and importance of technological development; (Mytelka 1991: 16–20; Kobrin 1997: 149–50) and dramatic improvements in transportation and communications technology (World Bank 1997: 36–7). Although multinational corporations (MNCs) had traditionally been very unwilling to share control of their technological assets up until the late 1970s, the changed parameters of technological development led many MNCs to view alliances with other MNCs as increasingly necessary to minimize the risks and costs of engaging in R&D and to increase the potential for innovation.[32] Concomitantly, the increased importance of technology coupled with the immense expense and difficulty involved in developing it also put a new premium on attracting FDI (United Nations Conference on Trade and Development (UNCTAD) 1995). At the same time, dramatic improvements in transportation and communications technology greatly increased the ease of coordinating different aspects of the production process across large geographic distances, thereby allowing many MNCs to rely ever more on international subcontracting (UNCTAD 1994: 143–5; World Bank 1997: 42–5) and to simultaneously disperse production and R&D globally wherever it was geographically most advantageous (Dunning 1993; UNCTAD 1993).

All of these global production changes were crucial to the course of the Cold War for two simple reasons: the Soviet Union and its allies were isolated from them; and they achieved their greatest salience among the Soviets' international competitors – the United States and its allies. Thus "globalization" was not global: it took sides in the Cold

---

[32] On the dramatic increase in interfirm alliances, see, for example, Mytelka (1991), Dunning (1995), and Kobrin (1997: 150–1). For example, one study of interfirm alliances in information technology and biotechnology found that from "a low of 6.5 in the 1970–75 period, the average number of agreements reported per year rose dramatically to 26.5 in the years 1976–79, quadrupling in 1980–83 to 110.8 and doubling once more in the 1984–87 period to reach a high 271.3" Mytelka (1991: 11). In turn, a variety of studies find that the complexity of technological development is the most important driving force behind the massive increase in interfirm alliances; see, for example, Hagedoorn (1993) and Kobrin (1997: 150–1).

War. While U.S. and Western MNCs were increasing their opportunities for technological innovation and reducing the risks and difficulty associated with R&D through a greatly expanding web of international interfirm alliances during the 1980s, the Soviets were completely isolated from this trend.[33] While the United States and Western Europe were able to exploit the latest technologies and production methods from throughout the world because of rapidly increasing FDI inflows, the Soviets were largely dependent on autonomous improvements in technology and production methods.[34] And instead of being able to disperse production throughout the world to reap various efficiencies as the United States and its main allies – Japan, West Germany, France, and Britain – were able to do, the Soviets were forced to make almost all of their key components and perform almost all of their production within the Eastern bloc.[35]

Of course, the Soviet Union had faced significant economic handicaps from the moment its foreign policy became equated with economic isolation in the 1920s. But these handicaps greatly increased in relative importance as the cost, complexity and difficulty of technological development spiraled upwards in the late 1970s and 1980s and as the globalization of production concomitantly accelerated. It is easy to see how isolation from the globalization of production increased the difficulty of keeping up with the West in terms of general economic and technological productivity, likely the key concern of many new thinkers. Less obvious is the fact that Soviet isolation from these global production changes simultaneously made it much more difficult to remain technologically competitive in the arms race – of foremost importance to old thinkers. Interfirm alliances in the 1980s were concentrated in those sectors with rapidly changing technologies and high entry costs, such as microelectronics, computers, aerospace, telecommunications,

---

[33]The overwhelming majority (more than 90 percent, by many estimates) of interfirm alliances during the 1980s were located within the triad of Western Europe, Japan, and North America (Kobrin 1997: 150).

[34]During the 1980s, the "annual average growth rate for FDI outflows reached 14 per cent" (Jones 1996: 52). As the absolute level of FDI rose dramatically in the 1980s, the Soviets remained isolated from these flows, while the share of FDI based in Western Europe, the United States and Canada increased from 62 percent of the world total in 1980 to 70 percent in 1993 (Kobrin 1997: 48, 54).

[35]In combination, these five Western countries accounted for 74 percent of the total world FDI stock in 1980 (Kobrin 1997: 47). One reflection of the enhanced degree to which the production of U.S. MNCs became strongly integrated internationally during this period is that "the value of United States intra-firm exports increased by nearly two-thirds between 1977 and 1982 and by over 70 per cent between 1982 and 1989" (UNCTAD 1994: 143). Another reflection of this trend is that the value of offshore outsourcing by the U.S. increased from US$48.8 billion in 1972 to US$356 billion in 1987 (World Bank 1997: 45).

transportation, new materials, biotechnology, and chemicals (Kobrin 1997: 150; Dicken 1998: 229). At the same time, production appears to have been most geographically dispersed in those sectors of manufacturing with high levels of R&D costs and significant economies of scale, such as machinery, computers, electronic components, and transportation (World Bank 1997: 42). These sectors read like a who's who of dual-use industries. Thus, the very sectors that were becoming most internationalized in the 1980s were those that provide much of the foundation for military power in the modern era. For this reason, Soviet isolation from ongoing global production changes became a tremendous handicap relative to the West in the 1980s in the military realm (Brooks 2001, chap. 5).

This analysis places the whole debate concerning technological lags and the end of the Cold War in a new perspective. As noted above, in the 1980s Soviet policymakers became increasingly concerned that the country was being left behind in the "scientific and technological revolution" (Parrott 1983). Many scholars have long argued that these concerns helped to forge a confluence of interests between the political elite and elements of the defense-industrial sector on the general need to reorient Soviet foreign policy (Bova 1988; Herspring 1990; Gaddy 1997). But this literature never explains why all this was happening in the 1980s and not earlier, when the technological lag also existed (as did Washington's efforts to exploit it), and why Moscow's technological lag led to international economic opening rather than to the traditional Russian response: hunkering down and allocating increased resources away from consumers and toward technological development. Technology-driven global production changes help account for both anomalies: they greatly accelerated in the late 1970s and 1980s; and they made a "hunkering down" strategy prohibitive, thereby generating powerful incentives that affected security maximizers as well as welfare maximizers.

The changing structure of global production and the reorientation of Soviet foreign policy

In the Soviet Union, there was a clear recognition at this time that the structure of global production was fundamentally changing. Soviet specialists saw that international economic linkages were increasing and changing qualitatively – in particular, that MNCs were becoming more significant and were leading to the "internationalization of production" (Hough 1986: 94–7). In his speech to the Twenty-seventh Party Congress in February 1986, Gorbachev noted that the reach of global firms had "gained strength rapidly.... By the early 1980s, the transnational corporations accounted for more than one-third of industrial production, more than one half of foreign trade, and nearly 80 percent of the patents for new machinery and technology in the capitalist world" (Gorbachev 1987, vol. 3: 192).

In response to the changed incentives noted above, analysts and, later, policymakers, eventually concluded that it was necessary to increase Soviet access to MNCs and the global economy to try to prevent a severe erosion of the country's technological capacity (Hough 1988a, 1988b; Geron 1990; Cooper 1991; Hewett and Gaddy 1992). Even a hard-line conservative such as Valery Boldin clearly recognized that the Soviets were falling behind technologically in the 1980s and that this was in significant part due to "our lack of world experience, our country's lack of access to world markets.... We stewed in our own juices for the simple reason that most of our electronics went to defense purposes, and defense was a completely closed sector" (Skvortsov interview with Boldin Feb. 24, 1999). Thus, when Secretary of State George Shultz, Secretary of the Treasury James Baker, and other U.S. officials lectured Gorbachev and Shevardnadze on the growing costs of Soviet isolation from the international economy, their arguments simply reinforced views that were already popular in Moscow (Oberdorfer 1998).

By the mid-1980s, even many Communist Party officials with impeccable defense-industrial credentials such as Prime Minister Ryzhkov and Lev Zaikov (the secretary on defense issues of the Central Committee), strongly supported greater integration to gain access to Western technology (Aslund 1991: 37–43). This stance on the part of such figures was important, given that they were more conservative in outlook than Gorbachev, not inclined toward market-based economic reform or strong efforts to improve consumer welfare, and were ideologically insulated from the appeals of pro-Western intellectuals. Indeed, much evidence suggests that practical men such as these were actually well ahead of Gorbachev himself concerning greater integration with the world economy in the early years of perestroika (Aslund 1991: 37–48).

To act on this assessment, however, policymakers had to confront the long-standing isolationist precepts of the old Soviet foreign policy. Because of the high political and ideological costs of doing so, Gorbachev's first impulse was to try to redress the growing technological gap with the West through "internal" means – specifically, "transfusions" of ideas and innovations from the defense-industrial sector to the civilian economy and, in turn, by establishing greater production linkages among its own socialist allies in the CMEA. By 1987, it was clear this route was doomed to failure. Gorbachev soon learned that the Soviet military sector was not truly efficient; rather, it succeeded only by "cannibalizing" the civilian economy (Gaddy 1997: 56).[36] And it quickly became clear that increased production linkages within CMEA would bear little fruit, in significant part because no country in the Eastern bloc could match Western technology using indigenous sources (Adomeit 1998: 227).

The serious push for international economic integration dates from the failure of Gorbachev's initial policy package. It was clear to Soviet policymakers that just enhancing "shallow" integration with the international economy would not be enough to reverse technological decline. "Arms-length trade" and "passive technology transfers" (simply purchasing or stealing technology) would be insufficient – it was necessary to attract foreign direct investment, joint ventures, and other cooperative endeavors between Soviet and foreign MNCs (Hough 1988b, 80–3; Cooper 1991: 48–9). This led to the decision in 1987 to legalize FDI within the Soviet Union for the first time since the 1920s. To be sure, initial Soviet moves regarding joint ventures were quite modest. But, as time progressed and as the nature of the country's technological lag became even more apparent, efforts to attract FDI expanded greatly. While majority Soviet equity in joint ventures had initially been the "*sine qua non* of the Soviet leadership," in December 1988 majority foreign ownership (theoretically up to 99 percent) of joint ventures was permitted in an effort to greatly increase the Soviet Union's attractiveness as a site for foreign investment (Geron 1990: 47).

Although the growing costs of Soviet isolation from the globalization of production played a key role in the move toward increased economic engagement, these pressures were most important because they increased the impetus to initiate retrenchment. For one thing, whereas most other countries that wanted to become more globally integrated in the 1980s merely had to change their economic policies, the Soviets also had to readjust their security policies due to the West's "economic containment" policies (Mastanduno 1992). There was a clear recognition within the Soviet Union that the only way to reduce these Western restrictions was by moderating foreign policy.[37] This not only

---

[36]Even conservative civilian officials shared Gaddy's assessment: Valery Boldin, for example, notes that "the military 'grabbed' not just what it needed, but often much more – and sometimes even everything there was" (Skvortsov interview with Boldin, February 24, 1999).

[37]As Marshal Akhromeev told Secretary of State George Shultz at the December 1987 Washington summit: "My country is in trouble, and I am fighting alongside Mikhail Sergeevich to save it. That is why we made such a lopsided deal on INF, and that is why we want to get along with you. We want to restructure ourselves and to be part of the

increased the desire among new thinkers to initiate retrenchment, but also made it easier to convince skeptical hardliners. As one contemporary analyst noted, "The failure of economic autarky to produce high-technology, high-quality growth leaves them [hardliners] without a convincing policy argument" (Hough 1988b: 218). At the same time, Gorbachev and other reformers in favor of change could "plausibly say that reform was indispensable. They could say that Russia would not remain a great power unless the Soviet Union raised its technology to world levels, and they could say an opening to the West was necessary for that end" (Hough 1988a: 25).

In marshaling support for change, Gorbachev and Shevardnadze highlighted the growing technological lag as a means of winning over skeptics. In particular, they cited the prospect of increased technology and capital from Western firms as an increasingly important benefit of foreign policy retrenchment.[38] Not all conservatives were convinced by this line of argument, though some (including Boldin, Zaikov, Ryzhkov, Vitaly Vorotnikov, and perhaps even Sergei Akhromeev) appear to have been. The important point is that the growing costs of Soviet isolation from ongoing global production changes shifted the burden of proof to hardliners to come up with a compelling argument for why the large potential economic gains from retrenchment were *not* worth pursuing. This is something they were unable to do.

Of course, some might argue that Gorbachev highlighted the growing technological lag with the West only for political reasons and that his true motivations instead were simply to open up the international economy to improve consumer welfare. The evidence on this score remains incomplete, but it certainly seems unlikely that redressing the Soviets' growing technological lag with the United States was Gorbachev's only motivation for seeking to dilute the Western economic containment policies. And it is difficult to believe that Gorbachev's underlying strategy was to use rapprochement to end Soviet economic isolation, reaping the benefits from the globalization of production and redressing the country's technological lag only to challenge the United States for military supremacy once again. Some hardliners may have thought this was what Gorbachev was arguing (and, indeed, Gorbachev

---

modern world. We cannot continue to be isolated" (Shultz 1993: 1011–12). See also Shevardnadze (1988).

[38] After spelling out the security gains from foreign policy retrenchment, Gorbachev noted in a comprehensive speech to workers in Kiev in February 1989: "Our foreign policy also serves the cause of perestroika in the sense that it clears the way for broader economic cooperation with the outside world and for the country to join in world economic processes" (Gorbachev 1987, vol. 7: 344; see also Shevardnadze 1988).

may have deliberately misled them on this score (Evangelista 2001), but it is hard to imagine that this is what he had in mind.

Even if Gorbachev was motivated completely by a desire to improve the commercial economy and consumer welfare, the fact that Soviet isolation from the globalization of production reduced the country's technological competitiveness is still of crucial importance. Soviet isolation from the globalization of production increased the difficulty of keeping up with the West technologically in general terms and also reduced the Soviets' competitiveness in key dual-use technologies. Given the punishingly high degree to which the Soviets were already pouring scarce economic resources – especially R&D – into the military, the possibility that this burden might increase even further was truly a frightening prospect for Gorbachev and many other policymakers.[39] By the mid-1980s, even important figures in the Soviet military shared this assessment. For example, Marshal Dmitry Yazov remembered reacting favorably to Gorbachev's portrayal of the problem at the April 1985 Central Committee plenum that followed his selection as general secretary. Yazov recalled: "There was nothing left for investment in the economy. It was necessary to think about reducing defense expenditures. It was necessary to think about more advanced technologies and about science-intensive production processes, etc" (Skvortsov interview with Yazov, December 16, 1998).

If Gorbachev's ultimate goal was to improve consumer welfare, the last thing he would want was for even fewer economic and technological resources to be available for this purpose. In the end, the growing economic costs of Soviet isolation from the globalization of production created strong incentives for engaging in retrenchment irrespective of what Gorbachev's underlying motivations were. And retrenchment made sense as a response to the growing costs of Soviet economic isolation even if taking this course did not make it possible for the Soviets quickly to enjoy the fruits of globalization. This helps to explain why the Soviets proceeded with major early shifts toward unilateral retrenchment even in the absence of solid guarantees of being able to join the Western international economic order and obtain technology and capital from Western MNCs.

Comparing new thinkers and old thinkers

Changed material conditions shifted the rules of the international political game against the old Soviet ways of doing things. The evidence indicates that changes in the structure of global production and Soviet

---

[39] As Gorbachev (1996: 215) notes, "Of 25 billion rubles in total expenditure on science, 20 billion went to the military for technical research and development." The most recent and best researched study that documents this dilemma is Gaddy (1997).

relative decline both had a strong independent effect on Soviet decision-makers. What is most significant, though, is that they had a powerful interactive effect: in combination, these two pressures undermined support for sustaining the foreign policy status quo and caused the logic of Soviet retrenchment to become extraordinarily compelling. This finding undermines existing ideational models of change, which are premised on the notion that shifts in ideas caused new Soviet strategies or interests independent of material change.

The fact that political actors during or after the event claim to have acted in response to changes in material pressures might conceivably reflect earlier changes in ways of thinking that led them to see these pressures in a new light. Or, even if their preferences did not change, Soviet decision-makers' beliefs about the world may have changed in other ways that relatively quickly led them to reevaluate which material things really mattered to them. Potential counterarguments such as these – which derive clearly from the basic precepts of constructivist and other ideational studies – demand that we go further and examine whether the meaning of the material pressures we analyzed above were strictly dependent on ideational shifts. That is the purpose of this section. The evidence shows that both new and old thinkers tended to perceive similar material constraints – and both had to struggle to come to terms with them.

The new thinkers' agonizing reappraisal

Even for many reform-oriented policymakers, the process of renouncing old Soviet approaches was, as one new thinker put it, "an unbearably bitter and excruciating experience." (Alexander Tsipko, in his preface to Yakovlev (1993), xvi). For even the most progressive new thinkers in the leadership, such as Shevardnadze and Aleksandr Yakovlev, a complete abandonment of old stereotypes only occurs sometime in 1988-9; and all of them believed that Gorbachev's own intellectual journey was slower than theirs (Cherniaev 1993; Shakhnazarov 1993; Brooks and Wohlforth 2003). Indeed, in hindsight many Soviet policy veterans castigate the Gorbachev leadership for moving far too slowly and hesitantly in reining in imperial expenditures (Ellman and Kontorovich 1998; Gaidar 1999). Medvedev explains the delay by arguing that the "defense first" mentality was so deeply ingrained in all top Soviet decision-makers: "Only gradually, under the pressure of extremely acute economic problems, did the scales fall from our eyes. It became obvious that without a reduction in military expenditures, it would not be possible to resolve the urgent socioeconomic problems. This, to a large extent, stimulated the development of a new military doctrine and a new foreign policy aimed at stopping the arms race." (Interview excerpted in Ellman and Kontorovich 1998).

Also significant is that for most of the new thinkers, it took concrete, observable evidence of the material failings of their society to begin and complete an assault on the long-standing tenets of Soviet foreign policy. Indeed, in response to attacks from old thinkers in contemporary debates, many new thinkers cite such material failings to argue for the inevitability of retrenchment given objective realities.[40]

Finally, a clear theme in nearly all new thinkers' accounts is the Soviet Union's performance relative to its reference group; that is, the United States and its allies. No new thinker's memoir is complete without passages describing the revelatory effect of increased information about either living standards or the military-technological superiority of the West; nearly all accounts of change in mass and elite attitudes cite the powerful effect of this comparison (Brown 1996; Gorbachev 1996; Shubin 1997a). Thus, many analysts agree with Russian historian Aleksandr Shubin that it was the comparison to the west that "led to a sharp crisis in the national superpower self-consciousness" (Shubin 1997b: 143).

Demonstration effects were thus of crucial importance, but they ultimately derived their importance because of Soviet observations of actual material conditions in the West. The lessons of specific experiences mattered, but they were reinforced by large-scale material shifts. The evidence also indicates that many policymakers and intellectuals who became idea entrepreneurs did so in part as they learned of the material failings of the Soviet system. And their ideas became saleable to those more skeptical about reform in significant part because they accorded with undeniable material trends.

Old thinkers face the facts

If the meaning and consequences of the material pressures facing the Soviet Union depended on ideational shifts, then people with different ideas should have had dramatically different strategic reactions to observable indications of material change. But this was not the case: a critical mass of old thinkers in the military, defense industry, the foreign ministry, the Communist Party apparatus, and the KGB saw

---

[40]Thus, for example, Shakhnazarov argues that economic costs constrained even the Brezhnev leadership from more forceful intervention in Poland in 1980–81. See his analysis of the documents of the Suslov Politburo Commission on Poland in Shakhnazarov (1993: 112–18).

essentially the same material constraints Gorbachev did, and so not only acquiesced to but were complicit in Gorbachev's strategic response. Before proceeding, it is useful to reemphasize that our focus is on the overall reorientation of Soviet foreign policy, not the collapse of the Soviet Union. This is essential, because when old thinkers criticize Gorbachev and argue that they would have done things differently, their focus is overwhelmingly on the breakup of the Soviet Union itself.

In addition, it is important to recognize that changing the Soviet Union's international course did not require conversion of all old thinkers into new-thinking enthusiasts; nor did it require that old thinkers support each detail of each specific foreign policy decision. Rather it required the acquiescence – grudging or otherwise – of hundreds of old-thinking high officials whose expertise and authority were necessary to implement Moscow's fundamental change of course. We will never know precisely to what extent old thinkers actually wanted to engage in retrenchment due to the free-rider problem: old thinkers did not need to take the lead on this issue because plenty of other policymakers were already doing so. Some appear to have concluded that retrenchment was necessary, while others clearly objected to this general course. The key issue is not whether old thinkers played a key role in the initiation of retrenchment, but rather whether they were going to expend any political capital to try to prevent it.

Most social science theory would predict massive opposition to Gorbachev's foreign policy. A major theme in the political science literature on Soviet politics concerns the deeply embedded institutional barriers to any major policy change (Roeder 1993; Stone 1996). After all, Gorbachev was taking on a formidable array of special interests representing perhaps a quarter of the country's economic activity. Constructivism and social psychology would expect fierce resistance to Gorbachev's assault on some of the political elite's most cherished ideological precepts. Against this baseline expectation, what is most striking about the evidence that has come to light so far is the haphazard, ineffectual, belated, and intellectually weak nature of the opposition to Gorbachev's overall course in world affairs.

To be sure, the Soviet Union's domestic structure and Gorbachev's leadership qualities helped defuse opposition to retrenchment (Brown 1996; Evangelista 1999). Defense and military industrial elites sought to defend their bureaucratic turf and budgetary allocations as best they could; they resisted loss of decision-making authority; and clearly they were more troubled by the course of events than the new thinkers. In the final analysis, however, traditional thinkers faced an uphill battle because they could not credibly deny the existence of the basic material trends to which Gorbachev claimed to be responding.

The extraordinary feature of the new evidence concerning Soviet conservatives and hardliners is not that many of them opposed specific concessions to the West (especially regarding arms control, such as the inclusion of the "Oka" missile in the INF talks, counting rules for strategic missiles on bombers, etc.), but how very many of them accepted the basic picture of the crisis facing the country outlined by Gorbachev. As Aleksandr Savel'ev and Nikolai Detinov recount in their discussion of the Soviet concessions on the Strategic Arms Reduction Treaty (START) negotiations, "In judging the impact of any compromise from the Soviet standpoint, we cannot ignore the obvious facts. The pressure of military expenditures necessary for building and maintaining huge armed forces had become an exorbitant burden for the country. This fact was clear to Soviet leaders, who had witnessed such a situation and knew it too well. Decisions had to be reached – and, in practice, these decisions were achieved as before: through an agreed view of all the participants in the process" (Savelev, Detinov, and Varhall 1995: 161).

Because they wish to blame Gorbachev for the Soviet collapse, conservative policy veterans face strong incentives to argue in hindsight that Moscow had ample capability to continue the rivalry. It is therefore striking that even in hindsight most hold that Moscow could not sustain the Cold War status quo.[41] This is true even of people who represented sectors with powerful interests in the status quo.

An important but typical example is Marshal Yazov, who was a key participant in the August 1991 anti-Gorbachev putsch. When asked in a recent interview whether the Soviet Union had to get out of the Cold War, Yazov responded: "Absolutely ... We simply lacked the power to oppose the USA, England, Germany, France, Italy – all the flourishing states that were united in the NATO bloc. We had to seek a dénouement.... We had to find an alternative to the arms race.... We had to continually negotiate, and reduce, reduce, reduce – especially the most expensive weaponry" (Skvortsov interview with Yazov, March 11, 1999).

Another important example is Marshal Akhromeev. When the August putsch collapsed, Akhromeev hanged himself in his Moscow apartment, leaving a note that said: "Everything I have worked for has been destroyed." This is not a man who had undergone a deep intellectual

---

[41] This generalization is reflected in Ellman and Kontorovich's analysis (1997) of more than seventy memoirs and substantiated by our own review of memoirs and interviews that became available subsequently.

shift toward new thinking. Yet, before the Soviet collapse, he wrote with his friend and fellow traditionalist former First Deputy Foreign Minister Georgy Kornienko that "All who knew the real situation in our state and economy in the mid-1980s, understood that Soviet foreign policy had to be changed. The Soviet Union could no longer continue a policy of military confrontation with the United States and NATO after 1985. The economic possibilities for such a policy had been exhausted" (Akhromeev and Kornienko 1992: 314–15).

These two men not only made such statements after the fact, but they acted in accordance with these beliefs as chief of the Soviet general staff and Gorbachev's military aide (Akhromeev), and Minister of Defense (Yazov). The same goes for a very long list of old thinkers, including many KGB staffers (Leonov 1994) and technocratic party conservatives of the Ligachev and Ryzhkov variety.[42] For example, at a session of the Big Five coordinating committee on arms policy that discussed Soviet concessions on START, Igor Belousov (head of the Military–Industrial Commission after 1988) noted that "We need START like we need bread and water. Our economy is nearly broken and we cannot stand the arms race. We are in an economic dead end. We can accept a 2:1 disadvantage – not only that, we could take worse, given the economic situation" (From handwritten notes of Ambassador Yuri Nazarkin, as quoted at the Mershon Center Conference at the Ohio State University, September 1999).[43]

In memoir after memoir, formerly loyal party men recall how knowledge of the Soviet Union's material decline sapped their *esprit de corps*, caused them to question old verities, and weakened their ability to respond to the arguments and analyses of new thinking intellectuals (Hollander 1999). In one sense, this finding is not surprising. After all, the Brezhnev, Andropov, and Chernenko politburos had fretted over Soviet relative decline in the early 1980s. It was hard to make the case in the latter part of the decade that the situation had somehow turned around.

This is not to say that traditionalists were at the forefront in calling for foreign policy restructuring. In his own account, Akhromeev claims to have been a key initiator of the move toward unilateral retrenchment

---

[42]We have in mind officials such as Boldin, Belousov, Zaikov, and Vorotnikov. Illuminating sources on this score include, Savelev, Detinov, and Varhall (1995), Vorotnikov (1995), Gaddy (1997), and Skvortsov interviews with Boldin, Feburary 24, 1999, and Yazov, December 16, 1998. See also the documents revealing Ligachev and Ryzhkov arguing for greater concessions on INF in NSA (1998, doc. no. 32). Further evidence is analyzed in Brooks and Wohlforth (2003).

[43]The Big Five comprised representatives of the Ministries of Defense and Foreign Affairs, the Central Committee, the KGB and the General Staff.

and defensive restructuring (Akhromeev and Kornienko 1992). Some analysts, however, doubt whether he played such a role (Evangelista 1999). It is certainly true that Akhromeev eventually came to be troubled by the West's failure to quickly reciprocate the Soviets' unilateral initiatives – hardly a surprising reaction from a career military officer. In the end, what is of fundamental importance is not whether Akhromeev and other traditionalists helped initiate these changes, but that they did nothing substantial to block the overall course of Gorbachev's foreign policy reforms and that many of them actively aided and abetted it. In discussing Gorbachev's unilateral reduction of a half-million troops announced at the United Nations in December 1988, Yazov recounts that Gorbachev did, in fact, consult with the military beforehand before taking this step, adding "We even gave him the data. It was a reasonable, well-founded step." More generally, Yazov notes that "We [the military] did not oppose reductions in military forces and weapons.... In other words, there was no conflict whatsoever between the political leadership and the military.... Moreover, we agreed to a reassignment of a whole series of defense enterprises to civilian production" (Skvortsov interview with Yazov, December 16, 1998).

However much Gorbachev's fiercest critics opposed some of what Gorbachev was saying and doing, they could not deny the existence of at least some of the critical material trends that undermined the foreign policy status quo, particularly after 1988. An important example on this point is Oleg Baklanov, the Central Committee Secretary for Defense Industry. Few leaders had as much to lose from Gorbachev's reforms as Baklanov. He consequently was a harsh contemporary critic of Gorbachev's foreign policy initiatives and has remained one since. Not surprisingly, Baklanov tried to undermine Gorbachev's call in the late 1980s for reducing the burden of defense spending by arguing that the military absorbed less than 12 percent of economic output – a figure far below Gorbachev's estimate of 20 percent. Later, however, when questioned by fellow conservative Valery Boldin, even Baklanov allowed that the figure may have been as high as 15 percent (Skvortsov interviews with Baklanov (n.d.) and Boldin, February 24, 1999). At any rate, the key issue is whether Baklanov's assertion that the military was not a massive burden on the economy was plausible to other decision-makers, given the information at their disposal. As was discussed earlier, his claim was clearly not compelling. While Baklanov was deeply opposed to Gorbachev's foreign policy initiatives, he was ultimately unable to make a case that the increasing material pressures on Soviet foreign policy that Gorbachev was pointing to were illusory. He consequently made little headway in blocking retrenchment.

An additional important example is KGB chief Vladimir Kryuchkov, another hardliner who was a critical organizer of the 1991 putsch. Kryuchkov could not deny that the Soviet Union "seriously lagged behind in the scientific-technological revolution" (Skvortsov interview with Kryuchkov, October 13, 1998). After all, he knew how much the Politburo allocated for industrial espionage. The argument that "we can always steal from the West" is not a particularly effective rebuttal to the sorts of arguments Gorbachev and his supporters were making, especially given that "passive" technology transfers (illegal or otherwise) were of declining marginal utility (Brooks 2001, chap. 5). As former KGB colonel Vladimir Putin reports, agents involved in industrial espionage abroad became increasingly frustrated by the repeated inability of the Soviet economy to absorb the fruits of their labor (Putin 2000: 86).

The overall pattern of evidence that has emerged concerning Soviet old thinkers can be explained only in light of the material trends examined above, which undermined opposition to retrenchment by helping to break up the intellectual coherence of the old approach. In the end, old thinkers simply could not deny the existence of the rapidly mounting material pressures on the Soviet Union's foreign policy. The argument frequently turned from "no concessions or cuts are needed" to "concessions and cuts may be needed, but not this one in particular." Each special interest tried to defend itself while admitting, or acquiescing to, the general need for change. Adding up these particular objections did not by itself amount to a plausible general alternative to retrenchment. As much as they opposed specific concessions, old thinkers had trouble coming up with a compelling strategic alternative. In the end, any old thinker who wished to forward an alternative to retrenchment faced daunting odds.

Conclusion

Scholars who have recently contributed to the literature on the role of ideas in world politics are right to emphasize that material incentives always leave uncertainty. To improve our understanding of how and to what degree ideas shape international behavior, however, we need an estimate of *how much* uncertainty characterizes various strategic situations given material incentives. A key problem with the large literature that examines how ideas influenced the Cold War's end is that it has developed in the absence of an accurate understanding of the material constraints facing Soviet policymakers in the 1980s.

In this chapter, we consequently aimed to provide a more complete understanding of the material pressures facing Soviet policymakers and how those changing incentives influenced decision-making. In so doing, we brought three new factors to bear. First, we introduced a new and key shift in the material environment – the changing structure of global production. Second, we provided a more in-depth understanding of how Soviet relative decline influenced Moscow's strategic choices. Third, we examined new sources of evidence concerning Soviet old thinkers and how their responses to material pressures compared with other policymakers.

In reviewing this evidence, our general finding is that material conditions undermined old Soviet ways of doing things to a much greater extent than scholars have recognized. As the material pressures on Soviet foreign policy became more significant, Gorbachev became increasingly disposed to undertake a radical shift toward retrenchment. All Soviet decision-makers were not, of course, equally enthusiastic about a fundamental reorientation of the country's foreign policy, and many were opposed. The escalating economic costs of maintaining the foreign policy status quo, however, systematically undercut the ability of Gorbachev's critics to come up with a compelling general foreign policy alternative.

Our conclusion that material incentives systematically undermined alternatives to retrenchment does not foreclose important pathways by which ideas may have altered behavior. In fact, the clearer picture of material constraints that we provide leaves open a number of potential roles for ideational factors in the end of the Cold War that may be clarified in future research. If our research withstands the test of further releases of new evidence, the examination of the role of ideas in this case may move away from analyzing why the Soviets opted for a fundamental reorientation of their foreign policy and shift instead toward examining different questions for which ideational models may prove to have much greater utility. In particular, future research may reveal that ideational factors are very important in explaining more finely grained decisions. It would be easy to caricature our analysis as one that views material pressures as leading to one and only one set of foreign policy decisions throughout the entire Cold War endgame. Our analysis should not be interpreted to mean that there were no differences between new and old thinkers – or that representatives of these orientations would have responded identically to each strategic incentive. We do not claim – no responsible analyst can – to account for each microanalytical decision or bargaining position adopted during the Cold War endgame. By outlining a more complete portrayal of the material conditions facing Moscow in this period, what our analysis does provide is the basis for a more productive dialogue concerning how ideas and material incentives interacted in more finely grained decision problems.

Beyond the end of the Cold War case, what are the more general theoretical implications of our analysis? It is certainly true that Soviet elites and leaders invested heavily in new ideas, and it is clear that the shift in world views they experienced in the 1980s was accompanied by personal anguish and political struggle. However, just because intellectual shifts are observed to be strongly in evidence and, in turn, policy changes dramatically, it does not necessarily follow that these shifts played a key causal role. This is a crucial point that is often overlooked in much recent empirical scholarship on the role of ideas in international relations. Establishing a strong, independent role for ideas will be particularly difficult when material constraints are especially significant and/or when there is relatively little lag between material and policy changes – as was the case with respect to Soviet retrenchment. It is precisely for this reason that scholars who focus on ideas are so driven to claim that the material environment facing the Soviets did not change much in the 1980s – a claim we showed to be unsustainable. While more research is needed, in our judgment many of the basic causal mechanisms that are featured in ideational models of this case are to a significant degree endogenous to material changes.

In advancing this endogenization point, we are not suggesting that ideas are just hooks, nor that all phenomena can be reduced to material underpinnings. Our point is simply that scholars who focus on ideas need to consider more carefully whether the origins and impact of the intellectual shifts they highlight are endogenous to a changing material environment. This key endogeneity issue has been ignored or marginalized in recent empirical work on ideas in international relations. While this problem is hardly uncommon in social science inquiry, and it certainly is not always easy to deal with, it must be confronted more forthrightly if the study of ideas in international relations is to move forward.

This raises a related theoretical point. Particularly for many constructivist scholars who have examined this case, the reorientation of Soviet foreign policy is understood to have gone beyond a simple change of policy, but rather involved what they would view as a change in the Soviets' fundamental interests, or indeed in the Soviet identity itself. Whether this is the case or not is very hard to tell. For one thing, exactly what a state identity consists of is extremely vague within the constructivist literature (Fearon 1997). In turn, in many constructivist analyses, identities are understood to be exogenous, given, and stable, which leads one to wonder how they can also be subject to abrupt changes and yet still have many of the effects that constructivists posit they do. Finally, in situations in which material incentives shift dramatically prior to the change in policy – as occurred in this case – it will be very difficult to distinguish between a change in strategy or behavior, on the one hand, and a change in fundamental interests or identity, on the other.

If this case can, in fact, be characterized as a change in the Soviets' fundamental interests or of the Soviet identity itself, then what are the more general theoretical implications of our analysis? The most important is that we should not necessarily be too quick to endorse a staged method of inquiry – whereby, as many scholars have recently suggested, constructivists can first explain why shifts in identities and fundamental interests occur and then 'pass the baton' to theorists who focus largely on material incentives in the environment (Lamborn 1997: 205; Checkel 1998: 346; Katzenstein, Keohane, and Krasner 1998: 682; Ruggie 1998: 866–7). This suggestion is premature at best, given that constructivists have yet to systematically address how identities and fundamental interests actually do change (Checkel 1998: 344). International relations scholars typically assume that focusing on material incentives in the international environment is not at all helpful for explaining how changes in fundamental goals or identities occur (for one prominent exception to this see Kowert and Legro (1996: 490–1)). Although it is true that scholars who highlight material incentives typically assume fixed preferences, there is no reason to think that changing material incentives in the environment cannot at least sometimes help explain shifts in actors' fundamental interests and/or in their very identities. When analyzing specific cases, constructivists themselves sometimes make brief throwaway arguments along these lines, but have so far been unwilling to explore this point in any depth (Wendt 1992: 420, 1999: 129; Herman 1996: 277; Bukovansky 1997: 217).

In the end, we can only truly know where the world of ideas begins if we know what international behavior can be explained by changing material incentives. Because ideas are not directly observable, some of the best evidence in favor of ideational arguments is often the existence of a poor fit between changes in material incentives and evolving state behavior. Ironically, to better understand the role of ideas, there is thus a strong need for scholars to develop a more useful conception of how material incentives in the international environment affect state behavior. In clarifying the role that material incentives played in the reorientation of Soviet foreign policy, we hope that this analysis will make it possible to further the dialogue concerning the role of ideas in the end of the Cold War and in international relations more generally.

Chapter 8

Perestroika without politics: how realism misunderstands the Cold War's end

Robert English

"The Cold War ended as it did – with the Soviet Union's remarkably rapid and peaceful retreat from empire, its capitulation in the arms race and in the larger contest for global influence – because the country was broke. The apparent drama of events, including bitter opposition to Mikhail Gorbachev's sweeping changes in longstanding Soviet domestic and foreign policies, should not distract from the essential inevitability of their outcome."

This narrative predominates in American media and policymaking circles, not to mention the popular outlook. "We won the Cold War because of our economic superiority," the argument goes, "even hastening its denouement thanks to Ronald Reagan's heightened military-technological challenge to Moscow. Gorbachev, admittedly an unusual Soviet leader, was nevertheless tightly constrained by severe material pressures; his liberal 'new thinking' ideas about demilitarized, cooperative international relations served mainly to rationalize the inevitable. The Soviets essentially gave up because they could no longer compete, their bankruptcy confirmed by the USSR's collapse close on the heels of the Cold War's end."

Prominent (in slightly modified form) in the scholarly literature as well, this interpretation suffers from several analytical flaws, not the least of which is its conflation of the two noted events – the Cold War's end, and the USSR's demise. The latter has distorted understanding of the former by imparting an implicit determinism to Soviet actions, by encouraging bias in the selection and evaluation of evidence, by discouraging serious counterfactual analysis, and as a consequence by ultimately confusing necessary and sufficient conditions for change.

Each of these problems is reflected in the realist explanation for Soviet behavior of the late 1980s advanced by Stephen Brooks and William Wohlforth (this volume, previous chapter). In the strongest such argument to date, the authors cite new evidence on Moscow's economic woes and their supposedly compelling effect on even hard-line Soviet officials; as for Gorbachev, his innovation was basically a response to necessity and his role essentially that of a "streetcar" (if not for him, another would have soon come along to do the same). His new-thinking ideas were in fact "endogenous" to structure and "largely a reflection of a changing material environment" (this volume, p. 197). In sum, ideas and leadership were at best intervening variables; economic crisis was both a necessary *and* sufficient condition for the Cold War's end.

Yet Brooks and Wohlforth's case is weakened by an evident bias in their selection of sources – and, in turn, in those sources' recollec-tions of the 1980s – that flows from hindsight of the Soviet Union's subsequent collapse and a consequently exaggerated sense of the in-evitability of retreat. Downplaying the hardliners' opposition to reform, the authors also overlook evidence of the liberals' *principled* belief in new thinking with the result that the alternatives to radical retrench-ment disappear, the critical contributions of leadership and ideas fade, and economic decline alone renders fairly straightforward and all but inevitable a sweeping foreign policy turn that was in fact the end result of a highly complex and contingent causal chain.

The bias of hindsight is compounded by assumptions Brooks and Wohlforth make about the "rationality" of pre-reform Soviet politics whereby the pervasive cynicism, careerism, and corruption of military-industrial officials is replaced by a kind of bureaucratically tempered realism. Had the Politburo of the mid-1980s indeed been subject to anything like the pressures that would weigh on the leaders of a plural-istic state in similar economic straits, then correlation of those straits with subsequent policy change might constitute primary evidence of causation. But the Kremlin faced few such pressures, at least until the late 1980s, by which time Mikhail Gorbachev had already launched his boldest new-thinking initiatives. Until then, the Soviet system had been stable, the alternatives to major retrenchment had seemed viable (at least they had to a conservative leadership majority), and perhaps the most critical (but still under-appreciated) change was the growth of ties between a reformist leadership minority and a group of academics and policy analysts who had been advocating major "Westernizing" changes for more than a decade.

Below I examine some interpretive problems concerning evidence that Brooks and Wohlforth cite on the beliefs and actions of Soviet old thinkers. I then outline some important but overlooked sources on the origins and influence of the new thinking. Next I suggest an alternative to Brooks and Wohlforth's materialist explanation of Soviet behavior, seeking to give leadership and ideas their due alongside power and arguing that economic pressures were a necessary but clearly insufficient condition for the Cold War's peaceful end. I also offer some observations on the difficulty of assimilating new evidence on such a rare, complex event as the Cold War's end, and conclude with an argument for better balance, closer attention to context, and greater discernment in distinguishing between claims of correlations versus causation and necessity versus sufficiency.

Economic decline and Soviet old thinking

Brooks and Wohlforth begin with a synthesis of recent research on Soviet economic trends prior to Gorbachev's accession as General Secretary in 1985, and follow them through the early years of perestroika. They argue that Soviet relative decline came sooner, and proceeded more rapidly, than most Western analysts understood at the time. Further, this was a qualitative and not just quantitative change; looking back from the perspective of capitalism's incipient globalization, Brooks and Wohlforth contend that by the mid-1980s the dilemma facing Moscow was arguably "modern history's worst case of imperial overstretch" (this volume, p. 210).

Of course, this assessment by itself adds little to the materialist/realist case; indeed, some nonrealists had no difficulty proceeding from similarly pessimistic views of the Soviet condition long before their acceptance by realists (Tucker 1987). Others cited the analyses of such "dissident" Soviet economists as Igor Birman and Grigory Khanin (ignored by many realists until well after the Soviet Union's collapse) to argue that Moscow's military burden far exceeded even the worst-case Western estimates. Such findings, though now more conclusively documented, hardly show that radical retrenchment had become unavoidable by the mid-1980s. Absent strong evidence that the situation was broadly understood in such dire terms by the Soviet leadership – and, moreover, that there was agreement on major retrenchment as a remedy – such data make only a circumstantial case for the priority of material forces. In fact Brooks and Wohlforth do offer evidence to this end, but with so many flaws and omissions that it substantially undermines their argument.

For example, having shown that the Soviet economy was weaker than previously understood, Brooks and Wohlforth claim that this problem was particularly acute because "what mattered most to Soviet policymakers ... was the direct comparison between their country's economic performance and that of their main rival, the United States" (this volume, p. 206). Further, "the Soviet elite's basic reference point was one in which Moscow was gaining rapidly vis-à-vis the United States. Anything short of that was devastating" (this volume, p. 209). This is clearly wrong. Such attitudes had faded by the late 1960s, and by the early 1980s most of the leadership was mired in corruption, often oblivious to foreign and even domestic economic trends, and largely content to muddle through indefinitely. Politburo members certainly valued the international respect that their military might had earned, but that did not seem at risk.[1] And neither their identity, nor their legitimacy, depended on overtaking the United States. On the contrary, the Soviet leadership's "basic reference point" lay not in the future but in the past, mainly in the experience of World War II and postwar privations, which the leadership frequently invoked to rationalize current economic difficulties.[2] Nor did a younger generation of elites suffer from any "catch up and surpass America" illusions. Though they were clearly concerned about the economy, the near desperation that Brooks and Wohlforth depict is much exaggerated.[3]

The authors' focus next turns to members of the Soviet military-industrial complex; if even they agreed that economic woes made missile cuts, troop reductions, and other elements of a radical retrenchment unavoidable, then perhaps material pressures really were paramount. Here Brooks and Wohlforth draw on new evidence – primarily memoirs and interviews – to support two claims: that there was consensus on the depth of crisis and the necessity of urgent measures; and that there was agreement on, or at least an absence of serious resistance to, sweeping arms reductions. What is actually remarkable about such retrospective

---

[1] In the recollection of a former Deputy General Staff Chief," Our senior military officers and the political leadership ... didn't care about SDI [i.e., the U.S. Strategic Defense Initiative]. Everything was driven by departmental and careerist concerns. Any serious issue was shunned.... Nobody took national security seriously, nobody.... You are looking for elements of intelligence, logic, or concern for the nation's welfare, but all these were lacking" (quoted in Ellman and Kontorovich 1998: 57–8).

[2] This is the picture that emerges from a broad range of sources on Brezhnev-era politics. An especially lively description – though still representative of numerous such testimonies – is that found in the memoirs of Boris Yeltsin (1990; Russian-language sources include Medvedev 1991 and Grachev 1994).

[3] The views of former Politburo Second Secretary Yegor Ligachev, the patron of these officials, are instructive. As William E. Odom notes, "Ligachev wanted reform but not at the expense of the Soviet Union's international military status." This meant weaning wasteful clients, quitting Afghanistan, and other cost-cutting steps. It did *not* mean one-sided retrenchment; any major arms cuts would have to be matched by equivalent U.S. steps (Odom 1998: 92). See below for discussion of the viability of conservative alternatives to new thinking.

accounts is their *lack* of agreement. For each former official arguing, "We couldn't have stayed afloat for another 20 years, we were under a lot of pressure," another claims "I did not foresee an impending crisis." Or, "The country could still have endured for years to come.... Imagine that Brezhnev is still alive.... things would be a little worse, but the country would be under control" (Ellman and Kontorovich 1998: 52, 55, 65).[4]

Equally problematic is the testimony of several former top officials – Defense Minister Dmitry Yazov, General Staff Chief Sergei Akhromeyev, and others. Here some have claimed that they agreed on the need for major military reductions, and that far from opposing such cuts they actively cooperated in making them. Though this would seem to offer convincing support for Brooks and Wohlforth, there are several reasons for skepticism. One is a large body of conflicting evidence that reveals how strongly the old thinkers disagreed with Gorbachev's incipient new thinking. A typical example concerns Marshal Yazov, who has since recalled how excitedly he received Gorbachev's initial call for reforms. But according to a close colleague, Yazov's early enthusiasm had instead to do with Gorbachev's promise to *strengthen* the country's defenses; Yazov worried about the cost of modern weapons only insofar as neglect of training, housing, and other needs hurt combat readiness – but not about the military's larger drain on the civilian economy (Ivashov 1993).[5]

An even stronger reason to doubt the old thinkers' retrospective claims of support for military cuts is that at the time they consistently (and often openly) opposed them. This line began with questioning of Gorbachev's mid-1985 unilateral moratorium on nuclear tests and his pursuit of a late-1985 summit meeting to discuss arms control with U.S. President Ronald Reagan in Geneva.[6] It also includes opposition to the mid-1986 Stockholm agreement on confidence-building measures in

---

[4]It is also evident that much of "the arms race bankrupted us" opinion is shaped by hindsight. That is, the surprising speed of the system's subsequent collapse has colored today's reflections on yesterday's perceptions. See below for more discussion of this critical point.

[5]It is also difficult to believe that Marshal Akhromeyev, who was warning about NATO's threat and lobbying for costly high-technology arms in 1984, and who admitted suspicion of Gorbachev's foreign policy steps in 1985, became convinced of the need for deep, one-sided cuts by 1986 (Akhromeev and Kornienko 1992: 34, 65–6, 91, 362; Ellman and Kontorovich 1998: 96; Cherniaev 2000: 8–9).

[6]Arms negotiator Oleg Grinevsky argues that, contrary to their later claims, Marshal Akhromeyev, Deputy Foreign Minister Georgy Kornienko, and other conservatives fought Gorbachev's policies (Zubok 2000: 263). In fact, Akhromeyev tried to block the 1986 Stockholm agreement, opposed the 1987 INF treaty, and resigned over Gorbachev's 1988 conventional force cuts. For its part, the Defense Ministry only grudgingly backed Gorbachev's proposals, and then only as propaganda with no expectation that they

Europe as well as to Gorbachev's radical disarmament proposals offered later that year at Reykjavik, to efforts toward a defensive restructuring of Soviet military doctrine, to the 1987 treaty banning Intermediate-Range Nuclear Forces (INF), and to Gorbachev's sweeping 1988 unilateral troop reductions (Savel'yev, Detinov, and Varhall 1995: 131–8; Odom 1998: 89, 107, 130–6).

By this time, Politburo Second Secretary Yegor Ligachev had clearly joined the opposition to Gorbachev, as seen in his sponsorship of the infamous "Nina Andreyeva letter" that sought to halt the ideological liberation (or, in Ligachev's view, decay) that supported perestroika and new thinking, and shortly thereafter in his speech attacking the erosion of traditional Leninist foreign policy precepts.[7] It is no secret that the hardliners applauded Ligachev; as William Odom argues, they understood well that the old-thinking ideology was the linchpin of the militarized party-state system that they sought to preserve (Odom, 1998: 94–8,113–15). And so, while paying lip service to the new thinking, Soviet hardliners campaigned vigorously to discredit it – efforts that began in 1987, grew stronger in 1989, and continued right up to the attempted putsch of August 1991.[8] Nor did their obstruction of new-thinking policies – of initiatives to restrict arms transfers abroad, reduce military secrecy, halt biological weapons research, and begin defense conversion – slacken in the least (Odom 1998: 206, 229, 257–8).[9] Neither was the August putsch the hardliners' first such effort, having been preceded by a move to replace Gorbachev with Ligachev in the summer of 1990 and another to sideline him via emergency legislation in the early summer of 1991. And even as this "parliamentary putsch" failed, hardliners were preparing a more forceful variant as seen in their

---

would become policy (Shakhnazarov 1993: 89–91; Savel'yev, Detinov, and Varhall 1995: 93; Shevardnadze, Grinevskii, Kvitsinskii, Komplektov, and Piadyshev 1997: 4).

[7]Ligachev defended the orthodox, class-based foundation of Soviet foreign policy, precisely that which Gorbachev was discarding with his argument that "universal human values" superseded class interests. As Odom (1998: 92) notes, Ligachev opposed steps that threatened the country's "international military status [while] Gorbachev was willing to set the Soviet Union's military status aside" (on Ligachev's 1988 speech see Garthoff 1994: 363).

[8]This was seen in their support of such rabid old thinkers as Gen. Viktor Filatov, editor of the Defense Ministry's hard-line *Voenno-Istoricheskii Zhurnal* [Military-historical journal], of the "black colonels" Viktor Alksnis and Nikolai Petrushenko, and of conservative officers' and veterans' groups, on the one hand, and their harassment of such military reformers as Col. Alexander Savinkin, Maj. Vladimir Lopatin, and the liberal group "Shield" on the other. The brass also sponsored "vicious" abuse of their civilian critics (Kokoshin 1989: 145–6; Arbatov 1991: 366, 369–70; Odom 1998: 150–3, 163–71).

[9]Noteworthy as well was the effort of KGB Director Vladimir Kryuchkov to discredit Gorbachev's new thinking and the country's nascent opening to the West by accusing the latter's security services – primarily the U.S. Central Intelligence Agency – of plotting to destroy the Soviet Union (Matlock 1995: 442–5).

backing of the militant anti-Gorbachev manifesto *A word to the people* (Matlock 1995: 539–40).[10]

Nevertheless, Brooks and Wohlforth argue that "what is most striking ... is the haphazard, ineffectual, belated, and intellectually weak nature of the opposition to Gorbachev's overall course in world affairs" (this volume, p. 229). Intellectually weak it may have been, but that reflects only the intellect of the new thinking's opponents, not the depth of their convictions. And as for being haphazard or ineffectual, it was concerted enough to delay arms control progress repeatedly while complicating other attempts to put Soviet–Western relations on a new footing.[11] Given the Soviet military's tradition of strict subservience to the party, its oppositional efforts during the mid-to-late 1980s were actually *extraordinary* and seem ineffectual or belated only in hindsight. If this was a case of the dog that failed to bark, it certainly snarled so much that its eventual bite surprised few (Odom 1998: 339, 394–7).

Mention of the putsch raises another problem in evaluating the hardliners' claims – one of credibility. It is not only that the testimony of those who violated their solemn oaths should be treated with caution.[12] It is that the events of 1991 and after created circumstances of which Brooks and Wohlforth seem unaware. They argue that "because they wish to blame Gorbachev for the Soviet collapse, conservative policy veterans face strong incentives to argue in hindsight that Moscow had ample capabilities to continue the rivalry. It is therefore striking that even in hindsight, most hold that Moscow could not sustain the Cold War status quo" (this volume, p. 230). In fact the domestic context has been rather more complicated than this suggests, beginning with a highly charged atmosphere in the aftermath of the putsch (when many hardliners "went public" for the first time). Jailed and facing trial for treason, and with popular opinion inflamed against them, they had good reason to downplay their opposition to Gorbachev and counter their image as "dinosaurs" who had long been scheming against efforts

---

[10]The July hardliners' manifesto, subsequently reprinted in other conservative publications, first appeared as "Slovo k narodu" in *Sovetskaia Rossiia,* July 23, 1991. Its signatories included ground forces commander Gen. Valentin Varennikov and Deputy Interior Minister Gen. Boris Gromov.

[11]Others cite the initial cover-up of the 1986 Chernobyl nuclear reactor disaster, and the arrest on phony espionage charges of American journalist Nicholas Daniloff on the eve of the Reykjavik summit, as further efforts to sabotage fast-improving U.S.–Soviet relations.

[12]Some have also engaged in flagrant falsehoods on other issues, ranging from a cover-up of the military-KGB role in various antinationalist crackdowns to efforts at implicating Gorbachev in the August coup. At least in the case of the latter, the known facts support Gorbachev's admonition concerning the hardliners: "Don't believe them. They are liars, dyed-in-the-wool liars." (Federal News Service (2001).

to demilitarize and liberalize the Soviet system. And having gone on the record thus, what remains of their tattered credibility depended on not changing their story (or at least not changing it too radically) yet again.

And notwithstanding the sea change in Russian attitudes toward the West over the difficult years since the Soviet Union's collapse, the hardliners still have good reason to shade the truth. This is so because for all their opposition and delay, most ultimately acquiesced in Gorbachev's policies. Thus they now face such questions as: Given the loss and humiliation those policies have caused, why did you not act sooner? Why, rather than resigning and denouncing him publicly, did you remain at Gorbachev's side and so lend your authority to his disastrous concessions? Were you more concerned about the prerequisites of your position than the defense of the Motherland?[13] Were you so dazzled by Gorbachev's charms that you could not see straight?[14] In a climate where current Russian President Vladimir Putin directs a rare public outburst at those "who destroyed the army, the navy, and the state" ("Putin Blames Disaster on Those Who 'Destroyed the State'," *RFE/RL Security Watch,* August 28, 2000: 1), the former officials who were complicit in that destruction face a strong incentive to argue exactly as they have: the economy seemed so weak that we truly believed there was no alternative to some cuts; it was only later that Gorbachev went too far and things got out of control.[15]

The preceding is not meant to accuse all hardliners of falsehood. But it should suffice to demonstrate why most such testimony cannot simply be taken at face value.[16] Still, one might wonder what difference

---

[13]In addition to careerist concerns and their traditional deference to the party, some old thinkers also made a rational calculation. Notwithstanding their differences with Gorbachev's policies, they thought that they would still have greater influence opposing him from within the Politburo, restraining even deeper and more ill-conceived military cuts, than if they broke openly and irrevocably with him. Gorbachev, for his part, feared letting "this lousy, rabid dog off the leash" and thought it was better to have the "mastodons" inside the tent spitting out than outside spitting in (Cherniaev 2000: 279–80, 325, 338).

[14]Yazov, in particular, appears to have been under the spell of Gorbachev's personality. He was also most indebted to Gorbachev, having been named Minister of Defense in 1987 over many more qualified officers and then promoted to Marshal in 1989. These were things of which, just a few years earlier, he had probably not even dared to dream (Stepankov and Lisov 1992: 25–9; Odom 1998: 183). On Gorbachev's tactic of compromising critics by giving them responsibility for selling and implementing his initiatives, see Evangelista (2001: 20–1).

[15]It should be noted that Gorbachev has faced corresponding incentives to downplay the conservatives' opposition to new thinking; before 1991 this served to project an image of party unity for the sake of perestroika, and since then to share blame for the results of policies that he authored. Still, on the whole, the reformers' public recollections of the events of 1985–91 have been far more consistent, and accord better with known facts, than those of most hardliners.

[16]Further fueling these doubts are other inconsistencies. Yazov, for example, while presenting a face of moderation to Western interlocutors, shows a different one to other

it makes if the hardliners fought Gorbachev's policies from the outset or only after the INF treaty and troop cuts of 1987–8, or if they dug in their heels only over the loss of Eastern Europe and German reunification in 1989–90. The answer is that it makes all the difference in the world. For whatever one believes about the old thinkers' acquiescence in Gorbachev's initiatives, it remains inconceivable that they would have launched similar initiatives without him, much less persevered when they failed to elicit equivalent Western concessions. Thus it would seem self-evident that the role of Gorbachev, supported by Foreign Minister Eduard Shevardnadze and Ideology Secretary Alexander Yakovlev, was essential.

Mikhail Gorbachev: new-thinking leader or overseer of retreat?

Or was it? In Brooks and Wohlforth's portrayal, Gorbachev is essentially the CEO of "Soviet Retrenchment, Inc." His searching discussions of foreign policy philosophy with Shevardnadze, Yakovlev, and a few other intimates over 1985–7 are absent.[17] So too are the vital analytical contributions and political support of many liberal Soviet, and some Western, interlocutors.[18] Brooks and Wohlforth's lack of attention to the influence on Gorbachev of reformist intellectuals – and in turn to the complex sources of their new thinking – is a striking omission. The authors simply ignore a mass of evidence on the nonmaterial origins of intellectual change, or they misinterpret it: in one glancing reference to such sources, they state that "no new thinker's memoir is complete without [revelations] about either living standards or the military-technological superiority of the West" (this volume, p. 228).

audiences – for example, his praise of North Korean socialism and of its president Kim Jong Il as "a great commander who has won important battles." This comment suggests his real attitude toward the collapse of East German socialism and reunification with West Germany, as well as his unconcern for the military burden on a crippled economy ("Visits of Russian Communists to North Korea," (1997), 1). Also eye-opening is Yazov's surly and disingenuous interview with the Czech *Lidove noviny* [The people's news] (2000): 1–5.

[17]An example of how Gorbachev quietly tapped the ideas of liberal intellectuals – and how quickly they led him to radical conclusions – is the testimony of Alexander Tsipko (cited in Ellman and Kontorovich 1998: 169–86; see also English 2000, chaps. 5 and 6).

[18]Brooks and Wohlforth claim that only in late 1988 or 1989 "did [Gorbachev] begin privately to rely on the more radical intellectual proponents of new thinking" (this volume, p. 217) by which time material pressures were so great that ideas played only a rationalizing or facilitating role. But this is decisively contradicted by numerous sources that reveal such a process well under way by late 1985–6. Of course, the devastating implications of this two- or three-year difference for the "power drove ideas" thesis are clear.

This is a serious misstatement, and a telling one. Those new
thinkers in whose memoirs revelations about Western military-economic
power figure little (if at all) in recollections of their evolving worldviews
range from Georgy Arbatov, Fedor Burlatskii, and Anatoly Cherniaev
(Burlatskii 1990; Arbatov 1991; Cherniaev 1995) to Yevgeny Velikhov,
Alexander Yakovlev, and Yuri Zamoshkin (Zamoshkin 1989; Iakovlev
1994; on Velikhov, see the testimony detailed in English 2000, chaps.
3–5). And there are many others in between. Of course, the West,
including its economic vigor, is present in the reminiscences of many;
after all, these are foreign affairs experts! But rarely does it figure in the
simplistic fashion that Brooks and Wohlforth suggest.[19] For some, new
thinking was born in the revival of cultural links to the West; for others
it was the personal relations they established through exchanges and
professional ties. Some new thinkers emphasize Western progress on
environmental, race, or labor issues; others stress their realization that
NATO was a democratic, non-threatening alliance. Many were taken
with Western freedoms and openness, and nearly all recall how lingering fears were supplanted by a desire for contact, collaboration, even
integration.[20] Often these experiences date back to the late 1950s and
1960s, and moved them to begin reformist advocacy by the late 1960s
or early 1970s (Evangelista 1999). Crucially, many were pioneering
new thinkers who, it bears repeating, exerted considerable influence on
Gorbachev – most of it well before 1988, and some even before 1985.

Ignoring this evidence, Brooks and Wohlforth instead depict the
early Gorbachev as largely orthodox. They cite an initial rise in defense
spending but fail to ask how much leeway he had over "his" first
budget given the cumbersome planning system and advanced state
of preparations for the Twelfth (1986–90) Five-Year Plan. They have
him approving an escalation of the war in Afghanistan but overlook

---

[19]Here again is seen the tension between Brooks and Wohlforth's claims for correlation
versus those for causation. For the former it may suffice simply to demonstrate
that economic concerns were widespread, even if not uppermost, among those who
championed the new thinking. But the latter requires closer attention to a wider range
of intellectual, social, and political changes in order to make a considered judgment
about the *relative* influence of these various factors.

[20]Brooks and Wohlforth fault constructivists for counterposing ideas against a "spare
and impoverished" understanding of material incentives (this volume, p. 199). But
at least in my own analysis of the new thinking's origins, economic problems figure
prominently in a detailed examination of the evolution of a "Westernizing" policy-
academic elite, as well as in that elite's subsequent influence on Gorbachev. Admittedly
an early effort to understand the complex sources of new thinking, this analysis
nevertheless proceeds from recognition of the need for a comprehensive, balanced
assessment of multiple factors before venturing claims about causation (English 2000,
chaps. 2–6).

his concerted efforts toward withdrawal.[21] They include the 1987 INF treaty among the concessions driven by economic need but forget that eliminating a new class of nuclear missiles actually cost Moscow more than maintaining them in service.[22] And they omit altogether Gorbachev's principled rejection of long-standing imperial practices toward the Soviet bloc while considering Eastern Europe only insofar as it represented an economic liability.[23]

Beyond these critical omissions, Brooks and Wohlforth also ignore the significance of Gorbachev's early initiatives – his 1985 nuclear test moratorium, his 1986 disarmament plan and later Reykjavik proposal, and his pathbreaking ideological revisions.[24] In addition, they over-look a basic political reality – how *any* major changes were necessarily delayed by the roughly two years that it took to clear the leadership of such hardliners as Prime Minister Nikolai Tikhonov, Defense Indus-try Secretary Grigory Romanov, and Defense Minister Sergei Sokolov (Brown 1996, chap. 4) as well as other conservatives such as Vladimir Shcherbitsky, Gaidar Aliev, and Andrei Gromyko.[25]

As further evidence for the primacy of material forces, Brooks and Wohlforth cite a pre-Reykjavik summit (October 1986) Politburo meeting where Gorbachev fought for backing of his radical proposals by warning that otherwise "we will be pulled into another round of the

---

[21] On Gorbachev's early commitment to leave Afghanistan, and on his efforts toward that end as well as vacillation in the face of hardliners' opposition to a rapid withdrawal, see Cherniaev (1995: 25–6, 41–3, 89–90, 106, 161–2). One of those who so strongly opposed a "hasty" (only by February 1989!) exit that he resigned in protest was Georgy Kornienko (1994: 207).

[22] At least this was so in the near term, because of the complex destruction and verification procedures that the treaty mandated. Even more problematic is that in emphasizing economically driven concessions, Brooks and Wohlforth overlook the critical military rationale for the INF treaty; the Soviets gave up theater-range missiles (able to strike Western Europe) in return for destruction of U.S. weapons of strategic reach (able to strike targets in or near Moscow) (Primakov 1999: 49–50).

[23] I have confined my critique mainly to Brooks and Wohlforth's arguments on defense policy, as did they in their chapter. However, Gorbachev's East European policy was also central to Soviet retrenchment and Wohlforth has discussed it extensively elsewhere (Wohlforth 1994/95, 115–19). Rather than engage these issues here, I refer readers to the analysis of Mark Kramer (2001).

[24] Just as Gorbachev's January 1986 disarmament plan (dismissed at the time as propaganda) outlined the concessions later offered at Reykjavik, and subsequently enshrined in the INF and START treaties, so did his report at the Twenty-seventh Party Congress in February 1986 clearly foreshadow the ideological revisions (e.g., elevating all-human concerns over class ones) that he openly embraced later that year.

[25] Akhromeyev suggested that Gorbachev concealed the scope of his early ambitions for changing Soviet foreign policy because, had he made them clear, they would have been seen as a sharp departure from "the entire understanding by the military leadership of the essence of the country's defense capability" and so presumably rejected (quoted in Evangelista 2001: 25).

arms race that is beyond our capabilities" (this volume, p. 215). Again, they fail to consider the context.[26] Suppose, as other sources show, that Gorbachev had already come to a sharply different view of the West, of "the threat," and so of defense priorities. And that he now saw the main opposition to progress not in Washington or London but seated around the Politburo table.[27] How best to sell his proposals to these skeptics? How to win over such dyed-in-the-wool old thinkers as Ligachev – by trying to explain the nuances of "mutual security" and convincing them of the primacy of "universal human values"? Or simply by stressing economic necessity? The answer is obviously the latter, and by no means can Gorbachev's use of a particular rationale, before a *very* particular audience, be taken at face value as conclusive evidence of his own priorities.[28]

Mention of Reykjavik raises another aspect of Gorbachev's policy-making that Brooks and Wohlforth overlook: his summit proposals – as everything else of significance that he undertook – were hatched in a small group of liberal advisers. This was no accident; dominated by conservative interests and ideology, the Politburo, Defense Council and Defense Ministry, Military Industrial Commission, the "Big Five" arms control advisory group, and even much of the Foreign Ministry consistently worked to stymie innovation. The notion that, absent Gorbachev, they would have come up with similar initiatives is simply not credible. Confirmation of a sort comes from the old thinkers themselves, in their

---

[26]Nor do they note that at the first post-Reykjavik Politburo meeting, Gorbachev argued exactly the opposite (*Zasedanie Politburo TsK KPSS,* "Ob itogakh vstrechi General'nogo sekretariia TsK KPSS M.S. Gorbacheva s Prezidentom SShA R. Reaganom v Reikiavike, 14 oktabria 1986 goda" [Session of the Politburo of the CC of the CPSU, On the results of the meeting of CC CPSU General Secretary M.S. Gorbachev with USA President R. Reagan in Reykjavik, 14 October 1986], 2–4, credit for attention to this source is owed to Mark Kramer).

[27]Five months earlier, in a "secret" speech, Gorbachev had castigated *Soviet* obstruction of progress on a broad range of foreign policy issues – Afghanistan, nuclear arms, China, Eastern Europe, even human rights. For detail on this, and on Gorbachev's frustration with the bureaucracy that prompted his Reykjavik initiative, see Cherniaev (1993: 77–84) and English (2000: 220). Gorbachev's May 1986 closed speech at the Foreign Ministry (an abridged version was only published a year later, and the full text did not appear in public until after the Soviet Union's collapse) is found in Gorbachev (1993: 46–55).

[28]Just as the scripted, ritualistic conduct of the Brezhnev-era Politburo (and the fact that real decisions were made elsewhere, in smaller leadership groupings) limits the value of their proceedings to historians, so does the absence of much off-the-record deliberation (and the tactics of Gorbachev's maneuvering around the conservatives) render perestroika-era Politburo records difficult to interpret. A further problem is that in the few cases where Gorbachev's Politburo meetings were recorded, the transcripts were subsequently edited – distorted, in the complaints of several staff secretaries – by future putschist Valery Boldin.

constant complaint that Gorbachev ignored their advice, shut them out of his planning, and consulted instead with "amateurs" – or worse, with Western "agents."[29] It is difficult indeed to reconcile these sentiments with a supposed consensus for radical retrenchment.

Although not addressing this directly, Brooks and Wohlforth have an indirect answer: "However much Gorbachev's fiercest critics opposed" his initiatives, "they could not deny ... the critical material trends" that made them necessary (this volume, p. 232).[30] Here we see that there are actually two arguments embedded in their case for the primacy of material forces. The strong version holds that Gorbachev and the hardliners were essentially of one mind on the necessity of radical retrenchment, a necessity they accepted fairly early as the economic crisis worsened. This, as I have shown, is contradicted by a large body of evidence. The weak version argues that even if the old thinkers sharply disagreed with Gorbachev's changes, economic woes left them unable to offer "a plausible general alternative" (this volume, p. 233). Leaving aside for now the plausibility of alternatives to new thinking, it is immediately evident how heavily this second argument depends on the role of Gorbachev as the initiator of change, on the centrality of leadership. And this, in turn, necessarily points back to the key contribution of ideas as well as the important extent to which they developed and operated independent of material pressures.[31]

Old and new thinkers: a different interpretation

The preceding suggests a third version of how material and ideational forces interacted in the genesis of Gorbachev's reforms. It indeed begins with increasing concern among part of the Soviet ruling elite as well

---

[29]This sentiment resounds through the testimonies of Ligachev, Yazov, Akhromeyev, and many other conservatives.

[30]The only case cited by Brooks and Wohlforth of a senior official strongly opposing Gorbachev's cuts is that of Oleg Baklanov, an apparent exception to the radical-retrenchment consensus that they explain as "not surprising" because, as head of the Military-Industrial Commission, "few leaders had as much to lose from Gorbachev's reforms" (this volume, p. 232). But it is hard to see how Baklanov's shrinking budgets were more painful for him to bear than were General Staff Chief Akhromeyev's vanishing missiles and tanks or Defense Minister Yazov's demoralized officers and degraded troops. The obvious alternative explanation is that Baklanov has simply been more forthright than the others about his opposition to new thinking.

[31]As Evangelista (2001: 30–1) succinctly puts it, "We cannot understand Gorbachev's initiatives without taking seriously the normative and ideational context: Gorbachev's antinuclearism, his affinity for West European social democrats and their ideas about common security and nonoffensive defense, and his commitment to 'freedom of choice' and nonintervention in Eastern Europe."

as relief, in 1985, that they finally had a vigorous leader capable of resolute action. But relief soon turned to worry as Gorbachev began consulting with suspect liberals and broaching heretical ideas. Still, his concrete steps were modest, and the old thinkers reassured themselves that his proposals – a nuclear test ban, reduced military spending, defensive restructuring of doctrine, and deep cuts in nuclear arms – were either just clever rhetoric or, at worst, temporary and reversible.[32] Their favored course, one of modest economic changes and a more cost-effective military program that preserved strategic parity and the country's global might, still seemed fully viable.[33]

But unbeknown to the old thinkers, Gorbachev was drawing different conclusions. Frustrated by the domestic opposition that stymied both his domestic and foreign plans, and driven by his private study and rethinking of core issues in world politics, Gorbachev was pushed across a critical threshold by the Chernobyl nuclear accident in early 1986. A catastrophe in human terms, Chernobyl was also a key catalyst of new thinking on both domestic politics (by exposing the bankruptcy of the Stalinist system's sloppiness and secrecy) and foreign affairs (by highlighting nuclear dangers, the absurdity of an obsession with parity, and the duplicity and venality of the military-industrial complex).[34] But the harder Gorbachev pushed, the more these military-industrial interests resisted. Angry, he decided to seek a breakthrough by scheduling an immediate U.S.-Soviet summit, tearing up the negotiating positions produced by the bureaucracy, and insisting on his own radical proposal. The hardliners gave their grudging consent – and breathed a huge sigh of relief when Reykjavik narrowly failed.[35] But Gorbachev took heart from how close he had come. And drawing heavily on the ideas of liberal advisers, he pondered new moves to break the deadlock. Glasnost, initially a means to engage public opinion in his domestic reforms, was spread to foreign and military affairs as new-thinking intellectuals

---

[32]They thought that "waiting out the reformers while pretending to be reformers themselves was a viable strategy. Wrongly, they believed that time was on their side" (Odom 1998: 201).

[33]This was particularly so given the slight economic upturn in Gorbachev's first year.

[34]On this critical but underexplored episode, and the "cognitive punch" it provided in catalyzing liberals' rethinking of domestic and foreign policy issues, see English (2000: 215–22).

[35]The summit collapsed not over the main issues of radical reductions in offensive nuclear weapons – on which Reagan and Gorbachev agreed – but over the secondary matter of a formula for acceptable research on strategic defenses. Soviet liberals blamed military hardliners for scuttling a potentially historic agreement by insisting that Gorbachev not yield on relatively minor issues that, in any case, were soon set aside (on Reykjavik see Oberdorfer 1991: 183–209).

enlisted wholesale in the campaign for change.[36] But the old thinkers struck back in bitter polemics over the policies, and philosophy, of world affairs. Still feigning solidarity with Gorbachev, they "did all they could to jam sticks in the spokes" of his foreign policy (Cherniaev 2000: 341). Only in May 1987, following a German teenager's shocking flight across the Soviet Union and scandalous landing on Red Square, did Gorbachev have a pretext to alter the "correlation of forces" at the top. The powerful, hard-line Defense Minister Sergei Sokolov was replaced by the weak, junior Dmitry Yazov.[37] Gorbachev also ordered far-reaching military reform, including a purge of the officer corps, that shattered the morale and unity of the brass. With his opponents temporarily reeling, and with public opinion both increasingly assertive and increasingly hostile to them, Gorbachev now prevailed in pushing through the concessions necessary for the INF treaty, for an Afghan settlement, and for progress on issues from human rights to third world conflicts.

The last political prisoners were freed, the jamming of foreign radio broadcasts was halted, and Gorbachev embraced the new thinking's core precept – a rejection of the confrontational, class-based approach to world politics – as an orgy of glasnost undermined all that the old thinkers held sacred.[38] The excesses of Brezhnev's military buildup were ridiculed; Stalin's blundering in World War II and blame for the Cold War were exposed; and Lenin's responsibility for the Soviet Union's decades of disastrous political, economic, and cultural isolation was denounced. Only then was Gorbachev's hand strong enough to push through major (not piecemeal) military budget cuts, force real (not rhetorical) defensive restructuring of doctrine, and make the deep, unilateral conventional-force reductions announced in his landmark United Nations speech of December 1988. A refreshing contrast to the

[36]Conservatives were dismayed at what one described as a hijacking of perestroika by "highly politicized research organizations of a pro-Western orientation." This was the characterization of Ligachev's assistant Valery Legostayev (1991: 2).

[37]In one insider's view, Gorbachev hoped to neutralize "the powerful opposition to his 'new thinking' that existed in military circles.... [So] Sokolov just wouldn't do. Many members of the defense ministry collegium saw no need for major changes in the military sphere. They were seriously concerned about the policy of concessions to the Americans and a clear violation of military strategic parity. So turnover in the high command of the armed forces ... became Gorbachev's main task" (Ivashov 1993: 19–20).

[38]Like much else, Brooks and Wohlforth essentially ignore Gorbachev's measures to liberalize, humanize, and open the country to the West (save for new laws permitting joint business ventures). On the central role of human rights in improving U.S.-Soviet ties, see Matlock (1995: 105-7, 121-3, 148-50); for Gorbachev's 1986-7 embrace of liberal-democratic values as key to establishing international trust, see English (2000: 215-22).

consensual, public relations–minded version of how these cuts were decided comes from Yazov's biographer Ivashov:

> Many generals and marshals persistently argued that we needed to maintain military parity, and around the ministry [*v kuluarakh*] they referred to one-sided reductions as a betrayal of the interests of the USSR and the Warsaw Pact. This position was strongly supported by the country's military-industrial complex.... The arguments offered for why we needed to go forward with disarmament were primarily economic ones. Obviously counting on Yazov's backing, and without a Supreme Soviet decision nor even agreement with its committees, Gorbachev announced a unilateral 500,000-man cut in the Soviet armed forces at the UN on December 7, 1988. It was like a slap in the face of the deputies. Some of them tried to express their concerns ... but were swept aside by the paeans of praise and support for Gorbachev from the West, from our democratic figures, from the mass media.... The defense ministry was simply presented with a fait accompli. Nobody consulted with the military or worked out what was to be cut and when. It was, as they liked to say in the 1960s, typical voluntarism. That's why the military reacted to Gorbachev's initiative with – to put it mildly – skepticism.[39]

Staggering from this onslaught, the old thinkers fought on. KGB Director Vladimir Kryuchkov channeled even more tendentious (than usual) information to Gorbachev with the aim of undermining relations with the West.[40] Akhromeyev, after repeated threats to do so, finally resigned when Gorbachev's latest cuts faced him with aiding and abetting "the destruction of that which he'd spent his entire life building."[41] Gromyko quietly complained that "Gorbachev and his Politburo friends" were mindlessly destroying the state's security (Gromyko 1997: 182; credit for this source is owed to Vlad Zubok). And Ligachev warned that Gorbachev's policies were leading to "a new Munich" (Garthoff 1994: 421, 428-9). Other old thinkers fought a rearguard action – attacking the spread of "pacifism," bewailing the influence of "so-called experts," and spreading alarm about "Western subversion" everywhere from the pages of *Krasnaya Zvezda* (*Red Star*, the Ministry of Defense organ) and

---

[39]This account directly contradicts Yazov's subsequent claim, cited by Brooks and Wohlforth, that "there was no conflict whatsoever between the political leadership and the military" on these cuts (this volume p. 232).

[40]Kryuchkov also used his agency's resources to harass and impede the liberals in smaller ways – for example, engineering the firing of Yakovlev's chief assistant on the basis of specious denunciations (Cherniaev 1993: 221, 281, 339).

[41]Here I paraphrase from the marshal's post-putsch suicide note. For detail, see the interview with Akhromeyev's widow quoted in Evangelista (2001: 26).

Sovietskaya Rossiya (*Soviet Russia*, a virulently antireform newspaper) to the halls of party conferences and Central Committee plenums.

Still, even if the preceding suffices to rebut the claim of a "solid consensus" behind Gorbachev's policies and that his opponents "did nothing substantial" to block them (this volume, pp. 218, 232), why did they not do even more when there was still time? Part of the answer is indeed that an economic downturn in 1988 strengthened arguments for at least some kinds of reductions – but only part.[42] Also crucial were factors such as the force of Gorbachev's personality and his skill as a political tactician; time and again he defused confrontations and put off potentially fateful showdowns with the hardliners (Evangelista 2001). The pace of events was also critical; the changes came so quickly during 1987–9 that by the time the old thinkers dug in on one issue, the battle had already shifted to another. A related factor was the unexpected power of public opinion that Gorbachev enlisted in the cause of new thinking, an arena in which party and especially military habits of centralized decision-making, unquestioning obedience, and unimaginative implementation served them poorly.[43] These weaknesses point up yet another reason for the hardliners' seeming passivity – their lack of a strong leader. Ligachev, although true to his principles, would not lead an open assault on the party line; he did what he could within the strictures of the old command system and, as best he understood it, the emerging democratic one. Gromyko, no longer in charge of

---

[42] The issue of timing is key, especially because much of the testimony that Brooks and Wohlforth cite to show conservatives' backing for arms cuts concerns the period *after* 1988. For example, in support of the crisis-drove-concessions thesis, they note testimony on the START negotiations (this volume, p. 231) that actually pertains to events in 1989–90, that is, *after* Gorbachev had launched his boldest new-thinking initiatives. Prior to that, Yazov was assuring colleagues that Gorbachev's innovations were mainly clever rhetoric. Akhromeyev, for his part, later wrote that the military agreed on the economic rationale for significant arms reductions only in 1988, yet he himself still strongly opposed the particular unilateral cuts that Gorbachev announced late that year (Akhromeev and Kornienko 1992: 72–3; Odom 1998,117).

[43] Compounding these disadvantages, many hardliners themselves had publicly endorsed such new-thinking principles as "reasonable sufficiency" in defense. As a variety of witnesses have noted, they did so only grudgingly, for propaganda purposes, and with no expectation of actually implementing attendant policies (see footnote 6). Illustrating the problem of taking such endorsements at face value is an analogous episode from domestic politics. In 1987–8 Gorbachev won grudging approval for a reform of the political system; a year later the party suffered stunning electoral defeats, was set further reeling by its critics' subsequent dominance of the new legislature, and rapidly lost its grip on power. Looking back, no serious analyst argues that the party bosses willingly endorsed their own demise. They consented only to cosmetic changes (who could publicly oppose democratization?), mistakenly believing that they could control the election process and badly underestimating how radical Gorbachev's intentions were. Foreign-policy old thinkers, I argue, found themselves in precisely the same situation as these domestic-policy conservatives.

the Foreign Ministry but still sitting on the Politburo, resisted too, although his influence (and health) were waning fast.[44] Akhromeyev, after resigning as Chief of the General Staff, sought to preserve what he could of the Soviet Union's might by staying on for a time as an adviser to Gorbachev – to his later regret. And Yazov, as even a hard-line admirer writes, was too weak, too indebted to Gorbachev, and too preoccupied with mitigating the damage already done to play the role of a Napoleon.[45] Others hardliners seethed, praying that their jobs would not be the next ones cut and thinking ever more seriously about "emergency measures" to turn back the clock.

Assimilating new evidence: problems and possibilities

This interpretation of the old thinkers' behavior, if even remotely ac-curate, can hardly be squared with another that sees their supposed passivity as an attempt to preserve "political capital," much less as "free riding" on initiatives with which they actually agreed. Nor, for their part, can the new thinkers' manifold impressions of the West be reduced to "demonstration effects" of its economic superiority. In their effort to capture such complex phenomena in a sparse, materialist framework is revealed a central problem in Brooks and Wohlforth's argument – they so completely privilege the material over the ideational that they ignore much evidence of the nonmaterial sources of ideas and influence. Such a model simply does not admit the possibility that a critical mass of new-thinking intellectuals were motivated by normative concerns; that they took personal and professional risks to promote reform out of principle; and that only the virtual accident of the Kremlin's occupation by an unusually open-minded and innovative leader made it possible to translate these principles into policy.[46]

[44]Cherniaev recalls Gorbachev's frustration with Gromyko, observing that "this senile old fool still sat next to Gorbachev in the highest leadership body and never took less than an hour speaking on various issues about which he hadn't the slightest idea. But always from the standpoint that everything in his time was good and right, while anything different was suspect" (Cherniaev 2000: 129).

[45]As Yazov himself put it, it was the role of a "Pinochet" that he rejected when subordinates repeatedly appealed for him to stop Gorbachev (Ivashov 1993: 26–7, 66).

[46]Sources on Gorbachev's selection as General Secretary reveal his colleagues' expecta-tions of modest domestic changes and a largely status quo foreign policy; in the words of one, "Nobody thought that he'd be a reformer.... He didn't turn out to be the man we'd voted for" (English 2000: 195–200, citation of Politburo member Gaidar Aliev from p. 198).

Indeed, analyzing the situation "rationally," and with the benefit of hindsight,[47] Brooks and Wohlforth find it all but inconceivable that modern history's most overextended empire could have chosen any path other than retreat.[48] But one might better begin by asking how the Soviet Union got into such a fix in the first place, and if the institutional-ideological causes of such blundering could have combined again to produce another "irrational" outcome. A state or regime in the habit of setting negative precedents should not be underestimated in its ability to act in ways that outsiders might not find "plausible" or "compelling." Here the testimony of former economic aide Gennady Zoteyev is suggestive:

> In 1988, while still working as an advisor to [Prime Minister] Ryzhkov, [Gosplan Director] Baibakov invited me for a discussion. For almost two hours, I tried to explain to Baibakov the past, the present, and the future of the Soviet economy. He listened rather lethargically, probably because he simply failed to comprehend many of the things I was saying. At the end of the conversation he snapped out of his slumber and asked a rhetorical question: "How can all this be happening? We worked so hard and accomplished so much. We have such a powerful industry, the energy sector, and here you are coming up with such gloomy assessment [sic] and forecasts." (quoted in Ellman and Kontorovich 1998: 141)

This describes *Gorbachev's* director of planning, in the increasingly difficult circumstances of 1988, still unable to respond "rationally" to what was ostensibly obvious years before. Or consider Marshal Yazov's plaintive post-putsch lament: "The unfortunate thing is that I didn't realize what had happened in the country, that we had different people already, and a lot of these people didn't share my political views, having their own views on everything. That was my mistake" (quoted in Odom 1998: 337).

---

[47]To be fair, it is also the hindsight of Brooks and Wohlforth's *sources* that is at issue. As previously noted, the suddenness of the system's subsequent collapse has clearly colored many participants' recollections of precollapse events. Knowledge of outcomes leads to a "certainty of hindsight" bias – a false sense of inevitability – that is strongest in brief and summary discussions. Even with subjects striving for honesty and objectivity, it usually requires detailed, probing, event-specific interviews to recall the contingencies and recapture the arguments and expectations of the past. For more on this problem in general, as well as evidence of its distorting effect on the recollections of Soviet officials in particular, see Lebow and Stein 2004: 212–14.

[48]Brooks and Wohlforth protest that it would be a "caricature" to view their analysis as "leading to one and only one" outcome, and that materialist arguments "do not foreclose important pathways by which ideas may have altered behavior" (this volume, p. 234). But in fact they do; at every critical juncture, economic "necessity" or "lack of alternatives" triumphed, leading to an outcome in which the only "important pathways" amenable to the influence of ideas concerned relatively unimportant details.

Given that these and many similar officials were putatively Gorbachev's men – those who had replaced their old-thinking, Brezhnev-era predecessors – is it so inconceivable that under a different General Secretary, with an even more "traditional" team of economic, defense and foreign-policy officials, a different course might have been chosen in 1985–9? (for an excellent counterfactual analysis that reaches similar conclusions, see Breslauer and Lebow 2004). Elsewhere I have speculated about alternatives to Gorbachev's conciliatory path for the late Soviet empire, more status quo or even hard-line options under which the Cold War might still be ongoing (English 2000: 229–30). And there is evidence that such options were indeed proposed. Consider the testimony of Gen. Makhmut Gareyev, former Deputy Chief of the General Staff, describing the military reforms advocated by him and then-General Staff Chief Marshal Nikolai Ogarkov (Akhromeyev's predecessor):

> The arms race was, in some sense, justifiable.... the problem was to participate in the arms race, but to do so in a sensible manner.... Many areas offered substantial savings. Just recall the huge amounts of money we wasted on Egypt, Ethiopia, Angola, Salvador.... I also proposed to steer clear of such ventures as Afghanistan. That war was very costly. We also advocated a more rational arms procurement policy focusing on specific weapons systems rather than all the weapons produced by the United States.... If the arms race had been conducted in a more sensible manner, we could have sustained it and still maintained strategic parity, we could have matched the Western powers and ensured global stability. We also had every opportunity to preserve the Soviet Union.... But our leadership was feeble; it was not prepared to make tough, willful decisions, to act decisively like Stalin. (Ellman and Kontorovich 1998: 61–3)

That such proposals existed comes as no surprise.[49] Nor should it be doubted that – in tandem with less disruptive reforms than the

---

[49]Brooks and Wohlforth brush aside this particular proposal as a "Brezhnev-era" initiative, as if a decade or more outdated by the mid-1980s (this volume, chapter 9). In fact it is better characterized as an Andropov-era proposal (i.e., on the eve of Gorbachev's accession) whose central idea of more efficient military spending to preserve strategic parity was, if anything, even *more* relevant two years later. Brooks and Wohlforth also suggest that the lack of other such documented proposals demonstrates that such ideas were not prevalent. Again, they misunderstand the Soviet context; aside from the fact that KGB, Central Committee, and Defense Ministry furnaces worked overtime for a few days in August 1991, the list of major Soviet-era initiatives that were not first detailed in written form would fill an entire volume.

budget-busting antialcohol campaign or Gorbachev's ill-conceived tampering with the planning mechanism – they were certainly viable.[50] Moreover, Gareyev's testimony seems to confirm Wohlforth's own 1994–5 argument that "a harder-line alternative to Gorbachev waited in the wings" (Wohlforth 1994–5: 125). Indeed, it is difficult to imagine a better summary of how material forces influenced the Cold War's end than Wohlforth's statement that "decline was a necessary condition of change, but clearly insufficient to determine the precise nature of change" (Wohlforth 1995: 186–7). But now that harder-line alternative has apparently vanished, and decline seems to have become a sufficient condition as well. Are these conclusions justified?

I think not, and have highlighted four problems in Brooks and Wohlforth's argument. First, in making a case for the old thinkers' agreement with (or acquiescence in) radical retrenchment, the authors ignore much evidence of disagreement (and opposition). Second is their inattention to the domestic political context – including the institutional and cultural legacies of the Soviet military, Gorbachev's maneuvering around his conservative opponents, and the image consciousness of these conservatives' subsequent self-portrayals – that renders problematic the taking at face value of much documentary as well as oral testimony. Third, the authors gloss over key differences between 1985–6 and 1988–9, such that the importance of Gorbachev's critical early initiatives (when material pressures were relatively modest yet intellectual ferment was great) is downplayed, with emphasis instead placed on post-1988 changes (when the main new-thinking breakthroughs had already been achieved and economic woes were indeed rapidly worsening).

This is linked to a fourth problem in Brooks and Wohlforth's analysis – namely, their disinterest in the nonmaterial sources of new-thinking beliefs and behavior. The policy analysts who began advocating major "Westernizing" changes in the 1970s, Gorbachev's exposure to much unorthodox thinking even before 1985, and especially the intense discussion of core philosophical issues of world politics among Gorbachev's inner circle during his first years in power – all this is absent. And it is in the justification for this inattention that the authors'

---

[50] Although their overall economic analysis is thorough, Brooks and Wohlforth do not explore the extent to which the post-1988 downturn grew out of earlier trends versus the extent to which it resulted from Gorbachev's own policies. Serious consideration of the viability of alternative paths requires study of what moderately reduced defense outlays combined with better-designed domestic reforms could have done. Mindful of the interpretive bias caused by the system's subsequent collapse, James Millar recently concluded a review of newly declassified Soviet economic data with the observation that "the Soviet economy was a lot sturdier than it appears in hindsight" (Millar, public remarks at Princeton University Conference on the CIA and the USSR, Princeton, New Jersey, March 10, 2001).

central analytical flaw is seen. That flaw is a framework that too explicitly privileges the material over the ideational – the justification being
that "we can only truly know where the world of ideas begins if we know
what international behavior can be explained by changing material incentives" (this volume, p. 236). Constructivists naturally object to such
an *a priori* relegation of ideas to picking up only where "the world of
power" leaves off. Others might agree that material constraints set the
general structure within which various forces interacted to produce the
Cold War's end. But it is an unjustified leap from this to an analytical
mode that examines those forces' interaction by designating power
the default explanation, with ideas, leadership, or any other factors
meriting consideration only when there is a sufficient "lag" or "poor fit"
between shifts in power and state behavior (this volume, pp. 235, 236).

Given realism's well-documented difficulty in specifying expected
behavior, as well as in measuring power, it is unlikely that the fit will
ever be judged poor enough that ideational analyses need apply. Yet
Brooks and Wohlforth assert that "our study indicates that it is now critical for scholars who focus on the causal role of ideas to pay much more
attention to the issue of endogeneity" (i.e., that ideas might *not* play
a causal role, this volume, p. 197). Surely scholars should be mindful
of alternative explanations in all cases; but in this one, the study that
so indicates is not a close analysis that weighs competing claims and
evidence, but rather one that systematically *excludes* evidence of ideas'
causal influence. Pitted against an understanding of ideational incentives as "spare and impoverished" as that which Brooks and Wohlforth
charge constructivists of having about material incentives, it would
indeed be surprising if it had concluded anything else.[51]

In closing, Brooks and Wohlforth suggest another reason for so
heavily privileging the material over the ideational: that the quantifi-
ability of power justifies its priority over more qualitative types of

---

[51]Brooks and Wohlforth justify their lack of attention to the impact of ideas because
others' focus here "had already provided the baseline for our own analysis" (this volume,
p. 269). In fact their analysis mostly ignores that baseline. In addition to the many cited
examples, perhaps most telling is their blanket dismissal of the extensive evidence on
Gorbachev's early new thinking: "We are far less confident than English in analysts'
ability to discern Gorbachev's precise expectations and desires at every juncture on
the basis of only memoirs and recollections" (this volume, p. 271). This is a frankly
amazing statement, given that the variety of evidence cited on Gorbachev's motivations
is far richer, more detailed, and consistent across multiple, credible sources than that
which they cite in support of their opposing case. It is also confirmed in important
documentary sources; can one seriously argue otherwise by citing out of context a
late-1986 Politburo transcript while simply ignoring Gorbachev's comprehensive early-
1986 "secret speech" to the Foreign Ministry? In this fashion, evidence that fits Brooks
and Wohlforth's thesis is uncritically cited, while a body of sources that dispute it are
summarily dismissed.

evidence. Material explanations should come first, they write, because "ideas are not directly observable" (this volume, p. 236). But for all its extensive economic documentation, their argument ultimately hinges on something equally unobservable – namely, *perceptions.* And no quantity of evidence on what actors *should have* been thinking can substitute for quality of evidence on what they *actually did* think. "In the end," Brooks and Wohlforth write, "growing economic costs ... created strong incentives for engaging in retrenchment irrespective of Gorbachev's underlying motivations" (this volume, p. 226). But no one seriously disputes the economic "incentives for engaging in re-trenchment." The issue is whether they were uppermost – for the old thinkers, as well as Gorbachev and the new thinkers – in the "underlying motivations" for their actions. If instead the former were primarily moved by bureaucratic-careerist concerns, and the latter as much by normative ones, then evidence of economic incentives tells at best only half the story. Absent better analysis of how material and ideational incentives actually operated, and especially of how various alternatives actually appeared at the time, Brooks and Wohlforth can only show correlation but cannot reach credible judgments on the conditions that were sufficient for the Cold War's remarkable end.

I highlight these problems not to dismiss the importance of the sources that Brooks and Wohlforth bring to bear or to deny the centrality of material constraints to the way the Cold War ended. Economic decline was clearly a necessary factor in the inception of Soviet reforms, and the authors have given us new insights into how such pressures also played an important facilitating role. But they are still far from establishing material forces as a sufficient condition. Yet there is a note of finality in Brooks and Wohlforth's claim that "if our research withstands the test of further releases of new evidence," then constructivists should acknowledge the primacy of material forces in shaping Gorbachev's foreign policy and "shift instead toward examining different questions for which ideational models may prove to have much greater utility" (this volume, p. 234). Such a claim is certainly premature, and before we look ahead to new releases of evidence, the materialist model might better be subjected to a stronger test of the sources we already have.

Perestroika's missing politics

Throughout the preceding I have highlighted three main flaws in Brooks and Wohlforth's materialist analysis. The first is their ignoring of extensive new-thinking preparations that long preceded the onset of economic crisis; struggling as it did against an array of personal and institutional incentives, this pioneering new thinking points up the vital ideational, principled origins of policy innovation. Also ignored is the early engagement of Gorbachev and his reformist inner circle with these "heretical" ideas; discussions had already begun by the late 1970s, intensified in the early-mid 1980s, and spurred key policy initiatives by 1986–7, i.e., *before* the post-1988 economic downturn that Brooks and Wohlforth see as the critical catalyst of change. And a third flaw is the failure to consider that this downturn – undeniably an accelerator of change – was itself a direct result of Gorbachev's own radical domestic policies.

Not only does each serve to highlight the non-material factors (e.g., ideas, leadership, domestic debates) in political change that Brooks and Wohlforth neglect, they also subtly remind us of the very real alternatives to radical new thinking that actually existed. And in this fashion these three main criticisms join a host of smaller ones in my effort to sketch out the policy process under Gorbachev, to characterize the politics of perestroika, in a way that more accurately reflects the possibilities as they appeared to key actors – reformers and hardliners – at the time. And this in turn leads to a more fundamental, underlying issue – that rather than one clear decision point we instead view the adoption of new thinking in Soviet foreign policy as an extended and highly contingent process, a complex chain rather than a single event.

The advantages of parsimony are clear, but we must also be mindful of its perils. A stylized model or abstraction of the political process serves many useful purposes, not the least being its portability for comparative analysis of similar events. But that abstraction must not excessively squeeze events into an ill-fitting framework or oversimplify to the extent that something essential is lost. Rarely does an interpretive debate turn so sharply on the initial assumptions made – and the respective analytical frameworks employed – as this one. And absent much stronger empirical support than they have mustered to date, Brooks and Wohlforth's materialist analysis still falls well short. The endogeneity of ideas cannot be established via a framework that essentially endogenizes them from the outset.

Chapter 9

New versus old thinking in qualitative research

Stephen G. Brooks and William C. Wohlforth

Robert English has provided a strongly written critique of our "Power, Globalization, and the End of the Cold War" (this volume, chapter 7). Unfortunately, English's reply may have the unintended consequence of reinforcing a pernicious but popular view among political scientists that qualitative research – especially on single cases – cannot generate progress. Here we have a case of seminal importance that has attracted the sustained attention of dozens of international relations scholars for over a decade, and yet it appears that scholars are still involved in what looks like an interminable historians' debate over causes. In this chapter, we show that such a reaction would be utterly unjustified.

We have two basic responses. First, much of English's critique misses the mark because it is based on a misunderstanding of our research design. Second, English's reply is nonetheless a test of our major findings conducted by a skeptical and talented researcher. Our analysis passes this tough test, though English does advance some useful criticisms.

We proceed in four sections. First, we show that major progress has been made in explaining the end of the Cold War and establishing its theoretical implications. The debate now turns mainly on how to assess the causal implications of widely accepted findings, which is why issues of qualitative research design are so important. In the second section, we demonstrate the importance of moving beyond the framework of necessary and sufficient conditions toward a more probabilistic approach. Because it is constrained by the old framework, English's reply cannot directly engage much of our analysis. Third, we explain how we designed our research on this case to assess endogeneity. A failure to appreciate why and how we tackled this key issue is the source of English's serious – and wrong – charge that our research was "biased." Finally, in this case, as in so many others, arguments over possible alternatives to the course actually chosen are crucial and so rigor is at a premium. The fourth section addresses English's most central empirical challenge concerning hard-line alternatives to Soviet retrenchment.

The issues at stake here concern not just the end of the Cold War or even the study of ideas in international relations, but qualitative research more generally. None of the methodological challenges we highlight has a generally accepted answer in social science (King, Keohane, and Verba 1994; Van Evera 1997; George and Bennett 2005). In our first chapter in this anthology, we sought to apply new thinking to these challenges. English's chapter shows that we were not entirely successful in articulating our method for accomplishing this. This chapter gives us a chance to do so.

Making progress on explaining the end of the Cold War

Ten years ago, the conventional wisdom was that Soviet material decline – often measured solely in terms of military capabilities – was small or nonexistent; that this factor consequently had little causal weight in the end of Cold War; and thus that other variables, particularly ideational ones, carried the day (Kegley 1993). A second wave of empirical scholarship that emerged in the mid-1990s shifted the conventional wisdom. Most now agreed that the Soviet material decline –measured more accurately in terms of overall capabilities – had actually been quite significant beginning in the early-to-mid 1980s and that it did play a significant causal role (Blacker 1993; Wohlforth 1994/95). Still, the standard conclusion was that while decline did prompt change in Soviet foreign policy, the resulting shift could have just as easily been toward aggression or a new version of muddling through rather than retrenchment and that other factors played the key role in resolving this uncertainty (Herman 1996).

Though the tone of his chapter might lead readers to overlook it, English actually concurs with two of our most important findings – each of which differed sharply from the previous conventional wisdom. First, we found that the economic burden on the Soviet Union was far greater than the second wave of scholarship had realized. In particular: (1) Soviet decline was more marked, occurred earlier, and generally placed a much greater strain on maintaining the foreign policy status quo than scholars had previously assumed; (2) the costs of Soviet isolation from the globalization of production were growing rapidly; and (3) the Soviet Union "arguably confronted modern history's worst case of imperial overstretch." English does not challenge this analysis, which comprised 40 percent of our chapter, and flatly accepts that the Soviet Union represented "modern history's most overextended empire" (this volume, p. 255).[1]

The second finding concerns endogeneity, in particular, the role of economic constraints in propelling the translation of new thinkers' ideas into policy. We found that the Soviet Union's declining material fortunes was the key factor that made the new thinkers' ideas saleable to those skeptical of retrenchment. English agrees, noting that Gorbachev found that "stressing economic necessity" was the "best" way to "sell his proposals" to his "main opposition...such dyed-in-the-wool old thinkers as Ligachev" and others in the Politburo (this volume, p. 248).

It is thus clear that empirical research is generating real progress on this case. These two new findings alone move the ball substantially down the field. English's response is wholly focused on how to assess empirically the causal effect of the material constraints we examined. The rest of this chapter is consequently devoted to this issue.

Probabilistic rather than deterministic causation

English's reply exemplifies a pervasive problem in qualitative research: the lack of a good general language for expressing levels of causality within a case. The popular language of necessity and sufficiency simply cannot capture the debate among scholars who all agree that such major causal factors as "ideas" and "material incentives" will always be necessary but insufficient to explain any important outcome. Lacking any better terminology for expressing their claims, however, qualitative researchers are often led to straw-man others' arguments as deterministic in order to highlight the significance of their own otherwise unremarkable finding that a different causal factor is necessary to explain a given

---

[1] English does, however, question the significance of the Soviet Union's rapid decline, arguing that "most of the leadership" had not cared much about the country's relative position since "the late 1960s" and was instead "mired in corruption, often oblivious to foreign and even domestic trends, and largely content to muddle through indefinitely" (this volume, p. 240). Doubtless some Soviet officials did not care much about the country's international position. But our analysis centered on Soviet foreign policy change, and our attention was consequently focused on the country's foreign policy elite, which all analysts agree was keenly focused on the country's international standing. Moreover, as we show on p. 208–p. 213 of our first chapter, there are four overlapping reasons why "the Soviet Union's international position made its grand strategy more sensitive to relative decline than were the strategies of other modern great powers" (this volume, chapter 7, p. 213).

event. The result is a literature bedeviled by the imputation to others of obviously untenable claims that some factor wholly determines an outcome which are then countered by obvious, and therefore banal, counterclaims that some other factor is really necessary for a complete explanation. The costs imposed by this practice become evident when we review English's specific claims regarding our research.

Debunking a straw man

Let us begin with our more detailed analysis. English marshals evidence in support of the following propositions:

(1) There was no "consensus for strategic retreat" among old thinkers, and they were not all simply "free riding on initiatives with which they actually agreed." We never claimed otherwise. Rather, we found that "a solid consensus emerged in the *political* leadership on the need for downsizing the military and scaling back the costs of empire.... Even many elements in the military leadership and the defense-industrial sector agreed on the general need to reduce the imperial burden" (this volume, p. 218).[2]

(2) The new thinkers "held beliefs motivated by ideals," and their ideas did not spring directly from rising economic constraints. Again, we never suggested otherwise. Instead, we found that "many policy-makers and intellectuals who became idea entrepreneurs did so in part as they learned of the material failings of the Soviet system. And their ideas became saleable to those more skeptical about reform in significant part because they accorded with undeniable material trends" (this volume, p. 228).

(3) Soviet old thinkers did try to "delay arms control progress" and obstruct "efforts to put Soviet–Western relations on a new footing." We agree. We simply found that "The extraordinary feature of the new evidence concerning Soviet conservatives and hardliners is not that many of them opposed specific concessions to the West (especially regarding arms control, such as the inclusion of the "Oka" missile in the INF talks, counting rules for strategic missiles on bombers, etc.), but how very many of them accepted the basic picture of the crisis facing the country outlined by Gorbachev.... Each special interest tried to defend itself while admitting, or acquiescing to, the general need for change. Adding up these particular objections did not by itself amount

---

[2]We have added emphasis here to the word "political" because of its great importance in accurately describing our empirical findings, because English obviously misses the significance of this key qualifier, and because he leaves it out when quoting from our first chapter.

to a plausible general alternative to retrenchment" (this volume, pp. 230, 233).

(4) Gorbachev's "skill as a political tactician" was helpful in overcoming obstructionism from skeptical officials. We never denied Gorbachev's political skills, but simply found that highlighting economic constraints was his most effective strategy for convincing those skeptical of foreign policy retrenchment and, in turn, that "the escalating economic costs of maintaining the foreign policy status quo.... systematically undercut the ability of Gorbachev's critics to come up with a compelling general foreign policy alternative" (this volume, p. 234).

In each of these instances, English translates our probabilistic finding into an obviously untenable deterministic one. And the same problem applies to our broader analysis. We found that the economic costs of maintaining Moscow's Cold War foreign policy were rapidly escalating, generating strong and growing incentives to retrench. Throughout his chapter, English is at pains to show that Gorbachev and company did not always act out of narrow rational calculation but rather deep normative conviction; that they sometimes did not see their policies as a strategic retreat but as a leap forward into a better world. All of this is true, but none of it bears on our findings. Incentives affect behavior by altering the relative costs of various courses of action. Our findings do not presuppose that people respond to incentives with automaton-like efficiency. On the contrary, people have dreams and hopes, they engage in wishful thinking, they seek to defy or deny incentives, they blunder. Could anyone with any knowledge of human affairs think otherwise? Over the longer run, however, changing incentives will tend to push people in certain overall directions.

In the aggregate, we found the driving force for embarking on new approaches was less the appeal of a clear forward-looking strategic vision than the need to move away from costly practices of the past. As Odom puts it, "The most remarkable thing about the beginnings of Gorbachev's new military policy [was] the lack of a well-developed analytic basis for it.... Its motive, in contrast, was clear. A surprisingly broad consensus existed among most of the Soviet elite that the Soviet economy was in serious trouble and that the burden of military expenditures was much to blame" (1998: 115). The same goes for the Soviets' sporadic efforts to put relations with Eastern Europe on a new footing. The documentary evidence that has come to light strongly endorses Alex Pravda's initial assessment: "It would be unrealistic to argue that the Gorbachev leadership had any well-defined idea of the relationship they wished to achieve. They were clearer about past features they wanted to avoid and the general direction in which the relationship should evolve" (Pravda 1992: 7; see also Brooks and Wohlforth 2002). What the Soviets wanted was to reduce the escalating economic burden of subsidies and other costs associated with their position in Eastern Europe, but their efforts to do so never added up to a plan for "strategic retreat." Had the citizens in Eastern Europe not organized to over-throw the existing regimes, the Soviet leadership – Gorbachev included – would have been quite happy to hold on to it. In the end, what changed was the Soviet willingness to pay high costs to maintain the status quo.

Beyond necessity and sufficiency

In the end, much of English's empirical analysis is effective only at debunking a non-existent straw man – namely the argument that eco-nomic constraints made retrenchment "unavoidable" and that ideas did "not play a causal role." Neither in our larger conclusions nor in our evaluation of more discrete patterns of evidence did we advance a deterministic claim. On the contrary, we carefully evaluated a series of probabilistic hypotheses and reached a series of probabilistic findings. Why then does English misinterpret our analysis as being determinist? We doubt that he deliberately "shifted the goal posts" in his favor to make it easier to critique our argument. Instead, his misinterpreta-tion likely derives from the problem with which we began this section: the terminology of necessary and sufficient conditions. The following quotation is telling: "I highlight these problems not to dismiss the importance of the sources that Brooks and Wohlforth bring to bear or to deny the centrality of material constraints to the way the Cold War ended. Economic decline was clearly a necessary factor in the inception of Soviet reforms, and the authors have given us new insights into how such pressures also played an important facilitating role. But they are still far from establishing material forces as a sufficient condition" (this volume, p. 259).

It is easy to understand why English resorts to the terminology of necessary and sufficient conditions. It is a lexicon we all understand. Unfortunately, it is simply incapable of expressing the issues at stake in this case and, indeed, in the larger dialogue concerning the relationship between ideas and material incentives. As we were at pains to stress: "Material incentives are never determinate" and, hence, "the question is clearly no longer whether but rather how and how much ideas matter under different conditions – and how best to model their influence on strategic behavior" (this volume, pp. 200, 196).

All qualitative researchers face the challenge of expressing levels of causality. We found that the economic constraints on the Soviet Union were far stronger than scholars had realized in the mid-1990s, when the consensus assessment was that material incentives were necessary but insufficient to explain Soviet retrenchment. How should we report this finding? Clearly, material shifts were still necessary and still insufficient, yet more important than understood previously. We struggled with this issue and concluded the best response was to frame our analysis in probabilistic terms. Thus, we concluded that "given the extent of relative decline, the odds were heavily stacked against those who stood for the status quo" (this volume, p. 218) and that "material incentives systematically undermined alternatives to retrenchment" (this volume, p. 234). By this we meant that rather than being simply one of many equally probable responses to Soviet material decline, retrenchment was the most likely one. Where we erred, and can accept some of the blame for English misinterpreting our analysis, is that while we carefully expressed our more detailed findings in probabilistic terms, we failed to stress that our overall finding was also probabilistic.

English faced the same challenge of conveying his estimate of causal weight. Stuck in the conceptual framework of necessity and sufficiency, he paid a price: he is not prompted to address the issue of probability, either with respect to his own analysis or ours. In the end, English's powerful prose conceals a weak argument: that material incentives are not sufficient to explain the Cold War's end, and thus "new thinking" ideas are necessary to explain it – a finding we never questioned. He states that other Soviet responses to decline were possible. Of course they were, though we concluded they were not likely. How probable does English think these alternatives were? He does not say.

While our focus in this chapter is to respond to English's, it is important to recognize that he is not the only contributor to this literature to run afoul of the straw man bias; numerous other analysts of the role of ideas in the end of Cold War case have fallen prey to this same methodological limitation. In a particularly prominent example, Margarita Petrova asserts that "Brooks and Wohlforth set out to demonstrate that in the Soviet case the material setting was in fact determinate" (Petrova 2003: 123). Like English, Petrova is content to argue against a deterministic straw man and ultimately conclude that ideas played a role. While there may be rare historical cases in which it is analytically useful to demonstrate that a single factor is alone insufficient to explain the outcome, the end of the Cold War is clearly not among them. Scholarship on this event has long since moved far beyond the point where showing the insufficiency of material incentives and the necessity of some other factor constitutes a contribution. All scholars now agree that material incentives were very important but do not explain every aspect of this case.

Nevertheless, even after the publication of our exchange with English, scholars who focus on ideas continue to tout as a noteworthy "finding" the fact that material incentives did not determine the precise outcome, and so that other outcomes were possible (Thomas 2005; English 2005). Such claims cannot advance the learned debate; indeed, they retard it. Progress will require a different approach. We have suggested that scholars should make greater efforts to express their causal findings and arguments probabilistically. After all, there is a widespread understanding in social science that most feasible causal inferences about complex events must be probabilistic in nature (George and Bennett 2005). Moreover, there is nothing about a probabilistic approach that "privileges" one causal factor over another. Hence we can only attribute the continued reluctance to move in this direction to the terminology of necessary and sufficient conditions itself, which effectively discourages scholars from considering causality in a probabilistic manner.

Research design

Like English, we are totally committed to nailing down the empirical details in this case. Yet if we don't get the research design right, evidence alone cannot generate progress.

Facing up to endogeneity

English concludes that our study "is not a close analysis that weighs competing claims and evidence, but rather one that systematically *excludes* evidence of ideas' causal influence" (this volume, p. 258). This is wrong. It reflects a profound misunderstanding of our motivation for highlighting the issue of endogeneity and our research design for addressing it.

Endogeneity is clearly one of the most important challenges facing scholars who study the role of ideas, not just in this case but in social science more generally. We focused on this issue not because we believe "that ideas are just hooks, nor that all phenomena can be reduced to material underpinnings" (this volume, p. 235), but rather because "this key endogeneity issue has been ignored or marginalized in recent empirical work on ideas in international relations" (this volume, p. 235). The end of the Cold War is simply a particularly prominent example of this general tendency to give short shrift to endogeneity.

To establish the causal role of ideas, scholars must demonstrate that the intellectual shifts they point to do not have the effects they do because of a changing material environment. Prior to the work discussed in our first chapter in this anthology, we lacked a comprehensive account of how economic constraints influenced Soviet policy makers. As a result, scholars who focused on the role of ideas were simply not in a position to grapple with endogeneity. Our purpose in providing a fuller account of material pressures facing Soviet policy makers was to make this possible.[3] Some scholars who focus on the role of ideas have recognized this purpose of our chapter.[4] English instead misinterprets our effort as being driven by a "framework that too explicitly privileges the material over the ideational" (this volume, p. 258).

We see no reason to privilege any causal factor in the abstract. As we stressed, "Ideas and material incentives clearly work together in complex ways, and their interaction varies across cases" (this volume, p. 200). The precise nature of this interaction is ultimately an empirical question. Scholars who focus on the role of ideas, English included, are often extremely concerned about where scholars should first direct their attention. But this concern is irrelevant to the literature on the end of Cold War, which has been overwhelmingly preoccupied with establishing the role of ideas. English is right; we do not spend much time directly discussing how ideational shifts might have influenced this case. But that is only because scholars' intensive focus on this question had already provided the baseline for our analysis.

Multiplying observable implications

A second criticism English directs at our empirical analysis is that it is limited to establishing correlation. This is also wrong. On the contrary, our focus on endogeneity demanded that we gauge the extent to which ideas influenced events independently of material shifts. To accomplish this, we examined as many specific observable implications as we could. It is important to stress that each observable implication was a separate

---

[3] As we noted, "the objective of a more sophisticated approach to the study of ideas is currently hampered less by the quantity of plausible models than by deficiencies in our understanding of the material incentives facing decision-makers ... ideational models are crucially dependent on a careful specification of the material incentives facing Soviet decision-makers" (this volume, p. 196).

[4] Nina Tannenwald, for example, notes in a recent paper that "for Brooks and Wohlforth, the proper starting point for assessing the role of ideas is to seek to nail down more tightly how constraining material conditions were.... [they] have very productively challenged ideationalists to tighten their arguments" (Tannenwald 2001).

test of central conclusions from the ideas literature in this case. These observable implications fall into three major categories.

Assessments of material conditions.   The conclusion emerging from the ideas literature on this case is that the underlying ideas held by new thinkers caused them to perceive the world very differently from old thinkers. This was a supposition, however, because relatively little data on old thinkers was available until recently. In our analysis, we found that: (1) the ways new thinkers and old thinkers perceived trends in the Soviet economy and the global economy during the 1980s were similar and matched up well with objective indicators; (2) pre-Gorbachev, old-thinking leaders perceived relative decline and the technological lag a few years after these trends accelerated in the late 1970s; and (3) that during the 1980s many in the Soviet military concluded that the Soviet Union could not continue to bear the costs of its international position.

Of these observable implications, English appears to question only the last. The evidence he marshals, however, once again only under-mines a deterministic claim we did not make: that *all* Soviet military officers concluded that the country could not long bear the costs of its foreign policy. What we actually reported was the striking fact that very many of them recollect having reached this assessment. Worthy of note is that the most exhaustively researched analysis of the Soviet military in the Gorbachev era reaches an even stronger conclusion: "In interviews and in their memoirs senior former Soviet military officers uniformly cited the burden of military spending as more than the Soviet economy could bear" (Odom 1998: 225, see also p. 91).

Relationship between economic constraints and the scope of policy change.   The ideas literature on this case suggests that the mounting economic problems facing the Soviet Union had relatively little to do with the rapid escalation in both the scope and depth of foreign policy change. In our analysis we found that: (1) many new thinkers and old thinkers cited growing economic constraints when initiating foreign policy changes; (2) increased economic pressures made old thinkers increasingly unable to oppose a major shift in Soviet foreign policy; (3) even for many of the most progressive new thinkers, the process of renouncing old foreign policy stereotypes was difficult and, in turn, the complete abandonment of these stereotypes only occurred in 1988–9; (4) concrete evidence that Soviet performance relative to the West was a contributing factor to many new thinkers' growing dissatisfaction with Soviet foreign policy; and (5) Gorbachev and large numbers of officials decided to opt for more radical foreign policy retrenchment only after the default-option reforms ("acceleration") had failed to revitalize the Soviet economy.

English's analysis challenges the last two of these observable implications. Regarding new thinkers' intellectual evolution, English again assaults a deterministic claim we never made: namely, that "western military-economic power" mechanistically drove the intellectual journey of *all* new thinkers. What we wrote is that new thinkers' recollections testify to the influence of "either living standards or the military-technological superiority of the West" (this volume, p. 228) on their intellectual evolution. In his book, English himself shows how new thinkers "emphasized the gathering 'scientific-technological revolution,' stressed Soviet weakness, and argued for drawing on Western experience to keep pace" (English 2000: 143). So too do the new thinkers whose recollections he cites to support his assertion that "western military-economic power figure[s] little, if at all" (this volume, p. 246) in many new thinkers' intellectual growth.[5] English's critique does nevertheless raise an important point: we should have been clearer that we were much more concerned with how the new thinkers' ideas became saleable to skeptics than on their particular origins.

Regarding the fifth observable implication noted above – the role of decline in the shift to more radical retrenchment – English does not deny that the most dramatic foreign policy moves were made after 1987. Moreover, he agrees that the "economic downturn in 1988 strengthened arguments for at least some kinds of reductions" (this volume, p. 253). But he stresses that the shift to radical retrenchment had been Gorbachev's intention all along. We are far less confident than English in analysts' ability to discern Gorbachev's precise expectations and desires at every juncture on the basis only of memoirs and recollections. For this reason, we focused on recently released internal documents in assessing Gorbachev's early policies and the transition to more significant foreign policy change. Moreover, we focused on how other decision-makers perceived Gorbachev's initial course through 1987 and find striking that many new thinkers *and* old thinkers criticize Gorbachev for initially moving too slowly and hesitantly in reining in imperial expenditures.

Ideas and responses to material decline.   A key theme underlying the ideas literature on this case is that because they held different ideas, the

---

[5] Examples of English's sources include Georgy Arbatov (1991) who details his efforts to direct the leadership's attention to the "scientific technological revolution" in the West, and Aleksandr Yakovlev (1991) who discusses his institute's analyses of Soviet economic decline.

new thinkers had dramatically different strategic reactions to observable indications of material change than did old thinkers. In our analysis we found that: (1) beginning in the early 1980s, Leonid Brezhnev, Yuri Andropov, and Konstantin Chernenko each successively labored to constrain Soviet defense spending; (2) decline was already strongly pushing the pre-Gorbachev leadership towards greater restraint in Eastern Europe; (3) not just new thinkers, but also many conservative officials strongly supported greater integration with Western firms to try to reduce the growing technological gap; (4) the economic reform alternatives to Gorbachev's post-acceleration plan – including the one favored by conservatives – were all weighted even more heavily to reducing defense spending; and (5) no evidence of a general alternative to retrenchment has come to light.

English only questions the last of these findings. This is, indeed, the most important observable implication, and much of English's critique is consequently devoted to challenging it. In the next section, we show that this challenge fails.

Concerning our research design, two points emerge. First, we did everything possible to conduct tests that went beyond merely establishing correlation to access the causal mechanisms in play. Second, we explicitly designed these tests to evaluate the conclusions that emerged from the ideas literature on this case. Our basic finding was that "many of the basic causal mechanisms that are featured in ideational models of this case are to a significant degree endogenous to material changes" (this volume, p. 235). While future research may uncover evidence that calls this conclusion into question, English presents none in his chapter.

Ideas, switchmen, and alternatives

Scholars do not have, and may never devise, ideal procedures for examining the argument that ideas can switch policy onto certain tracks rather than others. Yet for the study of ideas in international relations to progress, the "switchmen" issue must be addressed with rigor (Weber 1958). A standard way to do so is to look at how people with different ideas responded to material change. That is why we examined new evidence on Soviet hardliners or "old thinkers" so carefully, and why English spends so much of his chapter trying to undermine it.

Looking for alternatives

English agrees that "for all their opposition and delay, most [old thinkers] ultimately acquiesced in Gorbachev's policies" (this volume,

p. 244). In our chapter, we found that hardliners acquiesced because they could not come up with a coherent general alternative strategy to retrenchment and that this outcome, in turn, was intimately related to mounting material constraints. In short, we found the old thinkers acquiescence to be largely the product of their lack of a good alternative. English, in contrast, sees the old thinkers' acquiescence as being driven by other factors. The key question then becomes: was there an alternative?

Scholars have looked long and hard for evidence of alternatives to retrenchment. At the time we wrote our first chapter of this anthology, none had come to light. If any researcher has the motive and the background to uncover significant evidence of this kind, it is Robert English. Yet he did not do so. All English is able to offer to support his contention that some hardliners did, in fact, have an alternative to retrenchment is an excerpt from an interview with Gen. Makhmut Gareev (Deputy Chief of the General Staff under Marshal Nikolai Ogarkov) which spells out three elements of the "alternative" to retrenchment he and his boss favored: (1) cut and run from Third World dependencies; (2) avoid the "costly" war in Afghanistan; and (3) cut back on unnecessary military programs by stopping the practice of trying to match the American arsenal weapon for weapon. Unmentioned by English are the further reductions Gareev discusses in the same interview. Gareev reports that he and Ogarkov also concluded it was necessary to reduce the size of the armed forces; scale back the Soviet military presence in Eastern Europe; cut spending on civil defense and strategic defense; halt production of aircraft carriers; and reduce the number of branches of the armed forces from five to three, including abolishing the *PVO Strany* [Air Defense Forces] as an independent branch (Gareev 1996: 163–7; Ellman and Kontorovich 1998: 62).

Two points need to made about the "alternative" spelled out by Gareev. First, this was in *Brezhnev's* time. Had such a policy been adopted then, it would have been seen as a major retrenchment. After all it was, substantively, much more than Gorbachev accomplished in the 1985–8 period that English views as such a dramatic era of change. In short, the Gareev "alternative" English cites is actually a hardliner version of retrenchment in hindsight. Second, also unmentioned by English is that in the same interview, Gareev goes on to argue that the growing technological gap necessitated a drastic Soviet response: a crash course of investing resources and scientists in the development of military technology on the same scale as the Herculean effort to match U.S. thermonuclear and missile capabilities in the 1950s (Ellman and Kontorovich 1998: 63).[6] Any Soviet leader presented with such a proposal would likely have mentioned to Gareev that 80 percent of Soviet expenditures on science already went to military purposes (Gorbachev 1996: 215); that increasing the proportion yet further was unlikely to bring about a reversal of the growing military technological gap with the United States; and that it would impose major opportunity costs on the general health of the Soviet economy. Extremely telling on this score is that in this same interview, Gareev himself admits that many of the reforms he and Ogarkov favored "were doomed because our proposals were detached from an overall restructuring of our society, our political system, and our economy at large" (Ellman and Kontorovich 1998: 61).

Evaluating evidence about policy alternatives

English's effort to find evidence of an alternative aside, he also attempts to challenge our finding in several other ways. However, these critiques ignore four key issues that need to be considered when addressing the switchmen issue by examining the nature of opposition and policy alternatives.

First, place the nature of opposition in context. In examining the opposition to Gorbachev's foreign policy changes, we kept in mind the vast and well established literatures in social science that tell us that major policy departures always lead to significant opposition due to the influence of bureaucratic interests, institutional structures, and numerous other factors. The question is not the existence of opposition but its scope and effectiveness given the magnitude of change and the constituencies it threatens. Reorienting fundamentally the foreign policy course that the Soviet Union had followed for a generation was obviously a dramatic change. And given that the country's entire political economy was in critical ways geared toward the production of military power, retrenchment clearly threatened major constituencies. Had experts on Soviet politics and international relations been asked in the early 1990s what evidence of internal opposition to Gorbachev's foreign strategy would come to light, most surely would have expected evidence of a major alternative foreign policy course "waiting in the

---

[6]Gareev stresses that the technological gap was most pronounced in "reconnaissance technologies, navigation equipment, target identification systems, electronic countermeasures, computers – all the equipment which uses electronics" (Ellman and Kontorovich 1998: 61).

wings."[7] Measured against this expectation, what we find most striking about the evidence that came to light subsequently is the weakness of the opposition it reveals. Contention concerned the terms, rather than the advisability, of retrenchment.

English's reply frequently reflects a preoccupation with the specific details of individual decisions. When the analytical lens is concentrated on such finely grained decisions, differences of opinion are almost always evident. This is frequently the stuff of policy-making, and it is not surprising that participants focus on it when revisiting their roles in larger events. But explaining, for example, why the Soviets agreed to the inclusion of the "Oka" missile in the INF talks in 1987 is not the same as explaining why they opted for a grand strategy of retrenchment. We found the general pattern emerging from the dozens of critical decisions that add up the end of the Cold War to be consistent with our analysis. English, by contrast, interprets nearly any disagreement and disgruntlement from old thinkers about particular policy decisions as being evidence of "concerted" opposition. This is a standard of evidence that makes mountains out of what in a larger context are surprisingly small molehills.

Second, consider the free-rider problem carefully. By free-riding we do not mean that old thinkers could let Gorbachev do the tough work of implementing retrenchment policies with which they fully agreed. Rather, it means that most of the old thinkers were not in positions where they were forced to confront the trade-offs implicit in any effort to deal with the Soviet Union's growing problems. They could complain about Gorbachev's course without ultimately having to face the painful choices between guns and butter and between the present and the future. For example, English finds it very significant that Ligachev, in William Odom's estimation, "wanted reform but not at the expense of the Soviet Union's international military status" (Odom 1998: 92). Odom is no doubt correct on this score. English does not mention that Odom goes on to quote Ligachev himself that "we faced the task of curtailing military spending.... the economy could not breath normally with a military budget that comprised 18 percent of the national income" (Odom 1998: 92). In short, Ligachev wanted to slash defense without sacrificing military power. Doubtless Gorbachev would have loved to have accomplished this. Who wouldn't? Those in opposition are free to advance incompatible policy preferences without having to worry about how to resolve them.

---

[7]This was, indeed, the expectation of one of us writing at that time (Wohlforth 1994/95: 125).

Third, bear in mind that leaders will be prone to select lieutenants who agree with their basic assessments. Of course, these lieutenants may end up supporting new policy departures simply out of careerism. This is the basis upon which English objects to the many statements we presented in our first chapter from hardliners that no alterative to retrenchment existed. To make this point, English focuses on Marshal Dmitry Yazov – Gorbachev's Minister of Defense who was also a leading participant in the August 1991 anti-Gorbachev coup – who, as we quoted in our chapter, has stated unequivocally that there was no alternative to retrenchment and that the Soviet Union had to follow such a course (this volume, p. 230). English is skeptical of these statements and relies on a biography of Marshal Yazov penned by a like-minded friend and fellow officer, Lt. Gen. Leonid Ivashov, to try to undercut them (Ivashov 1993).

How can we determine whether these lieutenants' retrospective claims of support for a new policy shift are the product of careerism, as English claims is the case for Yazov? There are three basic steps to take, none of which English follows in his chapter: (1) examine evidence about the lieutenants from before they were appointed; (2) after they are appointed, examine what kinds of analyses and research they undertook before key policy shifts are undertaken and implemented; and (3) examine how they convinced others of the advisability of policy shifts. In each of these three dimensions, the evidence on Yazov from the very Ivashov source that English relies upon points to the significance of growing economic constraints. First, Ivashov makes clear that, as we reported in our first chapter, Yazov and many of his fellow officers were initially enthusiastic about Gorbachev. They recognized that the "The arms race and the military-strategic parity we had attained was exacting a stiff price" and associated Gorbachev with their "yearning for radical changes" (Ivashov 1993: 9–10). Second, Ivashov notes that after he was appointed Minister of Defense, Yazov had the Institute of Military History conduct an analysis of all military reforms in Russian and Soviet history dating back to the early 16th century. Ivashov reports that Yazov was struck by "the interdependence between the size and structure of the armed forces and the state's economic potential" and, of all the military reforms over the centuries, he was most compelled by the major troop cuts carried out after the Crimean War by Tsarist Defense Minister Dmitry Miliutin as part of a strategy for modernizing Russia (Ivashov 1993: 38). Third and finally, Ivashov notes that economic constraints were, precisely as we argued, at the center of the arguments Yazov deployed to persuade his military colleagues of the necessity of painful reductions.[8] In the end, the Yazov case is simply a single instance of the general research finding that we reported: old thinkers acquiesced in or abetted retrenchment because material conditions undermined any effort to do otherwise.

Fourth, when examining how incentives are likely to affect retrospective claims concerning the existence of policy alternatives, apply those incentives to all individuals, not just a select group. English argues that the lack of evidence of alternatives is due to the fact that hardliners face strong incentives to conceal it. We, by contrast, thought that these officials would, if anything, face incentives to show that "I proposed a more sensible course that would have worked, but Gorbachev ignored it." After all, by 1999, when the interviews we cited were conducted, the political climate in Russia had changed dramatically from the immediate years after the 1991 coup, when the putschists faced trial and jail. Nostalgia for the Soviet Union and regret at the loss of great power status were growing. If an old-thinking veteran had taken active measures to put forward an alternative to retrenchment, why not bring forth evidence to this effect? He would at least be able to demonstrate that he had tried – that he had used his position in the government to fight for the right course.

We found evidence of one old-thinking policy veteran who did take this course: Oleg Baklanov. He, as we noted, went to Gorbachev with a memo arguing that defense was not a major burden on the Soviet economy. While certainly not a full-fledged alternative to retrenchment, this represented a move in this direction by trying to undercut what was, as English admits, Gorbachev's strongest argument for proceeding with retrenchment. As we noted, Baklanov's initiative went nowhere – it did not provide a focal point for resistance to retrenchment. Why? We argue that it was because Baklanov's argument that defense was not a major economic burden was simply not credible – discussions at this time were carried out on the assumption that the military burden was punishing and had to be addressed.[9] Large numbers of individuals were

---

[8]English quotes at length from Ivashov's description of the military's disgruntlement over Gorbachev's unilateral conventional force reductions, announced in his famous speech to the UN General Assembly in December 1988. Missing from the passage English quotes is this key sentence from Ivashov's text: "At meetings of the [Defense Ministry's] Collegium and other gatherings he [Yazov] forcefully implemented the policy of reducing the military forces, and set forth the reasons – mainly economic – why we needed to go forward with disarmament" (Ivashov 1993: 27).

[9]As Odom notes, "In the first half of the 1980s a rather wide and informal consensus was taking shape among all sectors of the party that ... dramatic action, particularly

unlikely to stake their political careers on a patently wrong argument, and hence it is no surprise there is little documentary evidence of efforts that measured up even to what Baklanov attempted.

English, by contrast, argues that the dearth of Baklanov-type evidence has nothing to do with mounting economic constraints, but instead is due to the fact that all old thinkers not only face strong incentives to conceal all evidence showing the existence of alternatives but have also been completely effective in doing so. If this is the case, then how does English explain Baklanov? English's answer is that "Baklanov has simply been more forthright than the others about his opposition to new thinking" (this volume, p. 249). But this raises a key question: why does English's reading of current incentives not apply to Baklanov – whose revelations have done nothing to harm his sterling reputation among his comrades as a Soviet patriot? In the end, English is right to raise the issue of incentives, but apparently wants to have it both ways: old thinkers *can,* in fact, be trusted, but only if they provide evidence that matches up with his particular reading of events.

Conclusion

Robert English possesses the talent, knowledge and the incentive to subject our first chapter to extraordinarily thorough scrutiny. In the end, our analysis passes this tough test. English endorses two of our most central findings – concerning the nature and magnitude of Soviet material decline and the fact that it constituted the most powerful argument against opponents of foreign policy retrenchment. He fails to undermine our bottom-line conclusion that changing material incentives made retrenchment the most likely response. Most importantly, he was unable to find any evidence of an alternative to retrenchment. At a deeper level, however, his critique falls short because it does not come to grips with our probabilistic framework, and so is largely devoted to marshaling evidence against deterministic claims we never made.

Needless to say, some of English's criticisms hit home. While our analysis is simple, easily exportable to other cases, and readily falsifiable, English underscores its inevitable limitations. Obviously, no single factor can adequately explain everything that is interesting about this case. In addition, English rightly criticizes us for implying that our analysis applied equally to the origins of new thinking and its actual translation into policy. We needed to be much clearer that, in raising the issue of endogeneity, our focus was on the latter question. His

---

reductions in military spending, was imperative to deal with the impending crises. The officer corps shared this view with party conservatives and reformers alike" (1998: 91).

sharp criticisms also compelled us to clarify the sets of observable implications we examined to evaluate our causal inferences. Finally, his overall response reflects a misunderstanding of our probabilistic framework for evaluating causal weight that has prompted us to articulate our approach more forthrightly here.

The space constraints of this exchange inevitably prevented us from addressing all the issues English raises. In two subsequent publications, English has sharpened his critique of our work, highlighting Gorbachev's role to an even greater degree and stressing the importance of the timing of his turn to radical advisers, his choice of economic policies, and his reforms of Soviet domestic institutions (English 2003, 2005). For our part, in two further chapters we analyze carefully many of the key counterfactuals that English has raised in his response to our analysis (Brooks and Wohlforth 2003, 2004). These additional works help to clarify our debate even further, but they also reveal the depth and complexity of remaining disagreements. New evidence, more study, and especially new thinking about the methodological challenges of expressing judgments of causal weight in complex cases are clearly needed.

At this stage of the debate, three things are clear. First, ideas are clearly part of the explanation for the way the Cold War ended. To be sure, the end of the Cold War did not become the most important case study of the role of ideas in international relations because scholars surmised that ideas merely played a role. The event's landmark status in the study of ideas clearly owes something to the supposition that ideas were unusually or extraordinarily important. Our research does suggest that this initial supposition has not been borne out by the latest evidence, which reveals that retrenchment can no longer be considered to be simply one of many equally probable responses to material decline.

Second, although the Cold War's end is well documented, much archival evidence is not yet available. As English has argued elsewhere, such documents should not be seen as the final answer – particularly in the Soviet context (English 1997: 283–94). But they may well provide the wherewithal to render far more confident judgments. And they may well undermine our central findings.

Finally, whether we like it or not, our field learns about theories from events like the end of the Cold War. One of the main reasons for our rigorous focus on research design and our search for as much precision as possible on expressing causal weight is to ensure that further releases do generate progress. By so doing, we have translated our basic finding into a series of detailed predictions about patterns of evidence that will emerge (Wohlforth 1998: 675–9). If, by contrast, we stick with old thinking on qualitative research then all we will have are ambiguous claims about this or that cause "mattering" or being "necessary." And then every archive in Russia could be wide open for a decade, and nothing resembling progress would result.

Chapter 10

The elaboration model and necessary causes

James Mahoney

Methodologists often discuss the issues that arise in the explanation of outcomes that apply to multiple cases, such as the occurrence of wars, alliances, and trade agreements. They have comparatively less to say about the explanation of particular historical outcomes, such as the causes of World War I and the end of the Cold War. In this chapter, I build on Goertz and Levy's framework for the analysis of necessary condition counterfactuals in examining how scholars establish valid claims about the causes of singular events that occurred in the past.

Central attention is focused on the ways in which qualitative analysts use an "elaboration model" to assess their causal claims (Lazarsfeld, Pasanella, and Rosenberg 1972; Babbie 1998). With this model, the analyst evaluates an initial bivariate hypothesis about a necessary cause through the introduction of one or more test variables. These test variables may contextualize the original relationship or diminish it, thereby either strengthening or weakening one's confidence that the relationship reflects genuine causation. I show how qualitative researchers use this mode of elaboration to frame their arguments, structure their narratives, and assess the importance of competing hypotheses.

In order to illustrate the use of this elaboration model, I formally specify the arguments and logic used in the substantive chapters of this volume. In doing so, I convert the narrative analyses of these chapters into diagrams that explicitly identify causal relationships among key variables. To represent a necessary cause, I employ the following structure: $X - n \rightarrow Y$ which can read as "X is a necessary cause of Y." For a sufficient cause, the structure is similarly: $X - s \rightarrow Y$ which reads "X is a sufficient cause of Y." For a necessary and sufficient cause, the structure is: $X - n/s \longrightarrow Y$ (i.e., "X is a necessary and sufficient cause of Y").

Although the issues and arguments considered here are complex, I want to try to keep things as straightforward as possible, and thus I will not address the topic of probabilistic causes in historical research. Furthermore, I argue that "contributing causes" are best understood within a framework of causal sufficiency and can be diagramed within this framework.

The elaboration model and necessary causes

The elaboration model was originally developed by Paul Lazarsfeld and his associates at Columbia University as part of the move of early quantitative social science toward multivariate analysis and the effort to distinguish correlation from causation (Kendall 1982). The central procedure of this framework is to begin with a bivariate relationship, and then to elaborate this relationship through the introduction of a third test variable. In some cases, the introduction of the third variable strengthens the original relationship, increasing one's confidence that the initial relationship is causal. In other cases, elaboration through a third variable calls into question the initial relationship, leading one to believe it is a spurious correlation.

Although the elaboration model was developed for the analysis of correlational relationships, with some modifications it can be extended to the analysis of hypotheses that posit necessary causes. The basic application remains the same: the analyst begins with a bivariate relationship and further tests the relationship through the introduction of a third variable.

More specifically, the researcher begins with a bivariate relationship in which X is a hypothesized necessary cause of Y, i.e., $X - n \longrightarrow Y$. (X and Y can either be particular events like World War I or more general variables of which particular events are examples). Next, the researcher introduces Z as either an intervening variable, i.e., $X \longrightarrow Z \longrightarrow Y$, or an antecedent variable, i.e., $Z \longrightarrow X \longrightarrow Y$. The analyst then evaluates the original bivariate relationship in light of the new relationships introduced by the third variable. The use of the elaboration model by case study researchers does not preclude the application of other methods of hypothesis assessment. For example, the elaboration model can be employed in conjunction with the modes of counterfactual analysis described by Goertz and Levy in the introduction to this volume. Likewise, the elaboration model may be used informally in conjunction with narrative analysis and process tracing, as is true of most of the chapters in this volume. Hence, the elaboration model is best seen as one tool among many that are used by scholars who seek to explain particular outcomes.

Intervening test variables

One way of using the elaboration model is to introduce an intervening test variable – i.e., a third variable (Z) that stands temporally between the initial two variables (X and Y). If one begins with the finding that $X -n\!\!\rightarrow Y$, this intervening variable can generate different sets of relationships, four of which are examined here. The first is the creation of a chain of necessary causes:

$$X -n\!\!\rightarrow Z -n\!\!\rightarrow Y$$
$$\downarrow \underline{\qquad\qquad n \qquad\qquad} \uparrow$$

In this case, all relationships model necessary causation. For example, imagine that we start with X = female and Y = childbirth, and then we introduce an intervening variable such as Z = pregnancy. This kind of elaboration helps identify the so-called mechanisms through which variable X exerts its effect on variable Y. The scholar pursues "process analysis" (George and Bennett 2005) by transforming a bivariate relationship into a chain of necessary causes.

A second possibility is to generate the following relationship through the introduction of an intervening variable:

$$X -s\!\!\rightarrow Z -n\!\!\rightarrow Y$$
$$\downarrow \underline{\qquad\qquad n \qquad\qquad} \uparrow$$

In this example, X is sufficient for the intervening variable Z, which in turn is necessary for the outcome Y. The discovery of this kind of relationship helps contextualize the initial X/Y relationship. In particular, we discover that X is necessary for Y because it produces a more proximate cause that is itself necessary. For instance, if X = female and Y = pregnancy, then the intervening variable might refer to the more specific genetic features that make pregnancy possible in women but not men (e.g., Z = estrogen). This additional information is useful because it elaborates the effect of X on Y.

Another possibility is to identify an intervening variable that is sufficient for the outcome of interest. This relationship can be represented as follows:

$$X \xrightarrow{\;n\;} Z \xrightarrow{\;s\;} Y$$

Here X is necessary for Z, which in turn is sufficient for Y. For example, imagine now that X = female, Z = fertilized egg, and Y = pregnancy. X is necessary for the outcome Y, but its causal effect runs through Z. In other words, X exerts its effect on Y only by virtue of its effect on Z. These kinds of intervening mechanisms help us better understand the effects of X on Y. At the same time, however, the discovery of variable Z diminishes the importance of the original X/Y relationship by calling primary attention to the new X/Z and Z/Y relationships. For example, when we introduce the intervening variable of fertilized egg, we are more likely to conclude the initial female variable is really a necessary cause of fertilized egg, rather than pregnancy itself.

A final representation is not logically possible:

$$X \xrightarrow{\;s\;} Z \xrightarrow{\;s\;} Y$$

To see why this formulation is not possible, we must recall that we are assuming that X is necessary but not sufficient for Y; that is, our initial bivariate relationship holds that $X \xrightarrow{\;n\;} Y$. However, in the example, X is sufficient for Z, and Z is sufficient for Y, and therefore X itself must be sufficient for Y, which violates our initial assumption. The lesson is that scholars who assert that an initial bivariate relationship is marked by necessary causation (but not sufficient causation) cannot then introduce an intervening variable that implies the relationship is marked by sufficiency without imposing a logical contradiction.

Antecedent test variables

An alternative way of using the elaboration model is to introduce an *antecedent* test variable – i.e., a third variable (Z) that is temporally *prior* to both of the initial two variables (X and Y). Again, it is useful to consider four ways in which such a variable can be used to elaborate a bivariate necessary condition relationship.

Let us first assume that the third antecedent variable is both a necessary cause of the original necessary cause and a necessary cause of the outcome Y. We thereby form a chain of necessary causes:

$$Z \xrightarrow{\;n\;} X \xrightarrow{\;n\;} Y$$

In this case, the analyst has identified a deeper, more temporally remote necessary cause. In effect, the analyst has identified some of the historical roots of a necessary cause. Scholars who are attracted to root causes and seek to find the "causes of causes" (as is true of many historically-inclined researchers) may find this strategy useful.

A second possibility occurs when an antecedent variable Z is sufficient for both X and Y. The relationship looks like this:

$$Z - s \rightarrow X - n \rightarrow Y$$

Here the investigator learns that X is necessary for Y only because it is an inevitable outcome of variable Z, which is itself sufficient for Y. How should one interpret this finding? On the one hand, the initial relationship between X and Y might be seen as diminished in importance insofar as the main causal action is now between Z and Y, with variable X simply being one of several potential mechanisms that allow Z to exert its effect. However, the X/Y relationship still remains an important finding, in that the removal of X would guarantee the absence of Y, whereas the removal of Z would not necessarily entail the absence of X and Y. Hence, it is appropriate to view this finding as contextualizing the initial X/Y relationship rather than making it spurious. We might also note that this example illustrates how a factor (or combination of factors) that is sufficient for an outcome may produce necessary causes rather than contain these causes itself.

A third possibility uses an antecedent variable to show that a necessary cause hypothesis is spurious. A bivariate necessary cause relationship between X and Y becomes spurious when one identifies a third antecedent variable that is simultaneously sufficient for X and necessary for Y:

$$Z - s \rightarrow X - n \rightarrow Y$$

In this case, the effect of X is diminished through the introduction of variable Z. That is, once we recognize that Z always brings into being X, and that Z is itself necessary for Y, we tend to conclude that X does not tell us much causally relevant information beyond our knowledge of Z. If Z is present, X will always also be present. In this sense, X is a redundant necessary cause. And if Z is absent, we already know that a necessary cause is missing, and thus that the outcome will be absent. The issue of whether X is present or absent seems irrelevant.

For example, imagine that X = no beard, Y = pregnancy, and Z = estrogen. Here one would not want to conclude that the absence of a

TABLE 10.1: Using the elaboration model with an intervening variable

Relationship to be explored:
$$X \longrightarrow ? \rightarrow Z \longrightarrow ? \rightarrow Y$$
$$\vert \underline{\hspace{3cm} n \hspace{3cm}} \uparrow$$

X is a necessary cause of *Z* AND *Z* is a necessary cause of *Y* THEN
  initial relationship is contextualized.

X is a necessary cause of *Z* AND *Z* is a sufficient cause of *Y* THEN
  initial relationship is diminished in importance.

X is a sufficient cause of *Z* AND *Z* is a necessary cause of *Y* THEN
  initial relationship is contextualized.

X is a sufficient cause of *Z* AND *Z* is a sufficient cause of *Y* THEN
  not logically possible.

---

beard actually exerts a necessary causal effect on childbirth. Rather, the
absence of beard is an incidental consequence of the estrogen variable,
which does affect pregnancy as a necessary cause. As we shall see,
this strategy of introducing an antecedent variable to show that an
initial relationship is spurious is one of the most effective means of
diminishing the importance of a necessary cause hypothesis, and it is
commonly employed in the chapters in this volume.

A final relationship introduces a logical contradiction and thus is
not possible in practice. This logically impossible relationship emerges
when *Z* is necessary for *X*, and when *Z* is sufficient for *Y*:

$$Z \longrightarrow n \rightarrow X \longrightarrow n \rightarrow Y$$
$$\vert \underline{\hspace{3cm} s \hspace{3cm}} \uparrow$$

This relationship is logically impossible because any factor that is
sufficient for an outcome must include all necessary causes (i.e., if a necessary cause is missing, one cannot have a relationship of sufficiency).
But in the example, *Z* does not inevitably entail the necessary cause *X*.
Hence, it is logically impossible to conclude that *Z* is sufficient for *Y*.

Tables 10.1 and 10.2 summarize the implications of the eight different logical combinations discussed here. As these tables show, the
introduction of a test variable may contextualize an initial relationship,
make the initial relationship spurious, or represent a logical contradiction. All of these possibilities emerge in the chapters of this volume.

TABLE 10.2: Using the elaboration model with an antecedent test variable

Relationship to be explored:
$$Z - ? \rightarrow X - n \rightarrow Y$$

Z is a necessary cause of X AND *Z is a necessary cause of Y* THEN initial relationship is contextualized.

Z is a necessary cause of X AND *Z is a sufficient cause of Y* THEN not logically possible.

Z is a sufficient cause of X AND *Z is a necessary cause of Y* THEN initial relationship is diminished in importance.

Z is a sufficient cause of X AND *Z is a sufficient cause of Y* THEN initial relationship is contextualized.

A note on contributing causes in case study research

Scholars who work on case studies may prefer to characterize their understanding of causation in terms of what the editors call "contributing causes" rather than necessary or sufficient causes. However, in the context of case study research, a contributing cause is probably best understood as one cause within a broader combination of causes that are sufficient for the outcome of interest. In this sense, a contributing cause is what Mackie (1974) calls an INUS cause, and it has the same status as individual causes in the causal combinations that are used in qualitative comparative analysis as specified by Ragin (1987; 2000).

We can consider this issue a little more by comparing briefly the nature of causal inference when N = 1 to a large-N setting. A contributing cause is typically understood as a cause that, all by itself, increases the probability of an outcome occurring. In large-N research, this idea is reflected in a statistical understanding of causation, such that a given change on a variable produces, on average, a given change on another variable, net of all other variables.

However, what does it mean to say that a cause "increases the likelihood" of an outcome when the outcome refers to a singular and historical event, such as World War I or the end of the Cold War? For example, what would it mean to say that economic decline increased the likelihood that the Soviet Union would pursue a policy of retrenchment? Here one cannot easily think in terms of statistical correlations, since N = 1 and whether or not the proposition can be generalized is irrelevant to its truth value. For example, even if it is true that economic decline increased the likelihood of Soviet retrenchment, one cannot therefore conclude that economic decline increases the probability of retrenchment strategies in general. Rather, the statement applies to the specific context of the USSR.

I suggest that the statement means that economic decline is one cause among many, and that various combinations of these many causes would have been sufficient for the outcome. For example, perhaps there were seven main contributing causes, and any five of them would have been jointly sufficient for the outcome. No cause was individually necessary or individually sufficient for the outcome. However, they all "contributed" to the outcome in a sufficiency sense and possibly also in a necessity sense. In the sufficiency sense, they worked together to overdetermine the occurrence of an outcome (i.e., multiple combinations were present that were each sufficient for the outcome). In the necessity sense, it is possible that if *all* of these individual causes were absent, then the outcome would not have occurred, because no sufficiency combination would have been present. On the other hand, one cannot know this for certain, because perhaps the absence of all of these causes would have brought into being alternative causes that would have brought about the outcome.

The upshot of this discussion is that contributing causes are parts of combinations that are sufficient for outcomes. In what follows, therefore, I will specify contributing causes as a part of a combination of causes that are jointly sufficient for an outcome.

The causes of World War I

My goal in this section is two-fold. First, when appropriate, I want to formally diagram the narrative arguments found in the chapters by Jack S. Levy, Richard Ned Lebow, William Thompson, and Paul Schroeder about the origins of World War I. Most of these authors present complex arguments built around chains of causes. By visually diagramming these arguments, I suggest that we can better appreciate their core claims and underlying logic.

Second, I want to raise specific issues related to the ideas discussed above concerning the elaboration model. In particular, I try to show

how the authors implicitly use the elaboration model to contextualize
or call into question several hypotheses about necessary causation.

Levy

The Levy chapter is centrally concerned with the relative weight of policy
choices versus international and domestic structural constraints. Levy
argues that miscalculations and specific policy choices were necessary
conditions for the continental war. However, he contends that these
policy choices were themselves caused by antecedent events. In effect,
he implies that the relationship between policy choices and the continental war may be spurious – that is, there is an antecedent variable
that is simultaneously sufficient for the policy choices and necessary
for the continental war.

The main argument embodies three major causal chains (see figure 10.1). The first chain concerns the causes of the local war between
Austria and Serbia (i.e., cells 1–6). A pivotal claim here is that Germany's assumption about British neutrality was a necessary cause of
Germany's support for Austrian aggression (i.e., the link between cells
3 and 4). Hence, German misperception appears to have been a critical
necessary cause. However, Levy shows that Germany hardly could have
avoided arriving at this conclusion given that Britain did not make
its intentions clear. Furthermore, Britain itself could not easily have
made its intentions clear given its domestic political structure. Once we
recognize that Britain could not communicate its intentions, and that
Germany was therefore destined to be misinformed, the role of German
misperception in causing support for Austrian aggression is greatly
diminished. Causal responsibility appears to rest more with British
domestic structure, which set into motion the tightly linked stream of
events in the first place.

Levy's second major chain leads to the Russian and German mobilizations (i.e., cells 7–16). The Russian mobilization causal chain begins
with a series of factors (cells 7–10) that appear to be jointly sufficient
for delayed military action by the Austrians (cell 11). In turn, this delay
causes Austria to lose sympathy in the international community (cell
12), which along with the beliefs of Russian leaders (cell 13) and the
local war itself (cell 6) was sufficient for the Russian mobilization (cell
14). In turn, given the structure of the international system (cell 15),
the Russian mobilization was sufficient to trigger mobilization by the
Germans (cell 16).

The final chain brings together the two prior chains and takes us to
the general war (cells 17–20). The key step here is the emergence of the

James Mahoney

FIGURE 10.1: Diagram of Levy's argument

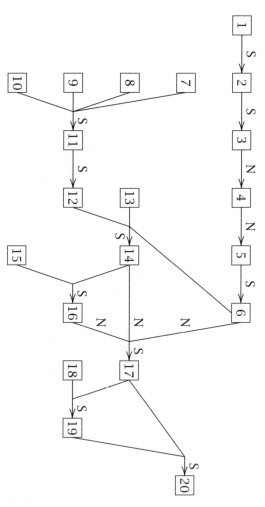

1. British domestic political structure. 2. British failure to make intentions clear to Germany. 3. German assumption that British will remain neutral so long as Germans do not mobilize before Russians. 4. Germans support Austrians without major conditions. 5. Austrians decide to initiate war. 6. Local war between Austria and Serbia. 7. Military organization. 8. Domestic structure and politics. 9. Organizational constraints. 10. State visit of Poincaré and Viviani. 11. Delayed military action by Austrians. 12. Austria loses some legitimacy. 13. Russian leaders' beliefs. 14. Russian mobilization. 15. Structure of alliance system. 16. German mobilization. 17. Continental war. 18. British leaders' beliefs. 19. British intervention. 20. General war.

continental war (cell 17). This event is produced by a conjuncture of three necessary causes that are jointly sufficient: the local war (cell 6), the Russian mobilization (cell 14), and the German mobilization (cell 16). In conjunction with British leaders' beliefs (cell 18), the continental war then leads to British intervention (cell 19). In turn, the combination of British intervention and the continental war was sufficient for the general war (cell 20).

In developing this argument, Levy explicitly explores the question of whether the war was "inadvertent," which in this context means whether individual political leaders could have made decisions that would have avoided the outcome of war while still protecting their vital interests. Levy's narrative shows that while different leader choices and perceptions could have stopped the war, these choices and perceptions could not have been avoided given external, internal, and informational constraints on political leaders. For example, while Germany's erroneous perception that the British would remain neutral was necessary for the local war, this perception could not have been avoided given the information that was provided to the Germans from Britain. And Britain itself could not have provided appropriate information given domestic political constraints. In this sense, the relationship between German misperception and war is spurious – i.e., it is explained away by antecedent variables that are simultaneously sufficient for the misperception and necessary for the war.

Likewise, Levy's analysis shows that the Austrian decision to delay military action may have been necessary for Russian mobilization, but this decision was itself so deeply embedded in prior causes that one wonders if it is a spurious cause. That is, the Austrians were led to their decision by a host of prior factors, and once we take into consideration those prior factors, the importance of the Austrian choice appears secondary. In these ways, Levy makes quite effective use of the logic of spurious necessary causes to assess the importance of different events in his causal chains. In doing so, he presents meaningful conclusions about which necessary conditions actually exert real causal effects.

FIGURE 10.2:   Basic structure of Lebow's argument

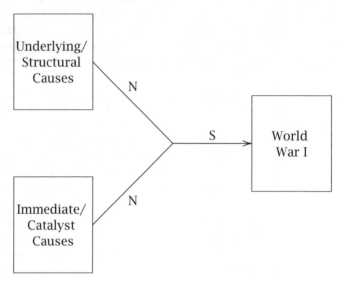

Lebow

Lebow's argument begins with the claim that underlying causes (i.e., structural factors) and immediate causes (i.e., catalysts) are individually necessary and jointly sufficient for World War I (see figure 10.2). The bulk of the article then entails specifying the causal chains that produced both the appropriate underlying causes and the appropriate immediate causes (see figures 10.3 and 10.4).

In the argument, three causal chains conjoin to produce the respective security dilemmas of Germany, Austria, and Russia, which taken together represent the underlying causes of World War I (i.e., cells 1–24 in figure 10.3). The causal chain leading to German insecurity is driven by a series of factors concerning unsuccessful competition by Germany in the European states systems (i.e., cells 1–8). I do not know if Lebow considers these factors to be necessary causes or sufficient causes; hence, I have not specified them in figure 10.3.

Austria's security dilemma ultimately grows out of a combination of the decision of short-sighted foreign ministers in Vienna and St. Petersburg to invade Bosnia–Herzegovina and the rise in Serbian power that followed the Italian occupation of Tripoli. These factors triggered the end of the Austrian-Russian cooperation and provoked Serbia toward hostility (see cells 10–16). Specifically, from the text, Lebow appears to argue that the rise in Serbian power (11), the end of Austrian-Russian

cooperation (14), and the embitterment of Serbia (15) were individually necessary and jointly sufficient for the Austrian security dilemma
(16). It bears emphasis that these necessary causes could be spurious
ones if certain antecedent factors in the chain were simultaneously
sufficient for them and necessary for Austria's security dilemma. For
example, if the Italian occupation of Tripoli (10) is sufficient for the rise
in Serbian power (11) and necessary for Austria's security dilemma (16),
then Lebow might conclude that the rise in Serbian power is a spurious
necessary cause.

Finally, Russia's security dilemma is driven most immediately by
two events that are treated as individually necessary and jointly sufficient causes: Russian external setbacks (18) and Russian internal
weaknesses (22). In turn, the internal problems are rooted in events
related to the Russian Revolution of 1905 (19–21), while the external
problems grow out of defeat in the Russo–Japanese War (17) and the
annexation of Bosnia and Herzegovina (13). Lebow does not say whether
these root causes might be sufficient for subsequent causes and necessary for Russia's security dilemma. If they are, however, Russia's
external setbacks and internal weaknesses would be diminished in
importance as necessary causes.

Lebow's other major causal chain concerns the immediate causes
of World War I (figure 10.4). The centerpiece of this discussion is the
assassinations (6), which are understood to produce a series of other
factors that together are a sufficient catalyst for the war. The narrative
considers both the causes and consequences of the assassinations. Concerning the causes, Lebow identifies five necessary causes (i.e., 1–5) that
involve relatively minor decisions often made by specific individuals.
For example, if Ferdinand had heeded warnings and cancelled the trip,
he might have lived a full life in a peaceful Europe. The focus on the decision of a specific individual is a common move when scholars develop
a necessary condition counterfactual claim. In particular, scholars often
are drawn to particular choices because these choices could have turned
out differently if the world was only slightly different. Arguments that
stress the importance of "contingency" thus often go hand-in-hand with
claims that small choices tip the balance toward one outcome and not
another.

Given that the assassination is viewed as a necessary cause of
World War I, the causes of this event can be seen as contextualizing this
necessary cause. In particular, these causes allow Lebow to construct a
chain of necessary causes that places the assassination as one specific
link in a highly contextualized narrative.

FIGURE 10.3:   Formal diagram of Lebow's underlying/structural causes

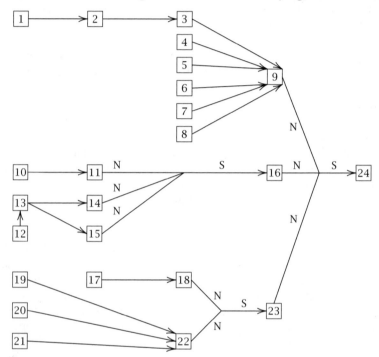

1. Russian access to French markets. 2. Russian industrialization. 3. Increased Russian power. 4. Germany's geographic position. 5. Prior German policies. 6. Bismark's failure to dissuade Wilhelm I. 7. Bismark's successors poor dealings with Russia. 8. Kaiser's unproductive naval race with England. 9. Germany's insecurity dilemma. 10. Italian occupation of Tripoli. 11. Decline in Ottoman power; rise in Serbian power. 12. Short-sighted foreign ministers in Vienna and St. Petersburg. 13. Annexation of Bosnia and Herzegovina. 14. Austrian-Russian cooperation ends. 15. Serbia embittered. 16. Austria's insecurity dilemma. 17. Russian defeat in Russo–Japanese War 18. Russian external setbacks. 19. Russian Revolution of 1905. 20. Alienation of middle classes. 21. Rise of powerful revolutionary movement. 22. Russian internal weaknesses. 23. Russia's insecurity dilemma. 24. Permissive underlying causes of WWI.

FIGURE 10.4: Formal diagram of Lebow's immediate/catalyst causes

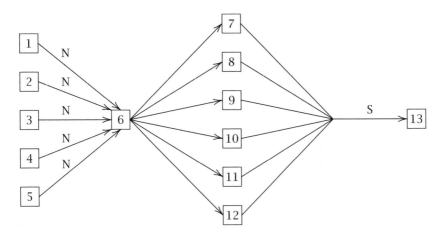

1. Princip does not obey order to abort assassination. 2. Austrian authorities in Belgrade do not take security seriously. 3. Franz Ferdinand does not cancel trip in response to warnings. 4. Franz Ferdinand chooses not to leave Sarajevo after ceremony. 5. Franz Ferdinand's cavalcade does not follow planned route. 6. Assassination of Franz Ferdinand and Sophie. 7. Austrian leaders believe they need to respond forcefully. 8. Franz Josef and Kaiser Wilhelm are receptive to calls for decisive action. 9. The principle spokesman in Vienna for peace is dead. 10. Bethmann-Hollweg experiences a gestalt shift. 11. It is possible for Bethmann-Hollweg to win the support of socialists. 12. Wilhelm and Bethmann-Hollweg believe they can proceed toward war in incremental steps. 13. Immediate/catalyst causes of WWI.

Concerning the consequences of the assassination, Lebow lists a series of implications that were made possible or brought into being by the death of Ferdinand. These immediate consequences are largely psychological in nature: actors moved toward a frame of mind such that they would act on the permissive structural environment. In this sense, the assassination was a necessary catalyst, pushing leaders to step through the window of opportunity that the underlying conditions had opened.

The idea of a conjuncture or a confluence – i.e., the coming together of separately determined sequences – is a central theme of the Lebow argument. It is not uncommon for scholars to argue – as does Lebow – that conjunctures are unpredictable and therefore contingent events. This contention typically assumes that a conjuncture occurs in a rela- tively constricted temporal domain, such that a slight alternation in the timing of one sequence would lead to a different outcome. The classical example, of course, involves a falling tile colliding with a pedestrian walking next to a building.

Lebow argues that a slight change in timing of either the sequence for underlying causes or the sequence for immediate causes would have prevented World War I. To make this argument plausible, he notes that the underlying causes entailed the conjuncture of three separate chains that happened to come together. Hence, the appropriate underlying causes were hardly an inevitable outcome, much as the assassination is cast as a contingent event. Since both the underlying and immediate causes could have been eliminated by slight changes in the world, Lebow concludes that the war itself was "contingent in both its underlying and immediate causes," and therefore not overdetermined (this volume, p. 85).

Thompson

The purpose of the chapter by Thompson is not to develop an explanation of World War I that employs the idea of necessary causes. Instead, Thompson seeks to draw out a structural explanation of the war. This explanation locates causal factors in the structure of rivalries and competition that make war in general more probable. In this sense, Thompson develops a theory of war that is understood to work like a probabilistic correlation – i.e., a set of factors that make an outcome more likely on average but not inevitable across a full population of cases.

The specific theory draws on four main variables: rivalry density, alliance bipolarization, global leader decline, and regional leader ascent. Thompson's table 5.3 presents scores of these variables for the period from 1815 to 1913. The table offers a dramatic presentation of results and appears be a stunning confirmation of the theory: all four of the variables reached record high levels during the 1910–13 period.

There are at least two ways to think about this argument. First, one could see Thompson's argument as a set of correlational hypotheses. Because these hypotheses were generated through the World War I case, most methodologists would not consider the chapter itself to offer a powerful test of the hypotheses. Rather, to really test the hypotheses, it would be necessary to introduce a broader range of cases, including cases that were not used in the development of the hypotheses. Thus, one possible reading of the Thompson chapter is as an exercise in the generation of a testable set of hypotheses that could be further evaluated using other cases.

Second, one could see the argument as an effort to identify a set of causes that are jointly sufficient (or almost sufficient) but not necessary for World War I. That is, to the extent that Thompson believes his four key causal factors made World War I quite likely, he has presented a probabilistic sufficiency argument. This interpretation suggests an affinity between correlational causes and joint sufficiency (see also Ragin 2000).

It is not clear that Thompson would endorse this latter interpretation, given that he expresses skepticism about the notions of necessary and sufficient causes. Indeed, he does not, for example, explicitly explore necessary condition counterfactuals by imagining that a particular variable assumes a different value. Furthermore, he writes that, "I worry that a renewed emphasis on necessary and sufficient causes may detract from developing relative weights for multivariate explanations" (this volume, p. 144). Yet, advocates of necessary/sufficient causation might respond that there are tools for evaluating the relative importance of necessary and sufficient causes, including both the technique emphasized by Goertz and Levy in the introduction and the elaboration modeling techniques highlighted here. Furthermore, one might stress that it is highly likely that Thompson's four variables interact in complex ways with one another. Accordingly, we should be concerned with the interactions among the variables as well as the isolated contributions of the variables. Insofar as frameworks for analyzing necessary/sufficient causation provide a good basis for examining these interactions, they also provide a useful set of tools for assessing key aspects of Thompson's theory.

Schroeder

Schroeder's argument uses ideas of necessary causation to call into question other scholars' explanations of World War I. He is particularly concerned with explanations that emphasize "subjective" factors, that is, factors related to the choices and decisions of specific powers. These subjective arguments emphasize the political agency of actors, and therefore may be linked to moral arguments. For example, Schroeder points out that many scholars believe Germany and Austria either actively chose to go to war or made decisions that created situations that would leave them with little choice but to go to war. That is to say, according to these scholars, Germany and Austria brought the war on themselves and therefore can be held morally accountable for it.

Schroeder casts doubt on this kind of reasoning by arguing that it relies on spurious necessary causes. As figure 10.5A shows, the

FIGURE 10.5:   The logic of Schroeder's skepticism regarding the subjective causes of World War I

A. The Moral Subjective Argument

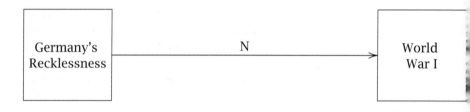

B. Schroeder's Alternative

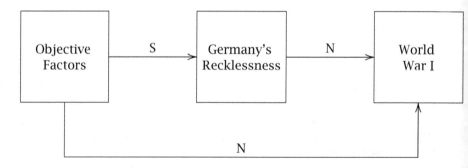

conventional wisdom identifies factors such as Germany's recklessness as necessary causes of World War I. Since this is a necessary cause, the counterfactual logic is that its absence would have prevented the insecurity crisis, and thus the war. However, Schroeder argues that, in fact, this necessary cause was produced by antecedent "objective" conditions that are simultaneously sufficient for the necessary cause and themselves necessary for the outcome of war (see figure 10.5B). Schroeder suggests that once we recognize that subjective necessary causes such as Germany's recklessness were produced by objective antecedent causes, the subjective factors appear to be only spuriously related to insecurity and war.

The thrust of this argument, therefore, is to illustrate that Germany and Austria really could not have chosen differently. For example, Schroeder points to many examples of conciliatory polices by the Germans and Austrians, and many other examples of unnecessarily aggressive policies by the other Europe powers. He concludes that, "Germany and Austria–Hungary were not in control of the international system, but being restrained and controlled by it. The initiative and leadership in European politics from 1890 to 1914 always lay with their opponents, increasingly so as time went on" (this volume, p. 164). Hence, Schroeder not only casts doubt on the importance of German and Austrian decisions, but also establishes agency for other European powers, showing that they had their own moral culpability.

Schroeder's positive argument takes the form of identifying the absence of a necessary condition for peace. Insofar as the absence of peace is equivalent to war, this argument can be seen as identifying a sufficient cause of war. At the most aggregate level, the structure of the argument can be diagrammed as in figure 10.6A and 10.6B. Schroeder argues that appropriate diplomatic responses to periodic crises are a necessary cause of sustained peace, as can be seen by the numerous uses of effective diplomacy in the decades before World War I. Accordingly, the absence of appropriate diplomatic responses to crises is a sufficient cause of the absence of sustained peace (i.e., war). In this sense, one might conclude that diplomatic failures caused World War I. However, Schroeder maintains that the absence of appropriate diplomatic responses was itself caused by an antecedent variable: change in foreign policy culture. In particular, European powers ceased to pursue diplomatic solutions as in the past because, "No one believed that a sane, rational foreign policy allowed any longer for this kind of collective response" (this volume, p. 192). Although Schroeder is not fully explicit, this change in foreign policy culture appears to be sufficient for the absence of appropriate diplomatic responses. As a

FIGURE 10.6:   Schroeder's positive argument

A. The Necessary Condition Formulation

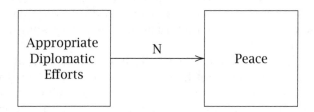

B. The Sufficient Condition Formulation

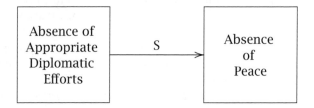

C. The Full Formulation

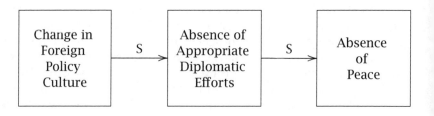

result, once we recognize the change in foreign policy culture, we are inclined to place less causal importance on the diplomatic response variable. In this way, too, Schroeder draws on the logic of a spurious necessary cause to weigh the importance of different factors.

The causes of the end of the Cold War

The second set of chapters in this volume is animated by a disagreement about the role of ideational conditions and material conditions in causing the Soviets to undertake the fundamental reorientation in foreign policy that composed their grand strategy of retrenchment and that effectively ended their animosity toward the United States. Stephen G. Brooks and William C. Wohlforth argue that many ideational scholars – Robert English included – have underemphasized the importance of long-run Soviet economic decline in producing the retrenchment. By contrast, English suggests that Brooks and Wohlforth greatly overstate and misinterepret the importance of this economic decline in producing the retrenchment and the end of the Cold War.

Here I seek to show how we can better understand the debate and the authors' contrasting views by viewing Brooks and Wohlforth's argument as an attempt to use an antecedent variable (material conditions) that diminishes the importance of ideational conditions as a necessary cause of the end of the Cold War. English attempts to rebut this argument by downplaying the importance of material conditions as an antecedent variable.

Brooks and Wohlforth

Brooks and Wohlforth are committed to a probabilistic mode of argument in which causes make outcomes more likely, but not inevitable. Although these authors contrast this approach with necessary and sufficient causation, the logic of their argument appears to rely on probabilistic necessary and probabilistic sufficient causes. Thus, they adopt a probabilistic framework, but one that still implicitly assumes necessary and sufficient causation.

Perhaps the most provocative aspect of the Brooks and Wohlforth argument is the claim that ideational conditions are endogenous to material changes. But what concretely does it mean to say that ideational conditions are endogenous? First, Brooks and Wohlforth explicitly state that ideational conditions are necessary but not sufficient for Soviet retrenchment. That is, foreign policy transformation would not have occurred without new ideas on the part of the Soviet leadership (see

FIGURE 10.7:   The debate over the end of the Cold War: the shared understanding

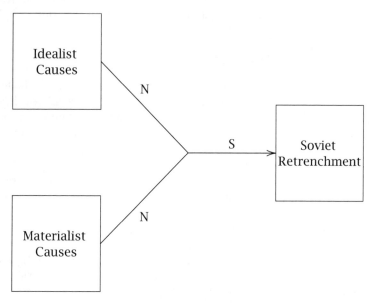

figure 10.7). Second, these authors also believe that changing material conditions – in particular, economic decline – were necessary but not sufficient for the foreign policy transformation. Why then are ideational conditions "endogenous" to materialist ones? For example, why do Brooks and Wohlforth not simply stop with the contention that both sets of conditions were individually necessary and jointly sufficient for the retrenchment?

The answer is that they believe that changing material conditions existed *prior to* changing ideational conditions, and that material conditions caused the transformation of Soviet thinking. The authors do not necessarily believe material conditions fully caused the change in ideational conditions, and thus their argument takes the form of a probabilistic sufficiency hypothesis. That is, the economic decline of the Soviet Union was probabilistically sufficient for the transformation of Soviet thinking. This idea is represented in figure 10.8.

Brooks and Wohlforth's argument thus involves identifying an antecedent causal variable (material conditions) that leads an initial bivariate relationship to become spurious. In this formulation, changes in material conditions are: (1) probabilistically sufficient for changes in ideational conditions; and (2) necessary for the outcome of Soviet retrenchment. By contrast, changes in ideational conditions are only necessary for the Soviet retrenchment. If this is true, the material condition hypothesis carries more causal weight than the ideational condition hypothesis.

One other aspect of Brooks and Wohlforth's argument deserves commentary. In addition to emphasizing the key role of economic decline, the authors stress other material conditions that worked in conjunction with economic decline to make the change in Soviet foreign policy especially likely. For example, they highlight the role of the bipolar international system, competition with the United States, the Soviet's overstretched empire and mounting defense spending, and the inability of the USSR to keep up with global technology. In effect, these causes represent a combination that made the change in Soviet foreign policy very likely. In this sense, the authors have identified a set of causes that together are understood to be (probabilistically) sufficient for the Soviet retrenchment.

English

English's argument attempts to undercut Brooks and Wohlforth's claim that material conditions drove changes in ideational conditions. This claim is at the core of Brooks and Wohlforth's overall contention that ideational models are endogenous to material models, and it represents the heart of their argument. In this sense, the debate in these chapters is largely about the causes of changes in Soviet thinking.

In developing his case, English accepts that changing material conditions were necessary for the end of the Cold War, but he disputes the idea that they played any leading role in reorienting Soviet thinking. First, he argues that Brooks and Wohlforth overstate the extent to which there was a consensus on the need for strategic retreat among old thinkers. Insofar as this consensus did not exist, material conditions did not systematically transform the ideational content of the Soviet leadership. Second, and more important for our purposes, English suggests that new thinking itself had important ideational causes, and thus that one cannot view changing ideational conditions as endogenous to a material model. In particular, English suggests the pattern of causation presented in figure 10.8.

In this model, ideational conditions are not endogenous to material conditions. Rather, the transformation of ideational conditions is a product of the interplay between both material conditions and ideational conditions. Both kinds of antecedent causes carry equal weight. Thus, idea-based factors are not a spurious necessary cause.

FIGURE 10.8:   The Brooks/Wohlforth and English debate over the end of the Cold War

Brooks and Wohlforth's Materialist Explanation

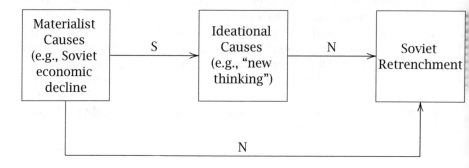

English's Rebuttal

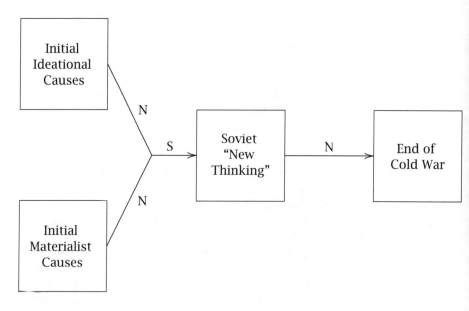

Much of the debate can be viewed as a disagreement about a specific counterfactual issue. Namely, is it true that, given their economic decline, Soviet leaders would have adopted a strategy of retreat regardless of their core values and preexisting ideologies? If they would have almost certainly adopted such a strategy even with a broad range of quite different ideologies and beliefs, then Brooks and Wohlforth's argument seems to have more merit. By contrast, if they would not have pursued retrenchment without the presence of specific preexisting ideas and ideologies, then English's argument seems to have the upper hand.

I am not qualified to judge who is correct in this debate. However, future research on the end of the Cold War by case experts could surely benefit by explicitly scrutinizing this specific counterfactual scenario.

Conclusion

The chapters in this volume are written by case experts whose goals are primarily substantive and explanatory in nature, not methodological. Nevertheless, in the course of making their substantive arguments, the authors illustrate the concrete issues that arise in the study of the necessary causes of particular events. In the introduction and first chapter of this book, Goertz and Levy systematically spell out many of these issues, including the role of counterfactuals, causal chains, turning points, windows of opportunity, powder keg metaphors, and the role of individuals and human agency.

In this conclusion I have focused on a slightly different issue: the ways in which scholars elaborate bivariate necessary causal claims through the introduction of intervening and antecedent variables. I have argued that the use of this elaboration model provides analysts with a concrete set of tools for contextualizing or diminishing the importance of specific hypotheses about necessary causes. Accordingly, one of the goals of this chapter was to illustrate a new methodological technique of hypothesis evaluation for scholars who work with necessary causal hypotheses.

In addition, I have sought to show how the elaboration model can help us view the specific arguments offered in this book in a new light. Above all else, this model encourages us to view these arguments in terms of diagrams composed of explicitly stated causal chains. I do not want to suggest that these "formal" presentations are any kind of substitute to the actual narratives in the text. However, the diagrams do help us see more clearly the ways in which their necessary and sufficient causal hypotheses are developed. Through the diagrams, we learn new things about the narrative arguments, including the specific ways in which they contextualize certain necessary causes and suggest others are spurious. Furthermore, any logical problems with an argument are more readily exposed in the diagrams. Hence, while formal diagrams cannot replace narrative, they may represent a useful supplement to it.

Appendix: Classroom exercises and website

This appendix provides exercises for the book *Explaining war and peace: case studies and necessary condition counterfactuals.* Answers to these exercises (except those that are open-ended or intended for general discussion) may be obtained by instructors from Gary Goertz (ggoertz@u.arizona.edu) or Jack Levy (jacklevy@rci.rutgers.edu). If you would like to be informed when these exercises are updated please contact us and we will put you on the emailing list.

The goal of these exercises is to provide material for classroom discussion and homework exercises. Some of the exercises deal with problems of logic. Other exercises involve the wider literature on World War I, the end of Cold War, or more generally the literature on international security, conflict, and war. A few have a more philosophical bent. We feel it is useful to see how the debates on World War I and the end of the Cold War appear in other debates about the causes of international conflict. Also, we have included exercises that might lead to different readings or interpretations. We think these can be useful in classroom discussions. Our goal is to provide a variety of possibilities and let the instructor choose those among them that fit within the scope and purpose of the class.

Most of the articles referred to in the following exercises are available electronically via library subscription in PDF format; complete references are found at the end. If possible we have chosen an electronically available article to a book. Some of the exercises appear briefly in the book itself and are answered there, but we have included them since we think an extended analysis would be a useful exercise in a classroom setting.

We welcome comments on these exercises and suggestions for new ones. We hope to expand this database of exercises over the next few years. You can check for updated versions of the exercises at: http://www.u.arizona.edu/~ggoertz/explaining_war_and_peace.html

1. A good way to understand the logic of necessary and sufficient condition is via 2×2 tables. Construct a 2×2 table (0=absence and 1=presence) and determine which cell must be zero if a necessary/sufficient condition is true.

2. A common error is to think a necessary condition counterfactual must involve dichotomous variables. Once you have completed the previous exercise plot the 2×2 table in a two-dimensional space, with one point per cell (i.e., 4 points at their (x,y) coordinates). By coding the necessary condition cell as zero and the other cells as one determine what a necessary condition scatter plot (i.e., continuous variables) would look like once you scatter more points around the three non-necessary condition cell (i.e., (x,y) coordinates) points.

3. The "democratic peace" idea is that democracies never fight wars with each other. This can be expressed as a either a necessary condition hypothesis or a sufficient condition hypothesis. Give both hypotheses.

4. It is not uncommon to confuse necessary condition counterfactuals with sufficient condition ones. See Fenoaltea (1973) for a beautiful discussion of this in the context of economic history. How does the following quote illustrate that:

> Immanual Kant's argument that democratic institutions ... are a necessary condition for peace has been empirically substantiated. (Risse-Kappen 1996: 366)

> The recent flurry of studies of the theory of the 'democratic peace' follows upon Kant's argument that a necessary condition for peace between states is constitutional republics. (Holsti 1996: 180)

5. Use the democratic peace to propose a specific counterfactual so that World War I does not occur.

6. Discuss the following claim by one of the most prominent historians today. Does it invoke a necessary or sufficient condition claim? Do a counterfactual analysis of it.

> The argument that British intervention in the war was made inevitable by the violation of Belgian neutrality has been repeated by historians ever since [Lloyd George]. (Ferguson 1999a: 231)

7. Here is a much more complicated exercise in logic. The following are the core hypotheses in Schweller's article. Explain how these two hypotheses are simultaneously (1) redundant and (2) contradictory.

Hint: think about contrapositives (i.e., "If X then Y" is equivalent to "If not-Y then not-X").

> 1. A power transition involving a declining democratic leader is both a necessary and sufficient condition for the absence of preventive war. 1a. When a decling democratic leader confronts a rising democratic challenger, accomodation results. 1b. When a declining democratic leader confronts a rising nondemocratic challenger, the leader tries to form a defensive alliance system to counterbalance the threat. 2. A power transition involving a decling nondemocratic state is a necessary but not sufficient condition for a preventive war, regardless of the regime type of the challenger. (Schweller 1992: 248–49)

8. The confusion of necessary with sufficient conditions also arises when defining what "cause" means. Explain how this works in Wendt's analysis of cause:

> In saying that 'X causes Y' we assume that: (1) X and Y exist independent of each other, (2) X precedes Y temporally, and (3) but for X, Y would not have occurred.... The logical empiricist model of causal explanation, usually called the deductive-nomological model or D-N model, is rooted in David Hume's seminal discussion of causality. Hume argued that when we see putative causes followed by effects, i.e., when we have met conditions (1) and (2), all we can be certain about is that they stand in relations of constant conjunction. The actual mechanism by which X causes Y is not observable (and thus uncertain), and appeal to it is therefore epistemically illegitimate. Even if there is necessity in nature, we cannot know it. How then to satisfy the third, counterfactual condition for causality, which implies necessity? (Wendt 1999: 79)

9. Quite a few different terms are often used to distinguish between different kinds of causes, e.g., "contributory cause," "remote cause," "intervening/mediating cause." Use Russett's very interesting analysis of World War I (1962) – in particular Fay's account – to discuss what these kinds of cause mean. See also Fischer's classic book (1970) which talks about eight kinds of cause: (1) all antecedents, (2) regularistic antecedents, (3) controllable antecedents, (4) rational and/or motivational antecedents, (5) abnormal antecedents, (6) structural antecedents, (7) contingent-series antecedents, (8) precipitant antecedents.

10. Brooks and Wohlforth argue for a *probabilistic* interpretation of their causal claims in their reponse to Wohlforth. For the philosophically

inclined, there is a major debate in philosophy about the "sense" that probably statements have for individual cases. Many argue that probability statements only make sense in over repeated events. This is called the "frequentist" position, e.g., "Our probability theory has nothing to do with questions such as: 'is there a probability of Germany being at some time in the future involved in a war with Liberia.' ... probability when it refers to a single event has no meaning at all for us" (von Mises 1957: 9, 11).

11. Van Evera's well-known article (1984) on World War I argues that the "cult of the offensive" was an important cause of the war. Find three key counterfactuals in that article that imply necessary condition hypotheses. One of the three should involve "window of opportunity" idea.

12. While the anthology focuses on necessary condition counterfactuals it is quite possible to construct a causal explanation with just sufficient conditions. Which chapter of the anthology best illustrates this? What is the sufficient condition argument?

13. What is the logical form of the hypothesis that U.S. military pressure would put such a strain on the Soviet Union "that the Soviet leadership would have little choice but to make substantial concessions on arms control" (Gaddis 1989: 13)?

14. Many historians feel that events like World War I were "over-determined." Explain why this would generally lead them to discount necessary condition counterfactuals, e.g., "The fact that so many plausible explanations for the outbreak of the war [World War I] have been advanced over the years indicates on the one hand that it was massively overdetermined, and on the other that no effort to analyze the causal factors involved can ever fully succeed" (Schroeder 1972: 320).

In general it is easy to make mistakes with the contrapositive that links necessary and sufficient conditions to each other.

15. Define the contrapositive: (1) starting with necessary conditions, (2) starting with sufficient conditions, (3) with multiple necessary conditions, (4) with multiple sufficient conditions.

16. The Schroeder chapter is a brillant example of how one can use the contrapositive to make a very provocative claim. (1) Explain what he did. (2) Do the same thing with a causal claim about the end of the Cold War.

17. The following quote summarizes the argument of Sagan (1986) on the causes of World War I:

> Sir Edward Grey's failure to present a clear and credible threat of British intervention early in the July crisis and the specific preemptive aspects of Germany's offensive war plans caused by the slow Russian mobilization and the Liege bottleneck are linked together as an immediate cause of the First World War. (Sagan 1986: 168; this is key thesis of whole article).

In the conclusions Sagan proposes the following counterfactual which is potentially *logically* inconsistent with the basic theory given above. What is that potential logical inconsistency? Can you give an interpretation which makes everything consistent?

> *If* Grey had given a clear warning earlier, *if* the Czar had further delayed Russian mobilization against Austria and then Germany, and *if* the German offensive war plans had not been able to depend upon a preemptive *coup de main* against Liege and the decisive battle in France before Russian mobilization was completed in the East, *then* it is possible, just possible, that Bethmann-Hollweg would have had the time and the courage necessary to apply sufficient pressure on Vienna to accept the "Halt in Belgrade." And if this had occurred, 1914 might today appear as only another one of a series of Balkan crises that almost led to a world war. (Sagan 1986: 169).

18. A key question in the causal analysis of individual cases is the relationship between temporal distance and causal importance. Should events or factors closer to the event to be explained receive greater or less causal importance. Analyze the quote below from Gerring (2005) who argues for increasing impact as temporal distance. Does it matter whether the cause is a necessary or sufficient condition?

> Consider the following path diagram. $X_1 \Rightarrow X_2 \Rightarrow X_3 \Rightarrow X_4 \Rightarrow Y$
> We are apt to consider X_1 to be the cause and causal factors $X_2 - X_4$ intermediate (and less important) causes, all other things being equal. Of course, all other things are rarely equal. We are likely to lose causal power (accuracy and completeness) as we move further away from the outcome. Yet, if we did not – e.g. if the correlations in this imaginary path diagram were perfect – we would rightly grant priority to X_1. Causes lying close to an effect are not satisfying as causes, precisely because of their proximity. Rather, we search for causes that are 'ultimate' or 'fundamental'.
> Consider a quotidian example. To say that an accident was caused because A ran into B is not to say much that is useful

about this event. Indeed, this sort of statement is probably better classified as descriptive, rather than explanatory. An X gains causal status as it moves back further in time from the event in question. If, to continue with this story, I claim that the accident was caused by the case of beer consumed by A earlier that evening, I have offered a cause that has greater priority and is, on this account at least, a better explanation. If I can show that the accident in question was actually a re-enactment of a childhood accident that A experienced 20 years ago, then I have offered an even more interesting explanation. Similarly, to say that the Civil War was caused by the attack on Fort Sumter, or that the First World War was caused by the assassination of the Archduke Francis Ferdinand at Sarajevo, is to make a causal argument that is almost trivial by virtue of its lack of priority. It does not illumine very much, except perhaps the mechanism that might be at work vis-a-vis some prior cause.

The further away we can get from the outcome in question, the more satisfying (ceteris paribus) our explanation will be. This explains much of the excitement when social scientists find 'structural' variables that seem to impact public policy or political behavior. It is not that they offer more complete or more accurate explanations; indeed, the correlations between X and Y are apt to be much weaker. It is not that they are more relevant; indeed, they are less relevant for most policy purposes, since they are apt to be least amenable to change. Priority often imposes costs on other criterial dimensions. Yet, such explanations will be better insofar as they offer us more power, more leverage on the topic. They are non-obvious. (Gerring 2005: 174–5)

19. The following is a well-known nursery verse that describes the cause of King Richard III's fall from power. Analyze the temporal distance causal claims embedded in it.

> For want of a nail the shoe was lost,
> For want of a shoe the horse was lost,
> For want of a horse the rider was lost,
> For want of a rider the battle was lost,
> For want of a battle the kingdom was lost,
> And all for the want of a horseshoe nail.

20. United States law gives particular importance to the person or action that was the last one which could have potentially avoided a bad event (e.g., car accident). What does this mean about the relative causal importance of recent or distant events.

21. How can you use the powder keg model to combine the arguments of English and Brooks/Wohlforth?

22. A key issue in the concept of a turning point revolves around whether a turning point should be defined in terms of points in history where things changed or should also include "potential" turning points but where things did not change. For example, Herrmann and Lebow do not include potential turn points in their definition: "We define a turning point in terms of two properties. First, it must be a change of significant magnitude, not an incremental adjustment but a substantial departure from previous practice. Second, it must be a change that would be difficult to undo" (Herrmann and Lebow 2004). Discuss the following example from A.J.P. Taylor regarding a turning point in German history where Germany did not turn:

> 1848 was the decisive year of German, and so of European, history: it recapitulated Germany's past and anticipated Germany's future. Echoes of the Holy Roman Empire merged into a prelude of the Nazi 'New Order'; the doctrines of Rousseau and the doctrines of Marx, the shade of Luther and the shadow of Hitler, jostled each other in bewildering succession. Never has there been a revolution so inspired by a limitless faith in the power of ideas; never has a revolution so discredited the power of ideas in its result. The success of the revolution discredited conservative ideas; the failure of the revolution discredited liberal ideas. After it, nothing remained but the idea of Force, and this idea stood at the helm of Germany history from then on. For the first time since 1521, the German people stepped on to the centre of the German stage only to miss their cues once more. German history reached its turning-point and failed to turn. This was the fateful essence of 1848. (Taylor 1945: 68; for a different perspective see Blackbourn and Eley 1984)

23. Use the idea of a *window of opportunity* to define all potential turning points. What is the role of necessary versus sufficient conditions?

24. Many historians feel that the "Pleiku" analysis of World War I is basically correct (i.e., that there were many Balkan crises and that one of them would have sparked a world war). Some similar arguments have been made with regard to the impact of the Versaille Treaty on the occurrence of World War II, that is made World War II very likely. What would be one counterfactual argument that strongly contests such views? Are there parallels to the end of the Cold War debate?

25. Can you make counterfactual arguments about the role of key individual decision-makers in the World War I case? End of Cold War?

26. Here are some claims that constitute core ideas of prominent work (both by political scientists and historians) on World War I (we do

not include those defended in various chapters of this anthology). In all cases these are central claims made by the author(s). The quotes below are obviously dramatic simplifications of complex arguments but they do capture the core of the scholar's argument and are useful for classroom discussion. Some are expressed in necessary condition counterfactual terms. Others are not; for these generate some necessary condition counterfactuals. More generally, analyze the causal explanations in them. These can be used as the basis for class discussion or additional reading.

Goemens:
I have to put the blame for four years of war and over ten million deaths squarely on the shoulders of Germany's regime. If Germany had not been a semirepressive, moderately exclusionary regime, would the war have ended sooner? Such counterfactual claims are notoriously hard to evaluate.... An argument can nevertheless be made that a nonrepressive, nonexclusionary Germany would have ended the war before 1918, with 1917 a likely termination year. (Goemans 2000: 314–15, in conclusions)

Ferguson:
Rather than joining the Allied war effect, he [Ferguson] said, Britain should have maintained its neutrality and allowed the Germans to win a limited Continental war against the French and the Germans. In that event, he postulated, Germany whose war aims in 1914 were relatively modest, would have respected the territorial integrity of Belgium, France, and Holland and settled for a German-led European federation. Had Britain "stood aside" he continued, it is likely that the century would have been spared the Bolshevik Revolution, the Second World War, and perhaps even the Holocaust. (Boynton 1999: 43; New Yorker piece on Ferguson's book)

Geiss:
The events of July and early August 1914 cannot be properly understood without a knowledge of the historical background provided by the preceding decades of Imperialism. On the other hand, that background alone is not sufficient to explain the outbreak of the First World War. Two general historical factors proved to be decisive, and both were fused by a third to produce the explosion known as the First World War. Imperialism, with Wilhelmine *Weltpolitik* as its specifically German version, provided the general framework and the basic tensions; the principle of national self-determination constituted, with its revolutionary potential, a permanent but latent threat to the old dynastic empires and built-up tensions in south-east Europe. The determination of the German Empire – then the most

powerful conservative force in the world after Tsarist Russia – to uphold the conservative and monarchic principles by any means against the rising flood of democracy, plus its *Weltpolitik* made war inevitable. (Geiss 1984: 46; original is the introduction of his book *July 1914*)

Taylor:
But there was only one decision which turned the little Balkan conflict between Austria-Hungary and Serbia into a European war. That was the German decision to start general mobilization on 31st July, and that was in turn decisive because of the academic ingenuity with which Schlieffen, now in his grave, had attempted to solve the problem of a two-front war. (Taylor 1969: 101)

Maier:
The irreversible momentum toward general war in 1914 is usually seen as a result of three factors: the hopeless, long-term instability of the Habsburg empire, the rigid structure of opposing alliances, and the inelectuable pull of military preparations. (Maier 1988: 822)

Williamson:
Of all the central actors in 1914, Conrad alone could have – by saying no to Berchtold or expressing hesitation to Franz Joseph or accepting some modified "Halt in Belgrade" – brought the crisis to a more peaceful conclusion. (Williamson 1988: 815–16)

Van Evera:
The consequences of the cult of the offensive are illuminated by imagining the politics of 1914 had European leaders recognized the actual power of the defense.... Thus the logic that led Germany to provoke the 1914 crisis would have been undermined, and the chain reaction by which the war spread outward from the Balkans would have been very improbable. In all likelihood, the Austro-Serbian conflict would have been a minor and soon-forgotten disturbance on the periphery of European politics. (Van Evera 1984: 105)

Snyder:
These war plans and the offensive doctrines behind them were in themselves an important and perhaps decisive cause of the war. (Snyder 1984: 108) In short, the European militaries cannot be blamed for the belligerent diplomacy that set the ball rolling towards World War I. Once the process began, however, their penchant for offense and their quickness to view war as inevitable created a slide towards war that the diplomats did not foresee. (Snyder 1984: 138–39)

Trachtenberg:
If in 1914 everyone understood the system and knew, for example,

that a Russian or German general mobilization would lead to war, and if, in addition, the political authorities were free agents – that is, if their hands were not being forced by military imperatives, or by pressure from the generals – then the existence of the system of interlocking mobilization plans could hardly be said in itself to have been a "cause" of war because, once it was set off, the time for negotiation was cut short. But if the working of the system was understood in advance, a decision for general mobilization was a decision for war; statesmen would be opting for war with their eyes open. To argue that the system was, in such a case, a "cause" of war makes about as much sense as saying that any military operation which marked the effective beginning of hostilities ... was a real "cause" of an armed conflict (Trachtenberg 1990–1: 122)

Sagan:

If Grey had given a clear warning earlier, *if* the Czar had further delayed Russian mobilization against Austria and then Germany, and *if* the German offensive war plans had not been able to depend upon a preemptive *coup de main* against Liege and the decisive battle in France before Russian mobilization was completed in the East, *then* it is possible, just possible, that Bethmann-Hollweg would have had the time and the courage necessary to apply sufficient pressure on Vienna to accept the "Halt in Belgrade." And if this had occurred, 1914 might today appear as only another one of series of Balkan crises that almost led to a world war. (Sagan 1986: 169)

Riker:

The process of confusion concerning the cause of α [World War I], which, being ambiguous, cannot properly be said to have a cause, starts with the assertion that the cause of B [the Austro-Serbian war] is the assassination at Sarajevo, event D. It can perhaps be demonstrated by valid arguments – or at least by arguments likely to be accepted by many historians – that the assassination of Franz Ferdinand is a sufficient condition of the Austro-Serbian war; and (somewhat dubiously, however) it can even be argued that it is was a necessary condition. (Riker 1957: 63–4)

References

Adomeit, H. 1998. *Imperial overstretch: Germany in Soviet policy from Stalin to Gorbachev.* Baden Baden: Nomos Verlagsgesellschaft.

Akhromeev, S., and Kornienko, G. 1992. *Glazami marshala i diplomata: kritich-eskii vzgliad na vneshniuiu politiku SSSR do i posle 1985 goda.* Moscow: Mezhdunarodnye Otnosheniia.

Albertini, L. 1980. *The origins of the war of 1914.* Westport: Greenwood.

Allain, J.-C. 1976. *Agadir 1911: une crise impérialiste en Europe pour la conquête du Maroc.* Paris: University of Paris.

Allison, G. 1971. *Essence of decision: explaining the Cuban missile crisis.* Boston: Little Brown.

Almond, G., and Genco, S. 1977. Clouds, clocks, and the study of politics. *World Politics* 29:489–522.

Arbatov, G. 1991. *Zatianuvsheesia vyzdorovlenie, 1953–1985: videtel'stvo sovre-mennika [A prolonged recovery (1953–1985) testimony of a contempo-rary].* Moscow: Mezhdunarodnye Otnosheniia.

Arbatov, Z. 1990. *Vozhdi i sovetniki. O Khrushcheve, Andropove, i ne tol'ko o nikh [Leaders and advisers: on Khrushchev, Andropov, and not only them].* Moscow: Politizdat.

Aron, R. 1951. *Les guerres en chaîne.* Paris: Gallimard.

———. 1986 (1938). *Introduction à la philosophie de l'histoire: essai sur les limites de l'objecivité historique,* 2nd edition. Paris: Gallimard.

Aslund, A. 1991. *Gorbachev's struggle for economic reform.* London: Pinter.

Babbie, Earl. 1998. *The practice of social research,* 8th edition. Belmont, CA: Wadsworth.

Barnes, H. 1926. *The genesis of the world war: an introduction to the problem of war guilt.* New York: Knopf.

Becker, A. 1994. Intelligence fiasco or reasoned accounting? CIA estimates of Soviet GNP. *Post-Soviet Affairs* 10:291–329.

Behschnitt, W. 1980. *Nationalismus unter Serben und Kroaten, 1830–1914.* Munich: Oldenbourg.

Bennett, A. 1999. *Condemned to repetition? The rise, fall, and reprise of Soviet-Russian military interventionism, 1973–1996.* Cambridge, MA: MIT Press.

Bennett, A., and Elman, C. 2006. Complex causal relations and case study methods: the example of path dependence. *Political Analysis* 14:250–67.

Berghahn, V. 1973. *Germany and the approach of war in 1914.* New York: Saint Martin's Press.

Bernstein, S., et al. 2000. God gave physics the easy problems. *European Journal of International Relations* 6:43-76.

Bhaskar, R. 1979. *The possibility of naturalism: a philosophical critique of the contemporary human sciences.* Brighton: Harvester.

Blackbourn, D., and Eley, G. 1984. *The peculiarities of German history: bourgeois politics and society in nineteenth century Germany.* Oxford: Oxford University Press.

Blacker, C. 1993. *Hostage to revolution: Gorbachev and Soviet security policy, 1985-1991.* New York: Council on Foreign Relations.

Boeckh, K. 1996. *Von den Balkankriegen zum Ersten Weltkrieg: Kleinstaaten-politik und ethnische Selbstbestimmung auf dem Balkan.* Munich: R. Oldenbourg.

Bova, R. 1988. The Soviet military and economic reform. *Soviet Studies* 40:385-405.

Boynton, R. 1999. Thinking the unthinkable: a young historian proposes that the Great War was England's fault. *New Yorker* 12:43-50.

Bracken, P. 1983. *The command and control of nuclear forces.* New Haven: Yale University Press.

Brams, S. 1985. *Superpower games: applying game theory to superpower conflict.* New Haven: Yale University Press.

Braumoeller, B., and Goertz, G. 2000. The methodology of necessary conditions. *American Journal of Political Science* 44:844-58.

Breslauer, G., and Lebow, R. 2004. Leadership and the end of the Cold War: a counterfactual thought experiment. In R. Herrmann and R. Lebow (eds.) *Ending the Cold War.* London: Palgrave.

Bridge, F. 1972. *From Sadowa to Sarajevo: the foreign policy of Austria-Hungary, 1866-1914.* London: Routledge & Kegan Paul.

———. 1990. *The Habsburg monarchy among the great powers, 1815-1918.* New York: Berg.

British documents on the origins of the war, 1898-1914, 11 vols. 1926-38. G. Gooch and H. Temperley (eds.). London: His Majesty's Stationary Office.

Brooks, S. 1997. Dueling realisms. *International Organization* 51:445-77.

———. 1999. The globalization of production and the changing benefits of conquest. *Journal of Conflict Resolution* 43:646-70.

———. 2001. The globalization of production and international security. Ph.D. Dissertation, Yale University.

Brooks, S., and Wohlforth, W. 2000. Power, globalization, and the end of the Cold War: reevaluating a landmark case for ideas. *International Security* 25:5-53.

———. 2002. From old thinking to new thinking in qualitative research. *International Security* 26:93-111.

———. 2003. Economic constraints and the end of the Cold War. In W. Wohlforth (ed.) *Cold War endgame: oral history, analysis, debates.* University Park: Pennsylvania State University Press.

————. 2004. Economic constraints and the turn toward superpower cooperation in the 1980s. In O. Njnillstad (ed.) *The last decade of the Cold War: from conflict escalation to conflict transformation: the Cold War in the 1980's.* London: Frank Cass.

Brown, A. 1996. *The Gorbachev factor.* Oxford: Oxford University Press.

Brown, J. 1988. *Eastern Europe and communist rule.* Durham: Duke University Press.

Brown, R., and Fish, D. 1983. The psychological causality implicit in language. *Cognition* 14:237-73.

Bueno de Mesquita, B. 1981. *The war trap.* New Haven: Yale University Press.

Bukovansky, M. 1997. American identity and neutral rights from independence to the War of 1812. *International Organization* 51:209-43.

Bunce, V. 1985. The empire strikes back: the evolution of the eastern bloc from Soviet asset to liability. *International Organization* 39:1-46.

Burkhardt, J. 1996. Kriegsgrund Geschichte? 1870, 1813, 1756 – historische Argumente und Orientierungen bei Ausbruch des Ersten Weltkriegs. In J. Burkhardt et al. (eds.) *Lange und Kurze Wege in den Ersten Weltkrieg.* Munich: Ernst Vögel.

Burlatskii, F. 1990. *Vozhdi i Sovetniki. O Khrushchev, Andropove, i ne tol'ko o nikh.* Moscow: Politizdat.

Butterfield, H. 1965. Sir Edward Grey in July 1914. *Historical Studies* 5:1-25.

Byman, D., and Pollack, K. 2001. Let us now praise great men: bringing the statesman back in. *International Security* 25:107-46.

Canis, K. 1997. *Von Bismarck zur Weltpolitik: Deutsche Aussenpolitik 1890 bis 1902.* Berlin: Akademie Verlag.

Cederman, L.-E. 1997. *Emergent actors in world politics: how states and nations develop and dissolve.* Princeton: Princeton University Press.

Checkel, J. 1993. Ideas, institutions, and the Gorbachev foreign policy revolution. *World Politics* 45:271-300.

————. 1997. *Ideas and international political change: Soviet/Russian behavior and the end of the Cold War.* New Haven: Yale University Press.

————. 1998. The constructivist turn in international relations theory. *World Politics* 50:324-48.

Cherniaev, A. 1993. *Shest' let s Gorbachevym: po dnevnikovym zapisiam [Six years with Gorbachev: notes from a diary].* Moscow: Progress.

————. 1995. *Moia zhizn' i moe vremia [My life and times].* Moscow: Mezhdunarodnye Otnosheniia.

————. 2000. *My six years with Gorbachev.* University Park: Pennsylvania State University Press.

Choucri, N., and North, R. 1975. *Nations in conflict: national growth and international violence.* San Francisco: W. H. Freeman.

Christensen, T., and Snyder, J. 1990. Chain gangs and passed bucks: predicting alliance patterns in multipolarity. *International Organization* 44:138-68.

Churchill, W. 1931. *The world crisis,* 4 vols. New York: Scribner.

Cioffi-Revilla, C. 1998. *Politics and uncertainty: theory, models and applications.* Cambridge: Cambridge University Press.

Clark, C. 1993. Relative backwardness in eastern Europe: an application of the technological gap hypothesis. *Economic Systems* 17:167–93.

Coetzee, M. 1990. *The German Army League: popular nationalism in Wilhelmine Germany.* New York: Oxford University Press.

Cohen, M. 1942. Causation and its application to history. *Journal of the History of Ideas* 3:12–29.

Colaresi, M., and Thompson, W. 2002. Hot spots or hot hands? Serial crisis behavior, escalating risks and rivalry. *Journal of Politics* 64:1175–98.

Collier, R., and Collier, D. 1991. *Shaping the political arena: critical junctures, the labor movement, and regime dynamics in Latin America.* Princeton: Princeton University Press.

Conrad von Hötzendorff, F. 1921–25. *Aus meiner Dienstzeit, 1906–1918, 5 vols.* Vienna: Rikola.

Cooper, J. 1991. Soviet technology and the potential of joint ventures. In Sherr. A. et al. (eds.) *International joint ventures: Soviet and western perspectives.* New York: Quorum Books.

Copeland, D. 1999–2000. Trade expectations and the outbreak of peace: détente 1970–1974 and the end of the Cold War 1985–1991. *Security Studies* 9:15–58.

———. 2000. *The origins of major war.* Ithaca: Cornell University Press.

Copi, I., and Cohen, C. 1990. *Introduction to logic,* 8th edition. London: Macmillan.

Craig, G. 1964. *The politics of the Prussian army, 1640–1945.* New York: Oxford University Press.

———. 1978. *Germany, 1866–1945.* Oxford: Oxford University Press.

Crampton, R. 1979. *The hollow détente: Anglo-German relations in the Balkans, 1911–1914.* Atlantic Highlands: Humanities Press.

D'Lugo, D. and Rogowski, R. 1993. The Anglo-German naval race and comparative constitutional "fitness." In R. Rosecrance and A. Stein (eds.) *The domestic bases of grand strategy.* Ithaca: Cornell University Press.

Dedijer, V. 1966. *The road to Sarajevo.* New York: Simon & Schuster.

Deudney, D., and Ikenberry, G. 1991–2. The international sources of Soviet change. *International Security* 16:74–118.

Dicken, P. 1998. *Global shift: transforming the world economy,* 3rd edition. London: Chapman.

Diehl, P., and Goertz, G. 2000. *War and peace in international rivalry.* Ann Arbor: University of Michigan Press.

Doran, C., and Parsons, W. 1980. War and the cycle of relative power. *American Political Science Review* 74:947–65.

Downs, G. 1989. The rational deterrence debate. *World Politics* 41:225–37.

Dray, W. 1957. *Laws and explanation in history.* Oxford: Oxford University Press.

Dunning, J. 1993. *Multinational enterprises and the global economy.* Reading: Addison-Wesley.

———. 1995. Reappraising the eclectic paradigm in an age of alliance capitalism. *Journal of International Business Studies* 26:461–91.

Easterly, W., and Fischer, S. 1995. The Soviet economic decline. *World Bank Economic Review* 9:347-71.

Eckstein, H. 1975. Case study and theory in political science. In F. Greenstein and N. Polsby (eds.) *Handbook of political science, vol. 7 Strategies of inquiry.* Reading: Addison-Wesley.

Eckstein, M. 1971. Sir Edward Grey and Imperial Germany in 1914. *Journal of Contemporary History* 6:121-31.

Eley, G. 1980. *Reshaping the German right: radical nationalism and political change after Bismarck.* New Haven: Yale University Press.

Ellman, M., and Kontorovich, V. 1997. The collapse of the Soviet system and the memoir literature. *Europe-Asia Studies* 49:259-79.

———. 1998. *The destruction of the Soviet economic system: an insider's account.* Armonk: M.E. Sharpe.

Elster, J. 1978. *Logic and society: contradictions and possible worlds.* New York: John Wiley & Sons.

English, R. 1997. Sources, methods, and competing perspectives on the end of the Cold War. *Diplomatic History* 21:283-94.

———. 2000. *Russia and the idea of the west: Gorbachev, intellectuals, and the end of the Cold War.* New York: Columbia University Press.

———. 2002. Power, ideas, and new evidence on the Cold War's end: a reply to Brooks and Wohlforth. *International Security* 26:70-92.

———. 2003. The road(s) not taken: causality and contingency in analysis of the Cold War's end. In W. Wohlforth (ed.) *Cold War endgame: oral history, analysis, debates.* University Park: Pennsylvania State University Press.

———. 2005. The sociology of new thinking: elites, identity change, and the Cold War's end. *Journal of Cold War Studies* 7:243-80.

Erdmann, K. 1984. War guilt 1914 reconsidered: a balance of new research. In H. Koch (ed.) *The origins of the first world war,* 2nd edition. Oxford: Oxford University Press.

Evangelista, M. 1995. The paradox of state strength: transnational relations, domestic structures, and security policy in Russia and the Soviet Union. *International Organization* 49:1-38.

———. 1999. *Unarmed forces: the transnational movement to end the Cold War.* Ithaca: Cornell University Press.

———. 2001. Norms, heresthetics, and the end of the Cold War. *Journal of Cold War Studies* 3:5-35.

Evans, R. 1988. The Habsburg monarchy and the coming of war. In R. Evans and H. von Strandmann (eds.) *The coming of the first world war.* Oxford: Oxford University Press.

Farrar, L. 1972. The limits of choice: July 1914 reconsidered. *Journal of Conflict Resolution* 16:1-25.

———. 1973. *The short-war illusion: German policy, strategy & domestic affairs, August-December 1914.* Santa Barbara: ABC-Clio.

Fay, S. 1966. *The origins of the world war.* New York: Free Press.

Fearon, J. 1991. Counterfactuals and hypothesis testing in political science. *World Politics* 43:169–95.

———. 1997. What is identity as we now use the word? Manuscript. University of Chicago.

Fenoaltea, S. 1973. The discipline and they: notes on counterfactuals in the new economic history. *Journal of European Economic History* 2:729–46.

Ferguson, N. 1999a. The kaiser's European Union: what if Britain had 'stood aside' in August 1914. In N. Ferguson (ed.) *Virtual history: alternatives and counterfactuals.* New York: Basic Books.

———. 1999b. Virtual history: towards a 'chaotic' theory of the past. In N. Ferguson (ed.) *Virtual history: alternatives and counterfactuals.* New York: Basic Books.

———. 1999c. *The pity of war: explaining World War I.* New York: Basic Books.

Feshbach, M., and Friendly, A. 1992. *Ecocide in the USSR: health and nature under siege.* New York: Basic Books.

Figes, O. 1998. *A people's tragedy: the Russian revolution 1891–1924.* New York: Penguin.

Firth, N., and Noren, J. 1998. *Soviet defense spending: a history of CIA estimates, 1950–1990.* College Station: Texas A&M Press.

Fischer, D. 1970. *Historians' fallacies: toward a logic of historical thought.* New York: Harper and Row.

Fischer, F. 1964. *Griff nach der Weltmacht: die Kriegszielpolitik des kaiserlichen Deutschland, 1914–18,* 3rd edition. Düsseldorf: Droste.

———. 1967. *Germany's aims in the first world war.* New York: Norton.

———. 1969. *Krieg der Illusionen: die deutsche Politik von 1911 bis 1914.* Düsseldorf: Droste.

———. 1974. *World power or decline: the controversy over Germany's aims in the First World War.* New York: Norton.

———. 1975. *War of illusions: German policies from 1911–1914.* New York: Norton.

———. 1988. The miscalculation of English neutrality. In S. Wank, et al. (eds.) *The mirror of history.* Santa Barbara, Calif.: ABC-Clio.

Fitzgerald, M. 1987. Marshall Ogarkov and the new revolution in Soviet military affairs. *Defense Analysis* 3:9–10.

Forsberg, T. 1999. Power, interests and trust: explaining Gorbachev's choices at the end of the Cold War. *Review of International Studies* 25:603–21.

Förster, S. 1995. Der deutsche Generalstab und die Illusion des kurzen Krieges, 1871–1914: Metakritik eines Mythos. *Militärgeschichtliche Mitteilungen* 54:61–95.

Franz, G. 1943. *Erzherzog Franz Ferdinand und die Pläne zur Reform der Habsburger Monarchie.* R. M. Rohrer: Brünn.

French, D. 1986. *British strategy and war aims, 1914–1916.* London: Allen and Unwin.

———. 1995. *The strategy of the Lloyd George coalition, 1916–1918.* Oxford: Oxford University Press.

Friedberg, A. 1988. *The weary titan: Britain and the experience of relative decline, 1895-1905.* Princeton: Princeton University Press.

Gaddis, J. 1989. Hanging tough paid off. *Bulletin of the Atomic Scientists* 45:11-14.

Gaddy, C. 1997. *The price of the past: Russia's struggle with the legacy of a militarized economy.* Washington, DC: Brookings Institution.

Gaidar, E. 1999. *Days of defeat and victory.* Seattle: University of Washington Press.

Galántai, J. 1989. *Hungary in the First World War.* Budapest: Akadémiai Kiadó.

Gallie, W. 1955. Explanations in history and the genetic sciences. *Mind* 64:160-80.

Gareev, M. 1996. Voenno-tekhnicheskaia politika: Retrospektivnyy analiz. *Problemy Prognozirovaniia* 3:163-7.

Garthoff, R. 1994. *The great transition: American-Soviet relations and the end of the Cold War.* Washington, DC: Brookings Institution.

Geiss, I. 1966. The outbreak of the first world war and German war aims. *Journal of Contemporary History* 1:75-91.

———. 1976. *German foreign policy, 1871-1914.* London: Routledge & Kegan Paul.

Geiss, I. (ed.) 1967. *July 1914: the outbreak of the First World War: selected documents.* London: Batsford.

George, A. (ed.) 1991a. *Avoiding war: problems of crisis management.* Boulder: Westview Press.

———. 1991b. The Persian Gulf crisis, 1990-1991. In A. George (ed.) *Avoiding war: problems of crisis management.* Boulder: Westview Press.

George, A., and Bennett, A. 2005. *Case studies and theory development.* Cambridge, MA: MIT Press.

Geron, L. 1990. *Soviet foreign economic policy under perestroika.* London: Pinter.

Gerring, J. 2005. Causation: a unified framework for the social sciences. *Journal of Theoretical Politics* 17:163-98.

Gilpin, R. 1981. *War and change in world politics.* Cambridge: Cambridge University Press.

Glymour, C. 1986. Statistics and causal inference: comment: statistics and metaphysics. *Journal of the American Statistical Association* 81:964-66.

Goemans, H. 2000. *War and punishment: the causes of war termination and the First World War.* Princeton: Princeton University Press.

Goertz, G. 1994. *Contexts of international politics.* Cambridge: Cambridge University Press.

———. 2004. Assessing the importance of necessary or sufficient conditions in fuzzy-set social science. Manuscript. University of Arizona.

———. 2005. Necessary condition hypotheses as deterministic or probabilistic: does it matter? (with discussion). *Qualitative Methods: Newsletter of the American Political Science Association Organized Section on Qualitative Methods* 3:23-32.

Goertz, G., and Starr, H. (eds.). 2003. *Necessary conditions: theory, methodology, and applications.* New York: Rowman & Littlefield.

Goldstein, J., and Keohane, R. (eds.). 1993. *Ideas and foreign policy: beliefs, institutions, and political change.* Ithaca: Cornell University Press.

Goldstein, J., and Keohane, R. 1993. Ideas and foreign policy: an analytic framework. In J. Goldstein and R. Keohane (eds.) *Ideas and foreign policy: belief institutions and political change.* Ithaca: Cornell University Press.

Gomulka, S., and Nove, A. 1984. *East-west technology transfer, vol 1.* Paris: Organization for Economic Cooperation and Development.

Gooch, G. 1923. *Franco-German relations, 1871–1914.* New York: Russell & Russell.

Gorbachev, M. 1987. *Izbrannye rechi i stat'i [Selected speeches and writings], vol 2.* Moscow: Izdatel'stvo Politicheskoi Literatury.

———. 1996. *Memoirs.* New York: Doubleday.

Gordon, M. 1974. Domestic conflict and the origins of the First World War: the British and German cases. *Journal of Modern History* 46:191–226.

Grachev, A. 1994. *Kremlevskaia khronika [Kremlin chronicle].* Moscow: EKSMO.

Grigg, J. 1985. *Lloyd George, from peace to war, 1912–1916.* London: Methuen.

Gromyko, A. 1997. *Andrei Gromyko. V labirintakh Kremlia. Vospominania i razmyshleniia syna.* Moscow: Avtor.

Hagedoorn, J. 1993. Understanding the role of strategic technology partnering: interorganizational modes of cooperation and sectoral differences. *Strategic Management Journal* 14:371–85.

Halberstam, D. 1972. *The best and the brightest.* New York: Random House.

Hanak, H. 1962. *Great Britain and Austria-Hungary during the First World War.* New York: Oxford University Press.

Harré, R., and Secord, P. 1972. *The explanation of social behaviour.* Oxford: Basil Blackwell.

Harrison, M. 1993. Soviet economic growth since 1928: the alternative statistics of GI Khanin. *Europe-Asia Studies* 45:141–67.

Hempel, C. 1942. The function of general laws in history. *Journal of Philosophy* 39:35–48.

Herman, R. 1996. Identity, norms, and national security: the Soviet foreign policy revolution and the end of the Cold War. In P. Katzenstein (ed.) *The culture of national security.* New York: Columbia University Press.

Herrmann, D. 1996. *The arming of Europe and the making of the first world war.* Princeton: Princeton University Press.

Herrmann, R., and Lebow, R. 2004. What was the Cold War? When and why did it end? In R. Herrmann and R. Lebow (eds.) *Learning from the Cold War.* London: Palgrave.

Herspring, D. 1990. *The Soviet high command, 1967–1989: personalities and politics.* Princeton: Princeton University Press.

Herwig, H. 1998. *The First World War: Germany and Austria-Hungary, 1914–1918.* London: Arnold.

Hewett, E., and Gaddy, C. 1992. *Open for business: Russia's return to the global economy.* Washington, DC: Brookings.

Hexter, J. 1971. *The history primer.* New York: Basic Books.

Hildebrand, K. 1995. *Das vergangene Reich: Deutsche Aussenpolitik von Bismarck zu Hitler, 1871-1945.* Stuttgart: Deutsche Verlags-Anstalt.

Hillgruber, A. 1966. Riezlers Theorie des kalkulieren Risikos und Bethmann Hollwegs politische Konzeption in der Julikrise 1914. *Historische Zeitschrift* 202:333-51.

Hinsley, F. 1995. The origins of the first world war. In K. Wilson (ed.) *Decisions for war, 1914.* New York: Saint Martin's Press.

Hoffmann, E., and Laird, R. 1982. *"The scientific-technological revolution" and Soviet foreign policy.* New York: Pergamon Press.

Holborn, H. 1951. *The political collapse of Europe.* New York: Alfred A. Knopf.

Holland, P. 1986a. Statistics and causal inference. *Journal of the American Statistical Association* 81:945-60.

——. 1986b. Statistics and causal inference: rejoinder. *Journal of the American Statistical Association* 81:968-70.

Hollander, P. 1999. *Political will and personal belief: the decline and fall of Soviet communism.* New Haven: Yale University Press.

Holsti, K. 1996. *The state, war, and the state of war.* Cambridge: Cambridge University Press.

Holsti, O. 1972. *Crisis, escalation, war.* Montreal: McGill-Queen's University Press.

Honoré, T., and Hart, H. L. A. 1985. *Causation in the law,* 2nd edition. Oxford: Oxford University Press.

Hoopes, T. 1969. *The limits of intervention: an inside account of how the Johnson policy of escalation was reversed.* New York: David McKay.

Hosking, G. 1997. *Russia: people and empire 1552-1917.* London: HarperCollins.

Hough, J. 1986. *The struggle for the third world: Soviet debates and American options.* Washington, DC: Brookings.

——. 1997. *Democratization and revolution in the USSR, 1985-1991.* Washington, DC: Brookings Institution.

——. 1988. *Opening up the Soviet economy.* Washington, DC: Brookings Institution.

——. 1988. *Russia and the west: Gorbachev and the politics of reform.* New York: Simon and Schuster.

Howard, M. 1998. Out of the trenches. *Times Literary Supplement* 13:23-4.

Humphreys, P. 1989. *The chances of explanation: causal explanation in the social, medical and physical sciences.* Princeton: Princeton University Press.

Ingram, E. 2001. Hegemony, global power and world power: Britain II as world leader. In C. Elman and M. Elman (eds.) *International history and international relations theory: bridges and boundaries.* Cambridge, MA: MIT Press.

Iakovlev, A. 1994. *Gorkaia chasha. Bol'shevizm i reformatsiia Rossii.* Iaroslavl': Verkhne-Volzhskoe.

Ivashov, L. 1993. *Marshal Iazov, Rokovoi avgust 91-go: Pravda o putche [Marshal Yazov, that fateful August of 1991: the truth about the putsch].* VelÕsk: VelÕti.

Janis, I., and Mann, L. 1977. *Decision-making: a psychological analysis of conflict, choice, and commitment.* New York: Free Press.

Jarausch, K. 1969. The illusion of limited war: chancellor Bethmann Hollweg's calculated risk, July 1914. *Central European History* 2:48–76.

———. 1973. *The enigmatic chancellor: Bethmann Hollweg and the hubris of Imperial Germany.* New Haven: Yale University Press.

Jelavich, B. 1991. *Russia's Balkan entanglements 1806–1914.* New York: Cambridge University Press.

Jervis, R. 1976. *Perception and misperception in international politics.* Princeton: Princeton University Press.

———. 1997. *System effects: complexity in political and social life.* Princeton: Princeton University Press.

Joll, J. 1984. *The origins of the First World War.* London: Longman.

———. 1992. *The origins of the First World War,* 2nd edition. London: Longman.

Jones, D., Bremer, S., and Singer, J. 1996. Militarized interstate disputes, 1816–1992: rationale, coding rules, and empirical patterns. *Conflict Management and Peace Science* 15:163–212.

Jones, G. 1996. *The evolution of international business.* London: Routledge.

Jones, J. 1980. *Britain and the world, 1649–1815.* Atlantic Highlands: Humanities Press.

Kahneman, D. 1995. Varieties of counterfactual thinking. In N. Roese and J Olson (eds.) *What might have been: the social psychology of counterfactual thinking.* Hillsdale: Lawrence Erlbaum.

Kahneman, D., and Tversky, A. 1979. Prospect theory: an analysis of decision under risk. *Econometrica* 47:263–92.

Kahneman, D., and Miller, D. 1986. Norm theory: comparing reality to its alternatives. *Psychological Review* 93:418–39.

Kaiser, D. 1983. Germany and the origins of the first world war. *Journal of Modern History* 55:442–74.

Kantorowicz, H. 1931. *The spirit of British policy and the myth of the encirclement of Germany.* London: Allen & Unwin.

Katzenstein, P. 1996. Introduction: alternative perspectives on national security. In P. Katzenstein (ed.) *The culture of national security: norms, identity, and world politics.* New York: Columbia University Press.

Katzenstein, P., Keohane, R., and Krasner, S. 1998. *International Organization* and the study of world politics. *International Organization* 52:645–85.

Kautsky, K. 1924. *Outbreak of the world war: German documents.* New York: Oxford University Press.

Kegley, C. 1993. The neoidealist moment in international studies? Realist myths and the new international realities. *International Studies Quarterly* 37:131–46.

Keiger, J. 1983. *France and the origins of the first world war.* New York: St. Martin's.

———. 1997. *Raymond Poincaré.* New York: Cambridge University Press.

Kendall, P. (ed.) 1982. *The varied sociology of Paul F. Lazarsfeld.* New York: Columbia University Press.

Kendall, P., and Wolf, K. 1949. The analysis of deviant cases in communications research. In P. Lazarsfeld and F. Stanton (eds.) *Communications research.* New York: Harper.

Kennedy, P. (ed.) 1979. *The war plans of the great powers, 1880–1914.* Boston: Allen & Unwin.

———. 1981. *The realities behind diplomacy: background influences on British external policy, 1865–1980.* London: Allen and Unwin.

———. 1982. The Kaiser and German Weltpolitik: reflections on Wilhelm II's place in the making of German foreign policy. In C. Röhl and N. Sombart (eds.) *Kaiser Wilhelm II: new interpretations.* Cambridge: Cambridge University Press.

———. 1987. *The rise and fall of the great powers: economic change and military conflict from 1500 to 2000.* New York: Random House.

Khanin, G. 1993. *Sovietskiy ekonomicheskiy rost: analiz zapadnykh otsenok [Soviet economic growth: An analysis of western assessments].* Novosibirsk: EKOR.

King, G., Keohane, R., and Verba, S. 1994. *Designing social inquiry: scientific inference in qualitative research.* Princeton: Princeton University Press.

Kingdon, J. 1984. *Agendas, alternatives, and public policies.* Boston: Little, Brown.

———. 1995. *Agendas, alternatives, and public policies,* 2nd edition. Boston: Little, Brown.

Knock, T. 1992. *To end all wars: Woodrow Wilson and the quest for a new world order.* Princeton: Princeton University Press.

Knopf, J. 1993. Beyond two-level games: domestic-international interaction in the intermediate-range nuclear forces negotiations. *International Organization* 47:599–628.

Kobrin, S. 1997. The architecture of globalization: state sovereignty in a networked global economy. In J. Dunning (ed.) *Governments, globalization and international business.* Oxford: Oxford University Press.

Koch, H. 1972a. Introduction. In H. Koch (ed.) *The origins of the first world war: great power rivalry and German war aims.* London: Macmillan.

———. (ed.) 1972b. *The origins of the first world war: great power rivalry and German war aims.* London: Macmillan.

Kokoshin, A. 1989. *Soviet strategic thought, 1917–1991.* Cambridge, MA: MIT Press.

Kolodziej, E. 1997. Order, welfare and legitimacy: a systemic explanation for the Soviet collapse and the end of the Cold War. *International Politics* 34:111–51.

Kontorovich, V. 1990. The long-run decline in Soviet R&D productivity. In H. Rowen and C. Wolf (eds.) *The impoverished superpower: perestroika and the Soviet military burden.* San Francisco: Institute for Contemporary Studies.

————. 1992. Technological progress and research and development. In M. Ell-man and V. Kontorovich (eds.) *The disintegration of the Soviet economic system.* London: Routledge.

Kornienko, G. 1994. *Kholodnaia voina: Svidetel'stvo ee uchastnika [The Cold War: testimony of a participant].* Moscow: Mezhdunarodnye Otnosheniia.

Koslowski, R., and Kratochwil, F. 1994. Understanding change in international politics: the Soviet empire's demise and the international system. *International Organization* 48:215–47.

Kotz, D. 1997. *Revolution from above: the demise of the Soviet system.* London: Routledge.

Kowert, P., and Legro, J. 1996. Norms, identity and their limits: a theoretical reprise. In P. Katzenstein (ed.) *The culture of national security: norms, identity, and world politics.* New York: Columbia University Press.

Kramer, K. 1996. The Soviet Union and eastern Europe: spheres of influence. In N. Woods (ed.) *Explaining international relations since 1945.* Oxford: Oxford University Press.

Kramer, M. 1999. Ideology and the Cold War. *Review of International Studies* 25:539–76.

————. 2001. Realism, ideology, and the end of the Cold War: a reply to William Wohlforth. *Review of International Studies* 27:119–30.

Kronenbitter, G. 1996. 'Nur los lassen' Österreich-Ungarn und der Wille zum Krieg. In Burkhardt et al. (eds.) *Lange und kurze Wege in den Ersten Weltkrieg: vier Augsburger Beiträge zur Kriegsursachenforschung.* München: Vögel.

Kupchan, C. 1994. *The vulnerability of empire.* Ithaca: Cornell University Press.

Lake, D., and Powell, R. (eds.). 1999. *Strategic choice and international relations.* Princeton: Princeton University Press.

Lakoff, G. 1973. Hedges: a study of meaning criteria and the logic of fuzzy concepts. *Journal of Philosophical Logic* 2:458–508.

Lamborn, A. 1997. Theory and the politics in world politics. *International Studies Quarterly* 41:187–214.

Larson, D. 1997. *Anatomy of mistrust: US–Soviet relations during the Cold War.* Ithaca: Cornell University Press.

Larson, D., and Shevchenko, A. 2003. Shortcut to greatness: the new thinking and the revolution in Soviet foreign policy. *International Organization* 57:77–109.

Lazarsfeld, P., Pasanella, A., and Rosenberg, M. (eds.). 1972.*Continuities in the language of social research.* New York: Free Press.

Lebow, R. 1981. *Between peace and war: the nature of international crisis.* Baltimore: Johns Hopkins University Press.

————. 1984. Windows of opportunity: do states jump through them? *International Security* 9:147–86.

————. 1985. The Soviet offensive in Europe: the Schlieffen Plan revisited? *International Security* 9:44–78.

————. 1987. *Nuclear crisis management: a dangerous illusion.* Ithaca: Cornell University Press.

——. 1994. The long peace, the end of the Cold War, and the failure of realism. *International Organization* 48:249-77.

——. 1995. The search for accommodation: Gorbachov in comparative perspective. In R. Lebow and T. Risse (eds.) *Understanding the end of the Cold War.* Baltimore: Johns Hopkins University Press.

——. 2000. What's so different about a counterfactual? *World Politics* 52:550-85.

——. 2003. A data set named desire: a reply to William R. Thompson. *International Studies Quarterly* 47:475-8.

Lebow, R., and Stein, J. 1994. *We all lost the Cold War.* Princeton: Princeton University Press.

——. 2004. Bridging levels of analysis: a nonlinear approach to the end of the Cold War. In R. Herrmann and R. Lebow (eds.) *Ending the Cold War.* London: Palgrave.

Legostayev, V. 1991. God 1987-yi – peremena logiki, *Den',* 14.

Leng, R. 1983. When will they ever learn? Coercive bargaining in recurrent crises. *Journal of Conflict Resolution* 27:379-419.

Leonov, L. 1994. *Likhlet'e [Cursed years].* Moscow: Mezhdunarodnye Otnosheniia.

Lévesque, J. 1997. *The enigma of 1989: the USSR and the liberation of eastern Europe.* Berkeley: University of California Press.

Levy, J. S. 1983. Misperception and the causes of war. *World Politics* 36:76-99.

——. 1986. Organizational routines and the causes of war. *International Studies Quarterly* 30:193-222.

——. 1987. Declining power and the preventive motivation for war. *World Politics* 40:82-107.

——. 1988. Domestic politics and war. *Journal of Interdisciplinary History* 18:653-73.

——. 1990/91. Preferences, constraints, and choices in July 1914. *International Security* 15:151-86.

——. 1994. Learning and foreign policy: sweeping a conceptual minefield. *International Organization* 48:279-312.

——. 2001. Explaining events and developing theories: history, political science, and the analysis of international relations. In C. Elman and M. Elman (eds.) *Bridges and boundaries: historians, political scientists, and the study of international relations.* Cambridge, MA: MIT Press.

——. 2002. Necessary conditions in case studies: preferences, constraints, and choices in July 1914. In G. Goertz and H. Starr (eds.) *Necessary conditions: theory, methodology, and applications.* New York: Rowman & Littlefield.

Levy, J. S., and Ali, S. 1998. From commercial competition to strategic rivalry to war: the evolution of the Anglo-Dutch rivalry, 1609-1652. In P. Diehl (ed.) *The dynamics of enduring rivalries.* Urbana: University of Illinois Press.

Levy, J., and Mabe, W. 2004. Politically motivated opposition to war. *International Studies Review* 6:65-83.

Lewis, D. 1973 *Counterfactuals.* Cambridge, MA: Harvard University Press.
———. 1986a. Causation. Postscripts to "Causation". *Philosophical papers,* vol. II. Oxford.: Oxford University Press.
Lieber, K. A. 2006. IR theory and the new historiography of World War I. Paper presented at the annual meeting of the American Political Science Association.
Lieberson, S. 2003. Review of "Fuzzy-set social science". *Cognitive Science* 30:331–4.
Lieven, D. 1983. *Russia and the origins of the first world war.* London: Macmillan.
Lijphart, A. 1971. Comparative politics and the comparative method. *American Political Science Review* 65:682–93.
Lloyd, J. 1993. Österreich-Ungarn vor dem Kriegsausbruch. In R. Melville (ed.) *Deutschland und Europa, 2 vols.* Munich: Oldenbourg.
Luhmann, N. 1997. *Die Gesellschaft der Gesellschaft, 2 vols.* Frankfurt am Main: Suhrkamp.
Lundestad, G. 1986. Empire by invitation: the United States and Western Europe, 1945–1952. *Journal of Peace Research* 23:263–77.
Lyakhovsky, A. 1995. *Tragediia i doblest' afgana [The tragedy and valor of the Afghan].* Moscow: GPI Iskona.
Lynn-Jones, S. 1986. Détente and deterrence: Anglo-German relations, 1911–1914. *International Security* 11:121–50.
Mackie, J. 1974. *The cement of the universe: a study of causation.* Oxford: Oxford University Press.
———. 1976. Causes and conditions. In M. Brand (ed.) *The nature of causation.* Urbana: University of Illinois Press.
Maddison, A. 1995. *Monitoring the world economy, 1820–1992.* Paris: OECD.
Mahoney, J. 1999. Nominal, ordinal, and narrative appraisal in macrocausal analysis. *American Journal of Sociology* 104:1154–96.
———. 2000. Path dependency in historical sociology. *Theory and Society* 29:507–48.
———. 2001. *The legacies of liberalism: path dependence and political regimes in Central America.* Baltimore: Johns Hopkins University Press.
———. 2004. Comparative-historical methodology. *Annual Review of Sociology* 30:81–101.
Mahoney, J., and Rueschemeyer, D. (eds.). 2003. *Comparative historical analysis in the social sciences.* Cambridge: Cambridge University Press.
Maier, C. 1988. Wargames: 1914–1919. *Journal of Interdisciplinary History* 18:819–49.
Marer, P. 1986. Reforms in the USSR and eastern Europe: is there a link? In A. Braun (ed.) *The Soviet-East European relationship in the Gorbachev era: the prospects for adaptation.* Boulder: Westview Press.
Mastanduno, M. 1992. *Economic containment: CoCom and the politics of east-west trade.* Ithaca: Cornell University Press.
Mastny, V. 1998. The Soviet non-invasion of Poland in 1980–81 and the end of the Cold War. Manuscript. Working Paper No. 23, Washington DC, Cold War International History Project.

Matlock, J. 1995. *Autopsy on an empire: the American ambassador's account of the collapse of the Soviet Union.* New York: Random House.

Mayer, A. 1967. Domestic causes of the first world war. In L. Krieger and F. Stern (eds.) *The responsibility of power: historical essays in honor of Hajo Holborn.* New York: Doubleday.

Mccullough, E. 1999. *How the first world war began: the Triple Entente and the coming of the great war of 1914-1918.* Montreal: Black Rose Books.

Mearsheimer, J. 2001. *The tragedy of great power politics.* New York: W.W. Norton.

Medvedev, R. 1991. *Lichnost' i epokha. Politicheskii portret L.I. Brezhneva.* Moscow: Novosti.

Mendelson, S. 1993. Internal battles and external wars: politics, learning, and the Soviet withdrawal from Afghanistan. *World Politics* 45:327-60.

———. 1998. *Changing course: ideas, politics, and the Soviet withdrawal from Afghanistan.* Princeton: Princeton University Press.

Miège, J.-L. 1961-1963. *Le Maroc et l'Europe 1830-1894,* 4 vols. Paris: Presses Universitaires de France.

Mises, R. von 1957 [1928]. *Probability, statistics, and truth.* Macmillan: New York.

Mommsen, W. 1966. The debate on German war aims. In Walter Laqueur and George Mosse (eds.) *1914: the coming of the First World War.* New York: Harper Torchbacks.

———. 1969. *Das Zeitalter des Imperialismus.* Frankfurt: Fischer Bücherei.

———. 1973. Domestic factors in German foreign policy. *Journal of Central European History* 6:3-43.

———. 1993. *Grossmachtstellung und Weltpolitik: die Aussenpolitik des Deutschen Reiches 1871 bis 1914.* Frankfurt: Propyläen.

Morrow, J. 1988. Social choice and system structure in world politics. *World Politics* 41:75-97.

Moses, J. 1975. *The politics of illusion: the Fischer controversy in German historiography.* London: George Prior.

Mueller, J. 1989. *Retreat from doomsday: the obsolescence of major war.* New York: Basic Books.

———. 1991. Is war still becoming obsolete? Paper presented at the annual meetings of the American Political Science Association.

———. 1995. *Quiet cataclysm: reflections on the recent transformation of world politics.* New York: HarperCollins.

Mytelka, L. 1991. Crisis, technological change, and the strategic alliance. In L. Mytelka (ed.) *Strategic partnerships: states, firms, and international competition.* Rutherford: Farleigh Dickinson University Press.

Nalebuff, B. 1986. Brinkmanship and nuclear deterrence: the neutrality of escalation. *Conflict Management and Peace Science* 9:19-30.

Neilson, K. 1995. *Britain and the last tsar: British policy and Russia, 1894-1917.* Oxford: Oxford University Press.

Nelson, D. 1989. Power at what price? security in the WTO. *Journal of Soviet Military Studies* 2:312-45.

Nichols, T. 1993. *The sacred cause: civil-military conflict over Soviet national security, 1917–1992.* Ithaca: Cornell University Press.

Oberdorfer, D. 1991. *The turn: from the Cold War to a new era: the United States and the Soviet Union, 1983–1990.* New York: Poseidon Books.

———. 1998. *From the Cold War to a new era: the United States and the Soviet Union, 1983–1991,* updated edition. Baltimore: Johns Hopkins University Press.

Odell, J. 2001. Case study methods in international political economy. *International Studies Perspectives* 2:161–76.

Odom, W. 1990. The Soviet military in transition. *Problems of Communism* 39:51–71.

———. 1998. *The collapse of the Soviet military.* New Haven: Yale University Press.

Organski, A. 1968. *World politics,* 2nd edition. New York: Knopf.

Organski, A., and Kugler, J. 1980. *The war ledger.* Chicago: University of Chicago Press.

Oye, K. 1995. Explaining the end of the Cold War: morphological and behavioral adaptations to the nuclear peace? In R. Lebow and T. Risse-Kappen (eds.) *International relations theory and the end of the Cold War.* New York: Columbia University Press.

Pakenham, T. 1991. *The scramble for Africa, 1876–1912.* London: Weidenfeld and Nicolson.

Papayoanou, P. 1999. *Power ties: economic interdependence, balancing, and war.* Ann Arbor: University of Michigan Press.

Parrott, B. 1983. *Politics and technology in the Soviet Union.* Cambridge, MA: MIT Press.

Patomäki, H. 1996. How to tell better stories about world politics. *European Journal of International Relations* 2:105–34.

Pennington, N. and Hastie, R. 1986. Evidence evaluation in complex decision making. *Journal of Personality and Social Psychology* 51:242-58.

Perrow, C. 1984. *Normal accidents: living with high risk technologies.* New York: Basic Books.

Petrova, M. 2003. The end of the Cold War: a battle or bridging ground between rationalist and ideational approaches in international relations? *European Journal of International Relations* 9:115–63.

Pierson, P. 2004. *Politics in time: history, institutions, and social analysis.* Princeton: Princeton University Press.

Pitzer, J., and Baukol, A. 1991. Recent GNP and productivity trends. *Soviet Economy* 7:46–82.

Poidevin, R. 1969. *Les relations économiques et financiers entre la France et l'Allemagne de 1898 à 1914.* Paris: Colin.

Powell, R. 1987. Crisis bargaining, escalation, and MAD. *American Political Science Review* 81:717–36.

———. 1988. Nuclear brinkmanship with two-sided incomplete information. *American Political Science Review* 82:155–78.

Pravda, A. 1992. Soviet policy towards eastern Europe in transition. In A. Pravda (ed.) *The end of outer empire: Soviet-East European relations in transition, 1985–1990.* Newbury Park: Sage Publications.

Primakov, E. 1999. *Gody v bol'shoi politiki [Years in high politics].* Moscow: Sovershenno Sekretno.

Przeworski, A., and Teune, H. 1970. *The logic of comparative social inquiry.* New York: John Wiley & Sons.

Putin, V. 2000. *First person: an astonishingly frank self-portrait by Russia's president.* New York: PublicAffairs.

Ragin, C. 1987. *The comparative method: moving beyond qualitative and quantitative strategies.* Berkeley: University of California Press.

———. 2000. *Fuzzy-set social science.* Chicago: University of Chicago Press.

Ragin, C., and Becker, H. 1992. *What is a case? Exploring the foundations of social inquiry.* Cambridge: Cambridge University Press.

Rapkin, D., Thompson, W., and Christopherson, J. 1979. Bipolarity and bipolarization in the Cold War era: conceptualization, measurement, and validation. *Journal of Conflict Resolution* 23:261-95.

Rasler, K., and Thompson, W. 1994. *The great powers and global struggle, 1490–1990.* Lexington: University Press of Kentucky.

———. 2000. Global war and the political economy of structural change. In M. Midlarsky (ed.) *Handbook of war studies II.* Ann Arbor: University of Michigan Press.

———. 2001. Malign autocracies and major power warfare: evil, tragedy and international relations theory. *Security Studies* 10:46-79.

Remak, J. 1971. 1914—the third Balkan war: origins reconsidered. *Journal of Modern History* 41:353-66.

Renouvin, P. 1928. *The immediate origins of the war (28th June-4th August 1914).* New Haven: Yale University Press.

Riezler, K. 1972. *Tagebücher, Aufsatze, Dokumente.* Göttingen: Vandenhoeck & Ruprecht.

Riker, W. 1957. *An economic theory of democracy.* New York: Harper.

Risse, T. 2000. "Let's argue!": communicative action in world politics. *International Organization* 54:1-39.

Risse-Kappen, T. 1994. Ideas do not float freely: transnational coalitions, domestic structures, and the end of the Cold War. *International Organization* 48:185-214.

———. 1996. Collective identity in a democratic community: the case of NATO. In P. Katzenstein (ed.) *The culture of national security: norms and identity in world politics.* New York: Columbia University Press.

Ritter, G. 1958. *The Schlieffen plan: critique of a myth.* New York: Praeger.

———. 1969-73. *The sword and the scepter: the problem of militarism in Germany,* 4 vols. Coral Gables: University of Miami Press.

Roeder, P. 1993. *Red sunset: the failure of Soviet politics.* Princeton: Princeton University Press.

Roese, N., and Olson, J. 1995. Counterfactual thinking: a critical overview. In N. Roese and J Olson (eds.) *What might have been: the social psychology of counterfactual thinking.* Hillsdale: Lawrence Erlbaum.

Rogger, H. 1966. Russia in 1914. In W. Laqueur and G. Mosse (eds.) *1914: the coming of the first world war.* New York: Harper and Row.

Röhl, J. (ed.) 1973. *1914: delusion or design? The testimony of two German diplomats.* New York: St. Martin's.

———. 1995. Germany. In K. Wilson (ed.) *Decisions for war, 1914.* New York: Saint Martin's Press.

Rosenbach, H. 1993. *Das deutsche Reich, Grossbritannien und der Transvaal, 1896-1902: Anfänge deutsch-britischer Entfremdung.* Göttingen: Vandenhoeck and Ruprecht.

Ruggie, J. 1998. What makes the world hang together? Neo-utilitarianism and the social constructivist challenge. *International Organization* 52:855-85.

Russett, B. 1962. Cause, surprise, and no escape. *Journal of Politics* 24:3-22.

Sagan, S. 1986. 1914 revisited: allies, offense, and instability. *International Security* 11:151-75.

Salmon, W. 1984. *Scientific explanation and the causal structure of the world.* Princeton: Princeton University Press.

Savelev, A., Detinov, N., and Varhall, G. 1995. *The big five: arms control decision-making in the Soviet Union.* Westport: Praeger.

Schilling, B. 1925. *How the war began in 1914: the diary of the Russian foreign office.* London: George Allen and Unwin.

Schmitt, B. 1930. *The coming of the war, 1914.* New York: Scribner's sons.

Schroeder, G. 1995. Reflections on economic Sovietology. *Post-Soviet Affairs* 11:197-234.

Schroeder, P. 1972. World War I as galloping Gertie: a reply to Joachim Remak. *Journal of Modern History* 44:319-45.

———. 1975. Romania and the great powers before 1914. *Revue Roumaine d'Histoire* 24:39-53.

———. 1994. *The transformation of European politics, 1763-1848.* Oxford: Oxford University Press.

———. 1999. A pointless enduring rivalry: France and the Habsburg monarchy, 1715-1918. In W. Thompson (ed.) *Great power rivalries.* Columbia: University of South Carolina Press.

———. 2004. Embedded counterfactuals and World War One as an unavoidable war. In D. Wetzel, R. Jervis, and J. S. Levy (eds.) *Systems, stability, and statecraft: essays on the international history of modern Europe.* London: Palgrave.

———. 2006. The life and death of a long peace, 1763-1914. In R. Vayrynen (ed.) *The waning of major war: theories and debates.* New York: Routledge.

Schweller, R. 1992. Domestic structure and preventive war: are democracies more pacific? *World Politics* 44:235-69.

———. 1998. *Deadly imbalances: tripolarity and Hitler's strategy of conquest.* New York: Columbia University Press.

Schweller, R., and Wohlforth, W. 2000. Power test: evaluating realism in response to the end of the Cold War. *Security Studies* 9:60–107.

Senator Gravel Edition. 1971. *Pentagon Papers: the Defense Department history of United States decisionmaking in Vietnam, 4 vols.* Boston: Beacon Press.

Shakhnazarov, G. 1993. *Tsena svobody: reformatsiia Gorbacheva glazami ego pomoshchnika [The price of freedom: Gorbachev's reformation through the eyes of his assistant].* Moscow: Rossika-Zevs.

Shaver, K. 1985. *The attribution of blame: causality, responsibility, and blameworthiness.* New York: Springer Verlag.

Shevardnadze, E. 1988 August 15. Doklad E.A. Shevardnadze. *Vestnik MID-SSSR* 15:27–48.

Shevardnadze, E., Grinevskii, O., Kvitsinskii, Iu., Komplektov, V., and Piadyshev, B. 1997 Feburary 19. Peregovorshchik-razoruzhenets. *Nezavisimaia Gazeta*, 2.

Shubin, A. 1997a. Sotsial'naia struktura SSSR v Kaun Perestroiki [The social structure of the USSR on the eve of peretroika]. *Otechestvenaiia istoriia* 4:131–46.

———. 1997b. *Istoki perestroiki 1978–1984 [The origins of perestroika], 2 vols.* Moscow.

Shultz, G. 1993. *Turmoil and triumph: my years as secretary of state.* New York: Scribner's.

Sinel'nikov, S. 1995. *Biudzhetnyi krisis v rossii, 1985–1995 gody [The budget crisis in Russia, 1985–1995].* Moscow: Evraziia.

Skocpol, T. 1979. *States and social revolutions: a comparative analysis of France, Russia, and China.* Cambridge: Cambridge University Press.

Skvortsov, O. (1998) Interview with Egor K. Ligachev, December 17, 1998, Cold War Oral History Project, Institute of General History, Moscow. (Transcript on file at the Institute of General History; and the Mershon Center at Ohio State University.)

Skvortsov, O. (n.d.) Interview with Oleg D. Baklanov, Cold War Oral History Project, Institute of General History, Moscow. (Transcript on file at the Institute of General History; and the Mershon Center at Ohio State University.)

Snel, G. 1998. A more defense strategy: the reconceptualisation of Soviet conventional strategy in the 1980s. *Europe-Asia Studies* 50:205–39.

Snyder, G. 1984. The security dilemma in alliance politics. *World Politics* 36:461–95.

Snyder, G., and Diesing, P. 1977. *Conflict among nations: bargaining and decision-making in international crises.* Princeton: University of Princeton Press.

Snyder, J. 1984. *The ideology of the offensive: military decision making and the disasters of 1914.* Ithaca: Cornell University Press.

———. 1991. *Myths of empire: domestic politics and international ambition.* Ithaca: Cornell University Press.

Soutou, G. 1970. *L'or et le sang.* Paris: Les Éditeurs Français Réunis.

Spitzmüller-Harmersbach, A. 1955. *Und hat auch Ursach, es zu Leben.* Vienna: William Frick.

Stein, J. 1995. Political learning by doing: Gorbachev as uncommitted thinker and motivated learner. In R. Lebow and T. Risse-Kappen (eds.) *International relations theory and the end of the Cold War.* New York: Columbia University Press.

Stein, J., et al. 1998. Five scenarios of the Israeli-Palestinian relationship in 2002: works in progress. *Security Studies* 7:195–212.

Steiner, Z. 1977. *Britain and the origins of the first world war.* London: Macmillan.

Stepankov, V., and Lisov, E. 1992. *Kremlevskii zagovor: Versiia sledstviia [Kremlin conspiracy: what the investigation revealed].* Moscow: Ogonek.

Stern, F. 1967. Bethmann Hollweg and the war: the limits of responsibility. In F. Stern and L. Krieger (eds.) *The responsibility of power: historical essays in honor of Hajo Holborn.* New York: Doubleday.

Stevenson, D. 1988. *The first world war and international politics.* Oxford: Oxford University Press.

———. 1996. *Armaments and the coming of war: Europe, 1904–1914.* Oxford: Clarendon Press.

———. 1997. Militarization and diplomacy in Europe before 1914. *International Security* 22:125–61.

Stone, N. 1966. Hungary and the crisis of July 1914. *Journal of Contemporary History* 1:153–70.

———. 1975. *The eastern front, 1914–1917.* New York: Scribner.

———. 1979. Moltke and Conrad: relations between the Austro-Hungarian and German general staffs, 1909–1914. In P. Kennedy (ed.) *The war plans of the great powers, 1880–1914.* Boston: Allen & Unwin.

Stone, R. 1996. *Satellites and commissars: strategy and conflict in the politics of Soviet-bloc trade.* Princeton: Princeton University Press.

Strandmann, H. von. 1988. Germany and the coming of war. In R. Evans and H. von Strandmann (eds.) *The coming of the first world war.* Oxford: Oxford University Press.

Strikwerda, C. 1993. The troubled origins of European economic integration: international iron and steel and labor migration in the era of World War I. *American Historical Review* 98:1106–29.

Sylvan, D., and Haddad, D. 1998. Reasoning and problem representation in foreign policy groups, individuals, and stories. In D. Sylvan and J. Voss (eds.) *Problem representation in foreign policy decision making.* Cambridge: Cambridge University Press.

Tammen, R., et al. 2000. *Power transitions: strategies for the 21st century.* Chatham: Chatham House.

Tannenwald, N. 2001. The role of ideas and the end of the Cold War: advancing the theoretical agenda on ideas. Paper presented at the annual meetings of the Conference on The Role of Ideas and the End of the Cold War, Brown University.

Taylor, A. 1945. *The course of German history: a survey of the development of Germany since 1815.* London: Hamish Hamilton.

——. 1954/1971. *The struggle for mastery in Europe, 1848-1918.* Oxford: Clarendon Press.

——. 1969. *War by time-table.* London: Macdonald.

——. 1974 (1969). War by timetable. *Purnell's history of the twentieth century.* New York: Purnell.

Taylor, R. 1976. Causation. In M. Brand (ed.) *The nature of causation.* Urbana: University of Illinois Press.

Tetlock, P., and Belkin, A. (eds.). 1996. *Counterfactual thought experiments in world politics: logical, methodological, and psychological perspectives.* Princeton: Princeton University Press.

Thomas, D. 2005. Human rights idea, the demise of communism, and the end of the Cold War. *Journal of Cold War Studies* 7:110-41.

Thompson, W. 1988. *On global war: historical-structural approaches to world politics.* Columbia: University of South Carolina.

——. 1992. Dehio, long cycles and the geohistorical context of structural transitions. *World Politics* 45:127-52.

——. 1999. The evolution of the Anglo-American rivalry. In W. Thompson (ed.) *Great power rivalries.* Columbia: University of South Carolina Press.

——. 2001. Identifying rivals and rivalries in world politics. *International Studies Quarterly* 45:557-86.

——. 2001. Venusian and Martian perspectives on international relations: Britain as system leader in the nineteenth and twentieth centuries. In C. Elman and M. Elman (eds.) *History and international relations theory: bridges and boundaries.* Cambridge, MA: MIT Press.

——. 2003. A streetcar named Sarajevo: catalysts, multiple causation chains, and rivalry structures. *International Studies Quarterly* 47:453-74.

Tirpitz, A. von. 1924-26. *Politisiche Dokumente.* Berlin: Cotta.

Trachtenberg, M. 1990-1. The meaning of mobilization in 1914. *International Security* 15:120-50.

Trulock, N. 1990. A Soviet view of nonnuclear strategic capabilities and future war. In K. Moss (ed.) *Technology and the future strategic environment.* Washington, DC: Wilson Center Press.

Trumpener, U. 1976. War premeditated? German intelligence operations in July 1914. *Central European History* 9:58-85.

Tsipko, A. 1993. Preface. In A. Yakovlev (ed.) *The fate of marxism in Russia.* New Haven: Yale University Press.

Tuchman, B. 1962. *The guns of August.* New York: Dell.

Tucker, R. 1987. *Political culture and leadership in Soviet Russia: from Lenin to Gorbachev.* Brighton: Wheatsheaf.

Turner, L. 1970. *Origins of the first world war.* New York: Norton.

——. 1979a. The significance of the Schlieffen Plan. In P. Kennedy (ed.) *The war plans of the great powers, 1880-1914.* London: Allen and Unwin.

——. 1979b. The Russian mobilisation in 1914. In P. Kennedy (ed.) *War plans of the great powers, 1880-1914.* London: Allen and Unwin.

UNCTAD. 1993. *World investment report 1993: transnational corporations and integrated international production.* Geneva: United Nations.

―――. 1994. *World investment report 1994: transnational corporations, employment and the workplace.* Geneva: United Nations.

―――. 1995. *World investment report 1995: transnational corporations and competitiveness.* Geneva: United Nations.

Van Evera, S. 1984. The cult of the offensive and the origins of World War I. *International Security* 9:58–107.

―――. 1997. *Guide to methods for students of political science.* Ithaca: Cornell University Press.

―――. 1999. *The causes of war: power and the roots of conflict.* Ithaca, NY: Cornell University Press.

Vandervort, B. 1998. *Wars of imperial conquest in Africa, 1830–1914.* Bloomington: Indiana University Press.

Vasquez, J. 1993. *The war puzzle.* Cambridge: Cambridge University Press.

Vermes, G. 1985. *István Tisza: the liberal vision and conservative statecraft of a Magyar nationalist.* New York: Columbia University Press.

Vorotnikov, V. 1995. *A bylo eto tak... Iz dnevnika chlena Politburo TsK KPSS [And so it was ... From the diary of a politburo member].* Moscow: Sovet Veteranov Knigoizdaniia.

Waltz, K. 1979. *Theory of international relations.* Boston: Addison-Wesley.

Wandruszka, A., and Urbanitsch, P. (eds.). 1993. *Die Habsburger-Monarchie 1848–1918, Vol VI: Die Habsburgermonarchie im System der Internationalen Beziehungen, Part 2.* Vienna: Austrian Academy.

Wayman, F. 1985. Bipolarity, multipolarity and the threat of war. In A. Sabrosky (ed.) *Polarity and war: the changing structure of international conflict.* Boulder: Westview Press.

Weber, M. 1949. Objective possibility and adequate causation in historical explanation. In *The methodology of the social sciences.* New York: Free Press.

―――. 1958. Max Weber: essays in sociology. In *The social psychology of the world religions.* Oxford: Oxford University Press.

Weber, S. 1997. Prediction and the Middle East peace process. *Security Studies* 6:167–79.

Wendt, A. 1992. Anarchy is what states make of it: the social construction of power politics. *International Organization* 46:391–425.

―――. 1998. On constitution and causation in international relations. *Review of International Studies* 24:101–17.

―――. 1999. *Social theory of international politics.* Cambridge: Cambridge University Press.

White, M. 1965. *The foundations of historical knowledge.* New York: Harper & Row.

Williams, P. 1976. *Crisis management: confrontation and diplomacy in the nuclear age.* New York: John Wiley & Sons.

Williamson, S. 1974. Influence, power, and the policy process: the case of Franz Ferdinand, 1906–1914. *Historical Journal* 17:417–34.

————. 1979a. Joffre shapes French strategy, 1911–1913. In P. Kennedy (ed.) *The war plans of the great powers*. London: Allen & Unwin.

————. 1979b. Theories of organizational process and foreign policy outcomes. In P. Lauren (ed.) *Diplomacy*. New York: Free Press.

————. 1988. The origins of world war I. *Journal of Interdisciplinary History* 18:795–818.

————. 1991. *Austria-Hungary and the origins of the first world war*. London: Macmillan.

Wilson, K. 1975. The British cabinet's decision for war, 2 August 1914. *British Journal of International Studies* 1:148–59.

————. 1985. *The policy of the entente: essays on the determinants of British foreign power 1904–1914*. Cambridge: Cambridge University Press.

Wilson, T. 1986. *The myriad faces of war: Britain and the great war, 1914–1918*. Cambridge: Polity Press.

Winiecki, J. 1986. Are Soviet-type economies entering an era of long-term decline? *Soviet Studies* 38:325–48.

Wohlforth, W. 1993. *The elusive balance: power and perceptions during the Cold War*. Ithaca: Cornell University Press.

————. 1994–5. Realism and the end of the Cold War. *International Security* 19:91–129.

————. 1995. Correspondence: realism and the end of the Cold War. *International Security* 20:186–87.

————. 1998. Reality check: revising theories of international politics in response to the end of the Cold War. *World Politics* 50:650–80.

Woodward, E. 1967. *Great Britain and the war of 1914–1918*. London: Methuen.

World Bank. 1997. *Global economic prospects and the developing countries*. Washington: World Bank.

Yakovlev, A. 1991. *Muki prochteniia bytiia-nadezhdy i real'nosti*. Moscow: Novosti.

Yeltsin, B. 1990. *Against the grain: an autobiography*. London: Cape.

Zamoshkin, I. 1989. Za novyi podkhod k probleme individualizma [For a new approach to the problem of individualism]. *Voprosy Filosofii [Philosophical Issues]* 6:3–16.

Zechlin, E. 1979. *Krieg und Kriegrisiko: Zur deutschen Politik im Ersten Weltkrieg*. Düsseldorf: Droste.

Zeman, Z. 1988. The Balkans and the coming of war. In R. Evans and H. von Strandmann (eds.) *The coming of the first world war*. Oxford: Oxford University Press.

Zuber, T. 2003. *Inventing the Schlieffen Plan : German war planning 1871–1914*. New York: Oxford University Press.

Zubok, V. 2000. Why did the Cold War end in 1989? Explanations of 'the turn'. In A. Westad (ed.) *Reviewing the Cold War: approaches, interpretation, theory*. London: Frank Cass.

Index

Aehrenthal, Alois Graf Lexa von
(Austro-Hungarian Minister for
Foreign Affairs, 1906-12), 192
alliances (1914) 22, 24n, 47, 49,
51, 85, 92, 93, 120n9, 175,
192; Austro-German, 51-53,
56, 56n19, 77, 127, 179, 192n;
Franco-Russian, 51, 55, 56n20,
93, 98, 101, 128, 156, 175;
Triple Alliance, 96, 101-102
Alsace-Lorraine, 91, 101, 118, 128,
131, 140, 170, 183
Andropov, Yuri (General Secretary
of the Communist Party of the
Soviet Union, 1982-84), 231,
272
Aron, Raymond, 2, 13-14
Austria-Hungary, 7, 17, 25, 28,
30, 32-33, 36, 38, 51-77, 81-
84, 86, 91-98, 101-104, 106-
111, 117-122, 127-130, 132,
134, 137, 144, 154-168, 170-
173, 176-180, 183-193, 292-
299; annexation of Bosnia-
Herzgovina, 91, 107, 118, 157,
162, 293; domestic politics,
36, 68-71, 157, 164-165, 188;
preferences in July crisis, 52-
53; Southern Slavs, 54, 72;
ultimatum to Serbia, 7, 51-54,
52n8, 53n12, 60, 66-69, 71-
73, 71n54, 98-99, 129, 154,
190-191; war plans, 69-71

balance of power, 61n31, 61n32,
66, 66n43, 85, 88, 96, 108,
166-170, 175, 188

Balkan Wars, 1, 65, 94, 96, 118-
119, 137, 156-157, 163, 167,
183
Balkans, 17, 23, 28, 38, 51, 52n8,
54-56, 60, 65-66, 68, 72, 75,
91, 95-99, 103, 106-107, 118-
119, 125, 128, 154, 156, 162-
164, 172, 178-179, 184-193,
339
Belgium (1914), 2, 43, 74, 79, 103,
169, 339; neutrality of, 29, 55,
66, 66n43, 66n44, 79, 79n79,
332,
Belkin, Aaron,; 50n6, 117n5, 149-
150, 152
Bennett, Andrew, 22, 29
Berchtold, Leopold Graf (Austro-
Hungarian Minister for Foreign Affairs, 1912-15), 52n10,
53, 68, 69, 70, 72, 73, 73n60
74n62, 93, 95, 97
Bethmann-Hollweg, Theobald von
(German Chancellor, 1909-
17), 28, 30, 56, 56n20, 57,
57n23, 60, 61, 60n28, 61n29,
61n32, 62, 62n34, 63, 65n40,
71n54, 71, 73, 73n59, 73n61,
74, 74n65 75, 74n66, 75, 78,
78n73, 78n74, 80n81, 89, 93,
97, 98, 99, 335, 339
bipolarity, 210-211
Bismarck, Otto von (German Chancellor, 1871-90), 14, 32-33, 84,
118, 155, 170, 179
blank cheque, 52, 52n10, 56, 60,
63, 68, 114, 179